Teach...
Inspire...
Lead...

With REA's FTCE Math 6–12 test prep, you'll be in a class all your own.

We'd like to hear from you!
*Visit **www.rea.com** to send us your comments or e-mail us at **info@rea.com**.*

Research & Education Association

The Best Teachers' Test Preparation for the

FTCE

Mathematics
6–12

Mel Friedman, M.S.
Adjunct Professor
Kutztown University

Leanne Wells, M.S.
Adjunct Professor
Florida International University

**And the Staff of
Research & Education Association**

Visit our Educator Support Center at:
www.REA.com/teacher

The competencies presented in this book were created and implemented by the Florida Department of Education. For further information visit the FTCE website at *www.firn.edu/doe/sas/ftcehome.htm.*

Research & Education Association
61 Ethel Road West
Piscataway, New Jersey 08854
E-mail: info@rea.com

The Best Teachers' Test Preparation for the Florida Teacher Certification Examination (FTCE) *Mathematics 6–12*

Printed in the United States of America

Library of Congress Control Number 2006930582

International Standard Book Number 0-7386-0162-4

REA® is a registered trademark of Research & Education Association, Inc.

About Research & Education Association

Founded in 1959, Research & Education Association is dedicated to publishing the finest and most effective educational materials—including software, study guides, and test preps—for students in middle school, high school, college, graduate school, and beyond.

REA's Test Preparation series includes books and software for all academic levels in almost all disciplines. Research & Education Association publishes test preps for students who have not yet entered high school, as well as for high school students preparing to enter college. Students from countries around the world seeking to attend college in the United States will find the assistance they need in REA's publications. For college students seeking advanced degrees, REA publishes test preps for many major graduate school admission examinations in a wide variety of disciplines, including engineering, law, and medicine. Students at every level, in every field, with every ambition can find what they are looking for among REA's publications.

REA's practice tests are always based upon the most recently administered exams and include every type of question that you can expect on the actual exams.

REA's publications and educational materials are highly regarded and continually receive an unprecedented amount of praise from professionals, instructors, librarians, parents, and students. Our authors are as diverse as the fields represented in the books we publish. They are well-known in their respective disciplines and serve on the faculties of prestigious high schools, colleges, and universities throughout the United States and Canada.

Today, REA's wide-ranging catalog is a leading resource for teachers, students, and professionals.

We invite you to visit us at *www.rea.com* to find out how "REA is making the world smarter."

Acknowledgments

We would like to thank REA's Carl Fuchs, President, for supervising development; Pam Weston, Vice President, Publishing, for setting the quality standards for production integrity and managing the publication to completion; Christine Reilley, Senior Editor, for project management and preflight editorial review; Diane Goldschmidt, Senior Editor, for post-production quality assurance; Vincent Biancomano and Sandra Rush for their editorial contributions; Christine Saul, Senior Graphic Artist, for cover design; and Jeff LoBalbo, Senior Graphic Artist, for post-production file mapping.

We also gratefully acknowledge the team at Aquent Publishing Services for typesetting and indexing the manuscript.

CONTENTS

CHAPTER 3   63

COMPETENCY 2: KNOWLEDGE OF FUNCTIONS

CHAPTER 4   73

COMPETENCIES 3 & 4: KNOWLEDGE OF GEOMETRY

CHAPTER 5   125

COMPETENCY 5: KNOWLEDGE OF TRIGONOMETRY

CHAPTER 15   247

PRACTICE TEST   251

INDEX   285

Passing
the Examination

About This Book

REA's *The Best Teachers' Preparation for the FTCE (Florida Teacher Certificate Examination) Mathematics Grade 6–12* is a comprehensive guide designed to assist you in preparing to take the FTCE required for teaching mathematics in grades 6–12. To enhance your chances of success in this important step toward your career as a teacher in Florida schools, this test guide

- presents an accurate and complete overview of the FTCE Mathematics Grade 6–12.
- identifies all of the important information and its representation on the exam
- provides a comprehensive review of every competency
- presents sample questions in the actual test format
- suggests tips and strategies for successfully completing standardized tests
- provides diagnostic tools to identify areas of strength and weakness
- provides a half-length diagnostic test to help pinpoint strengths and weaknesses
- provides a full-length practice test based on the most recently administered FTCE
- replicates the format of the official exam, including levels of difficulty

- provides the correct answer and detailed explanations for each question on the diagnostic and practice tests, which enables you to identify correct answers and understand why they are correct and, just as important, why the other answers are incorrect.

This guide is the result of studying many resources. The editors considered the most recent test administrations and professional standards. They also researched information from the Florida Department of Education, professional journals, textbooks, and educators. This guide includes the best test preparation materials based on the latest information available.

About the Test

Below are the competencies used as the basis for the FTCE Mathematics 6–12 examination, as well as the approximate percentage of the total test that each competency occupies. These competencies represent the knowledge that teams of teachers, subject area specialists, and district-level educators have determined to be important for beginning teachers. This book contains a thorough review of these competencies, as well as the specific skills that demonstrate each area.

Competencies	Percentage
1. Knowledge of Algebra	18%
2. Knowledge of Functions	8%
3. Knowledge of Geometry from a Synthetic Perspective	12%
4. Knowledge of Geometry from an Algebraic Perspective	6%
5. Knowledge of Trigonometry	6%
6. Knowledge of Statistics	6%
7. Knowledge of Probability	6%
8. Knowledge of Discrete Mathematics	5%
9. Knowledge of Calculus	6%
10. Knowledge of Number Sense and Mathematical Structure	5%
11. Knowledge of Mathematics as Communication	3%
12. Knowledge of Mathematics as Reasoning	4%
13. Knowledge of Mathematical Connections	3%
14. Knowledge of Instruction	6%
15. Knowledge of Assessment	6%

Can I Retake the Test?

If you do not achieve a passing grade on the FTCE, don't panic. The test can be taken again after 31 days, so you can seriously work on improving your score in preparation for your next FTCE. A score on the FTCE that does not match your expectations does not mean you should change your plans about teaching.

Who Administers the Test?

The Florida Department of Education develops and administers this test. Subject area knowledge tested on the Mathematics 6–12 examination of the FTCE was identified and validated by committees of content specialists from the state of Florida. Public school teachers made up the majority of the committee members, but the committees also included district supervisors and college faculty. Selection of committee members was based on recommendations by professional associations, experts, and teachers' unions. Development of the appropriate content and difficulty levels of the exam involved literature review, teacher interviews, beta tests, and professional judgment.

When Should the FTCE Be Taken?

Florida law requires that teachers demonstrate mastery of basic skills, professional knowledge, and content area of specialization. If you've graduated from a Florida state-approved teacher preparation program and made the decision to teach Mathematics 6–12, you need to begin the process by applying for a Florida Temporary Certificate in that subject. The Bureau of Educator Certification will only evaluate your eligibility in the subject/s you request on your application form. The Temporary Certificate is valid for three school years, which allows you time to complete the certification tests while teaching full-time.

For high school grads and out-of-state educators, the Bureau of Educator Certification will provide you with official information about which test(s) to take to complete requirements for the Professional Certificate.

The FTCE is usually administered four times a year in several locations throughout Florida. The usual testing day is Saturday, but the test may be taken on an alternate day if a conflict exists, such as a religious obligation. Special accommodations can also be made for applicants who are visually impaired, hearing impaired-physically disabled, or specific learning disabled.

To receive information on upcoming administrations of the FTCE you should consult the FTCE Registration Bulletin, which can be obtained by contacting:

All FTCE Inquiries

Florida Department of Education
325 West Gaines Street, Suite 414
Tallahassee, FL 32399-0400
Phone: (850) 488-8198 or (813) 974-2400
Website: *www.firn.edu/doe/sas/ftcehome.htm*
www.cefe.usf.edu/requestapp.aspx
Bureau of Educator Certification: *www.fldoe.org/edcert*

The FTCE Registration Bulletin also includes information regarding test retakes and score reports.

Is There a Registration Fee?

To take the FTCE, you must pay a registration fee. You may pay by personal check, money order, cashier's check, or Visa or MasterCard. Cash is not accepted. Utilize the contact information above with any questions.

How to Use This Book

How Do I Begin Studying?

1. Review the organization of this test preparation guide.
2. To best utilize your study time, follow our FTCE Independent Study Schedule. The schedule is based on a seven-week program, but can be condensed to four weeks if necessary.
3. Take the diagnostic test, and score it according to directions.
4. Review the format of the FTCE.
5. Review the test-taking advice and suggestions presented later in this chapter.
6. Pay attention to the information about competencies and skills, content, and topics on the test.
7. Spend time reviewing topics that stand out as needing more study.
8. Take the Practice Test, review the explanations to your answers carefully, study the competencies that your scores indicate need further review.
9. Follow the suggestions at the end of this chapter for the day before and the day of the test.

Note: Scientific calculators may be used during this test, so use one during the practice tests in this book. However, do not bring one on test day—calculators are provided by the testing center for the exam.

When Should I Start Studying?

It is never too early to start studying for the FTCE. The earlier you begin, the more time you will have to sharpen your skills. Do not procrastinate! Cramming is not an effective way to study, since it does not allow you the time to think about the content, review the competencies and the practice test. It is important, however, to review the material one last time the night before the test administration.

Studying for the FTCE Mathematics Grade 6–12

It is very important for you to choose the time and place for studying that works best for you. Some individuals may set aside a certain number of hours every morning to study, while others may choose to study at night before going to sleep. Other people may study during the day, while waiting in line, or even while eating lunch. Only you can determine when and where your study time will be most effective. Be consistent and use your time wisely. Work out a study routine and stick to it.

When you take the practice tests, simulate the conditions of the actual test as closely as possible. Turn your television and radio off, and sit down at a quiet table free from distraction. As you complete each practice test, score your test and thoroughly review the explanations to the questions you answered incorrectly; however, do not review too much at any one time. Concentrate on one problem area at a time by reviewing the question and explanation, and by studying our review until you are confident that you have mastered the material.

Keep track of your scores. By doing so, you will be able to gauge your progress and discover general weaknesses in particular sections. Give extra attention to the reviews that cover your areas of difficulty, as this will build your skills in those areas.

FTCE Mathematics Grade 6–12 Study Schedule

The following study schedule allows for thorough preparation for the FTCE. The course of study here is seven weeks, but you can condense or expand the timeline to suit your personal schedule. It is vital that you adhere to a structured plan and set aside ample time each day to study. The more time you devote to studying, the more prepared and confident you will be on the day of the test.

Week 1. Take the diagnostic exam. The score will indicate your strengths and weaknesses. Make sure you simulate real exam conditions when you take the test. Afterwards, score it and review the explanations, especially for questions you answered incorrectly.

Week 2. Review the explanations for the questions you missed, and review the appropriate chapter sections. Useful study techniques include highlighting key terms and information, taking notes as you review the book's sections, and putting new terms and information on note cards to help retain the information.

Weeks 3 and 4. Reread all your note cards, refresh your understanding of the exam's competencies and skills, review your college textbooks, and read over class notes you've previously taken. This is also the time to consider any other supplementary materials that your counselor or the Florida State Department of Education suggests. Review the Department's website at *http://www.fldoe.org.*

Week 5. Begin to condense your notes and findings. A structured list of important facts and concepts, based on your note cards and the book's competencies, will help you thoroughly review for the test. Review the answers and explanations for all missed questions.

Week 6. Have someone quiz you using the index cards you created. Take the practice test, adhering to the time limits and simulated test-day conditions.

Week 7. Review your areas of weakness using all study materials. This is a good time to re-take the practice test.

Format of the FTCE

The FTCE Mathematics Grade 6–12 addresses 15 main areas of competency identified by the Florida Department of Education as foundational to effective teaching. Divided between the 15 competencies are 118 skill areas that you will be questioned about to assess your mastery of Mathematics 6–12. Individual test items require a variety of different thinking levels, ranging from simple recall to evaluation and problem solving.

The competencies are broad statements written in a way to reflect the information that an entry-level educator needs in order to be a truly effective teacher. The competencies themselves will not be discussed in the actual FTCE test, only the skills.

All the questions on the FTCE are in multiple-choice format. Each question will have four options, lettered A through D, from which to choose. You should have plenty of time in which to complete the FTCE, but be aware of the amount of time you are spending on each question so that you allow yourself time to complete the test. Although speed is not very important, a steady pace should be maintained when answering the questions. Using the practice tests will help you prepare for this task.

Computer-Based Testing

As of this writing, computer-based testing is not available for the FTCE Subject Area Examination, Mathematics Grade 6–12. To verify, go to *http://www. cefe.usf.edu* and click on "Computer-Based Testing." Exams on the computer have the advantage of providing you with a notice of Pass/Fail immediately after completing the exam, which can be scheduled at a time that is convenient for you.

About the Review Sections

The reviews in this book are designed to help you sharpen the basic skills needed to approach the FTCE, as well as provide strategies for attacking the questions.

Each teaching competency is examined in a separate chapter. The skills required for all 15 competencies are extensively discussed to optimize your understanding of what the FTCE covers.

Your schooling has taught you most of what you need to answer the questions on the test. The education classes you took should have provided you with the know-how to make important decisions about situations you will face as a teacher. Our review is designed to help you fit the information you have acquired into specific competency components. Reviewing your class notes and textbooks together with our competency reviews will give you an excellent springboard for passing the FTCE.

Scoring the FTCE Mathematics Grade 6–12

How Do I Score My Practice Test?

There are approximately 80 multiple-choice questions on the FTCE Mathematics 6–12. This is a Pass or Fail test. You must get 66% or more of the 80 questions correct to pass.

If you do not achieve a passing score on the practice test, review the detailed explanations for the questions you answered incorrectly. Note which types of questions you answered wrong, and re-examine the corresponding review. After further review, you may want to re-take the practice tests.

When Will I Receive My Score Report and What Will It Look Like?

Approximately one month after you take the test, your score report will be mailed to you. Your scores will be submitted electronically to the Bureau of Educator Certification. A copy of your score report is provided to one Florida college or university and one Florida school district. You should have requested this information on your registration application.

When you receive your score report and have passed, only the word PASS will be reported. If you do not pass, you will receive a numeric score and will have to retake the test.

Test-Taking Tips

Although you may not be familiar with tests like the FTCE, this book will help acquaint you with this type of exam and help alleviate your test-taking anxieties. Listed below are ways to help you become accustomed to the FTCE, some of which may be applied to other tests.

Tip 1. Become comfortable with the format of the FTCE. When you are practicing, stay calm and pace yourself. After simulating the test only once, you will boost your chances of doing well, and you will be able to sit down for the actual FTCE with much more confidence.

Tip 2. Read all of the possible answers. Just because you think you have found the correct response, do not automatically assume that it is the best answer. Read through each choice to be sure that you are not making a mistake by jumping to conclusions.

Tip 3. Use the process of elimination. Go through each answer to a question and eliminate as many of the answer choices as possible. By eliminating two answer choices, you have given yourself a better chance of getting the item correct since there will only be two choices left from which to make your guess. Do not leave an answer blank; it is better to guess than to not answer a question on the FTCE test.

Tip 4. Place a question mark in your answer booklet next to answers you guessed, then recheck them later if you have time.

Tip 5. Work quickly and steadily. You will have two and one-half hours to complete the test, so work quickly and steadily to avoid focusing on any one problem too long. Taking the practice tests in this book will help you learn to budget your precious time.

Tip 6. Learn the directions and format of the test. Familiarizing yourself with the directions and format of the test will not only save time, but will also help you avoid anxiety (and the mistakes caused by getting anxious).

Tip 7. Be sure that the answer circle you are marking corresponds to the number of the question in the test booklet. Since the test is multiple-choice, it is graded by machine, and marking one wrong answer can throw off your answer key and your score. Be extremely careful.

The Day of the Test

Before the Test

On the day of the test, make sure to dress comfortably, so that you are not distracted by being too hot or too cold while taking the test. Plan to arrive at the test center early. This will allow you to collect your thoughts and relax before the test, and will also spare you the anguish that comes with being late.

You should check your FTCE Registration Bulletin to find out what time to arrive at the testing center.

Before you leave for the test center, make sure that you have your admission ticket and two forms of identification, one of which must contain a recent photograph, your name, and signature (i.e., driver's license). You will not be admitted to the test center if you do not have proper identification.

You must bring several sharpened No. 2 pencils with erasers, as none will be provided at the test center.

If you would like, you may wear a watch to the test center. However, you may not wear one that makes noise, because it may disturb the other test takers. Dictionaries, textbooks, notebooks, calculators, briefcases, or packages will not be permitted. Drinking, smoking, and eating are prohibited. NOTE: For this test, scientific calculators are permitted during the test, but they are provided at the test center. Do not bring a calculator of your own.

During the Test

The FTCE is given in one sitting with no breaks. Procedures will be followed to maintain test security. Once you enter the test center, follow all of the rules and instructions given by the test supervisor. If you do not, you risk being dismissed from the test and having your scores cancelled.

When all of the materials have been distributed, the test instructor will give you directions for filling out your answer sheet. Fill out this sheet carefully since this information will be printed on your score report.

Once the test begins, mark only one answer per question, completely erase unwanted answers and marks, and fill in answers darkly and neatly.

After the Test

When you finish your test, hand in your materials and you will be dismissed. Then, go home and relax—you deserve it!

FTCE

Florida Teacher Certification Examination
Mathematics 6–12

Diagnostic Test

Answer Sheet

1. (A) (B) (C) (D)
2. (A) (B) (C) (D)
3. (A) (B) (C) (D)
4. (A) (B) (C) (D)
5. (A) (B) (C) (D)
6. (A) (B) (C) (D)
7. (A) (B) (C) (D)
8. (A) (B) (C) (D)
9. (A) (B) (C) (D)
10. (A) (B) (C) (D)
11. (A) (B) (C) (D)
12. (A) (B) (C) (D)
13. (A) (B) (C) (D)
14. (A) (B) (C) (D)
15. (A) (B) (C) (D)
16. (A) (B) (C) (D)
17. (A) (B) (C) (D)
18. (A) (B) (C) (D)
19. (A) (B) (C) (D)
20. (A) (B) (C) (D)

21. (A) (B) (C) (D)
22. (A) (B) (C) (D)
23. (A) (B) (C) (D)
24. (A) (B) (C) (D)
25. (A) (B) (C) (D)
26. (A) (B) (C) (D)
27. (A) (B) (C) (D)
28. (A) (B) (C) (D)
29. (A) (B) (C) (D)
30. (A) (B) (C) (D)
31. (A) (B) (C) (D)
32. (A) (B) (C) (D)
33. (A) (B) (C) (D)
34. (A) (B) (C) (D)
35. (A) (B) (C) (D)
36. (A) (B) (C) (D)
37. (A) (B) (C) (D)
38. (A) (B) (C) (D)
39. (A) (B) (C) (D)
40. (A) (B) (C) (D)

FTCE Mathematics 6-12 Diagnostic Test

Note: This diagnostic test is half the length of the actual test. There is a full-length practice test following the review for the FTCE test competencies.

TIME: 75 minutes (1 hour and 15 minutes)
40 questions.

> **Directions:** Read each item and select the best response.

1. Use this graph to answer the question.

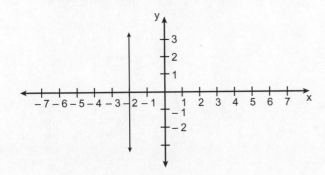

   Which equation is represented above?

   (A) $x = 2$ (C) $y = 2$

   (B) $x = -2$ (D) $y = -2$

2. Which is a factor of $6x^2 + 2x - 4$?

   (A) $(3x - 4)$ (C) $(x - 1)$

   (B) $(6x - 1)$ (D) $(3x - 2)$

3. From the following choices, select a good definition for the mathematics term *slope*

   (A) Rise over run.

   (B) The ratio of the change in the dependent variable to the change in the independent variable.

   (C) m

   (D) How steep something is compare to another thing that is not steep.

4. In an apartment building there are 9 apartments having terraces for every 16 apartments. If the apartment building has a total of 144 apartments, how many apartments have terraces?

   (A) 137   (C) 63

   (B) 81   (D) 102

5. Solve for x.
$$5x + 2y = -5$$
$$-3x + y = 3$$

   (A) 0   (C) 1

   (B) $-\frac{1}{11}$ (D) -1

6. Multiply.
$$(5x^2 + 2)(4x^2 - 7)$$

   (A) $20x^4 - 27x^2 - 14$

   (B) $20x^4 + 43x^2 - 14$

   (C) $20x^4 - 14$

   (D) $20x^4 - 35x^2 - 14$

7. If $f(x) = 7x^2 + 3$ and $g(x) = 2x - 9$, then $g(f(2)) =$

    (A) 53.   (C) 28.

    (B) 31.   (D) 19.

8. What is the domain of the function defined by

    $$y = f(x) = \sqrt{-x+1} + 5?$$

    (A) $\{x \mid x \geq 0\}$ (C) $\{x \mid 0 \leq x \leq 1\}$

    (B) $\{x \mid x \leq 1\}$ (D) $\{x \mid x \geq -1\}$

9. If $f(x) = x^3 - x - 1$, then the set of all c for which $f(c) = f(-c)$ is

    (A) {all real numbers}.

    (B) {0}.

    (C) {0, 1}.

    (D) {–1, 0, 1}.

10. A teacher starts class by showing students how to use algebra tiles to factor an algebraic expression. He then tells the students to use the tiles to factor several expressions found in the textbook. After a few minutes he notices that the students are using the paper and pencil method he taught them yesterday to find the answers and then grouping the tiles accordingly. What should he do?

    (A) Nothing, the students can get the answers. They get it.

    (B) Rearrange the unit plan so that in the future the manipulatives are used before the algebraic strategies in a discovery setting.

    (C) Forget about using the manipulatives in the next class. They are a waste of time.

    (D) Stop the class and repeat the example that he showed them at the start of the class.

11. While conducting informal observations of student progress on a problem involving ratios, a teacher gets the idea that the students should do a project on the golden ratio. He gets the attention of the students and tells them that they have a project due on the golden ratio in two weeks. He writes the terms golden ratio, golden mean, and divine proportion on the chalkboard. He then instructs the students to continue their work and goes back to the observations. All of the following are true except

    (A) The grades assigned to the project will have little meaning.

    (B) The students will learn about an intriguing and important concept in mathematics.

    (C) The projects will contain similar information.

    (D) The students will not gain much mathematical insight or understanding in doing the project.

12. If m $\overset{\frown}{ABC}$ is $\frac{3}{2}\pi$ radians, then y is equal to

    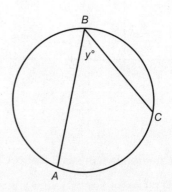

    (A) 90°.   (C) 45°.

    (B) 72°.   (D) 36°.

13. The best representation to highlight periodic behavior is a

    (A) line graph.

    (B) paragraph describing the amplitude.

    (C) trigonometric equation.

    (D) diagram of the unit circle.

14. The ceiling of George's bedroom must be painted. The diagram above represents his bedroom and includes a circular light fixture with a diameter of 2 feet. A gallon of paint covers 16 square feet and costs $8.95. How much will George have to spend on paint to cover the entire ceiling except for the light fixture?

(A) $44.75   (C) $35.80

(B) $50.20   (D) $42.99

15. What type of triangle is $\triangle ABC$?

(A) Right triangle

(B) Equilateral triangle

(C) Isosceles triangle

(D) Obtuse triangle

16. Select the statement that is the negation of the statement "If I am hungry, then I will have a snack."

(A) If I am not hungry, then I will not have a snack.

(B) I am not hungry and I will have a snack.

(C) I am hungry or I will not have a snack.

(D) I am hungry and I will not have a snack.

17. It is important for the teacher to anticipate and plan for likely student errors so that the teacher can

(A) gain insight into the concepts the students need to understand the new content.

(B) point out each potential error during the lesson.

(C) trick the students on multiple choice tests.

(D) plan for all the possible errors the students might make.

18. A certain arc of a circle has a measure of π radians. The ratio between the measure of the arc and the diameter is approximately

(A) 3.14   (C) 2

(B) 6.28   (D) 1.57

19. Which of the following sentences below concerning the equation of an ellipse

$$\frac{x^2}{a^2} + \frac{y^2}{b^2} = 1,$$

is true when $a = b = r$?

I.   The equation reduces to $x^2 + y^2 = r^2$.

II. The equation reduces to an equation of a circle with center at $(0, 0)$ and radius r.

III. The equation reduces to an equation of a circle, center $(0, r)$.

(A) I only.   (C) II and III only.

(B) I and II only.   (D) III only.

20. A circular region rotated 360° around its diameter as an axis generates a

(A) cube.   (C) cone.

(B) cylinder.   (D) sphere.

21. Read the graph and answer the question.

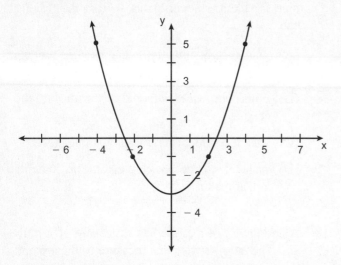

Which equation could be represented by the graph?

(A) $y = \frac{1}{2}x^2 + 3$ (C) $y = \frac{1}{2}x^2 - 3$

(B) $y = -\frac{1}{2}x^2 - 3$ (D) $y = -\frac{1}{2}x^2 + 3$

22. The distance between the point (2, 4) and the line $y + 2x - 3 = 0$ is

(A) 1.9   (C) 2.24

(B) 3.24   (D) 3.8

23. $\sin(x + y) = 0.9659$, $\sin(x) = 0.5$. Find $\cos(y)$.

(A) 0.425   (C) 0.707

(B) 0.034   (D) 0.816

24. $(\sin\theta \times \cot\theta)^2 + (\cos\theta \times \tan\theta)^2 =$

(A) 1   (C) $2\sin^2\theta$

(B) $2\cos^2\theta$ (D) $2\cot^2\theta$

25. Representatives to a student group are being selected to fill vacancies. Two of five freshmen will be selected and three of four sophomores will be selected. In how many different ways can these students be selected?

(A) 480   (C) 80

(B) 120   (D) 40

26. A zoo has eight elephants. On any given day three of the elephants are selected and lined up to give rides to the visitors. How many different arrangements of any three selected elephants are there?

(A) 21   (C) 336

(B) 24   (D) 6

27. Find the median of the following sample data: 6, 20, 7, 3, 18, 4, 8, 14.

(A) 7.5   (C) 10

(B) 8   (D) 80

28. The following plot represents an individual's shoe size and height.

Which of the following best describes the relationship between shoe size and height?

(A) There appears to be no relationship between shoe size and height.

(B) An increase in height causes an increase in shoe size.

(C) There appears to be a negative relationship between shoe size and height.

(D) There appears to be a positive relationship between shoe size and height.

29. If $f'(c) = 0$ for $f(x) = 3x^2 - 12x + 9$, where $0 \le x \le 4$, then $c =$

(A) 2   (C) 0

(B) 3   (D) 1

30. The position of a particle moving along a straight line at any time t is given by $S(t) = 2t^3 - 4t^2 + 2t - 1$. The least velocity during the time interval [0, 2] is

(A) 4.25   (C) −0.67

(B) 0.5   (D) −1.5

31. $\dfrac{dy}{dx} = x\cot(3x^2)$, then $y =$

(A) $\ln|\sin 3x^2| + c$

(B) $6\ln|\sin 3x^2| + c$

(C) $6\ln c|\sin 3x^2|$

(D) $\dfrac{1}{6}\ln|\sin 3x^2| + c$

32. If $\displaystyle\int_a^b f(x)\,dx = 8$, $a = 2$, f is continuous, and the average value of f on $[a, b]$ is 4, then $b =$

(A) 0   (C) 4

(B) 2   (D) 3

33. The area between the line $y = x$ and the curve $y = \dfrac{1}{2}x^2$ is

(A) 1   (C) $\dfrac{2}{3}$

(B) $\dfrac{1}{2}$ (D) $\dfrac{3}{2}$

34. $\displaystyle\lim_{h\to 0}\dfrac{e^{x+h} - e^x}{h}$ equals

(A) 0   (C) $+\infty$

(B) e^x (D) $-\infty$

35. Which equation expresses the relationship that the height (h) varies inversely as the square of the base (b)?

(A) $h = \dfrac{b^2}{k}$ (C) $h = \dfrac{k}{b^2}$

(B) $kb^2 = h$ (D) $kh = b^2$

36. Graphing calculators are an important part of the mathematics classroom because

(A) they offer students an easy way to get the right answers.

(B) students will have to know how to use a scientific calculator in order to succeed in college and in life.

(C) parents demand that teachers use technology.

(D) tedious math tasks become easier.

37. The graph below shows the relationship between temperature and sales of jackets in $1000 units. Which statement does this graph support?

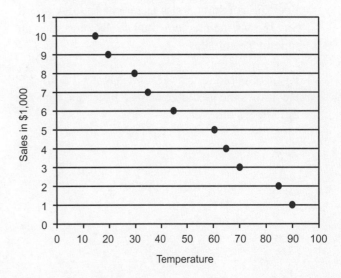

(A) As temperature decreases, sales of jackets increase.

(B) The sales of jackets are unchanged by temperature.

(C) As temperature increases, sales of jackets increase.

(D) The sales of jackets are unchanged as temperature increases.

38. $\log_3\left(\dfrac{1}{27}\right) =$

(A) −3   (C) $\dfrac{1}{3}$

(B) $-\dfrac{1}{3}$ (D) 3

39. To be eligible for the track team a student must be able to run a mile in less than 10 minutes and throw a medicine ball at least 12 feet. The student must also have a grade point average (GPA) of at least 2.5 and be taking a minimum of three classes.

The following students wish to try out for the team. Which ones, if any, are eligible?

<u>Sam</u> is taking 4 classes and has a GPA of 3.2. He runs a mile in 10.3 minutes and throws the medicine ball 14 feet.

<u>Lee Ann</u> is taking 3 classes and has a GPA of 3.8. She throws the medicine ball 12 feet and runs the mile in 9.9 minutes.

<u>Ryan</u> is taking 5 classes and has a GPA of 2.6. He throws the medicine ball 12.1 feet and runs the mile in 8.8 minutes.

(A) Sam and Ryan only

(B) Lee Ann only

(C) Lee Ann and Ryan only

(D) All of the students are eligible.

40. Which is a logical conclusion that can be drawn from the following?
All astronauts are highly skilled, trained professionals.
All highly skilled, trained professionals have college degrees.
Aaron has a college degree.

(A) Aaron is a highly skilled, trained professional.

(B) Aaron is an astronaut.

(C) Aaron is not an astronaut.

(D) None of these are logical.

Answer Key

1.	(B)	21.	(C)
2.	(D)	22.	(C)
3.	(B)	23.	(C)
4.	(B)	24.	(A)
5.	(D)	25.	(D)
6.	(A)	26.	(C)
7.	(A)	27.	(A)
8.	(B)	28.	(D)
9.	(D)	29.	(A)
10.	(B)	30.	(C)
11.	(B)	31.	(D)
12.	(C)	32.	(C)
13.	(A)	33.	(C)
14.	(A)	34.	(B)
15.	(A)	35.	(C)
16.	(D)	36.	(D)
17.	(A)	37.	(A)
18.	(D)	38.	(A)
19.	(B)	39.	(C)
20.	(D)	40.	(D)

Diagnostic Test
Detailed Explanations of Answers

1. (B)

The graphs of the equations represented by the other choices are as follows.

Answer choice (A): $x = 2$

Answer choice (C): $y = 2$

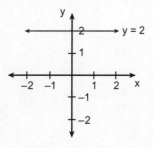

Answer choice (D): $y = -2$

The graph of $x = -2$ is parallel to the y-axis and passes through the point $(-2, 0)$.

2. (D)

$$6x^2 + 2x - 4 = 2(3x^2 + x - 2),$$

factoring out a 2 from each term. The $(3x^2 + x - 2)$ is further factored by finding the terms which multiply to $3x^2$, namely, $3x$ and x; and by finding the terms which multiply to -2, namely, -2 and 1 or $+2$ and -1. Here are the possibilities. Check the product of the inner terms and the product of the outer terms for each factor. We are looking for the middle term of $3x^2 + x - 2$, i.e., $+1x$.

$$3x^2 + x - 2 =$$

$$\overset{-3x}{(3x + 2)\,(x - 1)} \qquad \overset{+3x}{(3x - 2)\,(x + 1)}$$
$$\underset{-1x}{+2x} \qquad\qquad \underset{+1x}{-2x}$$
$$\times$$

$$\overset{-6x}{(3x + 1)(x - 2)} \qquad \overset{+6x}{(3x - 1)\,(x - 2)}$$
$$\underset{-5x}{+1x} \qquad\qquad \underset{+5x}{-1x}$$
$$\times$$

This says

$$3x^2 + x - 2 = (3x - 2)\,(x + 1).$$

Therefore,

$$6x^2 + 2x - 4 = 2(3x - 2)\,(x + 1),$$

and the factor which appears as one of the choices is $(3x - 2)$.

Answer choice (A) is incorrect because of a wrong use of the distributive law.

$$6x^2 + 2x - 4$$
$$2(3x^2 + x - 2) = 2(3x - 2)\,(x + 1)$$
$$2(3x - 2) = 3x - 4$$

Answer choice (B) is incorrect because of improper factoring out using the "F.O.I.L." method.

$$6x^2 + 2x - 4 = (6x - 1)(x + 4)$$

Answer choice (C) is also incorrect because of a change in sign.

$$6x^2 + 2x - 4 = 2(3x - 2)(x + 1), (x + 1)$$
$$= (x - 1)$$

3. (B)

The answer is (B). It is the mathematical definition of slope. The comparison shows how one variable changes with respect to change in another variable. Choice (A) is incorrect because although it is a common mnemonic device to remember the formula for slope, it provides very little information about what the slope actually is and requires the user to remember the definitions of rise and run. Choice (C) is simply a letter, perhaps a variable, but without any other reference the reader does not know if it is the 'm' from the equation for a linear function. Choice (D) is an explanation that a student with cursory understanding might provide. There is insufficient detail and lack of clarity.

4. (B)

$$\frac{9 \text{ apartments with terraces}}{16 \text{ apartments}} = \frac{?}{144 \text{ apartments}}$$

Solving this proportion for the "?"

$$? = \frac{9 \text{ apartments} \times 144 \text{ apartments}}{16 \text{ apartments}}$$

$$= \frac{1296 \text{ apartments}}{16 \text{ apartments}} = 81 \text{ apartments}$$

Answer (A) is incorrect because the apartments were subtracted.

$$144 - (16 - 9) = 144 - 7 = 137 \text{ apartments}$$

Answer (C) is incorrect because the number of apartments with terraces is 9 not $16 - 9$.

$$(144 \div 16) \times (16 - 9) = 9 \times 7 = 63$$

Answer (D) is incorrect due to a multiplication factor guess of 6.

$$144 - [(16 - 9) \times 6] = 102$$

5. (D)

$$5x + 2y = -5$$
$$-3x + y = 3$$

Multiply the bottom equation by –2 so that the terms in the *y*-column will cancel as follows (in this way if the *y*-terms cancel you will be solving for *x*).

$$5x + 2y = -5 \qquad\qquad 5x + 2y = -5$$
$$-2(-3x + y) = -2(3) \Rightarrow 6x - 2y = -6$$

$$\frac{11x}{11} = \frac{-11}{11}$$
$$x = -1$$

Add the coefficients/terms in the *x*-column and the constants on the right side. Then divide both sides by 11, the coefficient of the *x*-term.

Answer choice (A) is incorrect because it solved for the variable *y*.

$$3(\ 5x + 2y = -5) = 15x + 6y = -15$$
$$5(-3x + y = 3) = -15x + 5y = 15$$
$$11y = 0$$
$$y = 0$$

Answer choice (B) is incorrect because of an error in adding 2 negative numbers.

$$5x + 2y = -5$$
$$6x - 2y = -6$$
$$11x = -1, x = -\frac{1}{11}$$

Answer choice (C) is incorrect because of an error in signs.

$$5x + 2y = -5$$
$$-6x - 2y = -6$$
$$x = 1$$

6. **(A)**

Multiplication of binomials assumes that for

$$\overbrace{\underbrace{(5x^2 + 2)}_{first}\ (4x^2 - 7)}^{outer} =$$

(last, inner labels above; first, outer labels below)

we multiply the first terms $(5x^2)(4x^2)$ in the parentheses; then we multiply the outer terms $(5x^2)(-7)$ in the parentheses; then we multiply the inner terms $(2)(4x^2)$ in the parentheses; and then we multiply the last terms $(2)(-7)$ in the parentheses.

This means

$(5x^2 + 2)(4x^2 - 7) =$

$\underline{(5x^2)(4x^2)} + \underline{(5x^2)(-7)} + \underline{(2)(4x^2)} + \underline{(2)(-7)} =$

$20x^4 \quad - 35x^2 \quad + 8x^2 \quad - 14 \quad =$

$\begin{cases} \text{multiplying each} \\ \text{pair of terms and} \\ \text{adding exponents} \\ \text{in the first term} \end{cases}$

Combine the like terms $-35x^2 + 8x^2$ and we get

$20x^4 - 27x^2 - 14$

Answer (B) is incorrect due to an error in multiplying by a negative number.

$(5x^2 + 2)(4x^2 - 7)$
$= (5x^2)(4x^2) + (2)(4x^2) + (5x^2)(-7) + (2)(-7)$
$= 20x^4 + 8x^2 + (-35x^2) - 14$
$= 20x^4 + 8x^2 + 35x^2 - 14$
$= 20x^4 + 43x^2 - 14$

Answer (C) is incorrect because the product of inner and outer terms were not added.

$(5x^2 + 2)(4x^2 - 7) = (5x^2)(4x^2) + (2)(-7)$
$= 20x^4 - 14$

Answer (D) is also incorrect because the inner product was not added to the outer product.

$(5x^2 + 2)(4x^2 - 7) = (5x^2)(4x^2) +$
$(5x^2)(-7) + (2)(-7)$
$= 20x^4 - 35x^2 - 14$

7. **(A)**

$f(x) = 7x^2 + 3,\ g(x) = 2x - 9$

Substituting 2 into $f(x)$:

$f(2) = 7(2)^2 + 3 = 31.$

So $g(f(2)) = g(31).$

Substituting and solving:

$g(31) = 2(31) - 9 = 53$

8. **(B)**

The only restriction for the domain is that $-x + 1$ must be greater than or equal to zero.

$-x + 1 \geq 0$
$\Rightarrow x \leq 1$

9. **(D)**

$f(c) = c^3 - c - 1,\ f(-c) = -c^3 + c - 1$
$c^3 - c - 1 = -c^3 + c - 1$
$c^3 = c$
$\therefore c = -1,\ 0,\ \text{or}\ 1$

10. **(B)**

The teacher has misused the manipulatives. Manipulatives are not meant to confirm algebraic algorithms. Saying, "See the algebra I showed you works" will not improve a student's conceptual understanding of factoring polynomials. In fact, the students will become frustrated with this approach because they will question why they need to play with bits of plastic if they already know how to get the answers. The students should use the tiles to come up with their own ways of organizing the manipulatives with the teacher guiding them to method that later becomes algebraic algorithm.

Choice (A) is wrong. Getting the answer does not mean that the students understand the concept involved. Option (C) rejects the idea of reflective teaching. (D) does not work because repeating something that didn't work the first time rarely works the second time.

11. (B)

Therefore they will not learn because the assessment was not planned with any clear objective in mind and the students have no rubric for what is expected of them. Choice (D) is not true because they have not been asked to do anything that would require them to understand the mathematics of the golden ratio. Choice (C): In fact, they have not been asked to do anything other than a 'project'. This will likely result in reports on the topic with information gleaned from the internet. Choice (A): Any grades given will have little meaning because the students did not know on what they were being graded.

12. (C)

From a theorem we know that the measure of an inscribed angle is equal to $\frac{1}{2}$ the intercepted arc.

We are told that $m\,\overarc{ABC}$ is $\frac{3}{2}\pi$ radians. There are 2π radians in a circle. Therefore, the intercepted arc is the remaining $\frac{\pi}{2}$ radians.

Converting to degrees:

$$\left(\frac{\pi}{2}\right)\left(\frac{180}{\pi}\right) = 90°.$$

The angle y is half of this:

$$y = \frac{90°}{2} = 45°.$$

13. (A)

Choice (A) is the correct answer. A line graph allows the user to see trends in the data and to explore those trends. Choice (B) is incomplete in that it includes only a discussion of the amplitude of the periodic behavior. As well, written words would not provide the visual evidence and impact that is supplied by a graph. Choice (C) may provide a clue to the periodic nature of the behavior to someone that is already very comfortable with trigonometric functions and their graphs. However, the user that can see this behavior by looking at an equation is actually translating the information from the equation to the graph in their mind. To display

the nature of periodicity a graph is essential. Choice (D) is not correct for the same reasons as Choice (C).

14. (A)

In order to solve this problem, we must determine the area of the ceiling. This is accomplished by drawing a line that creates two rectangles as shown in the accompanying figure.

Determine the area of both rectangles using the formula

$$A = \text{length} \times \text{width}$$

The smaller rectangle will have an area of 5×4 or 20 sq. ft.

To find the length of the larger rectangle, use the information provided on the diagram. The lengths given on the bottom of the diagram are 7 and 5 which add up to 12.

Use the area formula and multiply 12 by 5 which yields 60 sq. ft.

Add the two areas together to obtain $60 + 20 = 80$.

Do not forget about the area of the light fixture. George does not want to paint over the fixture, so we must subtract the area of the light fixture from the total area of the ceiling.

The area of a circle is determined by the formula π times the radius squared.

We are given the diameter of the circle, 2 feet. The radius is half of the diameter, so our radius is 1 foot. Squaring this number leaves us with 1 still. So our formula is now π times 1. This will give us π which is equivalent to about 3.14.

Subtract the area of the light from the total area.

$$80 - 3.14 = 76.86$$

Next, determine how many times 16 (the number of square feet one gallon of paint covers) divides into 76.86.

$$76.86 \div 16 = 4.8.$$

To determine the cost of the project, multiply the number of gallons it will take to paint the ceiling by the price per gallon, $8.95.

Since the number of gallons did not come out to an even number, we must round this number up because you cannot buy 8/10 of a gallon.

4.8 rounds up to 5.

$$5 \text{ gallons} \times \$8.95 = \$44.75$$

15. (A)

is the correct answer. The two given angles sum to 90°. Since the angles of a triangle sum to 180°, this leaves 90° for $\angle A$. Since $\angle A$ is 90°, this makes $\triangle ABC$ a right triangle. There is no angle greater than 90°, so $\triangle ABC$ is not an obtuse triangle. Since the angles of $\triangle ABC$ are all different, the sides all have different measures which eliminates (B) and (C).

16. (D)

Let p = if I am hungry.

Let q = I will have a snack.

Then the original statement is: If p, then q.

The negation is: $\sim$ (if p, then q) = p and not q.

To negate a conditional: If p, then q, the result is p and not q. Therefore, the negation of the original statement is: "I am hungry and I will not have a snack."

17. (A)

The questions of what and how concepts will be assessed should occur at the start of the lesson planning stage. Therefore, when the teacher figures out the likely student errors, he can see which new concepts the students are going to have difficulty with and what prior knowledge is necessary for the new concepts to be accessible. Choice 'b' and 'd': Pointing out each possible

error is impossible as is planning for all possible errors. Choice 'c': Tests should not be tricks.

18. (D)

Call the arc AB. $AB = \pi r$ (given). If we multiply both sides by 2 we obtain:

$$2AB = 2\pi r = \pi d, AB = \frac{\pi}{2}d$$
$$\frac{AB}{d} = \frac{\pi}{2} \approx \frac{3.14}{2} = 1.57$$

Calculator: $\pi + 2 = 1.57$

19. (B)

If $a = b = r$, the given equation becomes

$$\frac{x^2}{a^2} + \frac{y^2}{b^2} = \frac{x^2}{r^2} + \frac{y^2}{r^2} = 1. \qquad (1)$$

Multiplying the last branch of the equality in equation (1) by r^2 yields

$$x^2 + y^2 = r^2. \qquad (2)$$

This is the equation of a circle with center at $C(0, 0)$ and radius r. Hence, we see that a circle is a special case of an ellipse.

20. (D)

A sphere is formed with a circle is rotated 360° about its diameter.

21. (C)

The graph passes through the points $(0, -3), (2, -1)$, $(-2, -1), (4, 5)$, and $(-4, +5)$. Also, the graph is a parabola which faces upward and, therefore, the coefficient of the x^2-term must be positive. These conditions are only satisfied by

$$y = \frac{1}{2}x^2 - 3$$

and, therefore, answer choices (A), (B), and (D) are incorrect.

22. (C)

The distance d of a point (x_0, y_0) to the line

$$Ax + By + C = 0$$

is $d = \dfrac{|Ax_0 + By_0 + C|}{\sqrt{A^2 + B^2}}$

For the problem given here, we therefore have

$$d = \frac{|2 \times 2 + 1 \times 4 - 3|}{\sqrt{2^2 + 1^2}} = \sqrt{5} = 2.236$$

23. (C)

$$x = \sin^{-1}(0.5) = 30°.$$
$$x + y = \sin^{-1}(0.9659) = 75°.$$

Then find y to be

$$y = 75° - 30° = 45°.$$

Then $\cos(y) = \cos(45°) = 0.707.$

24. (A)

$$(\sin\theta \times \cot\theta)^2 + (\cos\theta \tan\theta)^2$$

$$= \left(\sin\theta\left(\frac{\cos\theta}{\sin\theta}\right)\right)^2 + \left(\cos\theta\left(\frac{\sin\theta}{\cos\theta}\right)\right)^2$$
$$= \cos^2\theta + \sin^2\theta = 1$$

25. (D)

is the correct response. In how many ways can two of five freshmen be selected:

$$5C_2 \text{ or } \frac{5!}{2!3!} = \frac{5 \times 4 \times 3 \times 2 \times 1}{2 \times 1 \times 3 \times 2 \times 1} = 10$$

Three of four sophomores can be selected in the same manner.

$$4C_3 \text{ or } \frac{4!}{3!1!} = \frac{4 \times 3 \times 2 \times 1}{3 \times 2 \times 1 \times 1} = 4$$

Since the two events are independent, the values are multiplied (10 × 4 or 40) to determine the number of different ways these students can be selected. (A), (B), and (C) result from the use of inappropriate formulas.

26. (C)

is the correct response. Eight elephants are available to be selected for the first position. Given that the first elephant has been selected, only 7 elephants are left to be selected for the second position. The first and second positions have been selected, leaving 6 for the third position. Thus 8 × 7 × 6 = 336. (A), (B), and (D) are incorrect because they do not illustrate the fundamental counting principle for this example.

27. (A)

is the correct answer. The median is the middle number of a data set in numerical order. First arrange the set in order: 3, 4, 6, 7, 8, 14, 18, 20. Then locate the middle term. In this case the middle term would fall midway between 7 and 8, so the median is 7.5. (B) is from incorrectly rounding the median. (C) is the mean, and (D) is the sum total of the data set.

28. (D)

is the correct solution. We can see from the figure that as shoe size increases so does height, so there is a positive relationship which rules out (A) and (C). The problem with (B) is that neither variable causes a change in the other variable.

29. (A)

$$f'(x) = 6x - 12$$
$$f'(c) = 0$$
$$6c - 12 = 0$$
$$c = 2$$

30. (C)

The rate of movement of the particle is the velocity $s'(t)$. Use your graphic calculator to draw both $s(t)$ and $s'(t)$.

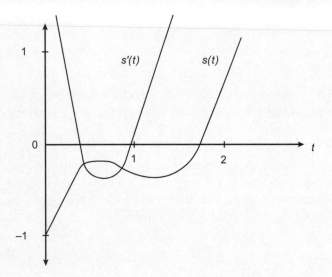

The velocity is given by $v(t) = 6t^2 - 8t + 2$.

The acceleration $a(t) = 12t - 8$ vanishes at $t = \dfrac{2}{3}$;

at this time the velocity has reached its minimum. This occurs during the interval $[0, 2]$.

Therefore, the minimum velocity of $v = -\dfrac{2}{3}$,

occurs at $t = \dfrac{2}{3}$.

31. (D)

By the method of substitution:

Let $u = 3x^2$

$\Rightarrow \dfrac{du}{dx} = 6x$

$\Leftrightarrow dx = \dfrac{du}{6}$, after cross multiplication and division.

Therefore, $\displaystyle\int x \cot(3x^2)\,dx = \dfrac{1}{6}\int \cot u\,du$

$= \dfrac{1}{6}\int \dfrac{\cos u}{\sin u}\,du$

$= \dfrac{1}{6}\ln|\sin u| + c$

$= \dfrac{1}{6}\ln\left|\sin\left(3x^2\right)\right| + c,$

(substituting u with $3x^2$).

32. (C)

Average value of f in

$$[a, b] = \dfrac{1}{b-a}\int_a^b f(x)\,dx$$

$$\Leftrightarrow 4 = \dfrac{1}{b-2} \times 8$$

substituting the given values

$\Leftrightarrow 4(b - 2) = 8$

$\Leftrightarrow b = 4.$

33. (C)

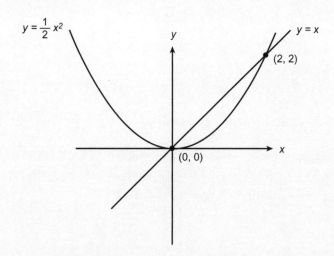

The curve is below the line, so

$\text{Area} = \displaystyle\int_0^2 \left(x - \dfrac{1}{2}x^2\right)dx = \left(\dfrac{x^2}{2} - \dfrac{x^3}{6}\right)\Bigg|_0^2 = 2 - \dfrac{8}{6} = \dfrac{2}{3}.$

34. (B)

$\displaystyle\lim_{h \to 0} \dfrac{e^{x+h} - e^x}{h}$ equals the derivative of e^x by using the definition of the derivative

$$f'(x) = \lim_{h \to 0} \frac{f(x+h) - f(x)}{h}$$
$$= e^x \quad \text{for} \quad f(x) = e^x$$

35. (C)

If x and y vary inversely as each other and k is the constant of variation, then $xy = k$. So if height (h) varies inversely as the square of the base (b^2) then $hb^2 = k$ Solving for h, we divide both sides of the equation $hb^2 = k$, by b^2 as follows:

$$\frac{hb^2}{b^2} = \frac{k}{b^2}$$
$$h = \frac{k}{b^2}$$

Answer (A) is incorrect because h varies directly as the square of the base,

$$h = \frac{b^2}{k},$$

if h increases then b^2 must also increase. Answer (B) is incorrect because h also varies directly as the square of the base,

$$kb^2 = h,$$

if h increases then b^2 must also increase. Answer (D) is incorrect because it takes the same form as answer (A) so the reasons are the same.

$$kh = b^2$$
$$h = \frac{b^2}{k}$$

36. (D)

Tedious tasks such as producing multiple graphs become easy. Therefore, the students can focus on the concepts behind the tasks rather than the tasks. However, just because a student is using a calculator does not mean that the answers are at her fingertips. Choice (A): Questions that require conceptual understanding will not be answered easily with or without a calculator

unless the concept is understood. However, if the student is good at following directions, the question "What is maximum value of the function f(x) = –x² + 4x?" can be readily answered using a graphing calculator or pencil and paper. Choices (B) and (D), scientific calculators are important tools but they are not essential to most people and, although parents do demand that teachers use technology, they often balk at calculators.

37. (A)

Draw a line through the set of data points. Notice that low values of temperature go with high sales, and that high-temperature values go with low sales. Next, evaluate the truth of each possible answer. The graph shows that as temperature decreases, sales of jackets increase.

38. (A)

$$\log_3\left(\frac{1}{27}\right) = \log_3\left(\frac{1}{3^3}\right) = \log_3(3^{-3}) = -3$$

We could also use the identity:

$$\log_a b^c = c\log_a b$$

and write:

$$\log_3 \frac{1}{27} = \log_3 3^{-3} = -3\log_3 3 = -3$$

39. (C)

is the correct answer. Sam is ineligible because he requires more than 10 minutes to run the mile. Both Lee Ann and Ryan are eligible, as they meet every requirement listed.

40. (D)

is the correct response. The set of astronauts is a subset of skilled, highly trained professionals which is in turn a subset of those with college degrees. However, even though Aaron has a college degree, he may or may not be in the set of highly skilled, trained professionals or astronauts.

Competency 1: Knowledge of Algebra

In algebra, letters or variables are used to represent numbers. A **variable** is defined as a placeholder, which can take on any of several values at a given time. A **constant,** on the other hand, is a symbol which takes on only one value at a given time. A **term** is a constant, a variable, or a combination of constants and variables. For example: 7.76, $3x$, xyz, $\dfrac{5z}{x}$, $(0.99)x^2$ are terms. If a term is a combination of constants and variables, the constant part of the term is referred to as the **coefficient** of the variable. If a variable is written without a coefficient, the coefficient is assumed to be 1.

- **EXAMPLES**

$3x^2$	y^3
coefficient: 3	coefficient: 1
variable: x	variable: y

An **expression** is a collection of one or more terms. If the number of terms is greater than 1, the expression is said to be the sum of the terms.

- **EXAMPLES**

$9, 9xy, 6x + \dfrac{x}{3}, 8yz - 2x$

An algebraic expression consisting of only one term is called a **monomial**; of two terms is called a **binomial**; of three terms is called a **trinomial**. In general, an algebraic expression consisting of two or more terms is called a **polynomial**.

Operations with Polynomials

A) **Addition of polynomials** is achieved by combining like terms, terms which differ only in their numerical coefficients, e.g.,

$P(x) = (x^2 - 3x + 5) + (4x^2 + 6x - 3)$

Note that the parentheses are used to distinguish the polynomials.

By using the commutative and associative laws, we can rewrite $P(x)$ as:

$P(x) = (x^2 + 4x^2) + (6x - 3x) + (5 - 3)$

Using the distributive law, $ab + ac = a(b + c)$, yields:

$(1 + 4)x^2 + (6 - 3)x + (5 - 3) = 5x^2 + 3x + 2$

B) **Subtraction of two polynomials** is achieved by first changing the sign of all terms in the expression which are being subtracted and then adding this result to the other expression, e.g.,

$(5x^2 + 4y^2 + 3z^2) - (4xy + 7y^2 - 3z^2 + 1)$

$= 5x^2 + 4y^2 + 3z^2 - 4xy - 7y^2 + 3z^2 - 1$

$= 5x^2 + (4y^2 - 7y^2) + (3z^2 + 3z^2) - 4xy - 1$

$= 5x^2 + (-3y^2) + 6z^2 - 4xy - 1$

$$= \left(\frac{6}{2}\right)\left(\frac{x}{1}\right)\left(\frac{y}{y^2}\right)\left(\frac{z^2}{z}\right)$$

$= 3xy^{-1}z$

$$= \frac{3xz}{y}$$

C) **Multiplication of two or more polynomials** is achieved by using the laws of exponents, the rules of signs, and the commutative and associative laws of multiplication. Begin by multiplying the coefficients and then multiply the variables according to the laws of exponents, e.g.,

$(y^2)(5)(6y^2)(yz)(2z^2)$

$= (1)(5)(6)(1)(2)(y^2)(y^2)(yz)(z^2)$

$= 60[(y^2)(y^2)(y)][(z)(z^2)]$

$= 60(y^5)(z^3)$

$= 60y^5z^3$

D) **Multiplication of a polynomial by a monomial** is achieved by multiplying each term of the polynomial by the monomial and combining the results, e.g.,

$(4x^2 + 3y)(6xz^2)$

$= (4x^2)(6xz^2) + (3y)(6xz^2)$

$= 24x^3z^2 + 18xyz^2$

E) **Multiplication of a polynomial by a polynomial** is achieved by multiplying each of the terms of one polynomial by each of the terms of the other polynomial and combining the result, e.g.,

$(5y + z + 1)(y^2 + 2y)$

$[(5y)(y^2) + (5y)(2y)] + [(z)(y^2) + (z)(2y)] +$

$[(1)(y^2) + (1)(2y)]$

$= (5y^3 + 10y^2) + (y^2z + 2yz) + (y^2 + 2y)$

$= (5y^3) + (10y^2 + y^2) + (y^2z) + (2yz) + (2y)$

$= 5y^3 + 11y^2 + y^2z + 2yz + 2y$

F) **Division of a monomial by a monomial** is achieved by first dividing the constant coefficients and the variable factors separately, and then multiplying these quotients, e.g.,

$6xyz^2 \div 2y^2z$

G) **Division of a polynomial by polynomial** is achieved by following the given procedure, called long division.

Step 1: The terms of both the polynomials are arranged in order of ascending or descending powers of one variable.

Step 2: The first term of the dividend is divided by the first term of the divisor which gives the first term of the quotient.

Step 3: This first term of the quotient is multiplied by the entire divisor and the result is subtracted from the dividend.

Step 4: Using the remainder obtained from Step 3 as the new dividend, Steps 2 and 3 are repeated until the remainder is zero or the degree of the remainder is less than the degree of the divisor.

Step 5: The result is written as follows:

$$\frac{\text{dividend}}{\text{divisor}} = \text{quotient} + \frac{\text{remainder}}{\text{divisor}}$$

divisor $\neq 0$

e.g., $(2x^2 + x + 6) \div (x + 1)$

$$
\begin{array}{r}
2x - 1 \\
(x+1)\overline{)2x^2 + x + 6} \\
-(2x^2 + 2x) \\
\hline
-x + 6 \\
-(-x - 1) \\
\hline
7
\end{array}
$$

The result is $(2x^2 + x + 6) \div (x + 1) = 2x - 1 + \dfrac{7}{x+1}$

Drill: Operations with Polynomials

Addition

DIRECTIONS: Add the following polynomials.

1. $9a^2b + 3c + 2a^2b + 5c =$

(A)　$19a^2bc$　　　　(C)　$11a^4b^2 + 8c^2$

(B)　$11a^2b + 8c$　　　(D)　$19a^4b^2c^2$

2.　　$14m^2n^3 + 6m^2n^3 + 3m^2n^3 =$

(A)　$20m^2n^3$　　　(C)　$23m^2n^3$

(B)　$23m^6n^9$　　　(D)　$32m^6n^9$

3.　　$3x + 2y + 16x + 3z + 6y =$

(A)　$19x + 8y$　　　(C)　$19x + 8y + 3z$

(B)　$19x + 11yz$　　(D)　$11xy + 19xz$

4.　　$(4d^2 + 7e^3 + 12f) + (3d^2 + 6e^3 + 2f) =$

(A)　$23d^2e^3f$　　　(C)　$33d^4e^6f^2$

(B)　$33d^2e^2f$　　　(D)　$7d^2 + 13e^3 + 14f$

5.　　$3ac^2 + 2b^2c + 7ac^2 + 2ac^2 + b^2c =$

(A)　$12ac^2 + 3b^2c$　　(C)　$11ac^2 + 4ab^2c$

(B)　$14ab^2c^2$　　　　(D)　$15ab^2c^2$

Subtraction

DIRECTIONS: Subtract the following polynomials.

6.　　$14m^2n - 6m^2n =$

(A)　$20m^2n$　　　(C)　$8m$

(B)　$8m^2n$　　　　(D)　8

7.　　$3x^3y^2 - 4xz - 6x^3y^2 =$

(A)　$-7x^2y^2z$　　　　　(C)　$-3x^3y^2 - 4xz$

(B)　$3x^3y^2 - 10x^4y^2z$　(D)　$-x^2y^2z - 6x^3y^2$

8.　　$9g^2 + 6h - 2g^2 - 5h =$

(A)　$15g^2h - 7g^2h$　(C)　$11g^2 + 7h$

(B)　$7g^4h^2$　　　　　(D)　$7g^2 + h$

9.　　$7b^3 - 4c^2 - 6b^3 + 3c^2 =$

(A)　$b^3 - c^2$　　　(C)　$13b^3 - c$

(B)　$-11b^2 - 3c^2$　(D)　$7b - c$

10.　$11q^2r - 4q^2r - 8q^2r =$

(A)　$22q^2r$　　　(C)　$-2q^2r$

(B)　q^2r　　　　(D)　$-q^2r$

Multiplication

DIRECTIONS: Multiply the following polynomials.

11.　$5p^2t \times 3p^2t =$

(A)　$15p^2t$　　　(C)　$15p^4t^2$

(B)　$15p^4t$　　　(D)　$8p^2t$

12.　$(2r + s)\,14r =$

(A)　$28rs$　　　　(C)　$16r^2 + 14rs$

(B)　$28r^2 + 14sr$　(D)　$28r + 14sr$

13.　$(4m + p)\,(3m - 2p) =$

(A)　$12m^2 + 5mp + 2p^2$

(B)　$12m^2 - 2mp + 2p^2$

(C)　$7m - p$

(D)　$12m^2 - 5mp - 2p^2$

14.　$(2a + b)\,(3a^2 + ab + b^2) =$

(A)　$6a^3 + 5a^2b + 3ab^2 + b^3$

(B)　$5a^3 + 3ab + b^3$

(C)　$6a^3 + 2a^2b + 2ab^2$

(D)　$3a^2 + 2a + ab + b + b^2$

15.　$(6t^2 + 2t + 1)\,3t =$

(A)　$9t^2 + 5t + 3$　　(C)　$9t^3 + 6t^2 + 3t$

(B)　$18t^2 + 6t + 3$　(D)　$18t^3 + 6t^2 + 3t$

Division

DIRECTIONS: Divide the following polynomials.

16.　$(x^2 + x - 6) \div (x - 2) =$

(A)　$x - 3$　　　(C)　$x + 3$

(B)　$x + 2$　　　(D)　$x - 2$

17.　$24b^4c^3 \div 6b^2c =$

(A)　$3b^2c^2$　　　(C)　$4b^3c^2$

(B)　$4b^4c^3$　　　(D)　$4b^2c^2$

18.　$(3p^2 + pq - 2q^2) \div (p + q) =$

(A) $3p + 2q$ (C) $3p - q$

(B) $2q - 3p$ (D) $3p - 2q$

19. $(y^3 - 2y^2 - y + 2) \div (y - 2)$

(A) $(y - 1)^2$

(B) $y^2 - 1$

(C) $(y + 2)(y - 1)$

(D) $(y + 1)^2$

20. $(m^2 + m - 14) \div (m + 4) =$

(A) $m - 2$ (C) $m - 3 + \dfrac{4}{m + 4}$

(B) $m - 3 + \dfrac{-2}{m + 4}$ (D) $m - 3$

Simplifying Algebraic Expressions

To factor a polynomial completely is to find the prime factors of the polynomial with respect to a specified set of numbers.

The following concepts are important while factoring or simplifying expressions.

A) The factors of an algebraic expression consist of two or more algebraic expressions which, when multiplied together, produce the given algebraic expression.

B) A **prime factor** is a polynomial with no factors other than itself and 1. The **least common multiple (LCM)** for a set of numbers is the smallest quantity divisible by every number of the set. For algebraic expressions, the least common numerical coefficients for each of the given expressions will be a factor.

C) The **greatest common factor (GCF)** for a set of numbers is the largest factor that is common to all members of the set.

D) For algebraic expressions, the greatest common factor is the polynomial of highest degree and the largest numerical coefficient which is a factor of all the given expressions.

Some important formulas, useful for the factoring of polynomials, are listed below.

$a(c + d) = ac + ad$

$(a + b)(a - b) = a^2 - b^2$

$(a + b)(a + b) = (a + b)^2 = a^2 + 2ab + b^2$

$(a - b)(a - b) = (a - b)^2 = a^2 - 2ab + b^2$

$(x + a)(x + b) = x^2 + (a + b)x + ab$

$(ax + b)(cx + d) = acx^2 + (ad + bc)x + bd$

$(a + b)(c + d) = ac + bc + ad + bd$

$(a + b)(a + b)(a + b) = (a + b)^3 = a^3 + 3a^2b + 3ab^2 + b^3$

$(a - b)(a - b)(a - b) = (a - b)^3 = a^3 - 3a^2b + 3ab^2 - b^3$

$(a - b)(a^2 + ab + b^2) = a^3 - b^3$

$(a + b)(a^2 - ab + b^2) = a^3 + b^3$

$(a + b + c)^2 = a^2 + b^2 + c^2 + 2ab + 2ac + 2bc$

$(a - b)(a^3 + a^2b + ab^2 + b^3) = a^4 - b^4$

$(a - b)(a^4 + a^3b + a^2b^2 + ab^3 + b^4) = a^5 - b^5$

$(a - b)(a^5 + a^4b + a^3b^2 + a^2b^3 + ab^4 + b^5) = a^6 - b^6$

$(a - b)(a^{n-1} + a^{n-2}b + a^{n-3}b^2 + \ldots + ab^{n-2} + b^{n-1}) = a^n - b^n$

where n is any positive integer (1, 2, 3, 4, ...).

$(a + b)(a^{n-1} - a^{n-2}b + a^{n-3}b^2 - \ldots - ab^{n-2} + b^{n-1}) = a^n + b^n$

where n is any positive odd integer (1, 3, 5, 7, ...).

The procedure for factoring an algebraic expression completely is as follows:

Step 1: First find the greatest common factor if there is any. Then examine each factor remaining for greatest common factors.

Step 2: Continue factoring the factors obtained in Step 1 until all factors other than monomial factors are prime.

• **EXAMPLE**

Factoring $4 - 16x^2$,

$4 - 16x^2 = 4(1 - 4x^2) = 4(1 + 2x)(1 - 2x)$

PROBLEM

Express each of the following as a single term.

(1) $3x^2 + 2x^2 - 4x^2$

(2) $5axy^2 - 7axy^2 - 3xy^2$

SOLUTION

(1) Factor x^2 in the expression.

$3x^2 + 2x^2 - 4x^2 = (3 + 2 - 4)x^2 = 1x^2 = x^2$

(2) Factor xy^2 in the expression and then factor a.

$$5axy^2 - 7axy^2 - 3xy^2 = (5a - 7a - 3)xy^2$$
$$= [(5 - 7)a - 3]xy^2$$
$$= (-2a - 3)xy^2$$

PROBLEM

Simplify $\dfrac{\dfrac{1}{x-1} - \dfrac{1}{x-2}}{\dfrac{1}{x-2} - \dfrac{1}{x-3}}$.

SOLUTION

Simplify the expression in the numerator by using the addition rule:

$$\frac{a}{b} + \frac{c}{d} = \frac{ad + bc}{bd}$$

Notice bd is the Least Common Denominator, LCD. We obtain

$$\frac{x - 2 - (x - 1)}{(x-1)(x-2)} = \frac{-1}{(x-1)(x-2)}$$

in the numerator.

Repeat this procedure for the expression in the denominator:

$$\frac{x - 3 - (x - 2)}{(x-2)(x-3)} = \frac{-1}{(x-2)(x-3)}$$

We now have

$$\frac{\dfrac{-1}{(x-1)(x-2)}}{\dfrac{-1}{(x-2)(x-3)}}$$

which is simplified by inverting the fraction in the denominator and multiplying it by the numerator and cancelling like terms

$$\frac{-1}{(x-1)(x-2)} \times \frac{(x-2)(x-3)}{-1} = \frac{x-3}{x-1}$$

Drill: Simplifying Algebraic Expressions

DIRECTIONS: Simplify the following expressions.

1. $16b^2 - 25z^2 =$

(A) $(4b - 5z)^2$ (C) $(4b - 5z)(4b + 5z)$

(B) $(4b + 5z)^2$ (D) $(16b - 25z)^2$

2. $x^2 - 2x - 8 =$

(A) $(x - 4)^2$ (C) $(x + 4)(x - 2)$

(B) $(x - 6)(x - 2)$ (D) $(x - 4)(x + 2)$

3. $2c^2 + 5cd - 3d^2 =$

(A) $(c - 3d)(c + 2d)$

(B) $(2c - d)(c + 3d)$

(C) $(c - d)(2c + 3d)$

(D) $(2c + d)(c + 3d)$

4. $4t^3 - 20t =$

(A) $4t(t^2 - 5)$ (C) $4t(t + 4)(t - 5)$

(B) $4t^2(t - 20)$ (D) $2t(2t^2 - 10)$

5. $x^2 + xy - 2y^2 =$

(A) $(x - 2y)(x + y)$ (C) $(x + 2y)(x + y)$

(B) $(x - 2y)(x - y)$ (D) $(x + 2y)(x - y)$

Linear Equations

A linear equation with one unknown is one that can be put into the form $ax + b = 0$, where a and b are constants, $a \neq 0$.

To solve a linear equation means to transform it in the form $x = \dfrac{-b}{a}$.

A) If the equation has unknowns on both sides of the equality, it is convenient to put similar terms on the same sides. Refer to the following example.

$$4x + 3 = 2x + 9$$
$$4x + 3 - 2x = 2x + 9 - 2x$$
$$(4x - 2x) + 3 = (2x - 2x) + 9$$
$$2x + 3 = 0 + 9$$
$$2x + 3 - 3 = 0 + 9 - 3$$
$$2x = 6$$
$$\frac{2x}{2} = \frac{6}{2}$$
$$x = 3$$

B) If the equation appears in fractional form, it is necessary to transform it, using cross-multiplication, and then repeat the same procedure as in A. We obtain:

$$\frac{3x + 4}{3} \diagdown\!\!\!\!\diagup \frac{7x + 2}{5}$$

By using cross-multiplication we would obtain:

$3(7x + 2) = 5(3x + 4)$.

This is equivalent to:

$21x + 6 = 15x + 20$,

which can be solved as in A.

$$21x + 6 = 15x + 20$$
$$21x - 15x + 6 = 15x - 15x + 20$$
$$6x + 6 - 6 = 20 - 6$$
$$6x = 14$$
$$x = \frac{14}{6}$$
$$x = \frac{7}{3}$$

C) If there are radicals in the equation, it is necessary to square both sides and then apply A.

$$\sqrt{3x + 1} = 5$$
$$(\sqrt{3x + 1})^2 = 5^2$$
$$3x + 1 = 25$$
$$3x + 1 - 1 = 25 - 1$$
$$3x = 24$$
$$x = \frac{24}{3}$$
$$x = 8$$

Slope of the Line

The slope of the line containing two points (x_1, y_1) and (x_2, y_2) is given by:

$$\text{Slope} = m = \frac{y_2 - y_1}{x_2 - x_1}$$

Horizontal lines have a slope of zero, and the slope of vertical lines is undefined. Parallel lines have equal slopes and perpendicular lines have slopes that are negative reciprocals of each other.

The equation of a line with slope m passing through a point $Q(x_0, y_0)$ is of the form:

$$y - y_0 = m(x - x_0)$$

This is called the *point-slope form* of a linear equation.

The equation of a line passing through $Q(x_1, y_1)$ and $P(x_2, y_2)$ is given by:

$$\frac{y - y_1}{x - x_1} = \frac{y_2 - y_1}{x_2 - x_1}$$

This is the *two-point form* of a linear equation.

The equation of a line intersecting the x-axis at $(x_0, 0)$ and the y-axis at $(0, y_0)$ is given by:

$$\frac{x}{x_0} + \frac{y}{y_0} = 1$$

This is the *intercept form* of a linear equation.

The equation of a line with slope m intersecting the y-axis at $(0, b)$ is given by:

$$y = mx + b$$

This is the *slope-intercept* form of a linear equation.

PROBLEMS ON LINEAR EQUATIONS:

A) Find the slope, the y-intercept, and the x-intercept of the equation $2x - 3y - 18 = 0$.

Solution: The equation $2x - 3y - 18 = 0$ can be written in the form of the general linear equation, $ax + by = c$.

$$2x - 3y - 18 = 0$$
$$2x - 3y = 18$$

To find the slope and y-intercept, we derive them from the formula of the general linear equation $ax + by = c$. Dividing by b and solving for y, we obtain:

$$\frac{a}{b}x + y = \frac{c}{b}$$
$$y = \frac{c}{b} - \frac{a}{b}x$$

where $\dfrac{-a}{b}$ = slope and $\dfrac{c}{b}$ = y-intercept

To find the x-intercept, solve for x and let $y = 0$:

$$x = \frac{c}{a} - \frac{b}{a}y$$
$$x = \frac{c}{a}$$

In this form we have $a = 2$, $b = -3$, and $c = 18$. Thus,

$$\text{slope} = -\frac{a}{b} = -\frac{2}{-3} = \frac{2}{3}$$
$$y\text{-intercept} = \frac{c}{b} = \frac{18}{-3} = -6$$
$$x\text{-intercept} = \frac{c}{a} = \frac{18}{2} = 9$$

B) Find the equation for the line passing through $(3, 5)$ and $(-1, 2)$.

Solution A): We use the two-point form with $(x_1, y_1) = (3, 5)$ and $(x_2, y_2) = (-1, 2)$. Then

$$\frac{y - y_1}{x - x_1} = \frac{y_2 - y_1}{x_2 - x_1}$$
$$\frac{y_2 - y_1}{x_2 - x_1} = \frac{2 - 5}{-1 - 3} \quad \text{thus} \quad \frac{y - 5}{x - 3} = \frac{-3}{-4}$$

Cross multiply, $-4(y - 5) = -3(x - 3)$.

Distribute, $-4y + 20 = -3x + 9$

Place in general form, $3x - 4y = -11$.

Solution B): Does the same equation result if we let $(x_1, y_1) = (-1, 2)$ and $(x_2, y_2) = (3, 5)$?

$$\frac{y_2 - y_1}{x_2 - x_1} = \frac{5 - 2}{3 - (-1)} \quad \text{thus} \quad \frac{y - 2}{x + 1} = \frac{3}{4}$$

Cross multiply, $4(y - 2) = 3(x + 1)$

Distribute $3x - 4y = -11$

Place in general form, $3x - 4y = -11$.

Hence, either replacement results in the same equation. Keep in mind that the coefficient of the x-term should always be positive.

C) (a) Find the equation of the line passing through $(2, 5)$ with slope 3.

   (b) Suppose a line passes through the y-axis at $(0, b)$. How can we write the equation if the point-slope form is used?

Solution C): (a) In the point-slope form, let $x_1 = 2$, $y_1 = 5$, $m = 3$.

The point-slope form of a line is:

$$y - y_1 = m(x - x_1)$$
$$y - 5 = 3(x - 2)$$
$$y - 5 = 3x - 6 \qquad \text{Distributive property}$$
$$y = 3x - 1 \qquad \text{Transposition}$$

(b) $y - b = m(x - 0)$
$$y = mx + b.$$

Notice that this is the slope-intercept form for the equation of a line.

PROBLEM

Construct the graph of the function defined by $y = 3x - 9$.

SOLUTION

This linear equation is in the slope-intercept form, $y = mx + b$.

A line can be determined by two points. Let us choose the intercepts. The x-intercept lies on the x-axis and the y-intercept is on the y-axis.

We can find the *y*-intercept by assigning 0 to *x* in the given equation and then find the *x*-intercept by assigning 0 to *y*. It is helpful to have a third point. We find a third point by assigning 4 to *x* and solving for *y*. Thus, we get the following table of corresponding numbers:

x	*y* = 3*x* − 9	*y*
0	$y = 3(0) - 9$	−9
3	$0 = 3x - 9, x = 9/3 = 3$	0
4	$y = 3(4) - 9$	3

The three points are (0, −9), (3, 0), and (4, 3). Draw a line through them as in Figure below.

PROBLEM

Graph the function defined by $3x - 4y = 12$.

SOLUTION

Solve for *y*:

$$3x - 4y = 12$$
$$-4y = 12 - 3x$$
$$y = -3 + \frac{3}{4}x$$
$$y = \frac{3}{4}x - 3$$

The graph of this function is a straight line since it is of the form $y = mx + b$. The *y*-intercept crosses (intersects)

the *y*-axis at the point (0, −3) since for $x = 0$, $y = b = -3$. The *x*-intercept crosses (intersects) the *x*-axis at the point (4, 0) since for $y = 0$, $x = (y + 3) \times \frac{4}{3} = (0 + 3) \times \frac{4}{3} = 4$.

These two points, (0, −3) and (4, 0) are sufficient to determine the graph (see Figure below). A third point, (8, 3), satisfying the equation of the function is plotted as a partial check of the intercepts. Note that the slope of the line is $m = \frac{3}{4}$. This means that *y* increases three units as *x* increases four units anywhere along the line.

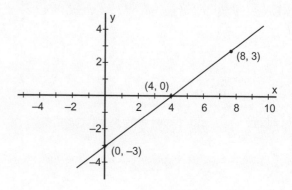

Two Linear Equations

Equations of the form $ax + by = c$, where *a*, *b*, *c* are constants and *a*, $b \neq 0$ are called **linear equations** with two unknown variables.

There are several ways to solve systems of linear equations with two variables.

Method 1: **Addition or subtraction**—If necessary, multiply the equations by numbers that will make the coefficients of one unknown in the resulting equations numerically equal. If the signs of equal coefficients are the same, subtract the equation, otherwise add.

The result is one equation with one unknown; we solve it and substitute the value into the other equations to find the unknown that we first eliminated.

Method 2: **Substitution**—Find the value of one unknown in terms of the other. Substitute this value in the other equation and solve.

Method 3: **Graph**—Graph both equations. The point of intersection of the drawn lines is a simultaneous solution for the equations, and its coordinates correspond to the answer that would be found analytically.

If the lines are parallel they have no simultaneous solution.

Dependent equations are equations that represent the same line; therefore, every point on the line of a dependent equation represents a solution. Since there is an infinite number of points on a line, there is an infinite number of simultaneous solutions. For example,

$$\begin{cases} 2x + y = 8 \\ 4x + 2y = 16 \end{cases}$$

These equations are dependent. Since they represent the same line, all points that satisfy either of the equations are solutions of the system.

A system of linear equations is consistent if there is only one solution for the system.

A system of linear equations is inconsistent if it does not have any solutions.

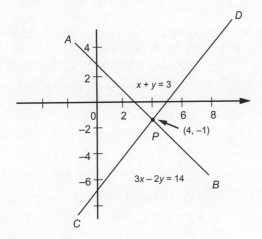

• EXAMPLE

Find the point of intersection of the graphs of the equations as shown in the previous figure.

$$x + y = 3$$

$$3x - 2y = 14$$

To solve these linear equations, solve for y in terms of x. The equations will be in the form $y = mx + b$, where m is the slope and b is the intercept on the y-axis.

$$x + y = 3$$

Subtract x from both sides: $y = 3 - x$

Subtract $3x$ from both sides: $3x - 2y = 14$

Divide by –2:
$$-2y = 14 - 3x$$
$$y = -7 + \frac{3}{2}x$$

The graphs of the linear functions, $y = 3 - x$ and $y = 7 + \frac{3}{2}x$ can be determined by plotting only two points. For example, for $y = 3 - x$, let $x = 0$, then $y = 3$. Let $x = 1$, then $y = 2$. The two points on this first line are $(0,3)$ and $(1,2)$. For $y = -7 + \frac{3}{2}x$ let $x = 0$, then $y = -7$. Let $x = 1$, then $y = -5\frac{1}{2}$. The two points on this second line are $(0,-7)$ and $(1,-5\frac{1}{2})$.

To find the point of intersection P of

$$x + y = 3 \text{ and } 3x - 2y = 14,$$

solve them algebraically. Multiply the first equation by 2. Add these two equations to eliminate the variable y.

$$\begin{array}{r} 2x + 2y = 6 \\ 3x - 2y = 14 \\ \hline 5x \quad\quad = 20 \end{array}$$

Solve for x to obtain $x = 4$. Substitute this into $y = 3 - x$ to get $y = 3 - 4 = -1$. P is $(4,-1)$. AB is the graph of the first equation, and CD is the graph of the second equation. The point of intersection P of the two graphs is the only point on both lines. The coordinates of P satisfy both equations and represent the desired solution of the problem. From the graph, P seems to be the point $(4,-1)$. These coordinates satisfy both equations, and hence are the exact coordinates of the point of intersection of the two lines.

To show that $(4,-1)$ satisfies both equations, substitute this point into both equations.

$x + y = 3$	$3x - 2y = 14$
$4 + (-1) = 3$	$3(4) - 2(-1) = 14$
$4 - 1 = 3$	$12 + 2 = 14$
$3 = 3$	$14 = 14$

• EXAMPLE

Solve the equations $2x + 3y = 6$ and $4x + 6y = 7$ simultaneously.

We have two equations and two unknowns,

$$2x + 3y = 6 \qquad (1)$$

and

$$4x + 6y = 7 \qquad (2)$$

There are several methods to solve this problem. We have chosen to multiply each equation by a different number so that when the two equations are added, one of the variables drops out. Thus,

Multiply equation (1) by 2: $\quad 4x + 6y = 12 \quad$ (3)

Multiply equation (2) by -1: $\underline{-4x - 6y = -7} \quad$ (4)

Add equations (3) and (4): $\qquad\qquad 0 = 5$

We obtain a peculiar result!

Actually, what we have shown in this case is that if there were a simultaneous solution to the given equations, then 0 would equal 5. But the conclusion is impossible; therefore, there can be no simultaneous solution to these two equations, hence no point satisfying both.

The straight lines which are the graphs of these equations must be parallel if they never intersect, but not identical, which can be seen from the graph of these equations (see the figure).

• EXAMPLE

Solve the equations $2x + 3y = 6$ and $y = -\left(\dfrac{2x}{3}\right) + 2$ simultaneously.

We have two equations and two unknowns.

$$2x + 3y = 6 \qquad (1)$$

and

$$y = -\left(\frac{2x}{3}\right) + 2 \qquad (2)$$

There are several methods of solution for this problem. Since equation (2) already gives us an expression for y, we use the method of substitution.

Substitute $-\left(\dfrac{2x}{3}\right) + 2$ for y in the first equation:

$$2x + 3(-\frac{2x}{3} + 2) = 6$$

Distribute: $\qquad 2x - 2x + 6 = 6$

$$6 = 6$$

The result $6 = 6$ is true, but indicates no solution. Actually, our work shows that no matter what real number x is, if y is determined by the second equation, then the first equation will always be satisfied.

The reason for this peculiarity may be seen if we take a closer look at the equation $y = -\left(\dfrac{2x}{3}\right) + 2$. It is equivalent to $3y = -2x + 6$, or $2x + 3y = 6$.

In other words, the two equations are equivalent. Any pair of values of x and y which satisfies one satisfies the other.

It is hardly necessary to verify that in this case the graphs of the given equations are identical lines, and that there are an infinite number of simultaneous solutions to these equations.

A system of three linear equations in three unknowns is solved by eliminating one unknown from any two of the three equations and solving them. After finding two unknowns substitute them in any of the equations to find the third unknown.

PROBLEM

Solve the system

$$2x + 3y - 4z = -8 \qquad (1)$$
$$x + y - 2z = -5 \qquad (2)$$
$$7x - 2y + 5z = 4 \qquad (3)$$

SOLUTION

We cannot eliminate any variable from two pairs of equations by a single multiplication. However, both x and z may be eliminated from equations (1) and (2) by multiplying equation (2) by -2. Then

$$2x + 3y - 4z = -8 \qquad (1)$$

$-2x - 2y + 4z = 10$ (4)

By addition, we have $y = 2$. Although we may now eliminate either x or z from another pair of equations, we can more conveniently substitute $y = 2$ in equations (2) and (3) to get two equations in two variables. Thus, making the substitution $y = 2$ in equations (2) and (3), we have

$x - 2z = -7$ (5)

$7x + 5z = 8$ (6)

Multiply equation (5) by 5 and multiply (6) by 2. Then add the two new equations. Then $x = -1$. Substitute x in either equation (5) or (6) to find z.

The solution of the system is $x = -1$, $y = 2$, and $z = 3$. Check by substitution.

A system of equations, as shown below, that has all constant terms $b_1, b_2, \ldots, b_n$ equal to zero is said to be a homogeneous system.

$$\begin{cases} a_{11}x_1 + a_{12}x_2 + \ldots + a_{1n}x_m = b_1 \\ a_{21}x_1 + a_{22}x_2 + \ldots + a_{2n}x_m = b_2 \\ \vdots \qquad \vdots \qquad \qquad \vdots \qquad \vdots \\ a_{n1}x_1 + a_{n2}x_2 + \ldots + a_{nn}x_m = b_n \end{cases}$$

A homogeneous system (one in which each variable can be replaced by a constant and the constant can be factored out) always has at least one solution which is called the trivial solution that is $x_1 = 0$, $x_2 = 0$, $\ldots$, $x_m = 0$.

For any given homogeneous system of equations, in which the number of variables is greater than or equal to the number of equations, there are non-trivial solutions.

Two systems of linear equations are said to be equivalent if and only if they have the same solution set.

Drill: Two Linear Equations

DIRECTIONS: Find the solution set for each pair of equations.

1. $3x + 4y = -2$
    $x - 6y = -8$

    (A) $(2, -1)$ (C) $(-2, -1)$

    (B) $(1, -2)$ (D) $(-2, 1)$

2. $2x + y = -10$
    $-2x - 4y = 4$

(A) $(6, -2)$ (C) $(-2, 6)$

(B) $(-6, 2)$ (D) $(2, 6)$

3. $6x + 5y = -4$
    $3x - 3y = 9$

    (A) $(1, -2)$ (C) $(2, -1)$

    (B) $(1, 2)$ (D) $(-2, 1)$

4. $4x + 3y = 9$
    $2x - 2y = 8$

    (A) $(-3, 1)$ (C) $(3, 1)$

    (B) $(1, -3)$ (D) $(3, -1)$

5. $x + y = 7$
    $x = y - 3$

    (A) $(5, 2)$ (C) $(2, 5)$

    (B) $(-5, 2)$ (D) $(-2, 5)$

Quadratic Equations

A second degree equation in x of the type $ax^2 + bx + c = 0$, $a \neq 0$, a, b, and c are real numbers, is called a quadratic equation.

To solve a quadratic equation is to find values of x which satisfy $ax^2 + bx + c = 0$. These values of x are called solutions, or roots, of the equation.

A quadratic equation has a maximum of two roots. Methods of solving quadratic equations:

A) Direct solution: Given $x^2 - 9 = 0$.

We can solve directly by isolating the variable x:

$x^2 = 9$

$x = \pm 3$

B) Factoring: Given a quadratic equation $ax^2 + bx + c = 0$, a, b, $c \neq 0$, to factor means to express it as the product $a(x - r_1)(x - r_2) = 0$, where r_1 and r_2 are the two roots.

Some helpful hints to remember are:

(a) $r_1 + r_2 = -\dfrac{b}{a}$.

(b) $r_1 + r_2 = \dfrac{c}{a}$.

Given $x^2 - 5x + 5 = 0$.

Since $r_1 + r_2 = \dfrac{-b}{a} = \dfrac{-(-5)}{1} = 5$, so the possible solutions are $(3, 2)$, $(4, 1)$, and $(5, 0)$. Also $r_1 r_2 = \dfrac{c}{a} = \dfrac{4}{1} = 4$; this equation is satisfied only by the second pair, so $r_1 = 4$, $r_2 = 1$ and the factored form is $(x - 4)(x - 1) = 0$.

If the coefficient of x^2 is not 1, it is necessary to divide the equation by this coefficient and then factor.

Given $2x^2 - 12x + 16 = 0$.

Dividing by 2, we obtain:

$x^2 - 6x + 8 = 0$

Since $r_1 + r_2 = \dfrac{-b}{a} = 6$, the possible solutions are $(6, 0)$, $(5, 1)$, $(4, 2)$, $(3, 3)$. Also $r_1 r_2 = 8$, so the only possible answer is $(4, 2)$ and the expression $x^2 - 6x + 8 = 0$ can be factored as $(x - 4)(x - 2)$.

C) Completing the square: If it is difficult to factor the quadratic equation using the previous method, we can complete the square.

Given $x^2 - 12x + 8 = 0$.

We know that the two roots added up should be 12 because $r_1 + r_2 = \dfrac{-b}{a} = \dfrac{-(-12)}{1} = 12$. The possible roots are $(12, 0)$, $(11, 1)$, $(10, 2)$, $(9,3)$, $(8, 4)$, $(7, 5)$, $(6, 6)$.

But none of these satisfy $r_1 r_2 = 8$, so we cannot use B).

To complete the square it is necessary to isolate the constant term,

$x^2 - 12x = -8$.

Then take $\dfrac{1}{2}$ coefficient of the x term, square it and add to both sides

$$x^2 - 12x + \left(\dfrac{-12}{2}\right)^2 = -8 + \left(\dfrac{-12}{2}\right)^2$$
$$x^2 - 12x + 36 = -8 + 36 = 28$$

Now we can use the previous method to factor the left side: $r_1 + r_2 = 12$, $r_1 r_2 = 36$ is satisfied by the pair $(6, 6)$, so we have:

$(x - 6)(x - 6) = (x - 6)^2 = 28$.

Now take the square root of both sides and solve for x. Remember when taking a square root that the solution can be positive or negative.

$(x - 6) = \pm\sqrt{28} = \pm 2\sqrt{7}$
$x = \pm 2\sqrt{7} + 6$

So the roots are: $x = 2\sqrt{7} + 6$, $x = -2\sqrt{7} + 6$

PROBLEM

Solve $2x^2 + 8x + 4 = 0$ by completing the square.

SOLUTION

Divide both members by 2, the coefficient of x^2.

$x^2 + 4x + 2 = 0$

Subtract the constant term, 2, from both members.

$x^2 + 4x = -2$

Add to each member the square of one-half the coefficient of the x-term.

$x^2 + 4x + 4 = -2 + 4$

Factor

$(x + 2)(x + 2) = (x + 2)^2 = 2$

Set the square root of the left member (a perfect square) equal to $\pm$ the square root of the right member and solve for x.

$x + 2 = \sqrt{2}$ or $x + 2 = -\sqrt{2}$

The roots are $\sqrt{2} - 2$ and $\sqrt{2} - 2$. Check each solution.

$$2\left(\sqrt{2} - 2\right)^2 + 8\left(\sqrt{2} - 2\right) + 4$$
$$= 2\left(2 - 4\sqrt{2} + 4\right) + 8\sqrt{2} - 16 + 4$$
$$= 4 - 8\sqrt{2} + 8 + 8\sqrt{2} - 16 + 4$$
$$= 0$$

$$2\left(-\sqrt{2} - 2\right)^2 + 8\left(-\sqrt{2} - 2\right) + 4$$
$$= 2\left(2 + 4\sqrt{2} + 4\right) - 8\sqrt{2} - 16 + 4$$
$$= 4 + 8\sqrt{2} + 8 - 8\sqrt{2} - 16 + 4$$
$$= 0$$

Quadratic Formula

Consider the polynomial:

$ax^2 + bx + c = 0$, where $a \neq 0$.

The roots of this equation can be determined in terms of the coefficients a, b, and c as shown below:

$$x = \frac{-b \pm \sqrt{b^2 - 4ac}}{2a}$$

where $(b^2 - 4ac)$ is called the discriminant of the quadratic equation.

Note that if the discriminant is less than zero $(b^2 - 4ac < 0)$, the roots are complex numbers, since the discriminant appears under a radical and square roots of negatives are complex numbers, and a real number added to an imaginary number yields a complex number.

If the discriminant is equal to zero $(b^2 - 4ac = 0)$, the result is one real root.

If the discriminant is greater than zero $(b^2 - 4ac > 0)$, then the roots are real and unequal. Further, the roots are rational if and only if a and b are rational and $(b^2 - 4ac)$ is a perfect square, otherwise the roots are irrational.

Example: Compute the value of the discriminant and then determine the nature of the roots of each of the following four equations:

A) $4x^2 - 12x + 9 = 0$

B) $3x^2 - 7x - 6 = 0$

C) $5x^2 + 2x - 9 = 0$

D) $x^2 + 3x + 5 = 0$

A) $4x^2 - 12x + 9 = 0$,

Here a, b, and c are integers,

$a = 4$, $b = -12$, and $c = 9$.

Therefore,

$b^2 - 4ac = (-12)^2 - 4(4)(9) = 144 - 144 = 0$.

Since the discriminant is 0, the roots are rational and equal.

B) $3x^2 - 7x - 6 = 0$

Here a, b, and c are integers,

$a = 3$, $b = -7$, and $c = -6$.

Therefore,

$b^2 - 4ac = (-7)^2 - 4(3)(-6) = 49 + 72 = 121 = 11^2$.

Since the discriminant is a perfect square, the roots are rational and unequal.

C) $5x^2 + 2x - 9 = 0$

Here a, b, and c are integers,

$a = 5$, $b = 2$, and $c = -9$.

Therefore,

$b^2 - 4ac = 2^2 - 4(5)(-9) = 4 + 180 = 184$.

Since the discriminant is greater than zero, but not a perfect square, the roots are irrational and unequal.

D) $x^2 + 3x + 5 = 0$

Here a, b, and c are integers,

$a = 1$, $b = 3$, and $c = 5$.

Therefore,

$b^2 - 4ac = 3^2 - 4(1)(5) = 9 - 20 = -11$.

Since the discriminant is negative, the roots are imaginary.

Example: Find the equation whose roots are $\dfrac{\alpha}{\beta}, \dfrac{\beta}{\alpha}$.

Solution: The roots of the equation are $x = \dfrac{\alpha}{\beta}$ and $x = \dfrac{\beta}{\alpha}$.

Subtract $\dfrac{\alpha}{\beta}$ from both sides of the first equation:

$$x - \frac{\alpha}{\beta} = \frac{\alpha}{\beta} - \frac{\alpha}{\beta} = 0$$

or

$$x - \frac{\alpha}{\beta} = 0$$

Subtract $\dfrac{\beta}{\alpha}$ from both sides of the second equation:

$$x - \frac{\beta}{\alpha} = \frac{\beta}{\alpha} - \frac{\beta}{\alpha} = 0$$

or

$$x - \frac{\beta}{\alpha} = 0$$

Therefore:

$$\left(x - \frac{\alpha}{\beta} \right)\left(x - \frac{\beta}{\alpha} \right) = (0)(0),$$

or

$$\left(x - \frac{\alpha}{\beta}\right)\left(x - \frac{\beta}{\alpha}\right) = 0. \qquad (1)$$

Equation (1) is of the form:

$(x - c)(x - d) = 0$, or

$x^2 - cx - dx + cd = 0$, or

$x^2 - (c + d)x + cd = 0. \qquad (2)$

Note that c corresponds to the root $\dfrac{\alpha}{\beta}$ and d corresponds

to the root $\dfrac{\beta}{\alpha}$. The sum of the roots is:

$$c + d = \frac{\alpha}{\beta} + \frac{\beta}{\alpha} = \frac{\alpha(\alpha)}{\alpha(\beta)} + \frac{\beta(\beta)}{\beta(\alpha)} = \frac{\alpha^2}{\alpha\beta} + \frac{\beta^2}{\alpha\beta}$$

$$= \frac{\alpha^2 + \beta^2}{\alpha\beta}$$

The product of the roots is:

$$c \times d = \frac{\alpha}{\beta} \times \frac{\beta}{\alpha} = \frac{\alpha\beta}{\beta\alpha} = \frac{\alpha\beta}{\alpha\beta} = 1$$

Using the form of Equation (2):

$$\left(x - \frac{\alpha}{\beta}\right)\left(x - \frac{\beta}{\alpha}\right) = x^2 - \left(\frac{\alpha^2 + \beta^2}{\alpha\beta}\right)x + 1 = 0.$$

Hence,

$$x^2 - \left(\frac{\alpha^2 + \beta^2}{\alpha\beta}\right)x + 1 = 0. \qquad (3)$$

Multiply both sides of Equation (3) by $\alpha\beta$

$$\alpha\beta\left[x^2 - \left(\frac{\alpha^2 + \beta^2}{\alpha\beta}\right)x + 1\right] = \alpha\beta(0)$$

Distributing,

$$\alpha\beta x^2 - (\alpha^2 + \beta^2)x + \alpha\beta = 0,$$

which is the equation whose roots are $\dfrac{\alpha}{\beta}, \dfrac{\beta}{\alpha}$.

Radical Equation

An equation that has one or more unknowns under a radical is called a radical equation.

To solve a radical equation, isolate the radical term on one side of the equation and move all the other terms to the other side. Then both members of the equation are raised to a power equal to the index of the isolated radical.

After solving the resulting equation, the roots obtained must be checked, since this method often introduces extraneous roots.

These introduced roots must be excluded if they are not solutions.

Given $\sqrt{x^2 + 2} + 6x = x - 4$

$$\sqrt{x^2 + 2} = x - 4 - 6x = -5x - 4$$

$$\left(\sqrt{x^2 + 2}\right)^2 = (-(5x + 4))^2$$

$$x^2 + 2 = (5x + 4)^2$$

$x^2 + 2 = 25x^2 + 40x + 16$

$24x^2 + 40x + 14 = 0$

Applying the quadratic formula, we obtain:

$$x = \frac{-40 \pm \sqrt{1600 - 4(24)(14)}}{2(24)} = \frac{-40 \pm 16}{48}$$

$$x_1 = \frac{-7}{6}, \quad x_2 = \frac{-1}{2}$$

Checking roots:

$$\sqrt{\left(\frac{-7}{6}\right)^2 + 2} + 6\left(\frac{-7}{6}\right) \stackrel{?}{=} \left(\frac{-7}{6}\right) - 4$$

$$\frac{11}{6} - 7 \stackrel{?}{=} \frac{-31}{6}$$

$$\frac{-31}{6} = \frac{-31}{6}$$

$$\sqrt{\left(\frac{-1}{2}\right)^2 + 2} + 6\left(\frac{-1}{2}\right) \stackrel{?}{=} \left(\frac{-1}{2}\right) - 4$$

$$\frac{3}{2} - 3 \stackrel{?}{=} \frac{-9}{2}$$

$$\frac{-3}{2} \neq \frac{-9}{2}$$

Hence, $-\dfrac{1}{2}$ is not a root of the equation, but $\dfrac{-7}{6}$ is a root.

PROBLEM

Solve for x: $4x^2 - 7 = 0$.

SOLUTION

This quadratic equation can be solved for x using the quadratic formula, which applies to equations in the form $ax^2 + bx + c = 0$ (in our equation $b = 0$). There is, however, an easier method that we can use:

Adding 7 to both sides, $4x^2 = 7$

Dividing both sides by 4, $x^2 = \dfrac{7}{4}$

Taking the square root of both sides, $x = \pm\sqrt{\dfrac{7}{4}} = \pm\dfrac{\sqrt{7}}{2}$.

The double sign $\pm$ (read "plus or minus") indicates that the two roots of the equation are $+\dfrac{\sqrt{7}}{2}$ and $-\dfrac{\sqrt{7}}{2}$.

PROBLEM

> Solve the equation $2x^2 - 5x + 3 = 0$.

SOLUTION

$2x^2 - 5x + 3 = 0$

The equation is a quadratic equation of the form $ax^2 + bx + c = 0$ in which $a = 2$, $b = -5$, and $c = 3$. Therefore, the quadratic formula $x = \dfrac{-b \pm \sqrt{b^2 - 4ac}}{2a}$ may be used to find the solutions of the given equation. Substituting the values for a, b, and c in the quadratic formula:

$$x = \dfrac{-(-5) \pm \sqrt{(-5)^2 - 4(2)(3)}}{2(2)}$$

$$x = \dfrac{5 \pm \sqrt{1}}{4}$$

$$x = \dfrac{5+1}{4} = \dfrac{3}{2} \text{ and } x = \dfrac{5-1}{4} = 1$$

Check: Substituting $x = \dfrac{3}{2}$ in the given equation,

$$2\left(\dfrac{3}{2}\right)^2 - 5\left(\dfrac{3}{2}\right) + 3 = 0$$

$$0 = 0$$

Substituting $x = 1$ in the given equation,

$$2(1)^2 - 5(1) + 3 = 0$$

$$0 = 0$$

So the roots of $2x^2 - 5x + 3 = 0$ are $x = \dfrac{3}{2}$ and $x = 1$.

Quadratic Functions

The function $f(x) = ax^2 + bx + c$, $a \pm 0$, where a, b, and c are real numbers, is called a quadratic function (or a function of second degree) in one unknown.

The graph of $y = ax^2 + bx + c$ is a curve known as a parabola.

The vertex of the parabola is the point $v\left(\dfrac{-b}{2a}, \dfrac{4ac - b^2}{4a}\right)$. The parabola's axis is the line $x = \dfrac{-b}{2a}$.

The graph of the parabola opens upward if $a > 0$ and downward if $a < 0$. If $a = 0$ the quadratic is reduced to a linear function whose graph is a straight line.

Figures below show parabolas with $a > 0$, and $a < 0$, respectively.

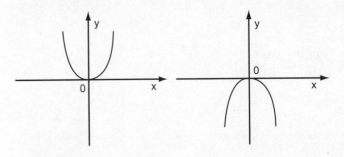

PROBLEM

> Solve the system
> $$y = -x^2 + 7x - 5 \qquad (1)$$
> $$y - 2x = 2 \qquad (2)$$

SOLUTION

Solving Equation (2) for y yields an expression for y in terms of x. Substituting this expression in Equation (1),

$$2x + 2 = -x^2 + 7x - 5 \qquad (3)$$

We have a single equation, in terms of a single variable, to be solved. Writing Equation (3) in standard quadratic form,

$$x^2 - 5x + 7 = 0 \qquad (4)$$

Since the equation is not factorable, the roots are not found in this manner. Evaluating the discriminant will indicate whether Equation (4) has real roots. The discriminant, $b^2 - 4ac$, of Equation (4) equals $(-5)^2 - 4(1)(7)$ $= 25 - 28 = -3$. Since the discriminant is negative, equation (4) has no real roots, and therefore the system has no real solution. In terms of the graph, figure shows that the parabola and the straight line have no point in common.

PROBLEM

Solve the system

$$y = 3x^2 - 2x + 5 \qquad (1)$$
$$y = 4x + 2 \qquad (2)$$

SOLUTION

To obtain a single equation with one unknown variable, x, substitute the value of y from Equation (2) in Equation (1),

$$4x + 2 = 3x^2 - 2x + 5. \qquad (3)$$

Writing Equation (3) in standard quadratic form,

$$3x^2 - 6x + 3 = 0. \qquad (4)$$

We may simplify equation (4) by dividing both members by 3, which is a factor common to each term:

$$x^2 - 2x + 1 = 0. \qquad (5)$$

To find the roots, factor and set each factor = 0. This may be done since a product = 0 implies one or all of the factors must = 0.

$$(x-1)(x-1) = 0$$
$$x - 1 = 0 \mid x - 1 = 0$$
$$x = 1 \mid \quad x = 1$$

Equation (5) has two equal roots, each equal to 1. For $x = 1$, from Equation (2), we have $y = 4(1) + 2 = 6$. Therefore, the system has but one common solution:

$$x = 1, \quad y = 6.$$

The figure indicates that our solution is probably correct. We may also check to see if our values satisfy Equation (1) as well:

Substituting in:
$$y = 3x^2 - 2x + 5$$
$$6 \overset{?}{=} 3(1)^2 - 2(1) + 5$$
$$6 \overset{?}{=} 3 - 2 + 5$$
$$6 = 6$$

Quadratic Equations in Two Unknowns and Systems of Equations

A quadratic equation in two unknowns has the general form:

$$ax^2 + bxy + cy^2 + dx + ey + f = 0$$

where a, b, and c are not all zero and a, b, c, d, e, and f are constants.

Graphing: If $b^2 - 4ac < 0$, $b \neq 0$ and $a \neq c$, the graph of $ax^2 + bxy + cy^2 + dx + ey + f$ is a closed curve called an ellipse. If $b = 0$ and $a = c$, the graph $ax^2 + bxy + cy^2 + dx + ey + f$ is a point or a circle, or else it does not exist.

If $b^2 - 4ac > 0$, the graph of $ax^2 + bxy + cy^2 + dx + ey + f = 0$ is a curve called a hyperbola.

If $b^2 - 4ac = 0$, the graph of $ax^2 + bxy + cy^2 + dx + ey + f = 0$ is a parabola or a pair of parallel lines which may be coincident, or else it does not exist.

Solving Systems of Equations Involving Quadratics

Some methods for solving systems of equations involving quadratics are given below:

A) One linear and one quadratic equation

Solve the linear equation for one of the two unknowns, then substitute this value into the quadratic equation.

B) Two quadratic equations

Eliminate one of the unknowns using the method given for solving systems of linear equations.

Example:

$$\begin{cases} x^2 + y^2 = 9 & (1) \\ x^2 + 2y^2 = 18 & (2) \end{cases}$$

Subtracting Equation (1) from (2), we obtain:

$y^2 = 9, y = \pm 3$

By substituting the values of y into (1) or (2), we obtain:

$x_1 = 0$ and $x_2 = 0$

So the solutions are:

$x = 0, y = 3$ and $x = 0, y = -3$

C) Two quadratic equations, one homogeneous

An equation is said to be homogeneous if it is of the form

$ax^2 + bxy + cy^2 + dx + ey = 0$.

Consider the system

$$\begin{cases} x^2 + 3xy + 2y^2 = 0 & (1) \\ x^2 - 3xy + 2y^2 = 12 & (2) \end{cases}$$

Equation (1) can be factored into the product of two linear equations:

$x^2 + 3xy + 2y^2 = (x + 2y)(x + y) = 0$

From this we determine that:

$x + 2y = 0 \Rightarrow x = -2y$
$x + y = 0 \Rightarrow x = -y$

Substituting $x = -2y$ into Equation (2), we find:

$$(-2y)^2 - 3(-2y)y + 2y^2 = 12$$
$$4y^2 + 6y^2 + 2y^2 = 12$$
$$12y^2 = 12$$
$$y^2 = 1$$
$$y = \pm 1, \text{ so } x = \pm 2$$

Substituting $x = -y$ into Equation (2) yields:

$$(-y)^2 - 3(-y)y + 2y^2 = 12$$
$$y^2 + 3y^2 + 2y^2 = 12$$
$$6y^2 = 12$$
$$y^2 = 2$$
$$y = \pm\sqrt{2}, \text{ so } x = \pm\sqrt{2}$$

So the solutions of Equations (1) and (2) are:

$x = 2, y = -1, x = -2, y = 1, x = \sqrt{2}, y = -\sqrt{2},$
and $x = -\sqrt{2}, y = \sqrt{2}$

D) Two quadratic equations of the form

$ax^2 + bxy + cy^2 = d$

Combine the two equations to obtain a homogeneous quadratic equation then solve the equations by the third method.

E) Two quadratic equations, each symmetrical in x and y

Note: An equation is said to be symmetrical in x and y if by exchanging the coefficients of x and y we obtain the same equation.

Example: $x^2 + y^2 = 9$.

To solve systems involving this type of equations, substitute $u + v$ for x and $u - v$ for y and solve the resulting equations for u and v.

Example: Given the system below:

$$\begin{cases} x^2 + y^2 = 25 & (1) \\ x^2 + xy + y^2 = 37 & (2) \end{cases}$$

Substitute:

$x = u + v$

$y = u - v$

If we substitute the new values for x and y into Equation (2) we obtain:

$$(u + v)^2 + (u + v)(u - v) + (u - v)^2 = 37$$

$$u^2 + 2uv + v^2 + u^2 - v^2 + u^2 - 2uv + v^2 = 37$$
$$3u^2 + v^2 = 37.$$

If we substitute for x and y into Equation (1), we obtain:

$$(u + v)^2 + (u - v)^2 = 25$$
$$u^2 + 2uv + v^2 + u^2 - 2uv + v^2 = 25$$
$$2u^2 + 2v^2 = 25.$$

The "new" system is:

$$\begin{cases} 3u^2 + v^2 = 37 \\ 2u^2 + 2v^2 = 25 \end{cases}$$

By substituting $a = u^2$ and $b = v^2$, these equations become:

$$\begin{cases} 3a + b = 37 \\ 2a + 2b = 25 \end{cases}$$

and

$$a = \frac{49}{4}, \quad b = \frac{1}{4}$$

So

$$u^2 = \frac{49}{4} \quad \text{and} \quad v^2 = \frac{1}{4}$$
$$u = \pm\frac{7}{2}$$
$$v = \pm\frac{1}{2}$$
$$x = \frac{7}{2} + \frac{1}{2} = 4 \quad \text{or} \quad \frac{-7}{2} - \frac{1}{2} = -4$$
$$y = \frac{7}{2} - \frac{1}{2} = 3 \quad \text{or} \quad \frac{-7}{2} + \frac{1}{2} = -3$$

Since x and y are symmetrical, the possible solutions are $(4, 3)$, $(-4, -3)$, $(3, 4)$, $(-3, -4)$.

Note that if the equation is symmetrical it is possible to interchange the solutions too. If $x = 3$, then $y = 4$ or vice-versa.

PROBLEM

Solve the system
$$2x^2 - 3xy - 4y^2 + x + y - 1 = 0$$
$$2x - y = 3.$$

SOLUTION

A system of equations consisting of one linear and one quadratic is solved by expressing one of the unknowns in the linear equation in terms of the other, and substituting the result in the quadratic equation. From the second equation, $y = 2x - 3$. Replacing y by this linear function of x in the first equation, we find

$$2x^2 - 3x(2x - 3) - 4(2x - 3)^2 + x + 2x - 3 - 1 = 0$$
$$2x^2 - 3x(2x - 3) - 4(4x^2 - 12x + 9) + x + 2x - 3 - 1 = 0$$

Distribute,

$$2x^2 - 6x^2 + 9x - 16x^2 + 48x - 36 + x + 2x - 3 - 1 = 0$$

Combine terms, $\qquad -20x^2 + 60x - 40 = 0$

Divide both sides by -20, $\quad \dfrac{-20x^2}{-20} + \dfrac{60x}{-20} - \dfrac{40}{-20} = \dfrac{0}{-20}$

$$x^2 - 3x + 2 = 0$$

Factoring, $\qquad\qquad\qquad (x - 2)(x - 1) = 0$

Setting each factor equal to zero, we obtain:

$$x - 2 = 0 \qquad\qquad x - 1 = 0$$
$$x = 2 \qquad\qquad\quad x = 1$$

To find the corresponding y-values, substitute the x-values in $y = 2x - 3$:

when $x = 1$,	when $x = 2$,
$y = 2(1) - 3$	$y = 2(2) - 3$
$y = 2 - 3$	$y = 4 - 3$
$y = -1$	$y = 1$

Therefore, the two solutions of the system are

$$(1, -1), \qquad\qquad (2, 1),$$

and the solution set is $\{(1, -1), (2, 1)\}$.

PROBLEM

Solve the system
$$2x^2 - 3xy + 4y^2 = 3 \qquad (1)$$
$$x^2 + xy - 8y^2 = -6 \qquad (2)$$

SOLUTION

Multiply both sides of the first equation by 2.

$$2(2x^2 - 3xy + 4y^2) = 2(3)$$
$$4x^2 - 6xy + 8y^2 = 6 \qquad (3)$$

Add Equation (3) to Equation (2):

$$x^2 + xy - 8y^2 = -6$$
$$\underline{4x^2 - 6xy + 8y^2 = 6}$$
$$5x^2 - 5xy = 0 \qquad (4)$$

Factoring out the common factor, $5x$, from the left side of Equation (4):

$$5x(x - y) = 0$$

Whenever a product $ab = 0$, where a and b are any two numbers, either $a = 0$ or $b = 0$ or both. Hence, either

$$5x = 0 \qquad\qquad \text{or} \qquad\qquad x - y = 0$$
$$x = 0/5 \qquad\qquad\qquad\qquad\qquad x = y$$
$$x = 0$$

Substituting $x = 0$ in Equation (1):

$$2(0)^2 - 3(0)y + 4y^2 = 3$$
$$0 - 0 + 4y^2 = 3$$
$$4y^2 = 3$$
$$y^2 = \frac{3}{4}$$

$$y = \pm\sqrt{\frac{3}{4}}$$
$$= \pm\frac{\sqrt{3}}{\sqrt{4}}$$
$$= \pm\frac{\sqrt{3}}{2}$$

Hence, two solutions are: $\left(0, \dfrac{\sqrt{3}}{2}\right), \left(0, -\dfrac{\sqrt{3}}{2}\right)$

Substituting x for y ($x = y$) in equation (1):

$$2x^2 - 3x(x) + 4(x)^2 = 3$$
$$2x^2 - 3x^2 + 4x^2 = 3$$
$$-x^2 + 4x^2 = 3$$
$$3x^2 = 3$$
$$x^2 = 3/3$$
$$x^2 = 1$$
$$x = \pm\sqrt{1} = \pm 1$$

Therefore, when $x = 1$, $y = x = 1$. Also, when $x = -1$, $y = x = -1$. Hence, two other solutions are: $(1, 1)$ and $(-1, -1)$. Thus the four solutions of the system are

$\left(0, \dfrac{\sqrt{3}}{2}\right), \left(0, -\dfrac{\sqrt{3}}{2}\right), (1,1), \text{ and } (-1,-1)$

Drill: Quadratic Equations

Solve for all values of x.

1. $x^2 - 2x - 8 = 0$

     (A)   4 and –2   (D)   –2 and 8

     (B)   4 and 8   (E)   –2

     (C)   4

2. $x^2 + 2x - 3 = 0$

     (A)   –3 and 2   (D)   –3 and 1

     (B)   2 and 1   (E)   –3

     (C)   3 and 1

3. $x^2 - 7x = -10$

     (A)   –3 and 5   (D)   –2 and –5

     (B)   2 and 5   (E)   5

     (C)   2

4. $x^2 - 8x + 16 = 0$

     (A)   8 and 2   (D)   –2 and 4

     (B)   1 and 16   (E)   4 and –4

     (C)   4

5. $3x^2 + 3x = 6$

     (A)   3 and –6   (D)   1 and –3

     (B)   2 and 3   (E)   1 and –2

     (C)   –3 and 2

6. $x^2 + 7x = 0$

     (A)   7   (D)   0 and 7

     (B)   0 and –7   (E)   0

     (C)   –7

7. $x^2 - 25 = 0$

(A) 5

(D) −5 and 10

(B) 5 and −5

(E) −5

(C) 15 and 10

8. $2x^2 + 4x = 16$

(A) 2 and −2

(D) 2 and −4

(B) 8 and −2

(E) 2 and 4

(C) 4 and 8

9. $2x^2 - 11x - 6 = 0$

(A) 1 and −3

(D) −4

(B) 0 and 4

(E) −½ and 6

(C) 1

10. $x^2 - 2x - 3 = 0$

(A) 0

(D) 2

(B) −1 and 3

(E) 1 and −2

(C) 5 and −3

ANSWER KEY

1. (A)
2. (D)
3. (B)
4. (C)
5. (E)

6. (B)
7. (B)
8. (D)
9. (E)
10. (B)

Absolute Value Equations

The absolute value of a, $|a|$, is defined as

$|a| = a$ when $a > 0$,

$|a| = -a$ when $a < 0$,

$|a| = 0$ when $a = 0$.

When the definition of absolute value is applied to an equation, the quantity within the absolute value symbol is considered to have two values. This value can be either positive or negative before the absolute value is taken. As a result, each absolute value equation actually contains two separate equations.

When evaluating equations containing absolute values, proceed as follows:

- **EXAMPLE**

$|5 - 3x| = 7$ is valid if either

$$5 - 3x = 7 \qquad \text{or} \qquad 5 - 3x = -7$$
$$-3x = 2 \qquad\qquad -3x = -12$$
$$x = -\frac{2}{3} \qquad\qquad x = 4$$

The solution set is therefore $x = \left(-\frac{2}{3}, 4\right)$.

Remember, the absolute value of a number cannot be negative. So, for the equation $|5x + 4| = -3$, there would be no solution.

Drill: Absolute Value Equations

DIRECTIONS: Find the appropriate solutions.

1. $|4x - 2| = 6$

   (A) -2 and -1 (C) 2

   (B) -1 and 2   (D) No solution

2. $\left|3 - \frac{1}{2}y\right| = -7$

   (A) -8 and 20   (C) 2 and -5

   (B) 8 and -20 (D) No solution

3. $2|x + 7| = 12$

   (A) -13 and -1 (C) -1 and 13

   (B) -6 and 6   (D) No solution

4. $|5x| - 7 = 3$

   (A) 2 and 4   (C) -2 and 2

   (B) $\frac{4}{5}$ and 3   (D) No solution

5. $\left|\frac{3}{4}m\right| = 9$

   (A) 24 and -16 (C) -12 and 12

   (B) $\frac{4}{27}$ and $-\frac{4}{3}$ (D) No solution

Inequalities

An inequality is a statement where the value of one quantity or expression is greater than ($>$), less than ($<$), greater than or equal to ($\geq$), less than or equal to ($\leq$), or not equal to ($\neq$) that of another.

- **EXAMPLE**

$5 > 4$

The expression above means that the value of 5 is greater than the value of 4.

A **conditional inequality** is an inequality whose validity depends on the values of the variables in the expression. That is, certain values of the variables will make the expression true, and others will make it false.

$3 - y > 3 + y$

is a conditional inequality for the set of real numbers, since it is true for any replacement less than zero and false for all others.

$x + 5 > x + 2$

is an **absolute inequality** for the set of real numbers, meaning that for any real value x, the expression on the left is greater than the expression on the right.

$5y < 2y + y$

is inconsistent for the set of non-negative real numbers. For any y greater than 0 the sentence is always false.

An expression is inconsistent if it is always false when its variables assume allowable values.

The solution of a given inequality in one variable x consists of all values of x for which the inequality is true.

The graph of an inequality in one variable is represented by either a ray or a line segment on the real number line.

The endpoint is not a solution if the variable is strictly less than or greater than a particular value.

- **EXAMPLE**

$x > 2$

2 is not a solution and should be represented as shown.

The endpoint is a solution if the variable is either (1) less than or equal to or (2) greater than or equal to a particular value.

- **EXAMPLE**

$5 > x \geq 2$

In this case 2 is a solution and should be represented as shown.

Properties of Inequalities

If x and y are real numbers, then one and only one of the following statements is true.

$x > y$, $x = y$, or $x < y$.

This is the order property of real numbers.

If a, b, and c are real numbers, the following statements are true:

  A) If $a < b$ and $b < c$ then $a < c$.

  B) If $a > b$ and $b > c$ then $a > c$.

This is the transitive property of inequalities.

If a, b, and c are real numbers and $a > b$, then $a + c > b + c$ and $a - c > b - c$. This is the **addition property of inequality.**

Two inequalities are said to have the same **sense** if their signs of inequality point in the same direction.

The sense of an inequality remains the same if both sides are multiplied or divided by the same positive real number.

- **EXAMPLE**

$4 > 3$

If we multiply both sides by 5, we will obtain

$4 \times 5 > 3 \times 5$

$20 > 15$

The sense of the inequality does not change.

The sense of an inequality becomes opposite if each side is multiplied or divided by the same negative real number.

- **EXAMPLE**

$4 > 3$

If we multiply both sides by -5, we would obtain

$4 \times -5 < 3 \times -5$

$-20 < -15$

The sense of the inequality becomes opposite.

If $a > b$ and a, b, and n are positive real numbers, then

$a^n > b^n$ and $a^{-n} < b^{-n}$

If $x > y$ and $q > p$, then $x + q > y + p$.

If $x > y > 0$ and $q > p > 0$, then $xq > yp$.

Inequalities that have the same solution set are called **equivalent inequalities.**

PROBLEM

Solve the inequality $2x + 5 > 9$.

SOLUTION

Add -5 to both sides: $2x + 5 + (-5) > 9 + (-5)$

Additive inverse property: $2x + 0 > 9 + (-5)$

Additive identity property: $2x > 9 + (-5)$

Combine terms: $2x > 4$

Multiply both sides by $\frac{1}{2}$: $\frac{1}{2}(2x) > \frac{1}{2} \times 4$

$x > 2$

The solution set is

$$X = \{x \mid 2x + 5 > 9\}$$
$$= \{x \mid x > 2\}$$

(that is all x, such that x is greater than 2).

Drill: Inequalities

DIRECTIONS: Find the solution set for each inequality.

1. $3m + 2 < 7$

   (A) $m \geq \dfrac{5}{3}$ (C) $m < 2$

   (B) $m > 2$ (D) $m < \dfrac{5}{3}$

2. $\dfrac{1}{2}x - 3 \leq 1$

   (A) $-4 \leq x \leq 8$ (C) $x \leq 8$

   (B) $x \geq -8$ (D) $2 \leq x \leq 8$

3. $-3p + 1 \geq 16$

   (A) $p \geq -5$ (C) $p \leq \dfrac{-17}{3}$

   (B) $p \geq \dfrac{-17}{3}$ (D) $p \leq -5$

4. $-6 < \dfrac{2}{3}r + 6 \leq 2$

   (A) $-6 < r \leq -3$ (C) $r \geq -6$

   (B) $-18 < r \leq -6$ (D) $-2 < r \leq -\dfrac{4}{3}$

5. $0 < 2 - y < 6$

   (A) $-4 < y < 2$ (C) $-4 < y < -2$

   (B) $-4 < y < 0$ (D) $-2 < y < 4$

Vectors

Definition 1:

A scalar is a quantity that can be specified by a real number. It has only magnitude.

Definition 2:

A vector is a quantity that has both magnitude and direction. Velocity is an example of a vector quantity.

A vector (AB) is denoted by $\overrightarrow{AB}$, where B represents the head and A represents the tail. This is illustrated in the Figure.

The length of a line segment is the magnitude of a vector.

If the magnitude and direction of two vectors are the same, then they are equal.

Definition 3:

Vectors that can be translated from one position to another without any change in their magnitude or direction are called free vectors.

Definition 4:

The unit vector is a vector with a length (magnitude) of one.

Definition 5:

The zero vector has a magnitude of zero.

Definition 6:

The unit vector $\bar{i}$ is a vector with magnitude of one in the direction of the x-axis.

Definition 7:

The unit vector $\bar{j}$ is a vector with magnitude of one in the direction of the y-axis.

Vector Properties

When two vectors are added together, the resultant force of the two vectors produces the same effect as the two combined forces. This is illustrated in the Figures.

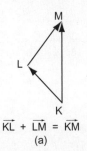

$$\overrightarrow{KL} + \overrightarrow{LM} = \overrightarrow{KM}$$
(a)

$$\overrightarrow{NO} + \overrightarrow{NP} = \overrightarrow{NQ}$$
(b)

In these diagrams, the vectors $\overrightarrow{KM}$ and $\overrightarrow{NQ}$ are the resultant forces.

Addition of Two Vectors

Let vector A be $<a_1, a_2>$ and vector B be $<b_1, b_2>$. Then

$$A + B = \left(a_1 + b_1\right)\vec{i} + \left(a_2 + b_2\right)\vec{j}$$

Multiplication of Vector by a Scalar

Let vector A be $\vec{a}i + \vec{b}j$ and let c be a constant. Then,

$$cA = c\left(\vec{a}i + \vec{b}j\right) = c\vec{a}i + c\vec{b}j$$

Additive and Multiplicative Properties of Vectors

Let s, t and u represent vectors and d and c represent real constants. All of the following are true:

1. $s + t = t + s$

2. $(s + t) + u = s + (t + u)$

3. $s + 0 = s$

4. $s + (-s) = 0$

5. $(c+d)s = cs + sd$

6. $c(s+u) = cs + cu$

7. $c(st) = (cs)\,t$

8. $1 \cdot s = s$

9. $0 \cdot s = 0$

10. $s \cdot s = |s|^2$

11. $c(ds) = (cd)s$

The magnitude $|s|$ of a vector $\vec{s} = a_1 i + a_2 j$ is

$$|s| = \sqrt{a_1^{\,2} + a_2^{\,2}}$$

The difference between vectors $\bar{a}$ and $\bar{b}$ is given by the formula

$$\bar{a} - \bar{b} = \bar{a} + (-\bar{b})$$

Scalar (DOT) Product

Two vectors are parallel if (a) one is a scalar multiple of the other; and (b) neither is zero.

Definition:

If vector A = $<a_1, a_2>$ and vector B = $<b_1, b_2>$, then the scalar product of A and B is given by the formula

$$A \cdot B = a_1 b_1 + a_2 b_2$$

Theorem:

If θ is the angle between the vectors $A = a_1\vec{i} + a_2\vec{j}$ and $B = b_1\vec{i} + b_2\vec{j}$ then

$$\cos\theta = \frac{a_1 b_1 + a_2 b_2}{|A||B|}$$

Definition:

Let vector $A = a_1\vec{i} + a_2\vec{j}$ and vector $B = b_1\vec{i} + b_2\vec{j}$ The projection of vector A on B (Proj$_B$A) is given by the quantity $|A|\cos\theta$, where θ is the angle between the two vectors.

Therefore,

$$\text{Proj}_B A = |A|\cos\theta = \frac{a_1 b_1 + a_2 b_2}{|B|} = \frac{A \cdot B}{|B|}$$

If the angle θ is acute, then $|A|\cos\theta$ is positive; if θ is obtuse, then $|A|\cos\theta$ is negative.

The scalar product of two non-zero vectors A and B is now redefined by the formula

$$A \cdot B = |A||B|\cos\theta = a_1b_1 + a_2b_2$$

PROBLEM

Which of the following vectors are equal to $\overrightarrow{MN}$ if M = (2, 1) and N = (3, –4)?

(a) $\overrightarrow{AB}$, where A = (1, –1) and B = (2, 3)

(b) $\overrightarrow{CD}$, where C = (–4, 5) and D = (–3, 10)

(c) $\overrightarrow{EF}$, where E = (3, –2) and F = (4, –7).

SOLUTION

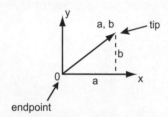

(a-0, b-0) represents the vector.

(c-a, d-b) represents the vector.

With each ordered pair in the plane there can be associated a vector from the origin to that point.

The vector is determined by subtracting the coordinates of the endpoint from the corresponding coordinates of the tip. As for $\overrightarrow{MN}$, the tip is the point corresponding to the second letter of the alphabetical notation, N, while the endpoint is the point corresponding to the first, M. In this problem the vectors are of a general nature wherein their endpoints do not lie at the origin.

We first find the ordered pair which represents MN.

$$\overrightarrow{MN} = (3-2,-4-1) = (1,-5)$$

Now, we find the ordered pair representing each vector.

(a) $\overrightarrow{AB} = (2-1,3-(-1)) = (1,4)$

(b) $\overrightarrow{CD} = ((-3)-(-4),10-5) = (1,5)$

(c) $\overrightarrow{EF} = (4-3,-7-(-2)) = (1,-5)$

Only $\overrightarrow{EF}$ and $\overrightarrow{MN}$ are equal.

Ratio, Proportion, and Variation

The ratio of two numbers x and y written $x:y$ is the fraction $\dfrac{x}{y}$ where $y \neq 0$. A proportion is an equality of two ratios. The laws of proportion are listed below:

If $\dfrac{a}{b} = \dfrac{c}{d}$, then:

A) $ad = bc$

B) $\dfrac{b}{a} = \dfrac{d}{c}$

C) $\dfrac{a}{c} = \dfrac{b}{d}$

D) $\dfrac{a+b}{b} = \dfrac{c+d}{d}$

E) $\dfrac{a-b}{b} = \dfrac{c-d}{d}$

Given a proportion $a:b = c:d$, then a and d are called the extremes, b and c are called the means, and d is called the fourth proportional to a, b, and c.

Problem Solving Examples:

PROBLEM

Solve the proportion $\dfrac{x+1}{4} = \dfrac{15}{12}$.

SOLUTION

Cross multiply to determine x; that is, multiply the numerator of the first fraction by the denominator of the second, and equate this to the product of the numerator of the second and the denominator of the first.

$$(x + 1)12 = 4 \times 15$$
$$12x + 12 = 60$$
$$x = 4$$

PROBLEM

If $a/b = c/d$, $a + b = 60$, $c = 3$, and $d = 2$, find b.

SOLUTION

We are given $\dfrac{a}{b} = \dfrac{c}{d}$. Cross multiplying, we obtain $ad = bc$.

Adding bd to both sides, we have $ad + bd = bc + bd$, which is equivalent to $d(a + b) = b(c + d)$ or

$$\frac{a+b}{b} = \frac{c+d}{d}$$

Replacing $(a + b)$ by 60, c by 3, and d by 2, we obtain

$$\frac{60}{b} = \frac{3+2}{2}$$
$$\frac{60}{b} = \frac{5}{2}$$

Cross multiplying, $5b = 120$
$$b = 24.$$

Variation

A) If x is directly proportional to y written $x \alpha y$, then $x = ky$ or $\dfrac{x}{y} = k$, where k is called the constant of proportionality or the constant of variation.

B) If x varies inversely as y, then $x = \dfrac{k}{y}$.

C) If x varies jointly as y and z, then $x = kyz$.

Example: If y varies jointly as x and z, and $3x:1 = y:z$, find the constant of variation.

Solution: A variable s is said to vary jointly as t and v if s varies directly as the product tv, that is, if $s = ktv$ where k is called the constant of variation.

Here the variable y varies jointly as x and z with k as the constant of variation.

$$y = kxz$$
$$3x:1 = y:z$$

Expressing these ratios as fractions,

$$\frac{3x}{1} = \frac{y}{z}$$

Solving for y by cross-multiplying,

$$y = 3xz$$

Equating both relations for y, we have:

$$kxz = 3xz$$

Solving for the constant of variation, k, we divide both sides by xz,

$$k = 3.$$

PROBLEM

If y varies directly with respect to x and $y = 3$ when $x = -2$, find y when $x = 8$.

SOLUTION

If y varies directly as x, then y is equal to some constant k times x; that is, $y = kx$ where k is a constant. We can now say $y_1 = kx_1$ and $y_2 = kx_2$ or $\dfrac{y_1}{x_1} = k$, $\dfrac{y_2}{x_2} = k$ which implies $\dfrac{y_1}{x_1} = \dfrac{y_2}{x_2}$ which is a proportion. We use the proportion $\dfrac{y_1}{x_1} = \dfrac{y_2}{x_2}$. Thus $\dfrac{3}{-2} = \dfrac{y_2}{8}$. Now solve for y_2:

$$8\left(\frac{3}{-2}\right) = 8\left(\frac{y_2}{8}\right)$$
$$-12 = y_2$$

When $x = 8$, $y = -12$.

PROBLEM

If y varies inversely as the cube of x, and $y = 7$ when $x = 2$, express y as a function of x.

SOLUTION

The relationship "y varies inversely with respect to x" is expressed as,

$$y = \frac{k}{x}$$

The inverse variation is now with respect to the cube of x, x^3, and we have,

$$y = \frac{k}{x^3}$$

Since $y = 7$ and $x = 2$ must satisfy this relation, we replace x and y by these values,

$$7 = \frac{k}{2^3} = \frac{k}{8}$$

and we find $k = 7 \times 8 = 56$. Substitution of this value of k in the general relation gives,

$$y = \frac{56}{x^3}$$

Which expresses y as a function of x. We may now, in addition, find the value of y corresponding to any value of x. If we had the added requirement to find the value of y when $x = 1.2$, $x = 1.2$ would be substituted in the function to give

$$y = \frac{56}{(1.2)^3} = \frac{56}{1.728} = 32.41$$

Other expressions in use are "is proportional to" for "varies directly," and "is inversely proportional to" for "varies inversely."

Drill: Ratios and Proportions

<u>DIRECTIONS</u>: Find the appropriate solutions.

1. Solve for n: $\dfrac{4}{n} = \dfrac{8}{5}$.

(A) 10 (C) 6

(B) 8 (D) 2.5

2. Solve for n: $\dfrac{2}{3} = \dfrac{n}{72}$.

(A) 12 (C) 64

(B) 48 (D) 56

3. Solve for n: $n : 12 = 3 : 4$.

(A) 8 (C) 9

(B) 1 (D) 4

4. Four out of every five students at West High take a mathematics course. If the enrollment at West is 785, how many students take mathematics?

(A) 628 (C) 705

(B) 157 (D) 655

5. At a factory, three out of every 1,000 parts produced are defective. In a day, the factory can produce 25,000 parts. How many of these parts would be defective?

(A) 7 (C) 750

(B) 75 (D) 7,500

6. A summer league softball team won 28 out of the 32 games they played. What is the ratio of games won to games played?

(A) 4 : 5 (C) 7 : 8

(B) 3 : 4 (D) 2 : 3

Real-World Problems Involving Proportion

PROBLEM

A chemist is preparing a chemical solution. She needs to add 3 parts sodium and 2 parts zinc to a flask of chlorine. If she has already placed 300 grams of sodium into the flask, how much zinc must she now add?

SOLUTION

Step 1 is to determine the ratio of sodium and zinc.

3 parts sodium, 2 parts zinc = 3:2

Step 2 is to write the problem as a proportion.

$$\frac{3}{2} = \frac{300}{?}$$

Step 3 is to put the proportion in the following format:

$AD = BC$ $\qquad\qquad$ 3(?) = 2(300)

Step 4 is to solve the right side of the proportion.

2(300) = 600

Step 5 is to rewrite the proportion.

3(?) = 600

Step 6 is to find the missing integer that solves the proportion. To do this, divide both sides by the known extreme, 3.

$$\frac{3(?)}{3} = ? \qquad\qquad \frac{600}{3} = 200$$

Step 7 is to rewrite the proportion.

? = 200

The solution is 200 grams of zinc.

PROBLEM

An automobile dealer has to sell 3.5 cars for every 1 truck to achieve the optimum profit. This year, it is estimated that 3,500 cars will be sold. How many trucks must he sell to achieve the optimum profit?

SOLUTION

Step 1 is to determine the ratio of cars to trucks.

3.5 cars, 1 truck = 3.5:1

Make both sides of the ratio an integer. To do this, multiply both sides of the ratio by 2.

2(3.5):2(1) = 7:2

Step 2 is to write the problem as a proportion.

$$\frac{7}{2} = \frac{3,500}{?}$$

Step 3 is to put the proportion in the following format:

$AD = BC$ $\qquad\qquad$ 7(?) = 2(3,500)

Step 4 is to solve the right side of the proportion.

2(3,500) = 7,000

Step 5 is to rewrite the proportion.

7(?) = 7,000

Step 6 is to find the missing integer that solves the proportion. To do this, divide both sides by the known extreme, 7.

$$\frac{7(?)}{7} = ? \qquad\qquad \frac{7,000}{7} = 1,000$$

Step 7 is to rewrite the proportion.

? = 1,000

The solution is 1,000 trucks.

PROBLEM

A baker is making a new recipe for chocolate chip cookies. He decides that for every 6 cups of flour, he needs to add 1 cup of sugar. He puts 30 cups of flour and 2 cups of sugar into the batter. How much more sugar does he need?

SOLUTION

Step 1 is to determine the ratio of flour to sugar.

6 cups flour, 1 cup sugar = 6:1

Step 2 is to write the problem as a proportion.

$$\frac{6}{1} = \frac{30}{?}$$

Step 3 is to put the proportion in the following format:

$AD = BC$ $\qquad\qquad$ 6(?) = 1(30)

Step 4 is to solve the right side of the proportion.

1(30) = 30

Step 5 is to rewrite the proportion.

$6(?) = 30$

Step 6 is to find the missing integer that solves the proportion.

To do this, divide both sides by the known extreme, 6.

$$\frac{6(?)}{6} = ?\qquad\qquad\frac{30}{6} = 5$$

Step 7 is to rewrite the proportion.

$? = 5$

The solution is that 5 cups of sugar must be added to the batter.

Step 8 is to determine how many more cups of sugar are needed.

$5 - 2 = 3$

Since only 2 cups have been added so far, the baker must still add 3 cups.

Algebra
Answer Key

Drill: Operations with Polynomials

1. (B)	6. (B)	11. (C)	16. (C)
2. (C)	7. (C)	12. (B)	17. (D)
3. (C)	8. (D)	13. (D)	18. (D)
4. (D)	9. (A)	14. (A)	19. (B)
5. (A)	10. (D)	15. (D)	20. (B)

Drill: Simplifying Algebraic Expressions

1. (C)	3. (B)	5. (D)
2. (D)	4. (A)	

Drill: Two Linear Equations

1. (D)	3. (A)	5. (C)
2. (B)	4. (D)	

Drill: Quadratic Equations

1. (A)	3. (B)	5. (D)
2. (D)	4. (C)	

Drill: Absolute Value Equations

1. (B)	3. (A)	5. (C)
2. (D)	4. (C)	

Drill: Inequalities

1. (D)	3. (D)	5. (A)
2. (C)	4. (B)	

Drill: Ratios and Proportions

1. (D)	3. (C)	5. (B)
2. (B)	4. (A)	6. (C)

Detailed Explanations of Answers

Drill: Operations with Polynomials

1. (B)

$$9a^2b + 3c + 2a^2b + 5c = (9a^2b + 2a^2b) + (3c + 5c)$$
$$= 11a^2b + 8c$$

2. (C)

$$14m^2n^3 + 6m^2n^3 + 3m^2n^3 = 23m^2n^3$$

3. (C)

$$3x + 2y + 16x + 3z + 6y = (3x + 16x) + (2y + 6y) + 3z$$
$$= 19x + 8y + 3z$$

4. (D)

$$(4d^2 + 7e^3 + 12f) + (3d^2 + 6e^3 + 2f) =$$
$$(4d^2 + 3d^2) + (7e^3 + 6e^3) + (12f + 2f) =$$
$$7d^2 + 13e^3 + 14f$$

5. (A)

$$3ac^2 = +2b^2c + 7ac^2 + 2ac^2 + b^2c =$$
$$(3ac^2 + 7ac^2 + 2ac^2) + (2b^2c + b^2c) =$$
$$12ac^2 + 3b^2c$$

6. (B)

$$14m^2n - 6m^2n = 8m^2n$$

7. (C)

$$3x^3y^2 - 4xz - 6x^3y^2 = (3x^3y^2 - 6x^3y^2) - 4xz$$
$$= -3x^3y^2 - 4xz$$

8. (D)

$$9g^2 + 6h - 2g^2 - 5h = (9g^2 - 2g^2) + (6h - 5h)$$
$$= 7g^2 + h$$

9. (A)

$$7b^3 - 4c^2 - 6b^3 + 3c^2 = (7b^3 - 6b^3) + (-4c^2 + 3c^2)$$
$$= b^3 - c^2$$

10. (D)

$$11q^2r - 4q^2r - 8q^2r = (11q^2r - 4q^2r) - 8q^2r$$
$$= 7q^2r - 8q^2r$$
$$= -q^2r$$

11. (C)

$$5p^2t \times 3p^2t = (5 \times 3)(p^2 \times p^2)(t \times t)$$
$$= 15p^4t^2$$

12. (B)

$$(2r + s)14r = (2r)(14r) + (s)(14r)$$
$$= 28r^2 + 14sr$$

13. (D)

$$(4m + p)(3m - 2p) = (4m)(3m) + (4m)(-2p)$$
$$+ (p)(3m) + (p)(-2p)$$
$$= 12m^2 [(-8mp) + 3mp] +$$
$$(-2p^2)$$
$$= 12m^2 - 5mp - 2p^2$$

14. (A)

$$(2a + b)(3a^2 + ab + b^2) = (2a)(3a^2) + (2a)(ab) +$$
$$(2a)(b^2) + (b)(3a^2) + (b)(ab) + (b)(b^2)$$
$$= 6a^3 + 2a^2b + 2ab^2 + 3a^2b$$
$$+ ab^2 + b^3 = 6a^3 + 5a^2b + 3ab^2 + b^3$$

15. (D)

$$(6t^2 + 2t + 1)(3t) = (6t^2)(3t) + (2t)(3t) + (1)(3t)$$
$$= 18t^3 + 6t^2 + 3t$$

16. (C)

$$(x^2 + x - 6) \div (x - 2) = \frac{x^2 + x - 6}{(x - 2)} = \frac{(x+3)(x-2)}{(x-2)} = x + 3$$

17. (D)

$$24b^4c^3 \div 6b^2c = \frac{\overset{4}{\cancel{24}} \overset{b^2}{\cancel{b^4}} \overset{c^2}{\cancel{c^3}}}{\cancel{6} \cancel{b^2} \cancel{c}} = 4b^2c^2$$

18. (D)

$$(3p^2 + pq - 2q^2) \div (p + q) = \frac{3p^2 + pq - 2q^2}{(p+q)}$$
$$= \frac{(3p - 2q)(p+q)}{(p+q)}$$
$$= 3p - 2q$$

19. (B)

$$(y^3 - 2y^2 - y + 2) \div (y - 2) = y - 2 \overline{)\begin{array}{l} y^2 - 1 \\ y^3 - 2y^2 - y + 2 \\ \underline{-(y^3 - 2y^2)} \\ \quad 0 - y + 2 \\ \quad \underline{-(-y + 2)} \\ \quad\quad 0 \end{array}}$$

20. (B)

$$(m^2 + m - 14) \div (m + 4) = m + 4 \overline{)\begin{array}{l} m - 3 \\ m^2 + m - 14 \\ \underline{-(m^2 + 4m)} \\ \quad -3m - 14 \\ \quad \underline{-(-3m - 12)} \\ \quad\quad -2 \end{array}}$$

$$= \frac{-2}{m + 4}$$

$$m - 3 + \frac{-2}{m + 4}$$

Drill: Simplifying Algebraic Expressions

1. (C)

$$16b^2 - 25z^2 = (4b + 5z)(4b - 5z)$$

2. (D)

$$x^2 - 2x - 8 = (x - 4)(x + 2)$$

3. (B)

$$2c^2 + 5cd - 3d^2 = (2c - d)(c + 3d)$$

4. (A)

$$4t^3 - 20t = 4t(t^2 - 5)$$

5. (D)

$$x^2 + xy - 2y^2 = (x - y)(x + 2y)$$

Drill: Two Linear Equations

1. (D)

$$3x + 4y = -2 \quad = \quad 3x + 4y = -2$$
$$-3(x - 6y = -8) \quad = \quad \underline{+\ -3x + 18y = 24}$$
$$0 + 22y = 22$$
$$y = 1$$

Substitute $y = 1$ in $x - 6y = -8$ to get

$$x - 6 = -8$$
$$\underline{+6 \quad +6}$$
$$x = 2$$

$$(-2, 1)$$

2. (B)

$$2x + y = -10$$
$$\underline{-2x - 4y = 4}$$
$$0 - 3y = -6$$

$$\frac{-3y}{-3} = \frac{-6}{-3}$$

$y = 2$ substitute in first equation to get

$$2x + 2 = -10$$
$$\underline{-2 = -2}$$
$$\frac{2x}{2} = \frac{-12}{2}$$

$(-6, 2)$

3. (A)

$$\begin{array}{rcl} 6x + 5y = -4 & = & 6x + 5y = -4 \\ (3x - 3y = 9)(-2) & = & \underline{-6x + 6y = -18} \\ & & 0 + 11y = -22 \\ & & \frac{11y}{11} = \frac{-22}{11} \\ & & y = -2 \end{array}$$

substitute in the second equation to get

$$3x - 3(-2) = 9$$
$$3x + 6 = 9$$
$$\underline{-6 \quad -6}$$
$$\frac{3x}{3} = \frac{3}{3}$$
$$x = 1$$

$(1, -2)$

4. (D)

$$\begin{array}{rcl} 4x + 3y = 9 & = & 4x + 3y = 9 \\ (2x - 2y = 8)(-2) & = & \underline{-4x + 4y = -16} \\ & & 0 + 7y = -7 \\ & & y = -1 \end{array}$$

substitute in the first equation to get

$$4x + 3(-1) = 9$$
$$4x - 3 = 9$$
$$\underline{+3 \quad = +3}$$
$$\frac{4x}{4} = \frac{12}{4}$$
$$x = 3$$

$(3, -1)$

5. (C)

$$\begin{array}{rcl} x + y = 7 & = & x + y = 7 \\ x = y - 3 & = & \underline{x - y = 3} \\ & & 2x = 4 \\ & & x = 2 \end{array}$$

substitute in the first equation

$$2 + y = 7$$
$$y = 5$$

$(2, 5)$

Drill: Quadratic Equations

1. (A)

$$(x^2 - 2x - 8) = 0$$
$$(x - 4)(x + 2) = 0$$

The values of x are 4 and -2.

2. (D)

$$x^2 + 2x - 3 = 0$$
$$(x + 3)(x - 1) = 0$$

The values of x are 3 and -1.

3. (B)

$$x^2 - 7x = -10$$
$$x^2 - 7x + 10 = 0$$
$$(x - 5)(x - 2) = 0$$

The values of x are 5 and 2.

4. (C)

$$x^2 - 8x + 16 = 0$$
$$(x - 4)(x - 4) = 0$$
$$(x - 4)^2 = 0$$

The value of x is 4.

5. (D)

$$3x^2 + 3x = 6$$
$$3x^2 + 3x - 6 = 0$$
$$3(x^2 + x - 2) = 0$$
$$3(x + 2)(x - 1) = 0$$

The values of x are -2 and 1.

Drill: Absolute Value Equations

1. (B)

$$|4x - 2| = 6 \quad 4x - 2 = 6 \quad \text{or} \quad 4x - 2 = -6$$
$$4x = 8 \qquad\qquad 4x = -4$$
$$x = 2 \quad \text{or} \qquad x = -1$$

2. (D)

$$|3 - \frac{1}{2}y| = -7$$

No solution. Absolute value must equal a positive number

3. (A)

$$2|x + 7| = 12$$
$$|x + 7| = 6 \quad x + 7 = 6 \quad \text{or} \quad x + 7 = -6$$
$$x = -2 \quad \text{or} \qquad x = -13$$

4. (C)

$$|5x| - 7 = 3$$
$$|5x| = 10 \quad 5x = 10 \quad \text{or} \quad 5x = -10$$
$$x = 2 \quad \text{or} \quad x = -2$$

5. (C)

$$\left|\frac{3}{4}m\right| = 9 \qquad \frac{3}{4}m = 9 \qquad\qquad \frac{3}{4}m = -9$$
$$\frac{4}{3}\left(\frac{3}{4}m\right) = 9\left(\frac{4}{3}\right) \quad \frac{4}{3}\left(\frac{3}{4}m\right) = (-9)\left(\frac{4}{3}\right)$$
$$m = 12 \qquad\qquad m = -12$$

Drill: Inequalities

1. (D)

$$3m + 2 < 7$$
$$\underline{-2 \quad -2}$$
$$\left(\frac{1}{3}\right)3m < 5\left(\frac{1}{3}\right)$$
$$m < \frac{5}{3}$$

2. (C)

$$\frac{1}{2}x - 3 \le 1$$
$$\underline{+3 \quad +3}$$
$$\frac{1}{2}x \le 4$$
$$(2)\frac{1}{2}x \le 4(2)$$
$$x \le 8$$

3. (D)

$$-3p + 1 \ge 16$$
$$\underline{-1 \quad -1}$$
$$-3p \ge 15$$
$$\left(-\frac{1}{3}\right)-3p \ge 15\left(-\frac{1}{3}\right)$$
$$p \le 5$$

4. (B)

$$-6 < \frac{2}{3}r + 6 \le 2$$
$$\underline{-6 \qquad -6 \quad -6}$$
$$-12 < \frac{2}{3}r \le -4$$
$$\frac{3}{2}\left(-12 < \frac{2}{3}r \le -4\right)$$
$$-18 < r \le -6$$

5. (A)

$$0 < 2 - y < 6$$
$$\frac{-2 - 2 \quad -2}{-2 < \ y < 4}$$
$$-1(-2 < -y < 4)$$
$$-4 < y < 2$$

4. (A)

$$4 : 5 = x : 785 \Rightarrow \qquad \frac{4}{5} = \frac{x}{785}$$
$$(785)(4) = 5x$$
$$\left(\frac{1}{5}\right)(785)(4) = (5x)\frac{1}{5}$$
$$(157)(4) = x$$
$$628 = x$$

Drill: Ratios and Proportions

1. (D)

$$\frac{4}{n} = \frac{8}{5} \qquad 5(4) = 8n$$
$$\left(\frac{1}{8}\right)20 = 8n\left(\frac{1}{8}\right)$$
$$\frac{20}{8} = n \Rightarrow 2.5 = n$$

5. (B)

$$3 : 1000 = y : 25000 \Rightarrow \qquad \frac{3}{1000} = \frac{y}{25000}$$
$$(3)(25,000) = y(1000)$$
$$\frac{(3)(25,000)}{1000} = y$$
$$75 = y$$

2. (B)

$$\frac{2}{3} = \frac{n}{72} \qquad 2(72) = 3n$$
$$\frac{1}{3}(144) = (3n)\frac{1}{3}$$
$$(2)(24) = n$$
$$48 = n$$

6. (C)

$$28 : 32 \Rightarrow \frac{28}{32} = \frac{7}{8} \Rightarrow 7 : 8$$

3. (C)

$$n : 12 = 3 : 4 \Rightarrow \quad \frac{n}{12} = \frac{3}{4}$$
$$4n = (12)(3)$$
$$4n = 36$$
$$n = 9$$

Competency 2: Knowledge of Functions

Elementary Functions

A **function** is any process that assigns a single value of y to each number of x. Because the value of x determines the value of y, y is called the **dependent variable** and x is called the **independent variable**. The set of all the values of x by which the function is defined is called the **domain** of the function. The set of corresponding values of y is called the **range** of the function.

PROBLEM

Is $y^2 = x$ a function?

SOLUTION

Graph the equation. Note that x can have two values of y. Therefore, $y^2 = x$ is not a function.

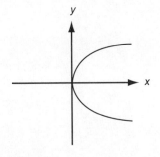

PROBLEM

Find the domain and range for $y = 5 - x^2$.

SOLUTION

First determine if there are any values that would make the function undefined (i.e., dividing by 0). There are none. The domain is the set of real numbers. The range can be found by putting some values in for x.

x	2	1	0	-1	-2
y	1	4	5	4	1

The range is the set of real numbers less than or equal to 5.

PROBLEM

Evaluate $f(1)$ for $y = f(x) = 5x + 2$.

SOLUTION

$$f(x) = 5x + 2$$

$f(1) = 5(1) + 2$

$= 5 + 2$

$= 7$

Functions can be added, subtracted, multiplied, or divided to form new functions.

a. $(f + g)(x) = f(x) + g(x)$

b. $(f - g)(x) = f(x) - g(x)$

c. $(f \times g)(x) = f(x) g(x)$

d. $(f / g)(x) = f(x) / g(x)$

PROBLEM

Let $f(x) = 2x^2 - 1$ and $g(x) = 5x + 3$. Determine the following functions:

(1) $f + g$ (2) $f - g$

(3) $f \times g$ (4) f / g

SOLUTION

(1) $(f + g)(x) = f(x) + g(x) = 2x^2 - 1 + 5x + 3$

$= 2x^2 + 5x + 2$

(2) $(f - g)(x) = f(x) - g(x) = 2x^2 - 1 - (5x + 3)$

$= 2x^2 - 1 - 5x - 3$

$= 2x^2 - 5x - 4$

(3) $(f \times g)(x) = f(x) g(x) = (2x^2 - 1)(5x + 3)$

$= 10x^3 + 6x^2 - 5x - 3$

(4) $(f / g)(x) = f(x) / g(x) = (2x^2 - 1) / (5x + 3)$

Note the domain of (4) is for all real numbers except $-\dfrac{3}{5}$.

The **composite function** $f \circ g$ is defined $(f \circ g)(x) = f(g(x))$.

PROBLEM

Given $f(x) = 3x$ and $g(x) = 4x + 2$. Find $(f \circ g)(x)$ and $(g \circ f)(x)$.

SOLUTION

$(f \circ g)(x) = f(g(x)) = 3(4x + 2)$

$= 12x + 6$

$(g \circ f)(x) = g(f(x)) = 4(3x) + 2$

$= 12x + 2$

Note that $(f \circ g)(x) \neq (g \circ f)(x)$.

PROBLEM

Find $(f \circ g)(2)$ if

$f(x) = x^2 - 3$ and $g(x) = 3x + 1$

SOLUTION

$(f \circ g)(2) = f(g(2))$

$g(x) = 3x + 1$

Substitute the value of x.

$g(2) = 3(2) + 1$

$= 7$

$f(x) = x^2 - 3$

Substitute the value of $g(2)$ in $f(x)$.

$f(7) = (7)^2 - 3$

$= 49 - 3$

$= 46$

The **inverse** of a function, f^{-1}, is obtained from f by interchanging the x and y and then solving for y.

Two functions f and g are inverses of one another if $g \circ f = x$ and $f \circ g = x$. To find g when f is given, interchange x and y in the equation $y = f(x)$ and solve for $y = g(x)$. Then replace y with $f^{-1}(x)$.

PROBLEM

Find the inverse of the functions

(1) $f(x) = 3x + 2$

(2) $f(x) = x^2 - 3$

SOLUTION

   (1) $f(x) = y = 3x + 2$

To find $f^{-1}(x)$, interchange x and y.

$$x = 3y + 2$$
$$3y = x - 2$$

Solve for y, then replace y with $f^{-1}(x)$.

$$f^{-1}(x) = \frac{x - 2}{3}$$

   (2) $f(x) = y = x^2 - 3$.

To find $f^{-1}(x)$, interchange x and y.

$$x = y^2 - 3$$
$$y^2 = x + 3$$

Solve for y, then replace y with $f^{-1}(x)$.

$$f^{-1}(x) = \sqrt{x + 3}$$

Logarithms and Exponential Functions and Equations

An equation

$$y = b^x$$

(with $b > 0$ and $b \neq 1$) is called an **exponential function.** The exponential function with base b can be written as

$$y = f(x) = b^x.$$

The inverse of an exponential function is the **logarithmic function,**

$$f^{-1}(x) = \log_b x.$$

PROBLEM

Write the following equations in logarithmic form:

$3^4 = 81$ and $M^k = 5$.

SOLUTION

The expression $y = b^x$ is equivalent to the logarithmic expression $\log_b y = x$. Therefore, $3^4 = 81$ is equivalent to the logarithmic expression

$$\log_3 81 = 4$$

and $M^k = 5$ is equivalent to the logarithmic expression

$$\log_M 5 = k.$$

PROBLEM

Find the value of $\log_5 25$ and $\log_4 x = 2$.

SOLUTION

$\log_5 25$ is equivalent to $5^x = 25$. Thus $x = 2$, since $5^2 = 25$.

$\log_4 x = 2$ is equivalent to $4^2 = x \times x = 16$.

Logarithm Properties

If M, N, p, and b are positive numbers and $b = 1$, then

  a. $\log_b 1 = 0$

  b. $\log_b b = 1$

  c. $\log_b b^x = x$

  d. $\log_b M\,N = \log_b M + \log_b N$

  e. $\log_b M\,/\,N = \log_b M - \log_b N$

  f. $\log_b M^p = p\,\log_b M$

PROBLEM

If $\log_{10} 3 = .4771$ and $\log_{10} 4 = .6021$, find $\log_{10} 12$.

SOLUTION

Since $12 = 4(3)$, $\log_{10} 12 = \log_{10} (4)\,(3)$

Remember

$$\log_b M\,N = \log_b M + \log_b N.$$

Therefore,

$$\log_{10} 12 = \log_{10} 4 + \log_{10} 3$$
$$= .6021 + .4771$$
$$= 1.0792$$

Properties of Functions

A) A function F is one to one if for every range value there corresponds exactly one domain value of x.

B) A function is even if $f(-x) = f(x)$ or

$$f(x) + f(-x) = 2f(x).$$

C) A function is said to be odd if $f(-x) = -f(x)$ or $f(x) + f(-x) = 0$.

D) Periodicity

A function f with domain X is periodic if there exists a positive real number p such that $f(x + p) = f(x)$ for all $x \in X$.

The smallest number p with this property is called the period of f.

Over any interval of length p, the behavior of a periodic function can be completely described.

E) Inverse of function

Assuming that f is a one-to-one function with domain X and range Y, then a function g having domain Y and range X is called the inverse function of f if:

$$f(g(y)) = y \text{ for every } y \in Y \text{ and}$$

$$g(f(x)) = x \text{ for every } x \in X.$$

The inverse of the function f is denoted f^{-1}.

To find the inverse function f^{-1}, you must solve the equation $y = f(x)$ for x in terms of y.

Be careful: This solution must be a function.

F) The identity function $f(x) = x$ maps every x to itself.

G) The constant function $f(x) = c$ for all $x \in R$.

The "zeros" of an arbitrary function $f(x)$ are particular values of x for which $f(x) = 0$.

(a)
Identity
function

(b)
Constant
function

x-intercept
(c)
Zeros of a
function

PROBLEM

Find the domain D and range R of the function

$$\left(x, \frac{x}{|x|} \right).$$

SOLUTION

Note that the y-value of any coordinate pair (x,y) is $\frac{x}{|x|}$. We can replace X in the formula $\frac{x}{|x|}$ with any number except 0, since the denominator, $|x|$, cannot equal 0. This is because division by 0 is undefined. Therefore, the domain D is the set of all real numbers except 0. If x is negative, i.e., $x < 0$, then $|x| = -x$ by definition. Hence, if x is negative, then $\frac{x}{|x|} = \frac{x}{-x} = -$. If x is positive, i.e. $x > 0$, then $|x| = x$ by definition. Hence, if x is positive, then $\frac{x}{|x|} = \frac{x}{x} =$. (The case where $x = 0$ has already been found to be undefined). Thus, there are only two numbers -1 and 1 in the range R of the function; that is, $R = \{-1,1\}$.

PROBLEM

If $f(x) = 3x + 4$ and $D = \{x \mid -1 \le x \le 3\}$, find the range of $f(x)$.

SOLUTION

We first prove that the value of $3x + 4$ increases when x increases. If $X > x$, then we may multiply both sides of the inequality by a positive number to obtain an equivalent inequality. Thus, $3X > 3x$. We may also add a number to both sides of the inequality to obtain an equivalent inequality. Thus,

$$3X + 4 > 3x + 4.$$

Hence, if x belongs to D, the function value $f(x) = 3x + 4$ is least when $x = -1$ and greatest when $x = 3$. Consequently, since $f(-1) = -3 + 4 = 1$ and $f(3) = 9 + 4 = 13$, the range is all y from 1 to 13; that is,

$$R = \{y \mid 1 \leq y \leq 13\}.$$

Graphing a Function

The Cartesian Coordinate System

Consider two lines x and y drawn on a plane region called R.

Let the intersection of x and y be the origin and let us impose a coordinate system on each of the lines.

If (x, y) is a point or ordered pair on the coordinate plane R then x is the first coordinate and y is the second coordinate.

To locate an ordered pair on the coordinate plane simply measure the distance of x units along the x-axis, then measure vertically (parallel to the y-axis) y units.

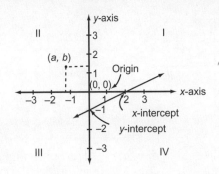

I, II, III, IV are called quadrants in the COORDINATE PLANE.

(a,b) is an ordered pair with x-coordinate a and y-coordinate b.

Drawing the Graph

There are several ways to plot the graph of a function. The process of computing and plotting points on the graph is always an aid in this endeavor. The more points we locate on the graph, the more accurate our drawing will be.

It is also helpful if we consider the symmetry of the function. That is,

a) A graph is symmetric with respect to the x-axis if whenever a point (x,y) is on the graph, then $(x,-y)$ is also on the graph.

b) Symmetry with respect to the y-axis occurs when both points $(-x,y)$ and (x,y) appear on the graph for every x and y in the graph.

c) When the simultaneous substitution of $-x$ for x and $-y$ for y does not change the solution of the equation, the graph is said to be symmetric about the origin.

Symmetric about the y-axis

(a)

Symmetric about the x-axis
Note: This is not a function of x.

(b)

Symmetric about the origin

(c)

Another aid in drawing a graph is locating any vertical asymptotes.

A vertical asymptote is a vertical line $x = a$, such that the functional value $|f(x)|$ grows indefinitely large as x approaches the fixed value a.

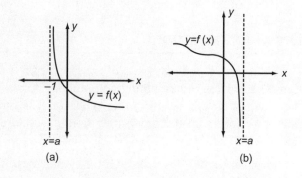

(a)   (b)

$x = a$ is a vertical asymptote for these functions

The following steps encapsulate the procedure for drawing a graph:

a) Determine the domain and range of the function.

b) Find the intercepts of the graph and plot them.

c) Determine the symmetries of the graph.

d) Locate the vertical asymptotes and plot a few points on the graph near each asymptote.

e) Plot additional points as needed.

PROBLEM

Construct the graph of the function defined by $y = 3x - 9$.

SOLUTION

An equation of the form $y = mx + b$ is a linear equation; that is, the equation of a line.

A line can be determined by two points. Let us choose intercepts. The x-intercept lies on the x-axis and the y-intercept on the y-axis.

We find the intercepts by assigning 0 to x and solving for y and by assigning 0 to y and solving for x. It is helpful to have a third point. We find the third point by assigning 4 to x and solving for y. Thus we get the following table of corresponding numbers:

x	$y = 3x - 9$	y
0	$y = 3(0) - 9 = 0 - 9 =$	-9
4	$y = 3(4) - 9 = 12 - 9 =$	3

Solving for x to get the x-intercept:

$$y = 3x - 9$$
$$y + 9 = 3x$$
$$x = \frac{y + 9}{3}$$

When $y = 0$, $x = \frac{9}{3} = 3$. The three points are $(0, -9)$, $(4, 3)$, and $(3, 0)$. Draw a line through them (see sketch).

PROBLEM

Are the following points on the graph of the equation $3x - 2y = 0$?

a) point $(2, 3)$?

b) point $(3, 2)$?

c) point $(4, 6)$?

$3x - 2y = 0$

SOLUTION

The point (a,b) lies on the graph of the equation $3x - 2y = 0$ if replacement of x and y by a and b, respectively, in the given equation results in an equation which is true.

a) Replacing (x,y) by $(2,3)$:

$$3x - 2y = 0$$
$$3(2) - 2(3) = 0$$
$$6 - 6 = 0$$
$$0 = 0, \text{ which is true.}$$

Therefore $(2,3)$ is a point on the graph.

b) Replacing (x,y) by $(3,2)$:

$$3x - 2y = 0$$
$$3(4) - 2(6) = 0$$
$$9 - 4 = 0$$
$$5 = 0, \text{ which is not true.}$$

Therefore $(3,2)$ is not a point on the graph.

c) Replacing (x,y) by $(4,6)$:

$$3x - 2y = 0$$
$$3(4) - 2(6) = 0$$
$$12 - 12 = 0$$
$$0 = 0, \text{ which is true.}$$

Therefore $(4,6)$ is a point on the graph.

This problem may also be solved geometrically as follows: draw the graph of the line $3x - 2 = 0$ on the coordinate axes. This can be done by solving for y:

$$3x - 2y = 0$$
$$-2y = -3x$$
$$y = \frac{-3}{-2}x = \frac{3}{2}x,$$

and plotting the points shown in the following table:

x	$y = \dfrac{3}{2}x$
0	0
1	$\dfrac{3}{2} = 1\dfrac{1}{2}$
2	3
−2	−3

(See accompanying figure.)

Observe that we obtain the same result as in our algebraic solution. The points $(2,3)$ and $(4,6)$ lie on the line $3x - 2y = 0$, whereas $(3,2)$ does not.

Polynomial Functions and Their Graphs

A polynomial in x is an expression of the form

$$a_n x^n + a_{n-1} x^{n-1} + \ldots + a_1 x + a_0,$$

where a_1, a_2, ... and a_n are real numbers and where all the exponents are positive integers. When $a_n \neq 0$, this polynomial is said to be of degree n. It is common to let $P(x)$ represent

$$a_n x^n + a_{n-1} x^{n-1} + \ldots + a_1 x + a_0.$$

Then $y = P(x)$ is a polynomial function. A function with the property that

$$P(-x) = P(x)$$

is an even function, while a function with the property

$$P(-x) = -P(x)$$

is an odd function. Even functions are symmetric with respect to the y-axis, while odd functions are symmetric with respect to the origin.

It would be possible to obtain the graph of a polynomial function $y = P(x)$ by simply setting up a table and plotting a large number of points; this is how a computer or a graphing calculator operates. However, it is often desirable to have some basic information about the graph prior to plotting points. The graph of the polynomial function, $y = a_0$ is a line which is parallel to the x-axis and $|a_0|$ units above or below the x-axis, depending on whether a_0 is positive or negative. A function of this type is called a constant function. The graph of the polynomial function

$$y = a_1 x + a_0$$

is a line with slope a_1 and with a_0 as the y-intercept. The graph of the polynomial function

$$y = a_2 x^2 + a_1 x + a_0$$

is a parabola.

It is much more difficult to graph a polynomial function with degree greater than two. However, here are three items which should be investigated.

(1) Find lines (x-axis and y-axis) of symmetry and find out whether the origin is a point of symmetry.

(2) Find out about intercepts. The y-intercept is easy to find but the x-intercepts are usually much more difficult to identify. If possible, factor $P(x)$.

(3) Find out what happens to $P(x)$ when $|x|$ is large. This procedure is illustrated in the following example.

• **EXAMPLE**

Graph

$$y = x^4 - 5x^2 + 4$$

(1) The graph has symmetry with respect to the y-axis.

(2) The y-intercept is at 4. Since

$$x^4 - 5x^2 + 4 = (x^2 - 4)(x^2 - 1)$$
$$= (x - 2)(x + 2)(x - 1)(x + 1),$$

the x-intercepts are at 1, 2, –1, and –2.

(3) As $|x|$ gets large, $P(x)$ gets large.

Here is a sketch of the graph.

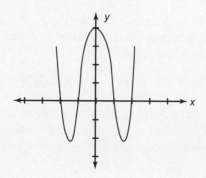

Rational Functions and Their Graphs

When $P(x)$ and $Q(x)$ are polynomials,

$$y = \frac{P(x)}{Q(x)}$$

is called a rational function. The domain of this function is the set of all real numbers x with the property that $Q(x) \neq 0$.

Graphing rational functions is rather difficult. As is the case for polynomial functions, it is desirable to have a general procedure for graphing rational functions. Here is the suggested method for

$$y = \frac{P(x)}{Q(x)}$$

where $P(x) = a_n x^n + a_{n-1} x^{n-1} + ... + a_1 x + a_0$ and $Q(x) = b_m x^m + b_{m-1} x^{m-1} + ... + b_1 x + b_0$.

(1) Find lines (x-axis and y-axis) of symmetry and determine whether the origin is a point of symmetry.

(2) Find out about intercepts. The y-intercept is at $\frac{a_0}{b_0}$ and the x-intercepts will be at values of x where $P(x) = 0$.

(3) Find vertical asymptotes. A line $x = c$ is a vertical asymptote whenever $Q(c) = 0$ and $P(c) \neq 0$.

(4) Find horizontal asymptotes

   (a) If $m = n$, then $y = \frac{a_n}{b_m}$ is the horizontal asymptote.

   (b) If $m > n$, then $y = 0$ is the horizontal asymptote.

   (c) If $m < n$, then there is no horizontal asymptote.

This procedure is illustrated in the following example

• **EXAMPLE**

Graph

$$y = \frac{x}{(x-1)(x+3)}$$

(1) The axes are not lines of symmetry, nor is the origin a point of symmetry.

(2) The x-intercept and the y-intercept are both at the origin.

(3) The lines $x = 1$ and $x = -3$ are both vertical asymptotes.

(4) The line $y = 0$ is the horizontal asymptote.

Here is a sketch of the graph.

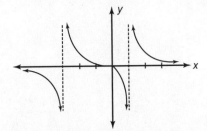

Special Functions and Their Graphs

It is possible to define a function by using different rules for different portions of the domain. The graphs of such functions are determined by graphing the different portions separately. Here is an example.

• **EXAMPLE**

Graph

$$f(x) = \begin{cases} x \text{ if } x \leq 1 \\ 2x \text{ if } x > 1 \end{cases}$$

Notice that point $(1,1)$ is part of the graph, but $(1, 2)$ is not.

Functions which involve absolute value can often be completed by translating them to a two-rule form. Consider this example.

• **EXAMPLE**

Graph

$$f(x) = |x| - 1$$

Since $|x| = \begin{cases} x \text{ if } x \geq 0 \\ -x \text{ if } x < 0 \end{cases}$

$f(x)$ can be translated to the following form.

$$f(x) = \begin{cases} x - 1 \text{ if } x \geq 0 \\ -x - 1 \text{ if } x < 0 \end{cases}$$

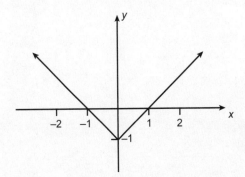

The greatest integer function, denoted by $f(x) = \left[|x| \right]$, is defined by $f(x) = j$, where j is the integer with the property that $j \leq x < j + 1$. The graph of this function follows.

Chapter

Competencies 3 & 4: Knowledge of Geometry

Points, Lines, and Angles

Geometry is built upon a series of undefined terms. These terms are those that we accept as known in order to define other undefined terms.

A) **Point:** Although we represent points on paper with small dots, a point has no size, thickness, or width.

B) **Line:** A line is a series of adjacent points that extends indefinitely. A line can be either curved or straight; however, unless otherwise stated, the term "line" refers to a straight line.

C) **Plane:** A plane is a collection of points lying on a flat surface that extends indefinitely in all directions.

Definitions

Definition 1

If A and B are two points on a line, then the **line segment** AB is the set of points on that line between A and B and including A and B, which are called the endpoints. The line segment is referred to as $\overline{AB}$.

Definition 2

A **half-line** is the set of all the points on a line on the same side of a dividing point, not including the dividing point, denoted by $\overleftrightarrow{AB}$.

Definition 3

Let A be a dividing point on a line. Then, a **ray** is the set of all the points on a half-line and the dividing point itself. The dividing point is called the endpoint or the vertex of the ray. The ray AB shown below is denoted by $\overrightarrow{AB}$.

Definition 4

Three or more points are said to be collinear if and only if they lie on the same line.

Definition 5

Let X, Y, and Z be three collinear points. If Y is between X and Z, then $\overrightarrow{YX}$ and $\overrightarrow{YZ}$ are called **opposite rays**.

Definition 6

The **absolute value** of x, denoted by $|x|$, is defined as

$$|x| = \begin{cases} x & \text{if} \quad x > 0 \\ 0 & \text{if} \quad x = 0 \\ -x & \text{if} \quad x < 0 \end{cases}$$

Definition 7

The absolute value of the difference of the coordinates of any two points on the real number line is the **distance** between those two points.

Definition 8

The **length** of a line segment is the distance between its endpoints.

Definition 9

Congruent segments are segments that have the same length. The sign for congruent is $\cong$.

Definition 10

The **midpoint** of a segment is defined as the point of the segment that divides the segment into two congruent segments. (The midpoint is said to bisect the segment.)

PROBLEM

Solve for x when $|x - 7| = 3$.

SOLUTION

This equation, according to the definition of absolute value, expresses the conditions that $x - 7$ must be 3 or -3, since in either case the absolute value is 3. If $x - 7 = 3$, we have $x = 10$; and if $x - 7 = -3$, we have $x = 4$. We see that there are two values of x that solve the equation.

PROBLEM

Find point C between A and B in the figure below such that $\overline{AC} \cong \overline{CB}$.

SOLUTION

We must determine point C in such a way that $\overline{AC} \cong \overline{CB}$, or $AC = CB$. We are first given that C is between A and B. Therefore, since the measure of the whole is equal to the sum of the measure of its parts:

(I) $AC + CB = AB$

Using these two facts, we can find the length of AC. From that we can find C.

First, since $AC = CB$, we substitute AC for CB in equation (I)

(II) $AC + AC = AB$

(III) $2(AC) = AB$

Dividing by 2 we have

(IV) $AC = (1/2) AB$

To find AC, we must know AB. We can find AB from the coordinates of A and B. They are 1 and 5, respectively. According,

(V) $AB = |5 - 1|$

(VI) $AB = 4$

We substitute 4 for AB in equation (IV)

(VII) $AC = (1/2)(4)$

(VIII) $AC = 2$.

Therefore, C is 2 units from A. Since C is between A and B, the coordinate of C must be 3.

Definition 11

The **bisector** of a line segment is a line that divides the line segment into two congruent segments.

Definition 12

An **angle** is a collection of points that is the union of two rays having the same endpoint. An angle such as the one illustrated the accompanying figure can be referred to in any of the following ways:

A) by a capital letter that names its vertex, ∡*A*;

B) by a lowercase letter or number placed inside the angle, ∡*x*;

C) by three capital letters, where the middle letter is the vertex and the other two letters are not on the same ray, i.e., ∡*CAB* or ∡*BAC*, both of which represent the angle illustrated in the above figure.

Definition 13

A set of points is **coplanar** if all the points lie in the same plane.

Definition 14

Two angles with a common vertex and a common side, but no common interior points, are called **adjacent angles.**

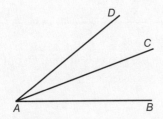

In the above figure, ∡DAC and ∡BAC are adjacent angles; ∡DAB and ∡BAC are not adjacent angles.

Definition 15

Vertical angles are two angles with a common vertex and with sides that are two pairs of opposite rays.

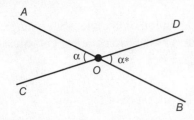

(∡α and ∡α* are vertical angles.)

Definition 16

An **acute angle** is an angle whose measure is larger that 0° but smaller than 90°.

Definition 17

An angle whose measure is 90° is called a **right angle.**

Definition 18

An **obtuse angle** is an angle whose measure is larger than 90° but less than 180°.

Definition 19

An angle whose measure is 180° is called a **straight angle.** Note: Such an angle is, in fact, a straight line.

Definition 20

An angle whose measure is greater than 180° but less than 360° is called a **reflex angle.**

Definition 21

Complementary angles are two angles, the sum of the measures of which equals 90°.

Definition 22

Supplementary angles are two angles, the sum of the measures of which equals 180°.

Definition 23

Congruent angles are angles of equal measure.

Definition 24

A ray **bisects** (is the bisector of) an angle if the ray divides the angle into two angles that have equal measure.

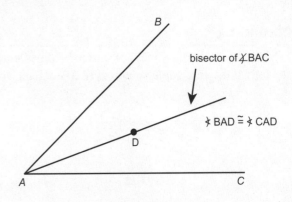

Definition 25

If the two non-common sides of adjacent angles form opposite rays, then the angles are called a **linear pair.** Note that α and β are supplementary.

Definition 26

Two lines are said to be **perpendicular** if they intersect and form right angles. The symbol for perpendicular (or, is perpendicular to) is ⊥; $\overleftrightarrow{AB}$ is perpendicular to $\overleftrightarrow{CD}$ is written as $\overleftrightarrow{AB} \perp \overleftrightarrow{CD}$.

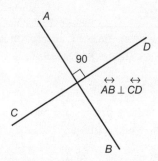

Definition 27

A line, a ray, or a line segment that bisects a line segment and is also perpendicular to that segment is called a **perpendicular bisector** of the line segment.

Definition 28

The **distance** from a point to a line is the measure of the perpendicular line segment from the point to that line. Note: This is the shortest possible distance from the point to the line.

Definition 29

Two or more distinct lines are said to be **parallel** (∥) if and only if they are coplanar and they do not intersect.

$$AB \parallel CD$$

Definition 30

The **projection of a given point** on a given line is the foot of the perpendicular drawn from the given point to the given line.

P_1 is the projection of P on $\overrightarrow{AB}$

The foot of a perpendicular from a point to a line is the point where the perpendicular meets the line.

Definition 31

The **projection of a segment** on a given line (when the segment is not perpendicular to the line) is a segment with endpoints that are the projections of the endpoints of the given line segment onto the given line.

$\overline{C_1D_1}$ is the projection of $\overline{CD}$ onto $\overleftrightarrow{AB}$

PROBLEM

The measure of the complement of a given angle is four times the measure of the angle. Find the measure of the given angle.

SOLUTION

By the definition of complementary angles, the sum of the measures of the two complements must equal 90°.

Accordingly,

(1) Let x = the measure of the angle

(2) Then $4x$ = the measure of the complement of this angle.

Therefore, from the discussion above,

$$x + 4x = 90°$$

$$5x = 90°$$

$$x = 18°$$

Therefore, the measure of the given angle is 18°.

PROBLEM

In the figure, we are given $\overrightarrow{AB}$ and triangle ABC. We are told that the measure of ∢1 is five times the measure of ∢2. Determine the measures of ∢1 and ∢2.

SOLUTION

Since ∢1 and ∢2 are adjacent angles whose non-common sides lie on a straight line, they are, by definition, supplementary. As supplements, their measures must sum to 180°.

If we let x = the measure of ∢1,

then $5x$ = the measure of ∢2.

To determine the respective angle measures, set $x + 5x = 180°$ and solve for x. $6x = 180°$. Therefore, $x = 30°$ and $5x = 150°$.

Therefore, the measure of ∢1 = 150° and the measure of ∢2 = 30°.

Postulates

Postulate 1 (The Point Uniqueness Postulate)

Let n be any positive number

Then there exists exactly one point N of $\overrightarrow{AB}$ such that $AN = n$. (AN is the length of n)

Postulate 2 (The Line Postulate)

Any two distinct points determine one and only one line that contains both points.

Postulate 3 (The Point Betweenness Postulate)

Let A and B be any two points. Then, there exists at least one point (and in fact an infinite number of such points) of $\overleftrightarrow{AB}$ such that P is between A and B, with $AP + PB = AB$.

Postulate 4

Two distinct straight lines can intersect at most at only one point.

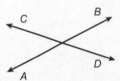

Postulate 5

The shortest line between any two points is a straight line.

Postulate 6

There is a one-to-one correspondence between the real numbers and the points of a line. That is, to every real number there corresponds exactly one point of the line and to every point of the line there corresponds exactly one real number. (In other words, a line has an infinite number of points between any two distinct points.)

Postulate 7

One and only one perpendicular can be drawn to a given line through any point on that line. Given point O

on line $\overleftrightarrow{AB}$, $\overrightarrow{OC}$ represents the only perpendicular to AB that passes through O.

PROBLEM

In the accompanying figure, point B is between points A and C, and point E is between points D and F. Given that $\overline{AB} \cong \overline{DE}$ and $\overline{BC} \cong \overline{EF}$. Prove that $\overline{AC} \cong \overline{DF}$.

SOLUTION

Two important postulates will be employed in this proof. The Point Betweenness Postulate states that if point Y is between points X and Z, then $XY + YZ = XZ$. Furthermore, the Postulate states that the converse is also true—that is, if $XY + YZ = XZ$, then point Y is between points X and Z.

The Addition Postulate states that equal quantities added to equal quantities yield equal quantities. Thus, if $a = b$ and $c = d$, then $a + c = b + d$.

Given: Point B is between A and C; point E is between points D and F; $\overline{AB} \cong \overline{DE}$; $\overline{BC} \cong \overline{EF}$

Prove: $\overline{AC} \cong \overline{DF}$

Statement	Reason
1. (For the given, see above)	1. Given.
2. $AB = DE$ $BC = EF$	2. Congruent segments have equal lengths.
3. $AB + BC = DE + EF$	3. Addition Postulate.
4. $AC = DF$	4. Point Between Postulate.
5. $\overline{AC} \cong \overline{DF}$	5. Segments of equal length are congruent.

PROBLEM

Construct a line perpendicular to a given line through a given point on the given line.

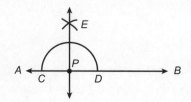

SOLUTION

Let line $\overleftrightarrow{AB}$ and point P be the given line and the given point, respectively.

We notice that $\sphericalangle APB$ is a straight angle. A line perpendicular to $\overleftrightarrow{AB}$ from point P will form adjacent congruent angles with $\overleftrightarrow{AB}$, by the definition of a perpendicular. Since $\sphericalangle APB$ is a straight angle, the adjacent angles will be right angles. As such, the required perpendicular is the angle bisector of $\sphericalangle APB$.

We can complete our construction by bisecting $\sphericalangle APB$.

1. Using P as the center and any convenient radius, construct an arc that intersects $\overleftrightarrow{AB}$ at points C and D.

2. With C and D as centers and with a radius greater in length than the one used in Step 1, construct arcs that intersect. The intersection point of these two arcs is point E.

3. Draw $\overrightarrow{EP}$.

$\overrightarrow{EP}$ is the required angle bisector and, as such, $\overrightarrow{EP} \perp \overleftrightarrow{AB}$.

PROBLEM

Present a formal proof of the following conditional statement:

If $\overrightarrow{CE}$ bisects $\sphericalangle ADB$, and if $\overleftrightarrow{FDB}$ and $\overleftrightarrow{CDE}$ are straight lines, then $\sphericalangle a \cong \sphericalangle x$. (Refer to the accompanying figure).

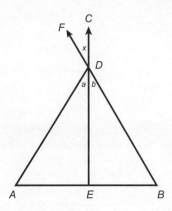

SOLUTION

In this problem, it will be necessary to recognize vertical angles and be knowledgeable of their key properties. Furthermore, we will need the definition of the bisector of an angle.

Vertical angles are two angles that have a common vertex, and whose sides are two pairs of opposite rays. Vertical angles are always congruent.

Lastly, the bisector of any angle divides the angle into two congruent angles.

Statement	**Reason**
1. $\overleftrightarrow{CE}$ bisects $\angle ADB$	1. Given.
2. $\angle a \cong \angle b$	2. A bisector of an angle divides the angle into two congruent angles.
3. $\overleftrightarrow{FDB}$ and $\overleftrightarrow{CDE}$ are straight lines	3. Given.
4. $\angle x$ and $\angle b$ are vertical angles	4. Definition of vertical angles.
5. $\angle b \cong \angle x$	5. Vertical angles are congruent.
6. $\angle a \cong \angle x$	6. Transitivity property of congruence of angles.

Note that step 3 is essential because without $\overleftrightarrow{FDB}$ and $\overleftrightarrow{CDE}$ being straight lines the definition of vertical angles would not be applicable to $\angle x$ and $\angle b$.

Postulate 8

The perpendicular bisector of a line segment is unique.

Postulate 9 (The Plane Postulate)

Any three non-collinear points determine one and only one plane that contains those three points.

Postulate 10 (The Points-in-a-Plane Postulate)

If two distinct points of a line lie in a given plane, then the line lies in that plane.

Postulate 11 (Plane Separation Postulate)

Any line in a plane separates the plane into two half planes.

Postulate 12

Given an angle, there exists one and only one real number between 0 and 180 corresponding to it. Note: $m\angle A$ refers to the measurement of angle A.

Postulate 13 (The Angle Sum Postulate)

If A is in the interior of $\angle XYZ$, then $m\angle XYZ = m\angle XYA + m\angle AYZ$.

Postulate 14 (The Angle Difference Postulate)

If P is in the exterior of $\angle ABC$ and in the same half-plane (created by edge $\overleftrightarrow{BC}$) as A, then

$$m\angle ABP = m\angle PBC - m\angle ABC.$$

PROBLEM

In the accompanying figure $\overline{SM}$ is the perpendicular bisector of $\overline{QR}$, and $\overline{SN}$ is the perpendicular bisector of $\overline{QP}$. Prove that $SR = SP$.

SOLUTION

Every point on the perpendicular bisector of a segment is equidistant from the endpoints of the segment.

Since point S is on the perpendicular bisector of $\overline{QR}$,

(I) $SR = SQ$

Also, since point S is on the perpendicular bisector of $\overline{QP}$,

(II) $SQ = SP$

By the transitive property (quantities equal to the same quantity are equal), we have:

(III) $SR = SP$.

PROBLEM

To construct an angle whose measure is equal to the sum of the measures of two given angles.

SOLUTION

To construct an angle equal to the sum of the measures of two given angles, we must invoke the theorem that states that the whole is equal to the sum of the parts. The construction, then, will duplicate the given angles in such a way as to form one larger angle equal in measure to the sum of the measures of the two given angles.

The two given angles, $\measuredangle A$ and $\measuredangle B$, are shown in the figure.

1. Construct any line $\overleftrightarrow{CD}$, and mark a point P on it.

2. At P, using $\overrightarrow{PD}$ as the base, construct $\measuredangle DPS \cong \measuredangle A$.

3. Now, using $\overrightarrow{PS}$ as the base, construct $\measuredangle SPT \cong \measuredangle B$ at point P.

4. $\measuredangle DPT$ is the desired angle, equal in measure to $m\measuredangle A + m\measuredangle B$. This follows because the measure of the whole, $\measuredangle DPT$, is equal to the sum of the measure of the parts, $\measuredangle A$ and $\measuredangle B$.

Theorems

Theorem 1

All right angles are equal.

Theorem 2

All straight angles are equal.

Theorem 3

Supplements of the same or equal angles are themselves equal.

Theorem 4

Complements of the same or equal angles are themselves equal.

Theorem 5

Vertical angles are equal.

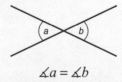

$$\measuredangle a = \measuredangle b$$

Theorem 6

Two supplementary angles are right angles if they have the same measure.

$$m \measuredangle \alpha = m \measuredangle \beta = 90°$$

Theorem 7

If two lines intersect and form one right angle, then the lines form four right angles.

PROBLEM

Find the measure of the angle whose measure is 40° more than the measure of its supplement.

SOLUTION

By the definition of supplementary angles, the sum of the measures of two supplements must equal 180°. Accordingly,

Let x = the measure of the supplement of the angle.

Then $x + 40°$ = the measure of the angle.

Therefore, $x + (x + 40°) = 180°$

$$2x + 40° = 180°$$

$$2x = 140°$$

$$x = 70° \text{ and } x + 40° = 110°.$$

Therefore the measure of the angle is 110°.

PROBLEM

What is the measure of a given angle whose measure is half the measure of its complement?

SOLUTION

When two angles are said to be complementary we know that their measures must sum, by definition, to 90°.

If we let x = the measure of the given angle,

then $2x$ = the measure of its complement.

To determine the measure of the given angle, set the sum of the two angle measures equal to 90 and solve for x. Accordingly,

$$x + 2x = 90°$$

$$3x = 90°$$

$$x = 30°$$

Therefore, the measure of the given angle is 30° and its complement is 60°.

PROBLEM

Given that straight lines $\overleftrightarrow{AB}$ and $\overleftrightarrow{CD}$ intersect at point E, that $\angle BEC$ has measure 20° greater than 5 times a fixed quantity, and that $\angle AED$ has measure 60° greater than 3 times this same quantity: Find a) the unknown fixed quantity, b) the measure of $\angle BEC$, and c) the measure of $\angle CEA$. (For the actual angle placement, refer to the accompanying diagram.)

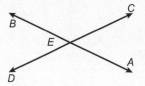

SOLUTION

a) Since $\overleftrightarrow{AB}$ and $\overleftrightarrow{CD}$ are straight lines intersecting at point E, $\angle BEC$ and $\angle AED$ are, by definition, vertical angles. As such, they are congruent and their measures are equal. Therefore, if we let x represent the fixed quantity, $\angle BEC = 5x + 20$ and $\angle AED = 3x + 60$; according to the information given. We can then set up the following equality, and solve for the unknown quantity.

$$5x + 20 = 3x + 60$$

$$5x - 3x = 60 - 20$$

$$2x = 40$$

$$x = 20$$

Therefore, the value of the unknown quantity is 20°.

b) From the information given about $\angle BEC$, we know that m$\angle BEC = (5x + 20)°$. By substitution, we have

$$m\angle BEC = 5(20°) + 20° = 100° + 20° = 120°.$$

Therefore, the measure of $\angle BEC$ is 120°.

c) We know that $\overleftrightarrow{AB}$ is a straight line; therefore, $\angle CEA$ is the supplement of $\angle BEC$. Since the sum of the measure of two supplements is 180°, the following calculation can be made:

$$m\sphericalangle CEA + m\sphericalangle BEC = 180°$$
$$m\sphericalangle CEA = 180° - m\sphericalangle BEC,$$

Substituting in our value for $m\sphericalangle BEC$, we obtain:

$$m\sphericalangle CEA = 180° - 120° = 60°$$

Therefore, the measure of $\sphericalangle CEA$ is 60°.

Theorem 8

Any point on the perpendicular bisector of a given line segment is equidistant from the ends of the segment.

$$\overline{PA} = \overline{PB}$$

Theorem 9

If a point is equidistant from the ends of a line segment, this point must lie on the perpendicular bisector of the segment.

Theorem 10

If two points are equidistant from the ends of a line segment, these points determine the perpendicular bisector of the segment.

Theorem 11

Every line segment has exactly one midpoint.

Theorem 12

There exists one and only one perpendicular to a line through a point outside the line. Take point C outside line $\overleftrightarrow{AB}$. $\overrightarrow{OC}$ represents the only perpendicular to $\overleftrightarrow{AB}$ that passes through C.

Theorem 13

If the exterior sides of adjacent angles are perpendicular to each other, then the adjacent angles are complementary.

α and β are complementary

Theorem 14

Adjacent angles are supplementary if their exterior sides form a straight line.

α and β are supplementary

Theorem 15

Two angles that are equal and supplementary to each other are right angles.

Congruent Angles and Congruent Line Segments

Definitions

Definition 1

Two or more geometric figures are congruent when they have the same shape and size. The symbol for congruence is ≅; hence, if triangle *ABC* is congruent to triangle *DEF*, we write $\triangle ABC \cong \triangle DEF$.

Definition 2

Two line segments are congruent if and only if they have the same measure.

Note: The expression "if and only if" can be used any time both a statement and the converse of that statement are true. Using definition 2, we can rewrite the statement as "two line segments have the same measure if and only if they are congruent." The two statements are identical.

Definition 3

Two angles are congruent if and only if they have the same measure.

PROBLEM

In the figure shown, $\triangle ABC$ is an isosceles triangle, such that $\overline{BA} \cong \overline{BC}$. Line segment $\overline{AD}$ bisects $\sphericalangle BAC$ and $\overline{CD}$ bisects $\sphericalangle BCA$. Prove that $\triangle ADC$ is an isosceles triangle.

SOLUTION

In order to prove $\triangle ADC$ is isosceles, we must prove that two of its sides, $\overline{AD}$ and $\overline{CD}$, are congruent. To prove $\overline{AD} \cong \overline{CD}$ in $\triangle ADC$, we have to prove that the angles opposite $\overline{AD}$ and $\overline{CD}$, $\sphericalangle 1$ and $\sphericalangle 2$, are congruent.

Statement	Reason
1. $\overline{BA} \cong \overline{BC}$	1. Given.
2. $\sphericalangle BAC \cong \sphericalangle BCA$ or $m\sphericalangle BAC = m\sphericalangle BCA$	2. If two sides of a triangle are congruent, then the angles opposite them are congruent.
3. $\overline{AD}$ bisects $\sphericalangle BAC$ $\overline{CD}$ bisects $\sphericalangle BCA$	3. Given.
4. $m\sphericalangle 1 = (1/2)m\sphericalangle BAC$ $m\sphericalangle 2 = (1/2)m\sphericalangle BCA$	4. The bisector of an angle divides the angle into two angles whose measures are equal.
5. $m\sphericalangle 1 = m\sphericalangle 2$	5. Halves of equal quantities are equal.
6. $\sphericalangle 1 \cong \sphericalangle 2$	6. If the measure of two angles are equal, then the angles are congruent.
7. $\overline{CD} \cong \overline{AD}$	7. If two angles of a triangle are congruent, then the sides opposite these angles are congruent.
8. $\triangle ADC$ is an isosceles triangle.	8. If a triangle has two congruent sides, then it is an isosceles triangle.

Theorems

Theorem 1

Every line segment is congruent to itself.

Theorem 2

Every angle is congruent to itself.

Let R be a relation on a set A. Then:

R is reflexive if aRa for every a in A.

R is symmetric if aRb implies bRa.

R is anti-symmetric if aRb and bRa imply $a = b$.

R is transitive if aRb and bRc imply aRc.

Note: The term aRa means the relation R performed on a yields a. The term aRb means the relation R performed on a yields b.

Postulates

By definition, a relation R is called an equivalence relation if relation R is reflexive, symmetric, and transitive.

Postulate 1

Congruence of segments is an equivalence relation.

(1) Congruence of segments is reflexive.

If $\overline{AB} \cong \overline{AB}$, $\overline{AB}$ is congruent to itself.

(2) Congruence of segments is symmetric.

If $\overline{AB} \cong \overline{CD}$, then $\overline{CD} \cong \overline{AB}$.

(3) Congruence of segments is transitive.

If $\overline{AB} \cong \overline{CD}$ and $\overline{CD} \cong \overline{EF}$, then $\overline{AB} \cong \overline{EF}$.

Postulate 2

Congruence of angles is an equivalence relation, that is, it is reflexive, symmetric, and transitive.

Postulate 3

Any geometric figure is congruent to itself.

Postulate 4

A geometric congruence may be reversed.

Postulate 5

Two geometric figures congruent to the same geometric figure are congruent to each other.

Theorem 3

Given a line segment $\overline{AB}$ and a ray $\overrightarrow{XY}$, there exists one and only one point O on $\overrightarrow{XY}$ such that $\overline{AB} \cong \overline{XO}$.

Theorem 4

If $\overline{AB} = \overline{CD}$, Q bisects $\overline{AB}$ and P bisects $\overline{CD}$, then $\overline{AQ} \cong \overline{CP}$ and $\overline{AQ} = \overline{CP}$.

Theorem 5

If $m\angle ABC = m\angle DEF$, and $\overrightarrow{BX}$ and $\overrightarrow{EY}$ bisect $\angle ABC$ and $\angle DEF$, respectively, then $m\angle ABC = m\angle DEF$.

Theorem 6

Let P be in the interior of $\angle ABC$ and Q be in the interior of $\angle DEF$. If $m\angle ABP = m\angle DEQ$ and $m\angle PBC = m\angle QEF$, then $m\angle ABC = m\angle DEF$.

Theorem 7

Let P be in the interior of $\angle XYZ$ and Q be in the interior of $\angle ABC$. If $m\angle XYZ = m\angle ABC$ and $m\angle XYP = m\angle ABQ$ then $m\angle PYZ = m\angle QBC$.

PROBLEM

Given triangle RST in the figure shown with $\overline{RT} \cong \overline{ST}$. Points A and B lie at the midpoint of $\overline{RT}$ and $\overline{ST}$, respectively. Prove that $\overline{RA} \cong \overline{SB}$.

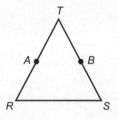

SOLUTION

This solution is best presented as a formal proof.

Statement	Reason
1. $\overline{RT} \cong \overline{ST}$ or $RT = ST$	1. Given.
2. A is the midpoint of $\overline{RT}$	2. Given.
3. $RA = (1/2)RT$	3. The midpoint of a line segment divides the line segment into two equal halves.
4. B is the midpoint of $\overline{ST}$	4. Given.
5. $\overline{SB} = (1/2)\overline{TS}$	5. The midpoint of a line segment divides the line segment into two equal halves.
6. $RA = SB$	6. Division Postulate: Halves of equal quantities are equal. Statements 3 and 5.

7. $\overline{RA} \cong \overline{SB}$

7. If two line segments are of equal length, then they are congruent.

Quiz: Method of Proof—Congruent Angles & Line Segments

Refer to the diagrams and find the appropriate solutions.

1. Find *a*.

   (A) 38°
   (B) 68°
   (C) 78°
   (D) 90°
   (E) 112°

2. Find *c*.

   (A) 32°
   (B) 48°
   (C) 58°
   (D) 82°
   (E) 148°

3. Determine *x*.

   (A) 21°
   (B) 23°
   (C) 51°
   (D) 102°
   (E) 153°

4. Find *z*.

   (A) 29°
   (B) 54°
   (C) 61°
   (D) 88°
   (E) 92°

5. In the figure shown, if $\overline{BD}$ is the bisector of angle *ABC*, and angle *ABD* is one-fourth the size of angle *XYZ*, what is the size of angle *ABC*?

   (A) 21°
   (B) 28°
   (C) 42°
   (D) 63°
   (E) 168°

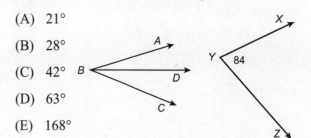

6. $\overrightarrow{BA} \perp \overrightarrow{BC}$ and $m\angle DBC = 53°$.

   Find $m\angle ABD$.

   (A) 27°
   (B) 33°
   (C) 37°
   (D) 53°
   (E) 90°

7. If $n \perp p$, which of the following statements is true?

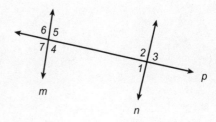

   (A) $\angle 1 \cong \angle 2$
   (B) $\angle 4 \cong \angle 5$
   (C) $m\angle 4 + m\angle 5 > m\angle 1 + m\angle 2$
   (D) $m\angle 3 > m\angle 2$
   (E) $m\angle 4 = 90°$

8. In the figure, if $p \perp t$ and $q \perp t$, which of the following statements is false?

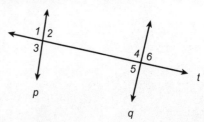

85

(A) $\sphericalangle 1 \cong \sphericalangle 4$

(B) $\sphericalangle 2 \cong \sphericalangle 3$

(C) $m\sphericalangle 2 + m\sphericalangle 3 = m\sphericalangle 4 + m\sphericalangle 6$

(D) $m\sphericalangle 5 + m\sphericalangle 6 = 180°$

(E) $m\sphericalangle 2 > m\sphericalangle 5$

9.   If $a \| b$, find z.

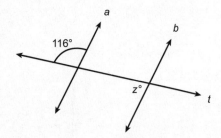

(A) 26°   (C) 64°   (E) 116°

(B) 32°   (D) 86°

10.   If $m \| n$, which of the following statements is not necessarily true?

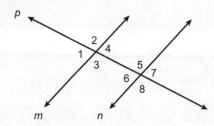

(A) $\sphericalangle 2 \cong \sphericalangle 5$

(B) $\sphericalangle 3 \cong \sphericalangle 6$

(C) $m\sphericalangle 4 + m\sphericalangle 5 = 180°$

(D) $\sphericalangle 1 \cong \sphericalangle 6$

(E) $m\sphericalangle 7 + m\sphericalangle 3 = 180°$

ANSWER KEY

1. (B)
2. (A)
3. (C)
4. (D)
5. (C)

6. (C)
7. (A)
8. (E)
9. (C)
10. (B)

Regular Polygons (Convex)

A **polygon** is a figure with the same number of sides as angles.

An **equilateral polygon** is a polygon all of whose sides are of equal measure.

An **equiangular polygon** is a polygon all of whose angles are of equal measure.

A **regular polygon** is a polygon that is both equilateral and equiangular.

PROBLEM

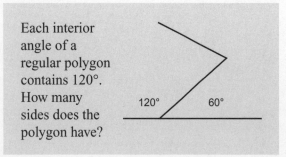

Each interior angle of a regular polygon contains 120°. How many sides does the polygon have?

120°   60°

SOLUTION

At each vertex of a polygon, we can draw an exterior angle that is supplementary to the interior angle, as shown in the diagram.

Since we are told that the interior angle measures 120°, we can deduce that the exterior angle measures 60°.

Each exterior angle of a regular polygon of n sides measure $\dfrac{360°}{n}$ degrees. We know that each exterior angle measures 60°, and, therefore, by setting $\dfrac{360°}{n}$ equal to 60°, we can determine the number of sides in the polygon. The calculation is as follows:

$$\frac{360°}{n} = 60°$$

$$60°n = 360°$$

$$n = 6$$

Therefore, the regular polygon, with interior angles of 120°, has six sides and is called a hexagon.

The **perimeter** of a regular polygon is the product of the length of a side(s) and the number of sides (n) $P = ns$.

The area of a regular polygon can be determined by using the **apothem** and **radius** of the polygon. The apothem (a) of a regular polygon is the segment from the center of the polygon perpendicular to a side of the polygon. The radius (r) of a regular polygon is the segment joining any vertex of a regular polygon with the center of that polygon.

(1) All radii of a regular polygon are congruent.

(2) The radius of a regular polygon is congruent to a side.

(3) All apothems of a regular polygon are congruent.

The **area** of a regular polygon equals one-half the product of the length of the apothem and the perimeter.

$$\text{Area} = \frac{1}{2}a \times p$$

PROBLEM

Find the area of a regular hexagon if one side has length 6.

SOLUTION

Since the length of a side equals 6, the radius also equals 6 and the perimeter equals 36. The base of the right triangle, formed by the radius and apothem, is half the length of a side, or 3. You can find the length of the apothem by using the Pythagorean theorem.

$$a^2 + b^2 = c^2$$
$$a^2 + (3)^2 = (6)^2$$
$$a^2 = 36 - 9$$
$$a^2 = 27$$
$$a = 3\sqrt{3}$$

The apothem equals $3\sqrt{3}$. Therefore, the area of the hexagon

$$= \frac{1}{2} a \times p$$
$$= \frac{1}{2}(3\sqrt{3})(36)$$
$$= 54\sqrt{3}$$

Drill: Regular Polygons (Convex)

Angle Measures

DIRECTIONS: Find the appropriate solutions.

1. Find the measure of an interior angle of a regular pentagon.

   (A) 55°　　　　(C) 90°

   (B) 72°　　　　(D) 108°

2. Find the sum of the measures of the exterior angles of a regular triangle.

   (A) 90°　　　　(C) 180°

   (B) 115°　　　　(D) 360°

Area(s) and Perimeter(s)

DIRECTIONS: Find the appropriate solutions.

3. A regular triangle has sides of 24 mm. If the apothem is $4\sqrt{3}$ mm, find the area of the triangle.

   (A) 72 mm²　　　　(C) 144 mm²

   (B) $96\sqrt{3}$ mm²　　　　(D) $144\sqrt{3}$ mm²

4. Find the area of a regular hexagon with sides of 4 cm.

   (A) $12\sqrt{3}$ cm²　　　　(C) $24\sqrt{3}$ cm²

   (B) 24 cm²　　　　(D) 48 cm²

5. Find the area of a regular decagon with sides of length 6 cm and an apothem of length 9.2 cm.

   (A) 55.2 cm²　　　　(C) 138 cm²

   (B) 60 cm²　　　　(D) 276 cm²

Similar Polygons

Definition

Two polygons are similar if there is a one-to-one correspondence between their vertices such that all pairs of corresponding angles are congruent and the ratios of the measures of all pairs of corresponding sides are equal. Note that although they must have the same shape, they may have different sizes.

Theorem 1

The perimeters of two similar polygons have the same ratio as the measure of any pair of corresponding line segments of the polygons.

Theorem 2

The ratio of the lengths of two corresponding diagonals of two similar polygons is equal to the ratio of the lengths of any two corresponding sides of the polygons.

Theorem 3

The perimeters of two similar polygons have the same ratio as the measures of any pair of corresponding sides of the polygons.

Theorem 4

Two polygons composed of the same number of triangles similar each to each, and similarly placed, are similar.

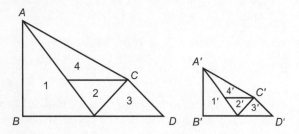

PROBLEM

> Prove that any two regular polygons with the same number of sides are similar.

SOLUTION

For any two polygons to be similar, their corresponding angles must be congruent and their corresponding sides proportional. It is necessary to show that these conditions always exist between regular polygons with the same number of sides.

Let us examine the corresponding angles first. For a regular polygon with n sides, each vertex angle is $\dfrac{(n-2)180}{n}$. Therefore, two regular polygons with the same number of sides will have corresponding vertex angles that are all of the same measure and, hence, are all congruent. This fulfills our first condition for similarity.

We must now determine whether the corresponding sides are proportional. It will suffice to show that the ratios of the lengths of every pair of corresponding sides are the same.

Since the polygons are regular, the sides of each one will be equal. Call the length of the sides of one

polygon ℓ_1 and the length of the sides of the other polygon ℓ_2. Hence, the ratio of the lengths of corresponding sides will be ℓ_1/ℓ_2. This will be a constant for any pair of corresponding sides and, hence, the corresponding sides are proportional.

Thus, any two regular polygons with the same number of sides are similar.

PROBLEM

> The lengths of two corresponding sides of two similar polygons are 4 and 7. If the perimeter of the smaller polygon is 20, find the perimeter of the larger polygon.

SOLUTION

We know, by theorem, that the perimeters of two similar polygons have the same ratio as the measures of any pair of corresponding sides.

If we let s and p represent the side and perimeter of the smaller polygon and s' and p' represent the corresponding side and perimeter of the larger one, we can then write the proportion

$$p : p' = s : s'$$

By substituting the given values, we can solve for p'.

$$20 : p' = 4 : 7$$
$$4\,p' = 140$$
$$p' = 35.$$

Therefore, the perimeter of the larger polygon is 35.

Triangles

A closed three-sided geometric figure is called a **triangle**. The points of the intersection of the sides of a triangle are called the **vertices** of the triangle.

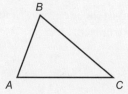

The **perimeter** of a triangle is the sum of the measures of the sides of the triangle.

A triangle with no equal sides is called a **scalene triangle**.

A triangle having at least two equal sides is called an **isosceles triangle**. The third side is called the **base** of the triangle, and the base angles (the angles opposite the equal sides) are equal.

AB = AC

A side of a triangle is a line segment whose endpoints are the vertices of two angles of the triangle.

An **interior angle** of a triangle is an angle formed by two sides and includes the third side within its collection of points.

An **equilateral triangle** is a triangle having three equal sides. $\overline{AB} = \overline{AC} = \overline{BC}$. An equilateral, triangle is also **equiangular**, with each angle equaling 60°.

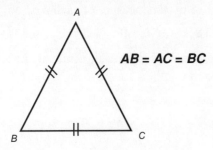

AB = AC = BC

The sum of the measures of the interior angles of a triangle is 180°.

A triangle with one obtuse angle (greater than 90°) is called an **obtuse triangle**.

An **acute triangle** is a triangle with three acute angles (less than 90°).

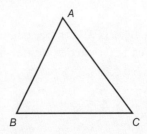

A triangle with a right angle is a **right triangle**. The side opposite the right angle in a right triangle is called the hypotenuse of the right triangle. The other two sides are called arms or legs of the right triangle. By the Pythagorean Theorem, the length of the three sides of a right triangle are related by the formula $c^2 = a^2 + b^2$ where c is the hypotenuse and a and b are the other sides (the legs).

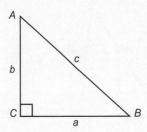

An **altitude** of a triangle is a line segment from a vertex of the triangle perpendicular to the opposite side.

The **area** of a triangle is given by $A = \frac{1}{2}bh$

where h is the altitude and b is the base to which the altitude is drawn.

A line segment connecting a vertex of a triangle and the midpoint of the opposite side is called a **median** of the triangle.

$BO = OC$

A line that bisects and is perpendicular to a side of a triangle is called a **perpendicular bisector** of that side.

An **angle bisector** of a triangle is a line that bisects an angle and extends to the opposite side of the triangle.

$$\angle\alpha = \angle\beta$$

The line segment that joins the midpoints of two sides of a triangle is called a **midline** of the triangle.

$AD = DC$
$BE = EC$

midline: DE

An **exterior angle** of a triangle is an angle formed outside a triangle by one side of the triangle and the extension of an adjacent side.

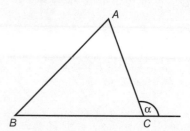

Three or more lines (or rays or segments) are **concurrent** if there exists one point common to all of them, that is, if they all intersect at the same point.

PROBLEM

The measure of the vertex angle of an isosceles triangle exceeds the measurement of each base angles by 30°. Find the value of each angle of the triangle.

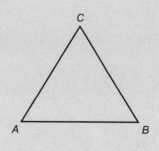

SOLUTION

We known that the sum of the values of the angles of a triangle is 180°. In an isosceles triangle, the angles opposite the congruent sides (the base angles) are, themselves, congruent and of equal value.

Therefore,

(1) Let x = the measure of each base angle.

(2) Then $x + 30$ = the measure of the vertex angle.

We can solve for x algebraically by keeping in mind the sum of all the measures will be 180°.

$$x + x + (x + 30) = 180$$
$$3x + 30 = 180$$
$$3x = 150$$
$$x = 50$$

Therefore, the base angles each measure 50°, and the vertex angle measures 80°.

Angle Measures

DIRECTIONS: Refer to the diagram and find the appropriate solution.

1. In $\triangle PQR$, $\angle Q$ is a right angle. Find $m\angle R$.

    (A) 27°   (C) 54°

    (B) 33°   (D) 67°

2. $\triangle MNO$ is isosceles. If the vertex angle, $\angle N$, has a measure of 96°, find the measure of $\angle M$.

    (A) 21°

    (B) 42°

    (C) 64°

    (D) 84°

3. Find x.

    (A) 15°

    (B) 25°

    (C) 30°

    (D) 45°

Similar Triangles

DIRECTIONS: Refer to the diagram and find the appropriate solution.

4. The two triangles shown are similar. Find b.

    (A) $2\frac{2}{3}$

    (B) 3

    (C) 4

    (D) 16

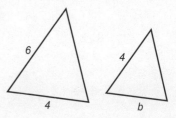

5. The two triangles shown are similar. Find a and b.

    (A) 5 and 10   (C) $4\frac{2}{3}$ and $7\frac{1}{3}$

    (B) 4 and 8   (D) $5\frac{1}{3}$ and 8

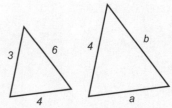

Area

DIRECTIONS: Refer to the diagram and find the appropriate solution.

6. Find the area of $\triangle MNO$.

    (A) 22

    (B) 49

    (C) 56

    (D) 84

7. Find the area of $\triangle PQR$.

    (A) 31.5

    (B) 38.5

    (C) 53

    (D) 77

8.   Find the area of $\triangle STU$.

   (A) $4\sqrt{2}$

   (B) $8\sqrt{2}$

   (C) $12\sqrt{2}$

   (D) $16\sqrt{2}$

9.   Find the area of $\triangle ABC$.

   (A)   54 cm²

   (B)   81 cm²

   (C)   108 cm²

   (D)   135 cm²

10.   Find the area of $\triangle XYZ$.

   (A)   20 cm²

   (B)   50 cm²

   (C) $50\sqrt{2}$ cm²

   (D)   100 cm²

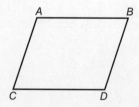

Quadrilaterals

A **quadrilateral** is a polygon with four sides.

Parallelograms

A **parallelogram** is a quadrilateral whose opposite sides are parallel.

Two angles that have their vertices at the endpoints of the same side of a parallelogram are called consecutive angles.

The perpendicular segment connecting any point of a line containing one side of a parallelogram to the line containing the opposite side of the parallelogram is called the altitude of the parallelogram.

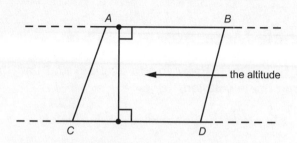

A diagonal of a polygon is a line segment joining any two nonconsecutive vertices.

The area of a parallelogram is given by the formula $A = bh$, where b is the base and h is the height drawn perpendicular to that base. Note that the height equals the altitude of the parallelogram.

$A = bh$

$A = (10)(3)$

$A = 30$

Rectangles

A **rectangle** is a parallelogram with right angles.

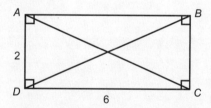

The diagonals of a rectangle are equal.

If the diagonals of a parallelogram are equal, the parallelogram is a rectangle.

If a quadrilateral has four right angles, then it is a rectangle.

The area of a rectangle is given by the formula $A = lw$, where l is the length and w is the width.

$A = lw$

$A = (3)(10)$

$A = 30$

Rhombi

A **rhombus** is a parallelogram that has two adjacent sides that are equal.

All sides of a rhombus are equal.

The diagonals of a rhombus are perpendicular to each other.

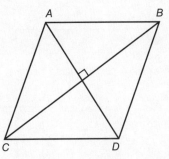

The area of a rhombus can be found by the formula $A = \frac{1}{2}(d_1 + d_2)$ where d_1 and d_2 are the diagonals.

The diagonals of a rhombus bisect the angles of the rhombus.

If the diagonals of a parallelogram are perpendicular, the parallelogram is a rhombus.

If a quadrilateral has four equal sides, then it is a rhombus.

A parallelogram is a rhombus if either diagonal of the parallelogram bisects the angles of the vertices it joins.

Squares

A **square** is a rhombus with a right angle.

A square is an equilateral quadrilateral.

A square has all the properties of parallelograms and rectangles.

A rhombus is a square if one of its interior angles is a right angle.

In a square, the measure of either diagonal can be calculated by multiplying the length of any side by the square root of 2.

The area of a square is given by the formula $A = s^2$, where s is the side of the square. Since all sides of a square are equal, it does not matter which side is used.

$A = s^2$

$A = 6^2$

$A = 36$

The area of a square can also be found by taking $\frac{1}{2}$ the product of the length of the diagonal squared.

$A = \frac{1}{2}d^2$

$A = \frac{1}{2}(8)^2$

$A = 32$

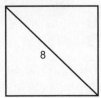

Trapezoids

A **trapezoid** is a quadrilateral with two and only two sides parallel. The parallel sides of a trapezoid are called **bases.**

The **median** of a trapezoid is the line joining the midpoints of the non-parallel sides.

median of trapezoid

The perpendicular segment connecting any point in the line containing one base of the trapezoid to the line containing the other base is the **altitude** of the trapezoid.

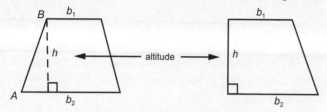

The area of a trapezoid equals one half the altitude times the sum of the bases, or $\frac{1}{2}h(b_1 + b_2)$.

An **isosceles trapezoid** is a trapezoid whose non-parallel sides are equal. A pair of angles including only one of the parallel sides is called a pair of base angles.

Pairs of base angles

The median of a trapezoid is parallel to the bases and equal to one-half their sum.

The base angles of an isosceles trapezoid are equal.

The diagonals of an isosceles trapezoid are equal.

The opposite angles of an isosceles trapezoid are supplementary.

Drill: Quadrilaterals

DIRECTIONS: Refer to the diagram and find the appropriate solution.

1. Quadrilateral *ABCD* is a parallelogram. If $m\angle B = (6x + 2)°$ and $m\angle D = 98°$, find *x*.

   (A) 12
   (B) 16
   (C) $16\frac{2}{3}$
   (D) 18

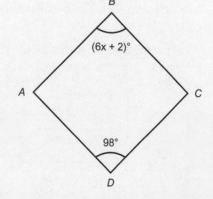

2. Find the area of parallelogram *STUV*.

   (A) 56
   (B) 90
   (C) 108
   (D) 162

3. In rectangle *ABCD*, $\overline{AD} = 6$ cm and $\overline{DC} = 8$ cm. Find the length of the diagonal $\overline{AC}$.

   (A) 10 cm   (C) 20 cm
   (B) 12 cm   (D) 28 cm

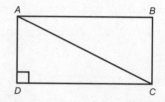

4. Find the area of rectangle *UVXY*.

   (A) 17 cm²
   (B) 34 cm²
   (C) 35 cm²
   (D) 70 cm²

5. Find the length of $\overline{BO}$ in rectangle *BCDE* if the diagonal $\overline{EC}$ is 17 mm.

   (A) 6.55 mm
   (B) 8 mm
   (C) 8.5 mm
   (D) 17 mm

6. In rhombus *GHIJ*, $\overline{GI} = 6$ cm and $\overline{HJ} = 8$ cm. Find the length of $\overline{GH}$.

   (A) 3 cm
   (B) 4 cm
   (C) 5 cm
   (D) $4\sqrt{3}$ cm

7. Find the area of the trapezoid *RSTU*.

(A) 80 cm²

(B) 87.5 cm²

(C) 140 cm²

(D) 175 cm²

8. *ABCD* is an isosceles trapezoid. Find the perimeter.

(A) 21 cm   (C) 30 cm

(B) 27 cm   (D) 50 cm

9. Find the area of trapezoid *MNOP*.

(A) $(17 + 3\sqrt{3})$ mm²   (C) $\dfrac{33\sqrt{3}}{2}$ mm²

(B) $\dfrac{33}{2}$ mm²   (D) 33 mm²

10. Trapezoid *XYZW* is isosceles. If $m\angle W = 58°$ and $m\angle Z = (4x - 6)°$, find *x*.

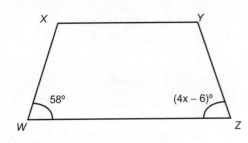

(A) 8   (C) 13

(B) 12   (D) 16

Circles

A **circle** is a set of points in the same plane equidistant from a fixed point, called its center. Circles are often named by their center point, circle *O*.

A **radius** of a circle is a line segment drawn from the center of the circle to any point on the circle.

A portion of a circle is called an **arc** of the circle.

A line that intersects a circle in two points is called a **secant**.

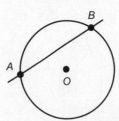

A line segment joining two points on a circle is called a **chord** of the circle.

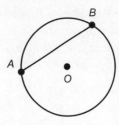

A chord that passes through the center of the circle is called a **diameter** of the circle.

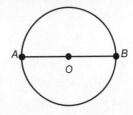

The line passing through the centers of two (or more) circles is called the **line of centers.**

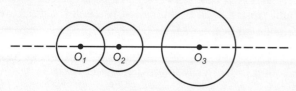

An angle whose vertex is on the circle and whose sides are chords of the circle is called an **inscribed angle** ($\angle$ BAC in the diagrams).

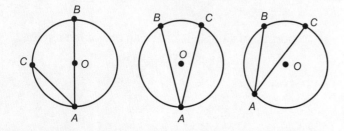

An angle whose vertex is at the center of a circle and whose sides are radii is called a **central angle.**

The measure of a minor arc is the measure of the central angle that intercepts that arc.

$$m\overarc{AB} = \alpha = m\angle AOB$$

The distance from a point P to a given circle is the distance from that point to the point where the circle intersects with a line segment with endpoints at the center of the circle and point P.

The distance of point P to the diagrammed circle with center O is the line segment $\overline{PB}$ of line segment $\overline{PO}$.

A line that has one and only one point of intersection with a circle is called a tangent to that circle, and their common point is called a **point of tangency.** In the diagram, Q and P are each points of tangency.

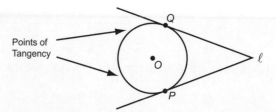

Congruent circles are circles whose radii are congruent.

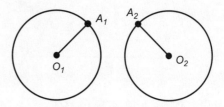

If $O_1A_1 \cong O_2A_2$, then $O_1 \cong O_2$.

The measure of a semicircle is 180°.

A **circumscribed circle** is a circle passing through all the vertices of a polygon. The polygon is said to be **inscribed** in the circle.

Circles that have the same center and unequal radii are called **concentric circles.**

Concentric Circles

The **circumference** of a circle is the length of its outer edge, given by $C = \pi d = 2\pi r$, where r is the radius, *d* is the diameter, and π(pi) is a mathematical constant approximately equal to 3.14.

The area of a circle is given by $A = 2\pi r^2$. A full circle is 360°. The length of arc intercepted by a central angle has the same ratio to the circle's circumference as the measure of the arc has to be 360°, the full circle. Therefore, arc length is given by $\frac{n}{360} \times 2\pi r$, where $n =$ measure of the central angle. The measure of an arc in degrees, however, is the same as the measure of its central angle.

A sector is the portion of a circle between two radii. Its area is given by $A = \frac{n}{360}(\pi r^2)$ where *n* is the central angle formed by the radii.

PROBLEM

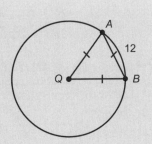

A and *B* are points on circle *Q* such that $\triangle AQB$ is equilateral. If the length of side $\overline{AB} = 12$, find the length of arc *AB*.

SOLUTION

To find the arc length of arc *AB*, we must find the measure of the central angle $\angle AQB$ and the measure of the radius $\overline{QA}$. $\angle AQB$ is an interior angle of the equilateral triangle $\triangle AQB$. Therefore,

$$m\angle AQB = 60°.$$

Similarly, in the equilateral $\triangle AQB$,

$$\overline{AQ} = \overline{AB} = \overline{QB} = 12.$$

Given the radius, *r*, and the central angle, *n*, the arc length is given by

$$\frac{n}{360} \times 2\pi r.$$

Therefore, by substitution,

$$\angle AQB = \frac{60}{360} \times 2\pi \times 12 = \frac{1}{6} \times 2\pi \times 12 = 4\pi.$$

Therefore, the length of arc $AB = 4\pi$.

DIRECTIONS: Determine the accurate measure.

1. Find the circumference of circle *A* if its radius is 3 mm.

   (A) 3π mm   (C) 9π mm

   (B) 6π mm   (D) 12π mm

2. Find the area of circle *I*.

   (A) 22 mm²

   (B) 121 mm²

   (C) 121π mm²

   (D) 132 mm²

3. The diameter of circle *Z* is 27 mm. Find the area of the circle.

   (A) 91.125 mm²   (C) 191.5π mm²

   (B) 182.25 mm²   (D) 182.25π mm²

4. The area of circle *B* is 225π cm². Find the length of the diameter of the circle.

   (A) 15 cm   (C) 30 cm

   (B) 20 cm   (D) 20π cm

5. The area of circle *X* is 144π mm² while the area of circle *Y* is 81π mm². Write the ratio of the radius of circle *X* to that of circle *Y*.

   (A) 3 : 4   (C) 9 : 12

   (B) 4 : 3   (D) 27 : 12

6. The radius of the smaller of two concentric circles is 5 cm while the radius of the larger circle is 7 cm. Determine the area of the shaded region.

   (A) 7π cm²

   (B) 24π cm²

   (C) 25π cm²

   (D) 36π cm²

7. Find the measure of arc $\overset{\frown}{MN}$ if $m\angle MON = 62°$.

(A) 16°

(B) 32°

(C) 59°

(D) 62°

8. Find the measure of arc $\overset{\frown}{AXC}$.

(A) 150°

(B) 160°

(C) 180°

(D) 270°

9. Find the measure of arc $\overset{\frown}{XY}$ in circle W.

(A) 40°

(B) 120°

(C) 140°

(D) 180°

10. Find the area of the sector shown.

(A) 4 cm²

(B) 2π cm²

(C) 16 cm²

(D) 8π cm²

Solid Geometry

Cubes, Cylinders

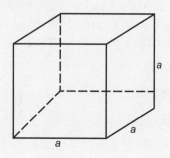

The volume of a cube with edge a is
$$V = a^3.$$
The surface area of a cube with edge a is
$$A = 6a^2.$$

The volume of a right circular cylinder with radius r and height h is
$$V = \pi r^2 h.$$

The surface area of a right circular cylinder with radius r and height h is
$$A = 2\pi r^2 + 2\pi rh.$$

Intersecting Planes

If two different planes intersect, they intersect in a straight line.

The angle between two planes is the angle between two rays on the two planes, each of which is perpendicular to the line of intersection of the planes.

Volume and Surface Area

Rectangular solid

The volume of a rectangular solid with length *l*, width *w*, and height *h* is

$$V = lwh.$$

Sphere

The volume of a sphere with radius *r* is

$$V = \frac{4}{3}\pi r^3.$$

The surface area of a sphere with radius *r* is

$$A = 4\pi r^2.$$

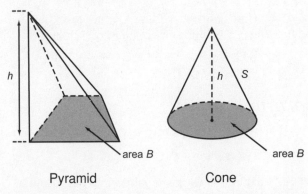

Pyramid   Cone

The volume of a pyramid or cone with base area *B* and height *h* is

$$V = \frac{1}{3}Bh.$$

If the base of the cone is a circle with radius *r*, then

$$A = \pi r^2,$$

so

$$V = \frac{1}{3}\pi r^2 h.$$

The total area of a cone is the sum of the surface area of the conical part (πrs), where *s* is the slant height, plus the area of the circular base, so $A = \pi rs + \pi r^2$.

PROBLEM

Calculate the circumference of a circle that has a radius of 12 inches.

SOLUTION

1. Write the formula for the circumference of a circle.

$$\text{circumference} = 2\pi r$$

2. Substitute the known values into the equation. Pi is approximately 3.14. The radius is 12.

$$\text{circumference} = 2(3.14)12$$

3. Solve the equation.

$$\text{circumference} = 75.4$$

The correct answer is that the circumference = 75.4 inches.

PROBLEM

Calculate the area of a circle that has a diameter of 10 meters.

SOLUTION

1. Write the formula for the area of a circle.

$$A = \pi r^2.$$

2. Substitute the known values into the equation. Pi is approximately 3.14. The diameter of the circle is 10 meters, so the radius is 5 meters.

$$A = \pi(5)^2$$

3. Solve the equation.

$$A = 78.5$$

The correct answer is that the area of the circle is 78.5 m².

PROBLEM

Calculate the volume of a sphere that has a radius of 2 meters.

SOLUTION

1. Write the formula for the volume of a sphere.

$$V = \frac{4}{3}\pi r^3$$

2. Substitute the known values into the equation. Pi is approximately 3.14 and the radius is 2 meters.

$$V = \frac{4}{3}\pi(2)^3$$

3. Solve the equation.

$$V = 33.49 \text{ or } {\sim}33.5$$

The correct answer is that the volume of the sphere is 33.5 m³.

PROBLEM

Calculate the perimeter of the triangle below.

SOLUTION

1. Write the formula for the perimeter of a triangle.

perimeter = length of side 1 + length of side 2 + length of side 3

2. Substitute the known values into the formula.

perimeter = 4 + 2 + 5

3. Solve the equation.

perimeter = 11

The correct answer is that the perimeter of the triangle is 11.

PROBLEM

Calculate the area of the triangle below.

SOLUTION

1. Write the formula for the area of a triangle.

$$A = \frac{1}{2}bh$$

2. Substitute the known values into the formula. The base of the triangle is 5 and the height is 6.

$$A = \frac{1}{2}(5)(6)$$

3. Solve the equation.

$$A = 15$$

The correct answer is that the area of the triangle is 15.

PROBLEM

Calculate the volume of the cube that has a length of 5, a height of 1.5, and a width of 4.

SOLUTION

1. Write the formula for the volume of a cube.

$$V = l \times w \times h$$

2. Substitute the known values into the formula.

$$V = 5 \times 4 \times 1.5$$

3. Solve the equation.

$$V = 30$$

The correct answer is that the volume of the cube = 30.

PROBLEM

Calculate the volume of a pyramid that has a height of 3 feet. The area of the base of the pyramid was calculated to be 15 square feet.

SOLUTION

1. Write the formula for the volume of a pyramid.

$V = \frac{1}{3}Bh$, where B is the area of the base of the pyramid.

2. Substitute the known values into the formula.

$$V = \frac{1}{3}(15)(3)$$

3. Solve the equation.

$$V = 15$$

The correct answer is that the volume of the pyramid is 15 cubic feet.

PROBLEM

Calculate the area of the triangle below.

SOLUTION

1. Write the formula for the area of a triangle.

$$A = \frac{1}{2}bh$$

2. Substitute the known values into the formula. The base of the triangle is 10 and the height is 15.

$$A = \frac{1}{2}(10)(15)$$

3. Solve the equation.

$$A = 75$$

The correct answer is that the area of the triangle is 75.

PROBLEM

Calculate the volume of the cone below.

SOLUTION

1. Write the formula for the volume of a cone.

$$V = \frac{1}{3}\pi r^2 h$$

2. Substitute the known values into the equation.

$$V = \frac{1}{3}\pi(2)^2(6)$$

3. Solve the equation.

$$V = 25.12$$

The correct answer is that the volume of the cone is 25.12 cubic inches.

PROBLEM

Calculate the volume of the cylinder below.

SOLUTION

1. Write the formula for the volume of a cylinder.

$$V = \pi r^2 h$$

2. Substitute the known values into the formula.

$$V = \pi(2)^2(11)$$

3. Solve the equation.

$$V = 138.16$$

The correct answer is that the volume is 138.16 m³.

PROBLEM

Calculate the total area of the cone below. Round to the nearest meter.

SOLUTION

1. Write the formula for the total area of a cone.

$$A = \pi rs + \pi r^2, \text{ where } s \text{ is the slant height}$$

2. Substitute the known values into the formula.

$$A = \pi(2)(5) + \pi(2)^2$$

3. Solve the equation.

$$A = 10\pi + 4\pi = \pi(10 + 4) = \pi(14)$$

$$A = 44$$

The correct answer is 44 m².

PROBLEM

Calculate the area of the trapezoid below.

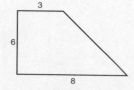

SOLUTION

1. Write the formula for the area of a trapezoid.

$$A = \frac{1}{2}h(b_1 + b_2), \text{ where } b_1 \text{ and } b_2 \text{ are the bases}$$

2. Substitute the known values into the formula.

$$A = \frac{1}{2}(6)(3 + 8)$$

3. Solve the equation.

$$A = 33$$

The correct answer is that the area of the trapezoid is 33 square feet.

PROBLEM

Calculate the area of the rhombus below.

SOLUTION

1. Write the formula for the area of a rhombus.

$$A = \frac{1}{2}(d_1 \text{ and } d_2), \text{ where } d_1 \text{ and } d_2 \text{ are the diagonals}$$

of the rhombus

2. Substitute the known values into the formula.

$$A = \frac{1}{2}(5)(4)$$

3. Solve the equation.

$$A = 10$$

The correct answer is that the area of the rhombus is 10 square feet.

PROBLEM

Calculate the area of the parallelogram below.

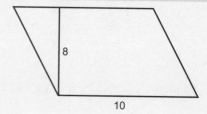

SOLUTION

1. Write the formula for the area of a parallelogram.

$A = bh$, where b is the base and h is the height

2. Substitute the known values into the formula.

$A = 10(8)$

3. Solve the equation.

$A = 80$

The correct answer is that the area of the parallelogram is 80.

Problem Solving with Triangles

PROBLEM

Using the Pythagorean theorem, calculate c in the figure below.

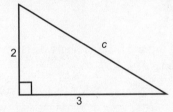

SOLUTION

1. Write the Pythagorean theorem.

$a^2 + b^2 = c^2$

2. Substitute the values of a and b into the equation.

$(3)^2 + (2)^2 = c^2$

3. Solve the left side of the equation.

$(3)^2 + (2)^2 = 13$

4. Rewrite the equation.

$13 = c^2$

5. Solve for c.

$\sqrt{13} = c$

The correct answer is $c = \sqrt{13}$.

PROBLEM

Using the Pythagorean theorem, calculate a in the figure below.

SOLUTION

1. Write the Pythagorean theorem.

$a^2 + b^2 = c^2$

2. Substitute the values of b and c into the equation.

$a^2 + (4)^2 = 7^2$

3. Simplify the equation.

$a^2 + 16 = 49$

4. Subtract 16 from both sides and rewrite the equation.

$a^2 = 33$

5. Solve for x.

$a = \sqrt{33}$

Coordinate Geometry

Coordinate geometry refers to the study of geometric figures using algebraic principles.

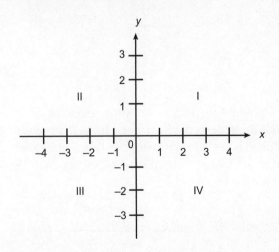

The graph shown is called the Cartesian coordinate plane. The graph consists of a pair of perpendicular lines called **coordinate axes.** The **vertical axis** is the *y*-axis and the **horizontal axis** is the *x*-axis. The point of intersection of these two axes is called the **origin**; it is the zero point of both axes. Furthermore, points to the right of the origin on the *x*-axis and above the origin on the *y*-axis represent positive real numbers. Points to the left of the origin on the *x*-axis or below the origin on the *y*-axis represent negative real numbers.

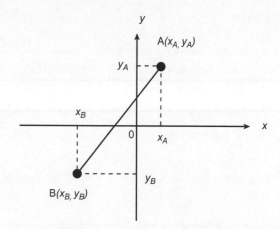

The four regions cut off by the coordinate axes are, in counterclockwise direction from the top right, called the first, second, third, and fourth quadrant, respectively. The first quadrant contains all points with two positive coordinates.

In the graph shown, two points *A* and *B* are shown. They can be identified by the ordered pair, (*x, y*) of numbers. The *x*-coordinate is the first number and the *y*-coordinate is the second number.

To plot a point on the graph when given the coordinates, draw perpendicular lines from the number-line coordinates to the point where the two lines intersect.

For any two points *A* and *B* with coordinates (x_A, y_A) and (x_B, y_B), respectively, the distance between *A* and *B* is represented by:

$$d = \sqrt{(x_A - x_B)^2 + (y_A - y_B)^2}$$

This is commonly known as the distance formula.

PROBLEM

Find the distance between the point *A*(1, 3) and *B*(5, 3).

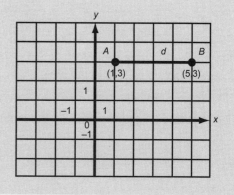

SOLUTION

In this case, where the ordinate of both points is the same, the distance between the two points is given by the absolute value of the difference between the two abscissas. In fact, this case reduces to merely counting boxes, as the figure shows.

Let, x_1 = abscissa of *A* y_1 = ordinate of *A*

x_2 = abscissa of *B* y_2 = ordinate of *B*

d = the distance

To find the coordinates of a given point on the graph, draw perpendicular lines from the point to the coordinates on the number line. The *x*-coordinate is written before the *y*-coordinate and a comma is used to separate the two.

In this case, point *A* has the coordinates (4, 2) and the coordinates of point *B* are (–3, –5).

Therefore, $d = |x_1 - x_2|$. By substitution, $d = |1 - 5|$ $= |-4| = 4$. This answer can also be obtained by applying the general formula for distance between any two points.

$$d = \sqrt{(x_1 - x_2)^2 + (y_1 - y_2)^2}$$

By substitution,

$$d = \sqrt{(1-5)^2 + (3-3)^2}$$
$$= \sqrt{(-4)^2 + (0)^2}$$
$$= \sqrt{16}$$
$$= 4$$

The distance is 4.

To find the midpoint of a segment between the two given endpoints, use the formula

$$MP = \left(\frac{x_1 + x_2}{2}, \frac{y_1 + y_2}{2} \right)$$

where x_1 and y_1 are the coordinates of one point, and x_2 and y_2 are the coordinates of the other point.

Conic Sections

Conic sections are the curves formed when a plane intersects the surface of a right circular cone. As shown below, these curves are the circle, the ellipse, the parabola, and the hyperbola.

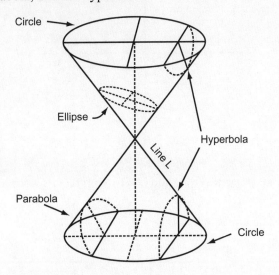

The Circle

As stated previously, a circle is defined to be the set of all points at a given distance from a given point. The given distance is called the radius, and the given point is called the center of the circle. Using the distance formula, it is easy to establish that an equation of a circle with center of (h,k) and radius of r is

$$(x - h)^2 + (y - k)^2 = r^2$$

An equation of this kind is said to be in standard form. Here are two examples that illustrate the practicality of the standard form.

• **EXAMPLES**

1. Find an equation of the circle with center of $(2,-3)$ with radius of 6.

$$(x - 2)^2 + [y - (-3)]^2 = 6^2$$
$$(x - 2)^2 + (y + 3)^2 = 36$$

2. Graph the equation listed below.

$$x^2 + y^2 - 6x + 10y + 30 = 0$$
$$(x^2 - 6x) + (y^2 + 10y) = -30$$

$$(x^2 - 6x + 9) + (y^2 + 10y + 25) = -30 + 34$$
$$(x - 3)^2 + (y + 5)^2 = 4$$

Notice, in the second example, how easy it is to graph

$$(x - 3)^2 + (y + 5)^2 = 4$$

and how difficult it would be to graph

$$x^2 + y^2 - 6x + 10y + 30 = 0$$

in that form.

Problem Solving Examples:

Write equations of the following circles:

(a) With center at $(-1,3)$ and radius 9.

(b) With center at (2,–3) and radius 5.

The equation of the circles with center at (*a,b*) and radius *r* is

$$(x - a)^2 + (y - b)^2 = r^2.$$

(a) Thus, the equation of the circle with center at (–1,3) and radius 9 is

$$[x - (-1)]^2 + (y - 3)^2 = 9^2$$
$$(x + 1)^2 + (y - 3)^2 = 81$$

(b) Similarly the equation of the circle with center at (2,–3) and radius 5 is

$$(x - 2)^2 + [y - (-3)]^2 = 5^2$$
$$(x - 2)^2 + (y + 3)^2 = 25$$

PROBLEM

Find the center and radius of the circle.

$$x^2 - 4x + y^2 + 8y - 5 = 0 \qquad (1)$$

SOLUTION

We can find the radius and the coordinates of the center by completing the square in both *x* and *y*. To complete the square in either variable, take half the coefficient of the variable term (i.e., the *x* term of the *y* term) and then square this value. The resulting number is then added to both sides of the equation. Completing the square in *x*:

$$\left[\frac{1}{2}(-4)\right]^2 = [-2]^2 = 4$$

Then equation (1) becomes:

$$(x^2 - 4x + 4) + y^2 + 8y - 5 = 0 + 4.$$

or

$$(x - 2)^2 + y^2 + 8y - 5 = 4 \qquad (2)$$

Before completing the square in *y*, add 5 to both sides of equation (2):

$$(x - 2)^2 + y^2 + 8y - \cancel{5} + \cancel{5} = 4 + 5$$

$$(x - 2)^2 + y^2 + 8y = 9 \qquad (3)$$

Now, completing the square in *y*:

$$\left[\frac{1}{2}(8)\right]^2 = [4]^2 = 16$$

Then equation (3) becomes:

$$(x - 2)^2 + (y^2 + 8y + 16) = 9 + 16,$$

or

$$(x - 2)^2 + (y + 4)^2 = 25 \qquad (4)$$

Note that the equation of a circle is:

$$(x - h)^2 + (y - k)^2 = r^2,$$

where (*h,k*) is the center of the circle and *r* is the radius of the circle. Equation (4) is in the form of the equation of a circle. Hence, equation (4) represents a circle with center (2,–4) and radius = 5.

PROBLEM

Find the equation of the circle of radius *r* = 9, with center on ℓ : *y = x* and tangent to both coordinate axes.

SOLUTION

As seen in the figure, there are two such circles, *O* and *O'*. Let the centers of *O* and *O'* be (*a,b*) and (*c,d*), respectively.

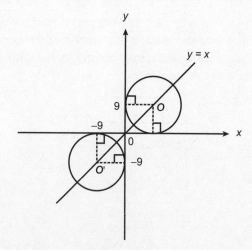

Since points (*a,b*) and (*c,d*) are on ℓ : *y = x*, we have *a = b* and *c = d*.

The equations will be

$$(x - a)^2 + (y - a)^2 = 9^2$$
$$\text{and } (x - c)^2 + (y - c)^2 = 9^2$$

Because the circles are tangent to both coordinate axes, we obtain $a = 9 = b$ and $c = -9 = d$ (see figure). Therefore, the equations are

$$(x - 9)^2 + (y - 9)^2 = 81 \text{ and}$$

$$(x + 9)^2 + (y + 9)^2 = 81$$

The Ellipse

An ellipse is defined to be the set of all points in a plane, the sum of whose distance from two fixed points is a constant. Each of the fixed points is called a focus. The plural of the word focus is foci. A simple method of constructing an ellipse comes directly from this definition. Mark two of the foci and call them F_1 and F_2, then insert a thumb tack at each focus. Next, take a string that is longer than the distance between F_1 and F_2 and tie one end at F_1 and the other end at F_2. Then, pull the string taut with a pencil and trace the ellipse. It will be oval shaped and will have two lines of symmetry and one point of symmetry.

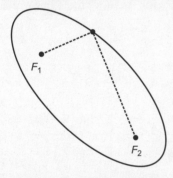

Using the distance formula, it is fairly easy to derive an equation of the ellipse with foci at $(c,0)$ and $(-c,0)$ with the sum of the distance of $2a$. The standard equation of such an ellipse is

$$\frac{x^2}{a^2} + \frac{y^2}{b^2} = 1,$$

where $b^2 = a^2 - c^2$. Obviously, $a^2 > b^2$. Here is a graph of such an ellipse.

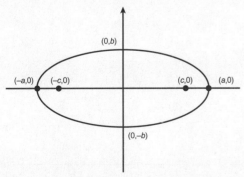

The center of the ellipse is the point midway between the foci. In this case, the center is at the origin. The segment from $(-a,0)$ to $(a,0)$ is called the major axis, and its length is $2a$. The segment from $(0,-b)$ to $(0,b)$ is called the minor axis, and its length is $2b$. In the ellipse, the x-axis and the y-axis are lines of symmetry, and the origin is a point of symmetry. The eccentricity e is defined to be $\frac{c}{a}$. When this ratio is close to 0, the ellipse resembles a circle, but when this ratio is close to 1, the ellipse is elongated.

It is very easy to graph an ellipse when the standard equation is given. In most cases, it is desirable to convert to that form. This process is illustrated in the example below.

• **EXAMPLE**

Graph

$$9x^2 + 16y^2 = 144$$

$$\frac{9x^2}{144} + \frac{16y^2}{144} = \frac{144}{144}$$

$$\frac{x^2}{16} + \frac{y^2}{9} = 1$$

$$\frac{x^2}{4^2} + \frac{y^2}{3^2} = 1$$

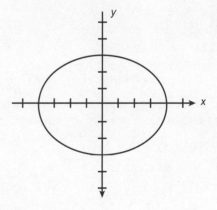

For an ellipse with foci at $(0,c)$ and $(0,-c)$, and with the sum of distances as $2a$, the standard equation is

$$\frac{y^2}{a^2} + \frac{x^2}{b^2} = 1$$

Here is a table that illustrates what happens when the center of the ellipse is not at the origin.

109

Center of ellipse	Sum of distance	Foci	Standard equation
(h,k)	$2a$	$(h+c,k)$ and $(h-c,k)$	$\dfrac{(x-h)^2}{a^2}+\dfrac{(y-k)^2}{b^2}=1$
(h,k)	$2a$	$(h,k+c)$ and $(h,k-c)$	$\dfrac{(y-k)^2}{a^2}+\dfrac{(x-h)^2}{b^2}=1$

In both cases, $b^2 = a^2 - c^2$.

Problem Solving Examples:

PROBLEM

Discuss the graph of $\dfrac{x^2}{25}+\dfrac{y^2}{9}=1$.

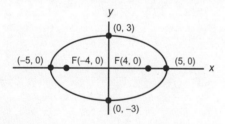

SOLUTION

Since this is an equation of the form $\dfrac{x^2}{a^2}+\dfrac{y^2}{b^2}=1$, with $a = 5$ and $b = 3$, it represents an ellipse. The simplest way to sketch the curve is to find its intercepts.

If we set $x = 0$, then

$$y = \sqrt{\left(1-\frac{x^2}{25}\right)9} = \sqrt{\left(1-\frac{0^2}{25}\right)9} = \pm 3$$

so that the y-intercepts are at $(0,3)$ and $(0,-3)$. Similarly the x-intercepts are found for $y = 0$:

$$x = \sqrt{\left(1-\frac{y^2}{9}\right)25}$$

$$= \sqrt{\left(1-\frac{0^2}{9}\right)25}$$

$$= \pm 5$$

to be at $(5,0)$ and $(-5,0)$ (see figure). To locate the foci we note that

$$c^2 = a^2 - b^2 = 5^2 - 3^2$$
$$c^2 = 25 - 9 = 16$$
$$c = \pm 4.$$

The foci lie on the major axis of the ellipse. In this case it is the x-axis since $a = 5$ is greater than $b = 3$. Therefore, the foci are $(\pm c, 0)$, that is, at $(-4,0)$ and $(4,0)$. The sum of the distances from any point on the curve to the foci is $2a = 2(5) = 10$.

PROBLEM

In the equation of an ellipse,
$$4x^2 + 9y^2 - 16x + 18y - 11 = 0,$$
determine the standard form of the equation, and find the values of a, b, c, and e.

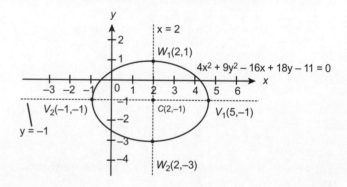

SOLUTION

By completing the squares, we can arrive at the standard form of the equation, from which the values of the parameters can be determined. Thus,

$$4(x^2 - 4x + 4) + 9(y^2 + 2y + 1) = 36.$$

or

$4(x-2)^2 + 9(y+1)^2 = 36$. Dividing by 36,

$$\frac{(x-2)^2}{9} + \frac{(y+1)^2}{4} = 1.$$

Thus, the center of the ellipse is at $(2, -1)$. Comparing this equation with the general form,

$\dfrac{x^2}{a^2} + \dfrac{y^2}{b^2} = 1$, where $a > b$, we see that

$a = 3$, $b = 2$, and

$c = \sqrt{a^2 - b^2} = \sqrt{5}$.

Finally, $e = \dfrac{c}{a} = \dfrac{\sqrt{5}}{3} \approx 0.745$.

PROBLEM

Find the equation of the ellipse that has vertices $V_1(-2,6)$, $V_2(-2,-4)$, and foci $F_1(-2,4)$, $F_2(-2,-2)$. (See figure.)

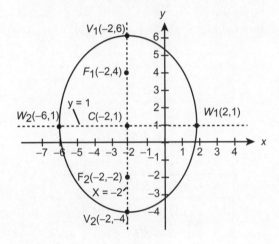

SOLUTION

Since the vertices and Foci are on the line $x = -2$, the major axis is on the line $x = -2$. The center has $x = -2$, the y value is half the difference between the vertices or $\frac{1}{2}(|6| - |-4|)$, or $\frac{1}{2}(10)$ or 5 units from either vertex, so the center is at $(-2,1)$. a, the length of the semimajor axis, equals the difference between the y-coordinates of V_1 (say) and the center, $a = 5$. From the coordinates of the foci, $c = 3$. Since $b^2 = a^2 - c^2$, $b = \sqrt{25 - 9} = 4$, and the ends of the minor axis, on $y = 1$, are at $W_1(2,1)$ and $W_2(-6,1)$. The equation can now be written, in the form

$$\frac{(y-k)^2}{a^2} + \frac{(x-h)^2}{b^2} = 1$$

$$\frac{(y-1)^2}{25} + \frac{(x+2)^2}{16} = 1.$$

The Parabola

A parabola is defined to be the set of all points in a plane equally distant from a fixed line and a fixed point not on the line. The line is called the directrix and the point is called the focus. The axis of a parabola is the line that passes through the focus and is perpendicular to the directrix. The vertex of the parabola is at the point halfway between the focus and the directrix. A picture of a parabola is shown in the figure.

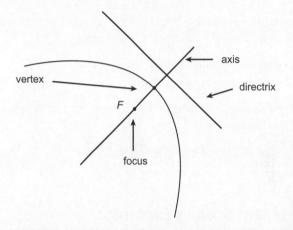

It is somewhat common for the undirected distance between the directrix and the focus to be labeled $2c$ (this means that $c > 0$.) The following table relates the standard equation to the position of the vertex, the position of the focus, and the equation of the directrix.

Directrix	Focus	Vertex	Standard Equation	Direction Parabola Opens
$y = -c$	$(0,c)$	$(0,0)$	$x^2 = 4cy$	Up
$x = -c$	$(c,0)$	$(0,0)$	$y^2 = 4cx$	Right
$y = c$	$(0,-c)$	$(0,0)$	$x^2 = -4cx$	Down
$x = c$	$(-c,0)$	$(0,0)$	$y^2 = -4cx$	Left
$y = -c + k$	$(h, c + k)$	(h,k)	$(x-h)^2 = 4c(y-k)$	Up
$x = -c + h$	$(c + h, k)$	(h,k)	$(y-k)^2 = 4c(x-h)$	Right
$y = c + k$	$(h, -c + k)$	(h,k)	$(x-h)^2 = -4c(y-k)$	Down
$x = c + h$	$(-c + h, k)$	(h,k)	$(y-k)^2 = -4c(x-h)$	Left

This table illustrates that once an equation for a parabola is in standard form, it is easy to characterize the parabola. Consider the following:

$$y^2 - 6y - 6x + 39 = 0$$
$$y^2 - 6y = 6x - 39$$
$$y^2 - 6y + 9 = 6x - 30$$
$$(y - 3)^2 = 6(x - 5)$$

This is a parabola with a standard equation of $(y - k)^2 = 4c(x - h)$, with vertex at (5,3) and focus at $(6\frac{1}{2},3)$. The equation of the directrix is $x = 3\frac{1}{2}$, and the parabola opens to the right (see line 6 in the table).

In general, equations of the form

$$y^2 + Dx + Ey + F = 0$$

are parabolas that open to the right or left, and equations of the form

$$x^2 + Dx + Ey + F = 0$$

are parabolas that open up or down.

Problem Solving Examples:

PROBLEM

Construct the graph of the function defined by
$$y = x^2 - 6x + 10.$$

SOLUTION

We are given the function $y = x^2 - 6x + 10$.

The most general form of the quadratic function is $y = ax^2 + bx + c$ where a, b, and c are constants. If a is

positive, the curve opens upward and it is U-shaped. If a is negative, the curve opens downward and it is inverted U-shaped.

Since $a = 1 > 0$ in the given equation, the graph is a parabola that opens upward. To determine the pairs of values (x,y) that satisfy this equation, express the quadratic function in terms of the square of a linear function of x.

$$y = x^2 - 6x + 10 = x^2 - 6x + 9 + 1$$
$$= (x - 3)^2 + 1$$

y is least when $x - 3 = 0$ This is true because the square of any number, be it positive or negative, is a positive number. Therefore y would always be greater than or equal to 1. Thus the minimum value of y is 1 when $x - 3 = 0$ or $x = 3$.

To plot the curve, select values for x and calculate the corresponding y values (see the table).

x	$x^2 - 6x + 10 =$	y
0	$(0)^2 - 6(0) + 10$	10
1	$(1)^2 - 6(1) + 10$	5
2	$(2)^2 - 6(2) + 10$	2
3	$(3)^2 - 6(3) + 10$	1
4	$(4)^2 - 6(4) + 10$	2
5	$(5)^2 - 6(5) + 10$	5
6	$(6)^2 - 6(6) + 10$	10

The points and graphs determined by the table are shown in the accompanying figure.

PROBLEM

Find the coordinates of the maximum point of the curve $y = -3x^2 - 12x + 5$, and locate the axis of symmetry.

SOLUTION

The curve is defined by a second degree equation $y = ax^2 + bx + c$. The coefficient of the x^2 term, a is negative. Hence, the graph of this curve is a parabola opening downward. The maximum point of the curve occurs at the vertex and has the x-coordinate:

$$-\frac{\text{coefficient of } x \text{ term}}{2(\text{coefficient of } x^2 \text{ term})} = -\frac{b}{2a} = -\frac{-12}{2(-3)} = \frac{12}{-6} = -2.$$

For $x = -2$, $y = -3(-2)^2 - 12(-2) + 5 = 17$. Hence the coordinates of the vertex are $(-2,17)$. The curve is symmetric with respect to the vertical line through its vertex. The axis of symmetry of this curve is the vertical line through the point $(-2,17)$, or the line $x = -2$.

PROBLEM

Discuss the graph of the equation $y^2 = 12x$.

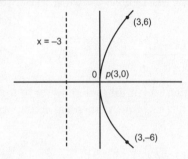

SOLUTION

The equation $y^2 = 12x$ is a quadratic equation of the form $y^2 = 4cx$ with the coefficient of the y^2 term positive. Therefore the graph is a parabola opening to the right. Since $f(x) = -f(x)$ the parabola is symmetric with respect to the x-axis. Point $(0,0)$ satisfies the equation and lies on the axis of symmetry. Hence the vertex of the parabola is at $(0,0)$ (see figure). The focus of the parabola lies on the axis of symmetry, $y = 0$, at the point $(c,0)$ where $4c =$ coefficient of x in the original equation: $4c = 12$, $c = 3$. Therefore the focus is at $(3,0)$. The directrix is the vertical line $x = -c = -3$. When $x = 3$, $y = \pm\sqrt{12x} = \pm\sqrt{12(3)} = \pm 6$. Therefore the points $(3,6)$ and $(3, -6)$ are points on the graph. The graph of this parabola is not the graph of a function, since for any given value of x there is more than one corresponding value of y.

PROBLEM

Write the equation of the parabola whose focus has coordinates $(0,2)$ and whose directrix has equation $y = -2$ (see figure).

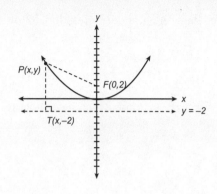

SOLUTION

Since, by definition, each point lying on a parabola is equidistant from both the focus and directrix of the parabola, the origin must lie on the specific parabola described in the statement of the problem (see figure).

To find the equation of the parabola, choose a point $P(x,y)$ lying on the parabola (see figure). By definition, then, the distance PT must equal the distance PF, where T lies on the directrix, directly below P. Since T also lies on $y = -2$, it has coordinates $(x,-2)$. Using the distance formula, we find for $PF = PT$:

$$\sqrt{(x-0)^2 + (y-2)^2} = \sqrt{(x-x)^2 + (y-(-2))^2}$$

$$\text{or } \sqrt{x^2 + (y-2)^2} = \sqrt{(y+2)^2}.$$

Squaring both sides of this equation, we obtain

$$x^2 + (y-2)^2 = (y+2)^2.$$

Expanding this,

$$x^2 + y^2 - 4y + 4 = y^2 + 4y + 4.$$

Subtracting y^2, $-4y$, and 4 from each side of this equation yields

$$x^2 = 8y.$$

Dividing both sides of this equation by 8 gives the equation of the parabola:

$$y = \frac{1}{8}x^2.$$

The Hyperbola

The hyperbola is defined to be the set of all points in a plane, the difference of whose distances from two fixed points is a constant. If the foci are at $(c,0)$ and $(-c,0)$, and if the difference of the distances is $2a$ with

$0 < a < c$, then the standard equation for this hyperbola is

$$\frac{x^2}{a^2} - \frac{y^2}{b^2} = 1,$$

where $b^2 = c^2 - a^2$. A graph of the hyperbola follows.

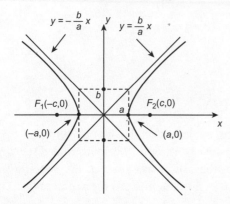

Notice that the hyperbola has two branches.

For the hyperbola, the focal axis is the line through the foci, the center is the point midway between the foci, and the conjugate axis is the line through the center, perpendicular to the focal axis. The hyperbola has symmetry with respect to those lines and that point. For the hyperbola in the figures, the focal axis is the x-axis, the conjugate axis is the y-axis, and the center is at the origin. Notice that, in this case, the lines

$$y = \frac{b}{a}x \quad \text{and} \quad y = \frac{-b}{a}x$$

are asymptotes for the hyperbola pictured, which means the hyperbola gets closer and closer to the lines but never crosses them. The fundamental rectangle is the dashed rectangle in the figure. The asymptotes are diagonal of this rectangle, which is bounded by the hyperbola.

If the foci are at $(0,c)$ and $(0,-c)$, and if the difference between the distances is still $2a$ with $0 < a < c$, then the standard equation for the hyperbola is

$$\frac{y^2}{a^2} - \frac{x^2}{b^2} = 1,$$

where $b^2 = c^2 - a^2$.

In this case, the center is at the origin, the focal axis is the y-axis, the conjugate axis is the x-axis, and the hyperbola has the lines

$$y = \frac{a}{b}x \quad \text{and} \quad y = \frac{-a}{b}x$$

as asymptotes. A graph of this hyperbola follows.

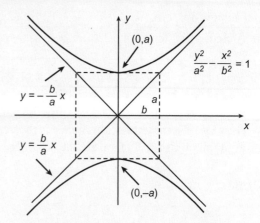

The standard form of the equation of the hyperbola with center at (h,k) and with focal axis parallel to the x-axis is

$$\frac{(x-h)^2}{a^2} - \frac{(y-k)^2}{b^2} = 1,$$

and the standard form for the equation of the hyperbola with center at (h,k) and with focal axis parallel to the y-axis is

$$\frac{(y-k)^2}{a^2} - \frac{(x-h)^2}{b^2} = 1.$$

Problem Solving Examples:

PROBLEM

Consider the equation

$$x^2 - 4y^2 + 4x + 8y + 4 = 0.$$

Express this equation in standard form, and determine the center, the vertices, the foci, and the eccentricity of this hyperbola. Describe the fundamental rectangle and find the equations of the two asymptotes.

SOLUTION

Rewrite the equation by completing the squares:

$$(x^2 + 4x + 4) - 4(y^2 - 2y + 1) = -4$$

or $(x + 2)^2 - 4(y - 1)^2 = -4$

or, dividing by -4 and rearranging terms, gives

$$\frac{(y-1)^2}{1} - \frac{(x+2)^2}{4} = 1.$$

The center, located at (h, k) in the equation

$\frac{(y-k)^2}{a^2} - \frac{(x-h)^2}{b^2} = 1$ is, therefore, at $(-2,1)$.

Furthermore, $a = 1$ and $b = 2$. Thus,

$$c = \sqrt{1^2 + 2^2} = \sqrt{5} \text{ and } e = \frac{c}{a} = \sqrt{5}.$$

The vertices are displaced $\pm a$ from the center, while the foci are displaced $\pm c$ (along the transverse- or focal-axis). Therefore, the vertices are $(-2, 1 \pm 1)$ and the foci are $(-2, 1 \pm \sqrt{5})$.

By definition, the fundamental rectangle is the rectangle whose vertices are at $(h \pm b, k \pm a)$. Hence, in this example, the coordinates of the vertices of the rectangle are $(0,2)$, $(-4, 2)$, $(-4, 0)$, and $(0,0)$. The equations of the two asymptotes are determined by finding the slopes of the lines passing through the center of the hyperbola and two of the vertices of its fundamental rectangle (see figure). Then,

$$m = \frac{\Delta y}{\Delta x} = \pm \frac{1}{2}$$

gives the two slopes, and the point-slope form, choosing the point $(-2,1)$ which is common to both asymptotes, gives

$$y - 1 = \pm \frac{1}{2}(x + 2),$$

the equation of the asymptotes.

PROBLEM

Find the equation of the hyperbola with vertices $V_1(8,0)$, $V_2(2,0)$ and eccentricity $e = 2$.

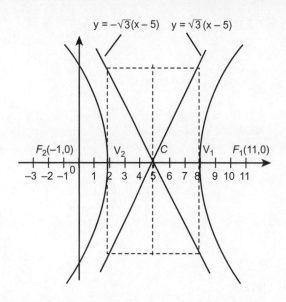

$y = -\sqrt{3}(x-5) \quad y = \sqrt{3}(x-5)$

$F_2(-1,0) \quad V_2 \quad C \quad V_1 \quad F_1(11,0)$

SOLUTION

There are two basic forms of the equation of a hyperbola that is not rotated with respect to the coordinate axes:

$$\frac{(x-h)^2}{a^2} - \frac{(y-k)^2}{b^2} = 1 \quad \text{and}$$

$$\frac{(y-k)^2}{a^2} - \frac{(x-h)^2}{b^2} = 1.$$

Which form is appropriate depends upon whether the transverse axis is parallel to the x-axis or to the y-axis, respectively. To determine the equation of a hyperbola, then, it is necessary to first discover which equation applies, then to determine the constants h, k, a, and c. The information about the vertices implies that the transverse axis is the x-axis.

Thus, the first form of the equation for a hyperbola applies. In this case, the center, which is the midpoint of the vertices is at $(5,0)$. The distance between the vertices is $2a = 6$; therefore, $a = 3$. In order to determine the value of b, we use the relation between eccentricity, e, c, and a: $e = c/a$. Thus, $c = e \times a = 2 \times 3 = 6$.

$$b = \sqrt{c^2 - a^2} = \sqrt{6^2 - 3^2} = \sqrt{27} \approx 5.2$$

Substituting for h, k, a, b, we have

$$\frac{(x-5)^2}{9} - \frac{y^2}{27} = 1,$$

or $3x^2 - y^2 - 30x + 48 = 0$.

PROBLEM

Discuss the graph of $\dfrac{x^2}{9} - \dfrac{y^2}{9} = 1$.

SOLUTION

$\dfrac{x^2}{9} - \dfrac{y^2}{9} = 1$ is an equation of the form $\dfrac{x^2}{a^2} - \dfrac{y^2}{b^2} = 1$ with $a = 3$ and $b = 3$. Therefore the graph is a hyperbola. The x-intercepts are found by setting $y = 0$:

$$\frac{x^2}{9} - \frac{y^2}{9} = 1$$
$$x^2 = 9$$
$$x = \pm 3.$$

Thus, the x-intercepts are at $(-3,0)$ and $(3,0)$. There are no y-intercepts since for $x = 0$, no real values of y satisfy the equation, that is, no real value of y satisfies

$$\frac{0^2}{9} - \frac{y^2}{9} = 1$$
$$y^2 = -9, \; y = \sqrt{-9}.$$

Solving the original equation for y:

$$y = \sqrt{\left(1 - \frac{x^2}{9}\right)(-9)} \;\; \text{or} \;\; y = \sqrt{x^2 - 9}$$

shows that there will be no permissible values of x in the interval $-3 < x < 3$. Such values of x do not yield real values for y. For $x = 5$ and $x = -5$, use the equation for y to obtain the ordered pairs $(5,4)$, $(5,-4)$, $(-5,4)$, and $(-5,-4)$ as indicated in the figure. The foci of the hyperbola are located at $(\pm c, 0)$, where

$$c^2 = a^2 + b^2$$
$$c^2 = 3^2 + 3^2 = 9 + 9 = 18$$
$$c = \pm\sqrt{18} = \pm 3\sqrt{2}.$$

Therefore, the foci are at $\left(-3\sqrt{2}, 0\right)$ and $\left(3\sqrt{2}, 0\right)$.

PROBLEM

Draw the graph of $xy = 6$.

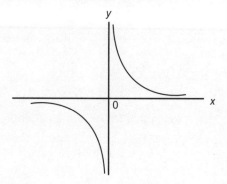

SOLUTION

Since the product is positive, the values of x and y must have the same sign, that is, when x is positive y must also be positive and when x is negative then y is also negative. Moreover, neither x nor y can be zero (or their product would be zero not 6), so that the graph never touches the coordinate axes. Solve for y and we obtain $y = \dfrac{6}{x}$. Substituting values of x into this equation, construct the following chart:

x:	-6	-3	-2	-1	1	2	3	6
y:	-1	-2	-3	-6	6	3	2	1

The graph is obtained by plotting the above points and then joining them with a smooth curve, remembering that the curve can never cross a coordinate axis. The graph of the equation, $xy = k$, is a hyperbola for all nonzero real values of k. If k is negative, then x and y must have opposite signs, and the graph is in the second and fourth quadrants as opposed to the first and third.

Quiz: Conic Sections

1. What is the center and radius of the circle given by $x^2 + y^2 + 6x - 10y = -32$?

(A) center $(-3,5)$ radius: $\sqrt{2}$

(B) center $(3,-5)$ radius: $\sqrt{2}$

(C) center $(-3,5)$ radius: 2

(D) center $(3,5)$ radius: 2

(E) center $(5,3)$ radius: $\sqrt{2}$

2. A circle is centered at point $(3,4)$. The endpoints of a diameter are A and B. The coordinates of point A are $(-2,1)$. What are the coordinates of point B?

(A) $(6,3)$.   (D) $(9,3)$.

(B) $(8,7)$.   (E) $(5,8)$.

(C) $(4,5)$.

3. An equation of a circle with center $\left(-\dfrac{2}{3}, \dfrac{1}{2}\right)$ and radius $\sqrt{7}$ is:

(A) $3x^2 + 4x + 3y^2 = 3y = 227$

(B) $36x^2 - 48x + 36y^2 + 36y = 259$

(C) $36x^2 + 48x + 36y^2 - 36y = 227$

(D) $3x^2 - 2x + y^2 + 2y = 7$

(E) $48x^2 - 36x + 36y^2 + 36y = 227$

4. The equation $6x^2 - 24x + 4y^2 + 32y = -52$ represents which of the following?

(A) circle   (D) ellipse

(B) hyperbola   (E) none of these

(C) parabola

5. The equation $x^2 - 2x + 2y^2 + 8y = -5$ is the equation of an ellipse. What are the coordinates of the foci of the ellipse?

(A) $(3,-2)$ and $(-1,-2)$

(B) $\left(1+\sqrt{2},-2\right)$ and $\left(1-\sqrt{2},-2\right)$

(C) $\left(1-\sqrt{3},2\right)$ and $\left(1,-2-\sqrt{2}\right)$

(D) $\left(1-\sqrt{3},2\right)$ and $\left(1+\sqrt{3},2\right)$

(E) $\left(-1+\sqrt{2},2\right)$ and $\left(-1-\sqrt{2},2\right)$

6. What is the equation of a parabola which is symmetrical about the y-axis and passes through points $(0,-2)$ and $(2,0)$?

(A) $y = x^2 - 2$ (D) $y = 2x^2 - 1$

(B) $y = \dfrac{1}{2}x^2 - 2$ (E) $y = 2x^2 - \dfrac{1}{2}$

(C) $y = \dfrac{3}{2}x^2 + \dfrac{1}{2}$

7. Find the center of the ellipse given by equation $x^2 + x + 3y + 2y^2 - 1 = 0$.

(A) $\left(\dfrac{1}{2}, -\dfrac{3}{2}\right)$

(B) $\left(\dfrac{1}{4}, \dfrac{3}{2}\right)$

(C) $\left(\dfrac{1}{2}, -\dfrac{3}{4}\right)$ (D) $\left(-\dfrac{1}{2}, -\dfrac{3}{4}\right)$

(E) $\left(1, -\dfrac{3}{4}\right)$

8. A parabola has the equation $y = \dfrac{-1}{2}x^2 + 3x - \dfrac{13}{2}$. What is the directrix of this parabola?

(A) $y = \dfrac{-5}{2}$ (D) $y = \dfrac{-3}{2}$

(B) $x = \dfrac{-3}{2}$ (E) $y = \dfrac{5}{2}$

(C) $x = \dfrac{-5}{2}$

9. What are the equations of the asymptotes for the hyperbola given by $\dfrac{(x+1)^2}{9} - \dfrac{(y-2)^2}{4} = 1$?

(A) $y = \dfrac{1}{3}x + \dfrac{2}{3}$ and $y = \dfrac{-1}{3}x - \dfrac{1}{3}$

(B) $y = \dfrac{2}{3}x + \dfrac{8}{3}$ and $y = \dfrac{-2}{3}x + \dfrac{4}{3}$

(C) $y = \dfrac{8}{3}x + \dfrac{-2}{3}$ and $y = \dfrac{-8}{3}x + \dfrac{4}{3}$

(D) $y = \dfrac{3}{3}x + 3$ and $y = \dfrac{-3}{2}x + \dfrac{1}{2}$

(E)   none of these

10.   Find a, b for the parabola

$y = ax^2 + bx + 3$

if the vertex is (2,4).

(A) $a = -\dfrac{1}{4}, b = 2$

(B) $a = -1, b = -2$

(C) $a = 1, b = 2$

(D) $a = -\dfrac{1}{3}, b = 1$

(E) $a = -\dfrac{1}{4}, b = 1$

Quiz: Conic Sections

ANSWER KEY

1. (A)
2. (B)
3. (C)
4. (D)
5. (B)

6. (B)
7. (D)
8. (D)
9. (B)
10. (E)

Geometry Review

ANSWER KEY

Drill: Regular Polygons (Convex)

1. (D)
2. (D)
3. (D)
4. (C)
5. (D)

Drill: Triangles

1. (D)   6. (C)
2. (B)   7. (B)
3. (C)   8. (D)
4. (A)   9. (A)
5. (D)   10. (B)

Drill: Quadrilaterals

1. (B)   6. (C)
2. (D)   7. (D)
3. (A)   8. (B)
4. (D)   9. (C)
5. (C)   10. (D)

Drill: Circles

1. (B)   6. (B)
2. (C)   7. (D)
3. (D)   8. (C)
4. (C)   9. (C)
5. (B)   10. (B)

Detailed Explanations of Answers

Drill: Regular Polygons (Convex)

1. (D)

A regular pentagon is both equiangular and equilateral. A pentagon is five sided. Therefore,

$$360° \div 5 = 72° \qquad 180° - 72° = 108°$$

2. (D)

$$(3 \times 180°) - 180° = 360°$$

3. (D)

$$a = 4\sqrt{3} \qquad P = \text{perimeter} = 3(24) = 72$$

$$A = \frac{1}{2}ap = \frac{1}{2}(4\sqrt{3})(72) = 144\sqrt{3} \text{ mm}^2$$

4. (C)

$s = 4$ therefore, radius = 4 too, which makes the apothem

$$\sqrt{(4)^2 - (2)^2} = 2\sqrt{3}$$

$$A = \frac{1}{2}ap = \frac{1}{2}(2\sqrt{3})(6)(4) = 24\sqrt{3} \text{ cm}^2$$

5. (D)

$$A = \frac{1}{2}ap = \frac{1}{2}a(s)(10) = \frac{1}{2}(9.2)(6)(10) = 276 \text{ cm}^2$$

Drill: Triangles

1. (D)

Since $\angle Q$ is a right angle, $m\angle Q = 90°$. Therefore,
$90° - 23° = 67°$

2. (B)

$$\frac{180° - 96°}{2} = \frac{84°}{2} = 42°$$

3. (C)

$$3x + 2x + x = 180$$

$$6x = 180$$

$$x = 30$$

4. (A)

$$6 : 4 = 4 : b \Rightarrow \frac{6}{4} = \frac{4}{b} \Rightarrow 6b = 16$$

$$b = \frac{16}{6} = 2\frac{4}{6} = 2\frac{2}{3}$$

5. (D)

$$3 : 6 = 4 : b \qquad b = 8$$

$$3 : 4 = 4 : a$$

$$\frac{3}{4} = \frac{4}{a}$$

$$3a = 16 \qquad a = 16\left(\frac{1}{3}\right) = 5\frac{1}{3}$$

6. (C)

$$A = \frac{1}{2}bh = \frac{1}{2}(14)(8) = 56$$

7. (B)

$$A = \frac{1}{2}bh = \frac{1}{2}(11)(7) = 38\frac{1}{2} \text{ or } 38.5$$

8. (D)

$$A = \frac{1}{2}bh = \frac{1}{2}(4)\left(8\sqrt{2}\right) = 16\sqrt{2}$$

9. (A)

Using the Pythagorean theorem,

$$\overline{AB} = \sqrt{\left(\overline{AC}\right)^2 - \left(\overline{BC}\right)^2} = \sqrt{(15)^2 - (9)^2} = \sqrt{144} = 12.$$

Then $A = \frac{1}{2}bh = \frac{1}{2}(9)(12) = 54 \text{ cm}^2$

10. (B)

This is an isosceles right triangle, so the legs are equal. Using the Pythagorean theorem,

$$(10\sqrt{2})^2 = a^2 + a^2$$
$$200 = 2a^2$$
$$a^2 = 100$$
$$a = 10$$

so the sides are 10 cm each.

$$A = \frac{1}{2}bh = \frac{1}{2}(10)(10) = 50 \text{ cm}^2$$

Drill: Quadrilaterals

1. (B)

$\angle B$ and $\angle D$ are opposite angles in the parallelogram and are equal. Therefore,

$$6x + 2 = 98$$
$$6x = 96$$
$$x = 16$$

2. (D)

$$A = bh = (18)(9) = 162$$

3. (A)

Using the Pythagorean Theorem,

$$\overline{AC} = \sqrt{\left(\overline{AD}\right)^2 + \left(\overline{DC}\right)^2}$$
$$= \sqrt{(6)^2 + (8)^2}$$
$$= \sqrt{36 + 64}$$
$$= \sqrt{100}$$
$$= 10 \text{ cm}$$

4. (D)

$$A = bh = (7)(10) = 70 \text{ cm}^2$$

5. (C)

$$\overline{EC} = \overline{BD} = 17$$
$$\overline{BO} = \frac{1}{2}\overline{BD} = \frac{1}{2}(17) = 8.5$$

6. (C)

Using the Pythagorean theorem,

$$\overline{GH} = \sqrt{\left(\frac{1}{2}\overline{GI}\right)^2 + \left(\frac{1}{2}\overline{HJ}\right)^2}$$
$$= \sqrt{\left[\left(\frac{1}{2}\right)(6)\right]^2 + \left[\left(\frac{1}{2}\right)(8)\right]^2}$$
$$= \sqrt{(3)^2 + (4)^2}$$
$$= \sqrt{25} = 5$$

7. (D)

$$A = \frac{1}{2}(b_1 + b_2)h$$
$$= \frac{1}{2}(14 + 21)(10)$$
$$= \frac{1}{2}(35)(10)$$
$$= 175$$

8. (B)

$$\overline{BC} = \overline{AD} = 6$$
$$P = 6 + 6 + 5 + 10 = 27$$

9. (C)

Use the Pythagorean Theorem to find the height.

$b^2 = b^2 + 3^2$

$b^2 = 27$

$b = 3\sqrt{3}$.

The area of this trapezoid is the area of the rectangle plus the area of the triangle, or

$$A = \underset{\text{rectangle}}{bh} + \underset{\text{triangle}}{\frac{1}{2}bh} = (4)\left(3\sqrt{3}\right) + \frac{1}{2}\left(3\sqrt{3}\right)(3)$$

$$= 12\sqrt{3} + \frac{9}{2}\sqrt{3} = \frac{33}{2}\sqrt{3}$$

10. (D)

The base angles of an isosceles trapezoid are equal.

Therefore, $\angle W = \angle Z$ so

$$58 = 4x - 6$$
$$64 = 4x$$
$$16 = x$$

Drill: Circles

1. (B)

$C = 2\pi r = 2(\pi)(3) = 6\pi$

2. (C)

$A = \pi r^2 = \pi(11)^2 = 121\pi$

3. (D)

$A = \pi r^2 \quad r = \frac{1}{2}d = \frac{1}{2}(27) = 13.5$

$A = \pi(13.5)^2 = 182.25\pi$

4. (C)

$A = 225\pi = \pi r^2$ so $r = \sqrt{225} = 15$

$d = 2r = 2(15) = 30$

5. (B)

$C_X = \pi r^2 = 144\pi \quad r_X = 12$

$C_Y = \pi r^2 = 81\pi \quad r_Y = 9$

$r_X : r_Y = 12 : 9 = 4 : 3$

6. (B)

Shaded Area = Larger Area – Smaller Area

$$= \pi r_1^2 - \pi r_2^2$$
$$= \pi(7)^2 - \pi(5)^5$$
$$= 49\pi - 25\pi$$
$$= 24\pi$$

7. (D)

Measure of arc = measure of central angle

8. (C)

The measure of a semicircle is 180°. Therefore, arc $\widehat{AXC} = 180°$.

9. (C)

Since $\widehat{XYZ}$ is semicircle, $180° - 40° = 140°$

10. (B)

$$\frac{45}{360}\pi r^2 = \frac{1}{8}\pi(4)^2 = \frac{16}{8}\pi = 2\pi$$

5

Competency 5: Knowledge of Trigonometry

Trigonometry is a field of mathematics that basically is used to solve triangles. With trigonometry, you can find the missing measures (lenghts of sides and angles) in a triangle if you have some information about the triangle. Extensions of the use of trigonometry include astronomy, geography, and even medical imaging. The values of trigonometric functions for any angle are available in "trig" tables or on most calculators.

Angles and Trigonometric Functions

The basic trigonometric functions are based on the right triangle, such as $\triangle ABC$, shown in the figure below:

Definition 1: Sine

$$\sin \angle A = \frac{BC}{AB}$$

$$= \frac{\text{measure of side opposite } \angle A}{\text{measure of hypotenuse}}$$

Definition 2: Cosine

$$\cos \angle A = \frac{AC}{AB}$$

$$= \frac{\text{measure of side adjacent to } \angle A}{\text{measure of hypotenuse}}$$

Definition 3: Tangent

$$\tan \angle A = \frac{BC}{AC}$$

$$= \frac{\text{measure of side opposite } \angle A}{\text{measure of side adjacent to } \angle A}$$

Definition 4: Cotangent

$$\cot \angle A = \frac{AC}{BC}$$

$$= \frac{\text{measure of side adjacent to } \angle A}{\text{measure of side opposite } \angle A}$$

Definition 5: Secant

$$\sec \angle A = \frac{AB}{AC}$$

$$= \frac{\text{measure of hypotenuse}}{\text{measure of side adjacent to } \angle A}$$

Definition 6: Cosecant

$$\csc \angle A = \frac{AB}{BC}$$

$$= \frac{\text{measure of hypotenuse}}{\text{measure of side opposite } \angle A}$$

The following table gives the values of sine, cosine, tangent, and cotangent for some special angles. The angles are given in radians and in degrees. A radian is a measure of the central angle in a circle and is usually expressed in terms of π. A full circle has $360°$, or 2π radians.

α	Sin α	Cos α	Tan α	Cot α
$0°$	0	1	0	∞
$\frac{\pi}{6} = 30°$	$\frac{1}{2}$	$\frac{\sqrt{3}}{2}$	$\frac{1}{\sqrt{3}}$	$\sqrt{3}$
$\frac{\pi}{4} = 45°$	$\frac{1}{\sqrt{2}}$	$\frac{1}{\sqrt{2}}$	1	1
$\frac{\pi}{3} = 60°$	$\frac{\sqrt{3}}{2}$	$\frac{1}{2}$	$\sqrt{3}$	$\frac{1}{\sqrt{3}}$
$\frac{\pi}{2} = 90°$	1	0	∞	0

A circle with center located at the origin of the rectangular coordinate axes with radius equal to one unit length is called a unit circle.

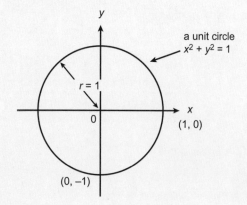

An angle whose vertex is at the origin of a rectangular coordinate system and whose initial side coincides with the positive x-axis is said to be in standard position with respect to the coordinate system.

A quadrant angle is an angle in standard position whose terminal side lies on one of the axes of a Cartesian coordinate system.

An angle in standard position with respect to a Cartesian coordinate system whose terminal side lies in the first (or second or third or fourth) quadrant is called a first (or second or third or fourth) quadrant angle.

If θ is a non-quadrantal angle in standard position and $P(x, y)$ is any point, distinct from the origin, on the terminal side of θ, then the six trigonometric functions of θ are defined in terms of the abscissa (x-coordinate), ordinate (y-coordinate), and distance $\overline{OP}$ as follows:

$$\text{sine } \theta = \sin\theta = \frac{\text{ordinate}}{\text{distance}} = \frac{y}{r}$$

$$\text{cosine } \theta = \cos\theta = \frac{\text{abscissa}}{\text{distance}} = \frac{x}{r}$$

$$\text{tangent } \theta = \tan\theta = \frac{\text{ordinate}}{\text{abscissa}} = \frac{y}{x}$$

$$\text{cotangent } \theta = \cot\theta = \frac{\text{abscissa}}{\text{ordinate}} = \frac{x}{y}$$

$$\text{secant } \theta = \sec\theta = \frac{\text{distance}}{\text{abscissa}} = \frac{r}{x}$$

$$\text{cosecant } \theta = \csc\theta = \frac{\text{distance}}{\text{ordinate}} = \frac{r}{y}$$

The signs of the functions in the quadrants depend on whether the ordinate or abscissa is positive or negative in that quadrant (the distance is always taken as positive). Thus, for $x < 90°$, if $\sin x = \underline{A}$, $\sin (x + 180) = -A$, or $\sin x = -\sin (x + 180)$.

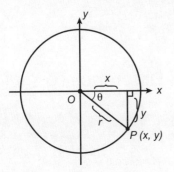

The value of trigonometric functions of quadrantal angles are given in the table.

θ	$\sin\theta$	$\cos\theta$	$\tan\theta$	$\cot\theta$	$\sec\theta$	$\csc\theta$
$0°$	0	1	0	$\pm\infty$	1	$\pm\infty$
$90°$	1	0	$\pm\infty$	0	$\pm\infty$	1
$180°$	0	-1	0	$\pm\infty$	-1	$\pm\infty$
$270°$	-1	0	$\pm\infty$	0	$\pm\infty$	-1

• **EXAMPLES**

1. Find $\sin\theta$ given $A = 30°$.

Obviously, $\theta = 180° + A = 210°$. Since sine is negative in the third quadrant, we have

$$\sin\theta = \sin 210° = -|\sin(210° - 180°)| = -\sin 30° = -\frac{1}{2}.$$

2. If $\sin 2x = -\cos(-x + 9°)$, find x.

$\sin 2x = -\cos(-x + 9°) = \cos(-x + 9° + 180°)$

But $2x - x + 9° + 180° = 90°$

$$x = -99°$$

Basic Identities

$\sin^2\alpha + \cos^2\alpha = 1$

$\tan\alpha = \dfrac{\sin\alpha}{\cos\alpha}$

$\cot\alpha = \dfrac{\cos\alpha}{\sin\alpha} = \dfrac{1}{\tan\alpha}$

$\csc\alpha = \dfrac{1}{\sin\alpha}$

$\sec\alpha = \dfrac{1}{\cos\alpha}$

$1 + \tan^2\alpha = \sec^2\alpha$

$1 + \cot^2\alpha = \csc^2\alpha$

One can find all the trigonometric functions of an acute angle when the value of any one of them is known.

• **EXAMPLES**

Given α is an acute angle and $\csc\alpha = 2$, then

$\sin\alpha = \dfrac{1}{\csc\alpha} = \dfrac{1}{2}$

$\cos^2\alpha + \sin^2\alpha = 1,\ \cos\alpha = \sqrt{1 - \sin^2\alpha}$

$$= \sqrt{1 - \left(\tfrac{1}{2}\right)^2}$$
$$= \sqrt{1 - \tfrac{1}{4}}$$
$$= \frac{\sqrt{3}}{2}$$

$\tan\alpha = \dfrac{\sin\alpha}{\cos\alpha} = \dfrac{\frac{1}{2}}{\frac{\sqrt{3}}{2}} = \dfrac{1}{\sqrt{3}} = \dfrac{\sqrt{3}}{3}$

$\cot\alpha = \dfrac{1}{\tan\alpha} = \sqrt{3}$

$\sec\alpha = \dfrac{1}{\cos\alpha} = \dfrac{1}{\frac{\sqrt{3}}{2}} = \dfrac{2}{\sqrt{3}} = \dfrac{2\sqrt{3}}{3}$

i) If θ is a first quadrant angle, and ϕ is in standard position, then

a) $\sin\theta = \sin\phi$ d) $\cot\theta = \cot\phi$
b) $\cos\theta = \cos\phi$ e) $\sec\theta = \sec\phi$
c) $\tan\theta = \tan\phi$ f) $\csc\theta = \csc\phi$

ii) If θ is a second quadrant angle:

   a) $\sin\theta = \sin\phi$ d) $\cot\theta = -\cot\phi$

   b) $\cos\theta = -\cos\phi$ e) $\sec\theta = -\sec\phi$

   c) $\tan\theta = -\tan\phi$ f) $\csc\theta = \csc\phi$

iii) If θ is a third quadrant angle, then

   a) $\sin\theta = -\sin\phi$ d) $\cot\theta = \cot\phi$

   b) $\cos\theta = -\cos\phi$ e) $\sec\theta = -\sec\phi$

   c) $\tan\theta = \tan\phi$ f) $\csc\theta = -\csc\phi$

iv) If θ is a fourth quadrant angle, then

   a) $\sin\theta = -\sin\phi$ d) $\cot\theta = -\cot\phi$

   b) $\cos\theta = \cos\phi$ e) $\sec\theta = \sec\phi$

   c) $\tan\theta = -\tan\phi$ f) $\csc\theta = -\csc\phi$

Addition and Subtraction Formulas

$$\sin(A \pm B) = \sin A \cos B \pm \cos A \sin B$$

$$\cos(A \pm B) = \cos A \cos B \pm \sin A \sin B$$

$$\tan(A \pm B) = \frac{\tan A \pm \tan B}{1 \pm \tan A \tan B}$$

$$\cot(A \pm B) = \frac{\cot A \cot B \pm 1}{\cot B \pm \cot A}$$

Double-Angle Formulas

$$\sin 2A = 2\sin A \cos A$$
$$\cos 2A = 2\cos^2 A - 1$$
$$= 1 - 2\sin^2 A$$
$$= \cos^2 A - \sin^2 A$$
$$\tan 2A = \frac{2\tan A}{1 - \tan^2 A}$$

Half-Angle Formulas

$$\sin\frac{A}{2} = \pm\frac{\sqrt{1-\cos A}}{2}$$

$$\cos\frac{A}{2} = \pm\frac{\sqrt{1+\cos A}}{2}$$

$$\tan\frac{A}{2} = \pm\sqrt{\frac{1-\cos A}{1+\cos A}}$$
$$= \frac{1-\cos A}{\sin A}$$
$$= \frac{\sin A}{1+\cos A}$$

$$\cot\frac{A}{2} = \pm\sqrt{\frac{1+\cos A}{1-\cos A}} = \frac{1+\cos A}{\sin A} = \frac{\sin A}{1-\cos A}$$

Sum and Difference Formulas

$$\sin\alpha + \sin\beta = 2\sin\left(\frac{\alpha+\beta}{2}\right)\cos\left(\frac{\alpha-\beta}{2}\right)$$

$$\sin\alpha - \sin\beta = 2\cos\left(\frac{\alpha+\beta}{2}\right)\sin\left(\frac{\alpha-\beta}{2}\right)$$

$$\cos\alpha + \cos\beta = 2\cos\left(\frac{\alpha+\beta}{2}\right)\cos\left(\frac{\alpha-\beta}{2}\right)$$

$$\cos\alpha - \cos\beta = -2\sin\left(\frac{\alpha+\beta}{2}\right)\sin\left(\frac{\alpha-\beta}{2}\right)$$

$$\tan\alpha + \tan\beta = \frac{\sin(\alpha+\beta)}{\cos\alpha\cos\beta}$$

$$\tan\alpha \times \tan\beta = \frac{\sin(\alpha-\beta)}{\cos\alpha\cos\beta}$$

Product Formulas of Sines and Cosines

$$\sin A \sin B = \frac{1}{2}[\cos(A-B) - \cos(A+B)]$$

$$\cos A \cos B = \frac{1}{2}[\cos(A+B) + \cos(A-B)]$$

$$\sin A \cos B = \frac{1}{2}[\sin(A+B) + \sin(A-B)]$$

$$\cos A \sin B = \frac{1}{2}[\sin(A+B) + \sin(B-A)]$$

- **EXAMPLE**

If $\sin\alpha = \dfrac{3}{5}$ and $\cos\beta = \dfrac{3}{5}$, find $\cos(\alpha+\beta)$.

Since $\cos(\alpha + \beta) = \cos\alpha\cos\beta - \sin\alpha\sin\beta$, we need to find $\cos\alpha$ and $\sin\beta$. But,

$$\cos\alpha = \sqrt{1-\sin^2\alpha} = \sqrt{1-\tfrac{9}{25}} = \sqrt{\tfrac{16}{25}} = \tfrac{4}{5}$$

$$\sin\beta = \sqrt{1-\cos^2\beta} = \sqrt{1-\tfrac{9}{25}} = \sqrt{\tfrac{16}{25}} = \tfrac{4}{5}$$

So,

$$\cos(\alpha+\beta) = \frac{4}{5}\times\frac{3}{5} - \frac{3}{5}\times\frac{4}{5} = 0$$

Properties and Graphs of Trigonometric Functions

The **sine function** is the graph of $y = \sin x$. Other trigonometric functions are defined similarly.

Sine Function

Cosine Function

Tangent Function

• **EXAMPLE**

Draw one period of the graph for the function $y = 0.5 \sin(4x + \frac{\pi}{6})$ and indicate its amplitude, period, and phase shift.

$$x = 0, y = 0.5 \sin \frac{\pi}{6}$$

$$x = \frac{\pi}{4}, y = 0.5 \sin(\pi + \frac{\pi}{6}) = -0.5 \sin \frac{\pi}{6}$$

$$x = \frac{\pi}{2}, y = 0.5 \sin(2\pi + \frac{\pi}{6}) = 0.5 \sin \frac{\pi}{6}$$

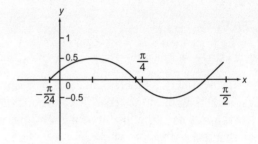

So, amplitude $= \dfrac{1}{2}$

period $= \dfrac{\pi}{2}$

phase shift $= -\dfrac{\pi}{24}$

Inverse Trigonometric Functions

If $-1 < x < 1$, then there are infinitely many angles whose sine is x, as we can see by looking at the graph of the sine function.

Definition:

$\arcsin x =$ the angle between $-\dfrac{\pi}{2}$ and $\dfrac{\pi}{2}$ whose sine is x.

$\operatorname{arccsc} x =$ the angle between $-\dfrac{\pi}{2}$ and $\dfrac{\pi}{2}$ whose cosecant is x.

$\arctan x =$ the angle between $-\dfrac{\pi}{2}$ and $\dfrac{\pi}{2}$ whose tangent is x.

$\arccos x =$ the angle between θ and π whose cosine is x.

$\operatorname{arcsec} x =$ the angle between θ and π whose secant is x.

$\operatorname{arccot} x =$ the angle between θ and π whose cotangent is x.

PROBLEM

Evaluate arcsin $\dfrac{1}{2}$.

SOLUTION

Since $\sin\dfrac{\pi}{6}=\dfrac{1}{2}$, arcsin$\dfrac{1}{2}=\dfrac{\pi}{6}$. The sine function and the arcsine function (abbreviated arcsin or sin^{-1}) are inverses of each other in the sense that the composition of the two functions is the identity function (that is the function that takes x back to x).

$\sin(\arcsin x) = x$

$\arcsin(\sin x) = x$

Periodicity

The **period** of a (repeating) function, f, is the smallest positive number p such that $f(x) = f(x + p)$ for all x.

The period of the tangent and cotangent function is π. This fact is clear from the graphs of the tangent and cotangent functions. Pick any angle, x, on the x-axis, and notice $x + \pi$ has the same tangent as x. The period of the other trigonometric functions is 2π.

If the period of a function f is p, and $g(x) = f(nx)$, then the period of g is p/n.

PROBLEM

What is the period of sin $3x$?

SOLUTION

Since the period of sin x is 2π, the period of sin $3x$ is $\dfrac{2\pi}{3}$.

Use Trigonometry to Solve Right-Triangle Problems

PROBLEM

Determine length of side AC in the figure below.

SOLUTION

1. Determine if sine, cosine, or tangent is needed.

Since the angle and hypotenuse are known, and the opposite side needs to be determined, use sine.

2. Write the ratio for sine.

sin $\angle B$ = opposite side/hypotenuse

3. Using a calculator, find the sine of $\angle B$.

sin $\angle B$ = sin(35°) = 0.574

4. Rewrite the ratio.

0.574 = opposite side/12

5. Multiply both sides of the equation by 12 to determine the length of the opposite side.

6.88 = length of AC

The correct answer is that the length of AC is 6.88.

PROBLEM

Determine the length of side AB in the figure below.

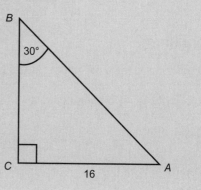

SOLUTION

1. Determine if sine, cosine, or tangent is needed. Since the angle and opposite side are known, and the hypotenuse needs to be determined, use sine.

2. Write the ratio for sine.

sin ∠B = opposite side/hypotenuse

3. Using a calculator, find the sine of ∠B.

sin ∠B = sin(30) = 0.50

4. Rewrite the ratio.

0.50 = 16/hypotenuse

5. Multiply both sides of the equation by the hypotenuse.

hypotenuse(0.50) = 16

6. Divide both sides of the equation by 0.50 to determine the length of the hypotenuse.

hypotenuse = 32

The correct answer is that the length of *AB* is 32.

PROBLEM

A carpenter is trying to determine the height of a flagpole so she can build a new flagpole. The distance from the flagpole to the carpenter is 30 feet. The angle of inclination (the line of sight from where the carpenter is standing to the top of the flagpole) is 30°. See the figure below.

What is the height of the flagpole?

SOLUTION

1. Determine if sine, cosine, or tangent is needed. Since the angle and adjacent side are known, and the opposite side needs to be determined, use tangent.

2. Write the ratio for tangent.

tan ∠B = opposite side/adjacent side

3. Using a calculator, find the tangent of ∠B.

tan ∠B = tan(30) = 0.577

4. Rewrite the ratio. 0.577 = opposite side/30 feet

5. Multiply both sides of the equation by 30 to determine the length of *AC*.

17.31 = length of *AC*.

The correct answer is that the height of the flagpole is 17.31 feet.

PROBLEM

A man is playing billiards with his friend. The cue ball hits the 7 ball at point *C*. The ball travels to point *B* and is deflected toward point *A* (the pocket). If the distance of *CB* is 14 inches, angle *C* is 60°, and ∠B is 90°, what is the length of *AB*? See the figure below.

SOLUTION

1. Determine if sine, cosine, or tangent is neeed. Since the angle and adjacent side are known, and the opposite side needs to be determined, use tangent.

2. Write the ratio for tangent.

$\tan \angle C$ = opposite side/adjacent side

3. Using a calculator, find the tangent of $\angle C$.

$\tan \angle C = \tan(60) = 1.73$

4. Rewrite the ratio.

1.73 = opposite side/14 inches

5. Multiply both sides of the equation by 14 to determine the length of AB.

24.22 = length of AB

The correct answer is that the distance to the pocket is 24.22 inches.

Drill: Trigonometry

1. $\tan^{-1}(-\sqrt{3}) =$

    (A) $-60°$ (C) $30°$

    (B) $60°$ (D) $-30°$

2. Calculate $\dfrac{\sin^{-1}\frac{1}{2}}{\tan^{-1}1}$.

    (A) $\dfrac{1}{2}$ (C) $45°$

    (B) $30°$ (D) $\dfrac{2}{3}$

3. Find $\cos[\arcsin(-1)]$.

    (A) $\dfrac{1}{2}$ (C) 0

    (B) $\dfrac{\sqrt{3}}{2}$ (D) $-\dfrac{\sqrt{3}}{2}$

4. If x is inside $[0, 2\pi]$, one solution for the equation $\sqrt{1+\sin^2 x} = \sqrt{2}\sin x$ is

    (A) $\dfrac{5}{2}\pi$.   (C) $\dfrac{3}{2}\pi$.

    (B) $\dfrac{\pi}{6}$.   (D) $\dfrac{\pi}{2}$.

5. $\sec^2\theta - \tan^2\theta =$

    (A) $\dfrac{4}{5}$ (C) -1

    (B) $\dfrac{1}{2}$ (D) 1

6. $\dfrac{\sin(45° + x) + \sin(45° - x)}{\cos x} =$

    (A) $\sqrt{2}$ (C) $\dfrac{\sqrt{2}}{2}$

    (B) $\tan x$ (D) $\dfrac{\sqrt{2}}{2}\cos x$

7. The amplitude of $y = \dfrac{\sqrt{3}}{3}\sin x + \cos x$ is

    (A) $\dfrac{\sqrt{3}}{2}$.   (C) $\dfrac{\sqrt{3}}{4}$.

    (B) $\dfrac{\sqrt{2}}{2}$ (D) $\dfrac{2\sqrt{3}}{3}$.

8. $\dfrac{\csc x}{2\cos x} =$

    (A) $\cos 3x$ (C) $\sin 2x$

    (B) $\tan 2x$ (D) $\csc 2x$

Answer Key

1. (A)
2. (D)
3. (C)
4. (D)

5. (D)
6. (A)
7. (D)
8. (D)

Detailed Explanations of Answers

1. **(A)**

   Using the table, you will find $\tan^{-1}\left(-\sqrt{3}\right)=60°$ in the 2nd or 4th quadrant.

2. **(D)**

   $$\frac{\sin^{-1}\frac{1}{2}}{\tan^{-1}1}=\frac{30}{45}=\frac{2}{3}$$

3. **(C)**

   $\cos[\arcsin(-1)]=\cos(-90)=0$

4. **(D)**

   $$\left[\sqrt{1+\sin^2 x}\right]^2=\left[\sqrt{2}\sin x\right]^2\Rightarrow 1+\sin^2 x=2\sin^2 x$$

   Subtract $-2\sin^2 x$:

   $$\begin{array}{rcc} & -2\sin^2 x & -2\sin^2 x \\ 1-\sin^2 x & = & 0 \\ \cos^2 x & = & 0 \end{array}$$

   $\cos x=0$ at $\dfrac{\pi}{2}$ or $\dfrac{3}{2}\pi$

   $\dfrac{3}{2}\pi$ won't satisfy the original equation

   So $\dfrac{\pi}{2}$ is the answer.

5. **(D)**

   $\sec^2\theta-\tan^2\theta=(\tan^2\theta+1)-\tan^2\theta=1$

6. **(A)**

   $$\frac{\sin(45°+x)+\sin(45°-x)}{\cos x}$$

   $$=\frac{\sin 45\cos x+\cos 45\sin x+\sin 45\cos x-\cos 45\sin x}{\cos x}$$

   $$=\frac{2\sin 45\cos x}{\cos x}$$

   $$=2\sin 45$$

   $$=2\left(\frac{\sqrt{2}}{2}\right)$$

   $$=\sqrt{2}$$

7. **(D)**

   $$y=\frac{\sqrt{3}}{3}\sin x+\cos x$$

   Test reference angles 0, 30, 45, 60, and 90 to determine that 30 is the greatest

   $$\frac{\sqrt{3}}{3}\sin(30)+\cos(30)=\frac{\sqrt{3}}{3}\left(\frac{1}{2}\right)+\left(\frac{\sqrt{3}}{2}\right)$$

   $$=\frac{\sqrt{3}}{6}+\frac{\sqrt{3}}{2}$$

   $$=\frac{\sqrt{3}}{6}+\frac{3\sqrt{3}}{6}$$

   $$=\frac{4\sqrt{3}}{6}$$

   $$=\frac{2\sqrt{3}}{3}$$

8. **(D)**

   $$\frac{\csc x}{2\cos x}=\frac{\frac{1}{\sin x}}{2\cos x}=\frac{1}{2\sin x\cos x}=\frac{1}{\sin 2x}=\csc 2x$$

Competency 6:
Knowledge of
Statistics

Data Description:
Graphs

Repeated measurements yield data, which must be organized according to some principle. The data should be arranged in such a way that each observation can fall into one, and only one, category. A simple graphical method of presenting data is the pie chart, which is a circle divided into parts that represent categories.

• **EXAMPLE**

2006 Budget

38% came from individual income taxes

28% from social insurance receipts

13% from corporate income taxes

12% from borrowing

5% from excise taxes

4% other

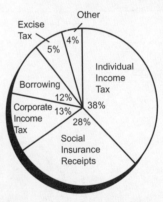

This data can also be presented in the form of a bar chart or bar graph.

• **EXAMPLE**

The population of the United States for the years 1860 and 1960 is shown in the table below,

Year	1860	1870	1880	1890	1900	1910
Population in millions	31.4	39.8	50.2	62.9	76.0	92.0
Year	1920	1930	1940	1950	1960	
Population in millions	105.7	122.8	131.7	151.1	179.3	

in this graph,

and in this bar chart.

(−3, 4) (−2, 0) (−1, −2) (0, −2) (1, 0) (2, 4) (3, 10)

The curve shown is called a parabola. The general equation for a parabola is

$$y = ax^2 + bx + c, \ a \neq 0$$

where *a*, *b*, and *c* are constants.

PROBLEM

• **EXAMPLE**

A quadratic function is given by

$$y = x^2 + x - 2$$

We compute the values of *y* corresponding to various values of *x*.

x	−3	−2	−1	0	1	2	3
y	4	0	−2	−2	0	4	10

From this table, the points of the graph are obtained:

Twenty students are enrolled in the foreign language department, and their major fields are as follows: Spanish, Spanish, French, Italian, French, Spanish, German, German, Russian, Russian, French, German, German, German, Spanish, Russian, German, Italian, German, and Spanish.

(a) Make a frequency distribution table.

(b) Make a frequency bar graph.

SOLUTION

(a) The frequency distribution table is constructed by writing down the major field and next to it the number of students.

Major Field	Number of Students
German	7
Russian	3
Spanish	5
French	3
Italian	2
Total	20

(b) A bar graph follows:

In the bar graph, the fields are listed and spaced evenly along the horizontal axis. Each specified field is represented by a rectangle, and all have the same width. The height of each, identified by a number on the vertical axis, corresponds to the frequency of that field.

A **box-and-whiskers** plot is a graph that displays five statistics. A minimum score, a maximum score, and three percentiles. A percentile value for a score tells you the percentage of scores lower than it. The beginning of the box is the score at the 25th percentile. The end of the box represents the 75th percentile. The score inside of the box is the median, or the score at the 50th percentile. Attached to the box you will find two whiskers. The score at the end of the left whisker is the minimum score. The score at the end of the right whisker is the maximum score.

• EXAMPLE

In the box-and-whiskers plot below, the minimum score is 70, the score at the 25th percentile is 78, the median score is 82, the score at the 75th percentile is 90, and the maximum score is 94.

Scores on a Test

PROBLEM

Using the box-and-whiskers plot above, what was the median score on the geography test?

SOLUTION

The median score is 84. On a box-and-whiskers plot, the median score is the score on the inside of the box.

• EXAMPLE

A **stem-and-leaf plot** is a way of displaying scores in groups. A stem-and-leaf plot gives you a picture of the scores, as well as the actual numbers themselves in a compact form. In this type of plot, a score is broken into a stem and a leaf. The leaf consists of the smallest digit and the stem consists of the remaining larger digits.

Task: Create a stem and leaf plot using the following scores.

Scores: 64, 48, 61, 81, 63, 59, 70, 54, 76, 61, 55, 31

Solution: The first step is to take these scores and create a set of "ranked ordered scores," ordering the scores from smallest to largest. Notice that the minimum score is 31, while the maximum score is 81.

Ranked Ordered Scores: 31, 48, 54, 55, 59, 61, 61, 63, 64, 70, 76, 81

The second step is to list the range of scores for the stems in a column. The stem of our smallest score (31) is 3, and that of our largest score (81) is 8. List all of the whole numbers between 3 and 8.

The third step is to put the leaves on the stems. Take each score, one at a time and put the last digit in a column next to its stem. For example, the last digit of 31 is 1, so put a 1 next to its stem of 3. The last digit of 48 is 8, so put an 8 next to its stem of 4. Do this for the remaining scores.

Stems	Leaves
8	1
7	0 6
6	1 1 3 4
5	4 5 9
4	8
3	1

A stem-and-leaf plot gives you a picture of how the scores are grouped so that you can begin to understand their meaning. In this example, you can see that 4 people got a score in the 60s. You can also see that the high score was 81, and the low score war 31.

PROBLEM

Stems	Leaves
6	5
5	3 6
4	0 1 7
3	2 9
2	4

The stem-and-leaf plot above was created using what set of scores?

SOLUTION

In this stem-and-leaf plot, the stems are the first digit, and the leaves are the remaining digits. Starting from the bottom, the first score is 24, the second score is 32, then comes 39, 40, 41, 53, 56, and 65.

• EXAMPLE

A **scatter-plot** is a graph that shows the relationship between two variables. A scatter-plot is a set of (x, y)

coordinates. Each coordinate is a point on the graph. x represents a value of one variable, while y represents the value of another variable. Remember, a variable is just a measurement that can take on more than one value. A scatter-plot is useful because in one picture you can see if there is a relationship between two variables. It has been said mat, "A picture is worth a thousand words." Likewise, "A graph is worth a thousand numbers."

Given: Variable x represents Grade level. Variable y represents Hours of Homework each week.

Task: Using the data below, construct a scatter-plot.

Question: What is the relationship between these two variables?

x	**Grade Level**	1	2	3	4	5	6	7	8	9	10	11	12
y	**Hours of Homework**	2	3	3	6	4	10	7	10	12	9	14	15

Answer: You can think of these two variables as one set of (x, y) coordinates on a graph. Remember, a coordinate is just a point. Graph the following points: (1, 2), (2, 3), (3, 3), (4, 6), (5, 4), (6, 10), (7, 7), (8, 10), (9, 12), (10, 9), (11, 14), and (12, 15). This graph shows that as grade level increases, the number of homework hours per week tends to increase.

Scatterplot

A statistic called **correlation** tells you if two measurements go together along a straight line. A scatter-plot is one way of looking at correlation. There are three different types of correlation.

POSITIVE CORRELATION

As one measurement increases, the other measurement also increases.

ZERO CORRELATION

The two measurements are not related to each other along a straight line.

NEGATIVE CORRELATION

As one measurement increases, the other measurement decreases.

Types of Frequency Curves

In applications we find that most of the frequency curves fall within one of the categories listed.

1. One of the most popular is the bell-shaped or symmetrical frequency curve.

Bell-shaped or Symmetrical

Note that observations equally distant from the maximum have the same frequency. The normal curve has a symmetrical frequency curve.

2. The U-shaped curve has maxima at both ends.

U-shaped

3. A curve can also be skewed to one side. Askew to the left is when the slope to the right of the maximum is steeper than the slope to the left. The opposite holds for the frequency curve skewed to the right.

Skewed to the left (negative skew)   Skewed to the right (positive skew)

4. A J-shaped curve has a maximum at one end.

J-shaped

5. A multimodal (bimodal) frequency curve has two or more maxima.

Multimodal

PROBLEM

What are two ways to describe the form of a frequency distribution? How would the following distributions be described?

(a)   (b)

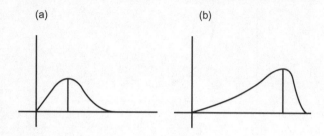

SOLUTION

The form of a frequency distribution can be described by its departure from symmetry or skewness and its degree of peakedness or kurtosis.

If the few extreme values are higher than most of the others, we say that the distribution is "positively skewed" or "skewed" to the right.

If the few extreme values are lower than most of the others, we say that the distribution is "negatively skewed" or "skewed" to the left.

(a) This distribution has extreme values in the upper half of the curve and is skewed to the right or positively skewed.

(b) The extreme values of this distribution are in the lower half of the curve. Thus, the distribution is negatively skewed or skewed to the left.

Numerical Methods of Describing Data

Introduction

Once we have a sufficient number of measurements, it is easy to find the frequency distribution. Graphic methods, however, are very often impractical or difficult to convey.

To remedy the situation, one can use a few numbers that describe the frequency distribution without drawing a real graph. Such numbers are called numerical descriptive measures, and each one describes a certain aspect of the frequency distribution. None of them yields the exact shape of the frequency distribution. Rather, they give us some notion of the general shape of the whole graph or parts of it.

For example, saying that somebody is 6'4" and weighs 250 lbs. does not describe the person in detail, but it does give us the general idea of a stout man.

It is important to describe the center of the distribution of measurements as well as how the measurements behave about the center of the distribution. For that purpose, we define central tendency and variability. In practical applications, we deal with one of two essentially different situations:

1. The measurements are gathered about the whole population.

    Numerical descriptive measures for a population are called **parameters.**

2. The measurements are gathered about the sample. Numerical descriptive measures for a sample are called **statistics.**

If we only have statistics, we are not able to calculate the values of parameters. But, using statistics, we can make reasonable estimates of parameters that describe the whole population. The most popular mathematical means of describing frequency distribution is an average. An **average** is a value that is representative or typical of a set of measurements.

Usually, averages are called measures of central tendency. We will be using different kinds of averages, such as the arithmetic mean, the geometric mean, and the harmonic mean. A different average should be applied depending on the data, the purpose, and the required accuracy.

Notation and Definitions of Means

By

$$x_1, x_2, \ldots, x_n$$

we denote the measurements observed in a sample of size n. The letter i in x_i is called a subscript or index. It stands for any of the numbers $1, 2, \ldots, n$.

We will be using the summation notation. The symbol

$$\sum_{i=1}^{n} x_i$$

denotes the sum of all x_i's, that is,

$$\sum_{i=1}^{n} x_i = x_1 + x_2 + \ldots + x_{n-1} + x_n$$

- **EXAMPLE**

$$\sum_{i=1}^{4} x_i y_i = x_1 y_1 + x_2 y_2 + x_3 y_3 + x_4 y_4$$

- **EXAMPLE**

Let a be a constant. Then

$$\sum_{k=1}^{n} a x_k = a x_1 + a x_2 + \ldots + a x_n$$
$$= a(x_1 + x_2 + \ldots + x_n)$$
$$= a \sum_{k=1}^{n} x_k$$

In general,

$$\sum a x_k = a \sum x_k$$

and

$$\sum (ax + by) = a \sum x + b \sum y$$

Often, when no confusion can arise, we write $\sum_{k} x_k$ instead of $\sum_{k=1}^{n} x_k$.

Definition of Arithmetic Mean

The arithmetic mean, or mean, of a set of measurements is the sum of the measurements divided by the total number of measurements.

The arithmetic mean of a set of numbers x_1, x_2, . . ., x_n is denoted by $\bar{x}$ (read "x bar").

$$\bar{x} = \frac{\sum_{i=1}^{n} x_1}{n} = \frac{x_1 + x_2 + \ldots + x_n}{n}$$

- **EXAMPLE**

The arithmetic mean of the numbers 3, 7, 1, 24, 11, and 32 is

$$\bar{x} = \frac{3 + 7 + 1 + 24 + 11 + 32}{6} = 13$$

- **EXAMPLE**

Let $f_1, f_2, \ldots, f_n$ be the frequencies of the numbers x_1, $x_2, \ldots, x_n$ (i.e., number x_i occurs f_i times). The arithmetic mean is

$$\bar{x} = \frac{f_1 x_1 + f_2 x_2 + \ldots + f_n x_n}{f_1 + f_2 + \ldots + f_n} = \frac{\sum_{i=1}^{n} f_i x_i}{\sum_{i=1}^{n} f_i}$$
$$= \frac{\sum fx}{\sum f}.$$

Note that the total frequency, that is, the total number of cases, is $\sum_{i=1}^{n} f_i$.

- **EXAMPLE**

If the measurements 3, 7, 2, 8, 0, and 4 occur with frequencies 3, 2, 1, 5, 10, and 6, respectively, then the arithmetic mean is

$$\bar{x} = \frac{3 \times 3 + 7 \times 2 + 2 \times 1 + 8 \times 5 + 0 \times 10 + 4 \times 6}{3 + 2 + 1 + 5 + 10 + 6} \approx 3.3$$

Keep in mind that the arithmetic mean is strongly affected by extreme values.

- **EXAMPLE**

Consider four workers whose annual salaries are $2,500, $3,200, $3,700, and $48,000. The arithmetic mean of their salaries is

$$\frac{\$57,400}{4} = \$14,350$$

The figure $14,350 can hardly represent the typical annual salary of the four workers.

- **EXAMPLE**

The deviation d_i of x_i from its mean $\bar{x}$ is defined to be

$$d_i = x_i - \bar{x}$$

The sum of the deviations of $x_1, x_2, ..., x_n$ from their mean $\bar{x}$ is equal to zero. Indeed,

$$\sum_{i=1}^{n} d_1 = \sum_{i=1}^{n} (x_i - \bar{x}) = 0$$

Thus,

$$\sum_{i=1}^{n} (x_i - \bar{x}) = \sum_{i=1}^{n} x_i - n\bar{x} = \sum x_i - n\frac{\sum x_i}{n}$$

$$= \sum x_i - \sum x_i = 0.$$

- **EXAMPLE**

If $z_1 = x_1 + y_1, ..., z_n = x_n + y_n$, then $\bar{z} = \bar{x} + \bar{y}$. Indeed,

$$\bar{x} = \frac{\sum x}{n}, \bar{y} = \frac{\sum y}{n}, \text{ and } \bar{z} + \frac{\sum z}{n}.$$

We have

$$\bar{z} = \frac{\sum z}{n} = \frac{\sum (x+y)}{n} = \frac{\sum x}{n} + \frac{\sum y}{n} = \bar{x} + \bar{y}.$$

The arithmetic mean plays an important role in statistical inference.

We will be using different symbols for the sample mean and the population mean. The population mean is denoted by μ, and the sample mean is denoted by $\bar{x}$. The sample mean $\bar{x}$ will be used to make inferences about the corresponding population mean μ.

- **EXAMPLE**

Suppose a bank has 500 savings accounts. We pick a sample of 12 accounts. The balance on each account in dollars is

657	284	51
215	73	327
65	412	218
539	225	195

The sample mean $\bar{x}$ is

$$\bar{x} = \frac{\sum_{i=1}^{12} x_i}{12} = \$271.75$$

The average amount of money for the of 12 sampled accounts is \$271.75. Using this information, we estimate the total amount of money in the bank to be

$$\$271.25 \times 500 = \$135{,}875.$$

PROBLEM

The following measurements were taken by an antique dealer as he weighed to the nearest pound his prized collection of anvils. The weights were 84, 92, 37, 50, 50, 84, 40, and 98. What was the mean weight of the anvils?

SOLUTION

The average or mean weight of the anvils is

$$\bar{x} = \frac{\text{sum of observations}}{\text{number of observations}}$$

$$= \frac{84 + 92 + 37 + 50 + 50 + 84 + 40 + 98}{8}$$

$$= \frac{535}{8} = 66.88 \cong 67 \text{ pounds}$$

An alternate way to compute the sample mean is to rearrange the terms in the numerator, grouping the numbers that are the same. Thus,

$$\bar{x} = \frac{(84 + 84) + (50 + 50) + 37 + 40 + 90 + 98}{8}$$

We see that we can express the mean in terms of the frequency of observations. The frequency of an observation is the number of times a number appears in a sample.

$$\bar{x} = \frac{2(84) + 2(50) + 37 + 40 + 90 + 98}{8}$$

The observations 84 and 50 appear in the sample twice, and thus each observation has frequency 2.

PROBLEM

> The numbers 4, 2, 7, and 9 occur with frequencies 2, 3, 11, and 4, respectively. Find the arithmetic mean.

SOLUTION

To find the arithmetic mean, $\bar{x}$, multiply each different number by its associated frequency. Add these products, then divide by the total number of numbers.

$$\bar{x} = \left[(4)(2) + (2)(3) + (7)(11) + (9)(4)\right] \div 20$$
$$= (8 + 6 + 77 + 36) \div 20$$
$$= 127 \div 20 = 6.35$$

All means can also be computed for the grouped data, that is, when data are presented in a frequency distribution. Then, all values within a given class interval are considered to be equal to the class mark, or midpoint, of the interval.

Measures of Central Tendency

Definition of the Mode

The mode of a set of numbers is that value which occurs most often (with the highest frequency).

Observe that the mode may not exist. Also, if the mode exists, it may not be unique. For example, for the numbers 1, 1, 2, and 2, the mode is not unique.

• EXAMPLE

The set of numbers 2, 2, 4, 7, 9, 9, 13, 13, 13, 26, and 29 has mode 13.

The set of numbers that has two or more modes is called **bimodal.**

For grouped data – data presented in the form of a frequency table – we do not know the actual measurements, only how many measurements fall into each interval. In such a case, the mode is the midpoint of the class interval with the highest frequency.

Note that the mode can also measure popularity. In this sense, we can determine the most popular model of car or the most popular actor.

• EXAMPLE

One can compute the mode from a histogram or frequency distribution.

The shaded area indicates the modal class, that is, the class containing the mode.

$$Mode = L + c\left[\frac{\Delta_1}{\Delta_1 + \Delta_2}\right]$$

where

L is the lower class boundary of the modal class

c is the size of the modal class interval

Δ_1 is the excess of the modal frequency over the frequency of the next lower class

Δ_2 is the excess of the modal frequency over the frequency of the next higher class

PROBLEM

> Find the mode of the sample 14, 19, 16, 21, 18, 19, 24, 15, and 19.

SOLUTION

The mode is another measure of central tendency in a data set. It is the observation or observations that occur with the greatest frequency. The number 19 is observed three times in this sample, and no other observation appears as frequently. The mode of this sample is therefore 19.

PROBLEM

Find the mode or modes of the sample 6, 7, 7, 3, 8, 5, 3, and 9.

SOLUTION

In this sample the numbers 7 and 3 both appear twice. There are no other observations that appear as frequently as these two. Therefore, 3 and 7 are the modes of this sample. The sample is called "bimodal."

PROBLEM

Find the mode of the sample 14, 16, 21, 19, 18, 24, and 17.

SOLUTION

In this sample all the numbers occur with the same frequency. There is no single number that is observed more frequently than any other. Thus, there is no mode or all observations are modes. The mode is not a useful concept here.

Definition of Median

The median of a set of numbers is defined as the middle value when the numbers are arranged in order of magnitude.

Usually, the median is used to measure the midpoint of a large set of numbers. For example, we can talk about the median age of people getting married. Here, the median reflects the central value of the data for a large set of measurements. For small sets of numbers, we use the following conventions:

- For an odd number of measurements, the median is the middle value.

- For an even number of measurements, the median is the average of the two middle values.

In both cases, the numbers have to be arranged in order of magnitude.

• EXAMPLE

The scores of a test are 78, 79, 83, 83, 87, 92, and 95. Hence, the median is 83.

• EXAMPLE

The median of the set of numbers 21, 25, 29, 33, 44, and 47 is $\frac{29+33}{2} = 31$.

It is more difficult to compute the median for grouped data. The exact value of the measurements is not known; hence, we know only that the median is located in a particular class interval. The problem is where to place the median within this interval.

For grouped data, the median obtained by interpolation is given by

$$\text{Median} = L + \frac{c}{f_{\text{median}}}\left(\frac{n}{2} - \left(\sum f\right)_{\text{cum}}\right)$$

where
L = the lower class limit of the interval that contains the median

c = the size of the median class interval

f_{median} = frequency of the median class

n = the total frequency

$\left(\sum f\right)_{\text{cum}}$ = the sum of frequencies (cumulative frequency) for all classes before the median class

PROBLEM

Find the median of the sample 34, 29, 26, 37, and 31.

SOLUTION

The median, a measure of central tendency, is the middle number. The number of observations that lie above the median is the same as the number of observations that lie below it.

Arranged in order we have 26, 29, 31, 34, and 37. The number of observations is odd, and thus the median is 31. Note that there are two numbers in the sample above 31 and two below 31.

PROBLEM

Find the median of the sample 34, 29, 26, 37, 31, and 34.

SOLUTION

The sample arranged in order is 26, 29, 31, 34, 34, and 37. The number of observations is even and thus the median, or middle number, is chosen halfway between the third and fourth numbers. In this case, the median is

$$\frac{31+34}{2} = 32.5$$

• EXAMPLE

The weight of 50 men is depicted in the table below in the form of frequency distribution.

Weight	Frequency
115 – 121	2
122 – 128	3
129 – 135	13
136 – 142	15
143 – 149	9
150 – 156	5
157 – 163	3
TOTAL	50

Class 136 – 142 has the highest frequency.

The mode is the midpoint of the class interval with the highest frequency.

$$Mode = \frac{135.5 + 142.5}{2} = 139$$

We can also use the formula

$$Mode = L + c\left(\frac{\Delta_1}{\Delta_1 + \Delta_2}\right)$$

where L = 135.5

c = 7

Δ_1 = 2 (15 – 13 = 2)

Δ_2 = 6 (15 – 9 = 6)

$$Mode = 135.5 + 7 \times \frac{2}{2+6} = 137.25$$

The median is located in class 136 – 142.

We have

$$Median = L + \frac{c}{f_{median}}\left[\frac{n}{2} - \left[\sum f\right]_{cum}\right]$$

where L = 135.5

c = 7

f_{median} = 15

n = 50

$\left(\sum f\right)_{cum}$ = 2 + 3 + 13 = 18

Hence,

$$Median = 135.5 + \frac{7}{15}\left[\frac{50}{2} - 18\right] = 138.77$$

To compute the arithmetic mean for grouped data, we compute midpoint x_i of each of the intervals and use the formula

$$\bar{x} = \frac{\sum\limits_{i=1}^{n} f_i x_i}{\sum\limits_{i=1}^{n} f_i}$$

We have

$$\bar{x} = \frac{118 \times 2 + 125 \times 3 + 132 \times 13 + 139 \times 15 + 146 \times 9 + 153 \times 5 + 160 \times 3}{50}$$

$$= 139.42$$

For symmetrical curves, the mean, mode, and median all coincide.

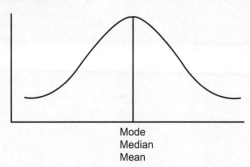

Mode
Median
Mean

For skewed distributions, we have the following.

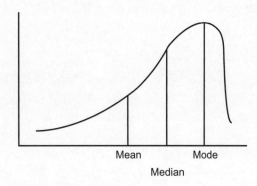

Mean   Mode
Median

The distribution is skewed to the left

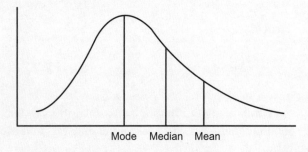

Mode   Median   Mean

The distribution is skewed to the right.

Class Boundaries	Class Weights	Frequencies
58.5 – 61.5	60	4
61.5 – 64.5	63	8
64.5 – 67.5	66	12
67.5 – 70.5	69	13
70.5 – 73.5	72	21
73.5 – 76.5	75	15
76.5 – 79.5	78	12
79.5 – 82.5	81	9
82.5 – 85.5	84	4
85.5 – 88.5	87	2

PROBLEM

Find the median weight from the previous table.

SOLUTION

There are 100 observations in the sample. The median will be the 50th observation. When using an even-numbered sample of grouped data, the convention is to call the $\frac{n}{2}$th observation the median. There are 37 observations in the first four intervals, and the first five intervals contain 58 observations. The 50th observation is in the fifth class interval.

We use the technique of linear interpolation to estimate the position of the 50th observation within the class interval.

The width of the fifth class is three, and there are 21 observations in the class. To interpolate we imagine that each observation takes up $\frac{3}{21}$ units of the interval. There are 37 observations in the first four intervals, and thus the 13th observation in the fifth class will be the median. This 13th observation will be approximately $13\left(\frac{3}{21}\right)$ units from the lower boundary of the fifth class interval. The median is thus the lower boundary of the fifth class plus $13\left(\frac{3}{21}\right)$ or

$$\text{median} = 70.5 + \frac{13}{7} = 72.36.$$

PROBLEM

A sample of drivers involved in motor vehicle accidents was categorized by age. The results appear as:

Age	Number of Accidents
16 – 25	28
26 – 35	13
36 – 45	12

46 – 55	8
56 – 65	19
66 – 75	20

What is the value of the median?

SOLUTION

We seek the $\frac{100}{2} = 50^{th}$ number, which appears in the third class (36 – 45).

The total number of accidents is 100. The median is the $\frac{100}{2} = 50^{th}$ number when the numbers are arranged in ascending order. (In this case, we have intervals of numbers instead of just numbers.) The two intervals 16 – 25 and 26 – 35 consist of 41 count. We need nine numbers from the interval 36 – 45. Use the lower boundary of this interval 36 – 45, which is 35.5, and add $\frac{9}{12}$ of the width of the interval (10).

Then

$$35.5 + \frac{9}{12}(10) = 43$$

Measures of Variability

Range and Percentiles

The degree to which numerical data tend to spread about an average value is called the **variation** or **dispersion** of the data. We shall define various measures of dispersion.

The simplest measure of data variation is the range.

Definition of Range

The **range** of a set of numbers is defined to be the difference between the largest and the smallest number of the set. For grouped data, the range is the difference between the upper limit of the last interval and the lower limit of the first interval.

• **EXAMPLE**

The range of the numbers 3, 6, 21, 24, and 38 is $38 – 3 = 35$.

Definition of Percentiles

The nth percentile of a set of numbers arranged in order of magnitude is that value which has $n\%$ of the numbers below it and $(100 – n)\%$ above it.

• **EXAMPLE**

The 70th percentile of a set of numbers

Percentiles are often used to describe the results of achievement tests. For example, someone graduates in the top 10% of the class. Frequently used percentiles are the 25th, 50th and 75th percentiles, which are called the lower quartile, the middle quartile (median), and the upper quartile, respectively.

Definition of Interquartile Range

The interquartile range, abbreviated IQR, of a set of numbers is the difference between the upper and lower quartiles.

Now, we shall introduce an important concept of deviation.

The deviation of a number x from its mean $\bar{x}$ is defined to be

$$x - \bar{x}$$

Using deviations, we can construct many different measures of variability.

Observe that the mean deviation for any set of measurements is always zero. Indeed, let $x_1, x_2, \ldots, x_n$ be measurements. Their mean is given by

$$\bar{x} = \frac{\sum x_i}{n}$$

The deviations are $x_1 - \bar{x}, x_2 - \bar{x}, \ldots, x_n - \bar{x}$, and their mean is equal to

$$\frac{\sum_{i=1}^{n}(x_i - \bar{x})}{n} = \frac{\sum x_i}{n} - \bar{x} = 0$$

PROBLEM

> Find the range of the sample composed of the observations 33, 53, 35, 37, and 49.

SOLUTION

The range is a measure of the dispersion of the sample and is defined to be the difference between the largest and smallest observations.

In our sample, the largest observation is 53 and the smallest is 33. The difference is $53 - 33 = 20$, and the range is 20.

The range is not a very satisfactory measure of dispersion as it involves only two of the observations in the sample.

PROBLEM

> In a sample of data, the 75th percentile is the number 23. If the interquartile range is 10, what number represents the 25th percentile?

SOLUTION

The interquartile range = the difference between the 75th percentile and the 25th percentile. If $x = 25$th percentile, we have $23 - x = 10$, so $x = 13$.

Definition of Standard Deviation

The standard deviation of a set $x_1, x_2, \ldots, x_n$ of n numbers is defined by

$$s = \sqrt{\frac{\sum_{i=1}^{n}(x_i - \bar{x})^2}{n}} = \sqrt{\overline{(x - \bar{x})^2}}$$

The sample standard deviation is denoted by s, while the corresponding population standard deviation is denoted by σ.

For grouped data, we use the modified formula for standard deviation. Let the frequencies of the numbers $x_1, x_2, \ldots, x_n$ be $f_1, f_2, \ldots, f_n$, respectively. Then,

$$s = \sqrt{\frac{\sum f_i(x_i - \bar{x})^2}{\sum f_i}} = \sqrt{\frac{\sum f(x - \bar{x})^2}{\sum f}}$$

Often, in the definition of the standard deviation, the denominator is not n but $n - 1$. For large values of n, the difference between the two definitions is negligible.

Definition of Variance

The variance of a set of measurements is defined as the square of the standard deviation. Thus,

$$s^2 = \frac{\sum_{i=1}^{n}(x_i - \bar{x})^2}{n - 1}$$

or

$$s^2 = \frac{\sum_{i=1}^{n}f_i(x_i - \bar{x})^2}{\sum_{i=1}^{n}f_i}$$

Usually, the variance of the sample is denoted by s^2, and the corresponding population variance is denoted by σ^2.

• **EXAMPLE**

A simple manual task was given to six children, and the time each child took to complete the task was measured. Results are shown in the table.

x_i	$x_i - \bar{x}$	$(x_i - \bar{x})^2$
12	2.5	6.25
9	−0.5	0.25
11	1.5	2.25
6	−3.5	12.25
10	0.5	0.25
9	−0.5	0.25
Total 57	0	21.5

For this sample, we shall find the standard deviation and variance.

The average $\bar{x}$ is 9.5.

$$\bar{x} = 9.5$$

The standard deviation is

$$s^2 = \sqrt{\frac{21.5}{5}} = 2.07$$

and the variance is

$$s^2 = 4.3$$

PROBLEM

A couple has six children whose ages are 6, 8, 10, 12, 14, and 16. Find the variance in ages.

SOLUTION

The variance in ages is a measure of the spread or dispersion of ages about the sample mean.

To compute the variance, we first calculate the sample mean.

$$\bar{X} = \frac{\sum X_i}{n} = \frac{\text{sum of observations}}{\text{number of observations}}$$

$$= \frac{6 + 8 + 10 + 12 + 14 + 16}{6} = \frac{66}{6} = 11$$

The variance is defined to be

$$s^2 = \frac{\sum_{i=1}^{n}(X_i - \bar{X})^2}{n-1}$$

$$= \frac{(6-11)^2 + (8-11)^2 + (10-11)^2 + (12-11)^2 + (14-11)^2 + (16-11)^2}{5}$$

$$= \frac{25 + 9 + 1 + 1 + 9 + 25}{5} = \frac{70}{5} = 14$$

Sampling

Sample quantities, such as sample mean, deviation, etc., are called **sample statistics** or **statistics**. Based on these quantities, we estimate the corresponding quantities for population, which are called **population parameters** or **parameters**. For two different samples, the difference between sample statistics can be due to chance variation or some significant factor. The latter case should be investigated, and possible mistakes corrected. The statistical inference is a study of inferences made concerning a population and based on the samples drawn from it.

Probability theory evaluates the accuracy of such inferences. The most important initial step is the choice of samples that are representative of a population. The methods of sampling are called the **design** of the experiment. One of the most widely used methods is random sampling.

Random Sampling

A sample of n measurements chosen from a population N $(N > n)$ is said to be a random sample if every different sample of the same size n from the population has an equal probability of being selected.

One way of obtaining a random sample is to assign a number to each member of the population. The population becomes a set of numbers. Then, using the random number table, we can choose a sample of desired size.

- **EXAMPLE**

Suppose 1,000 voters are registered and eligible to vote in an upcoming election. To conduct a poll, you need a sample of 50 persons, so to each voter you assign a number between one and 1,000. Then, using the random number table or a computer program, you choose at random 50 numbers, which are 50 voters. This is your required sample.

Sampling With and Without Replacement

From a bag containing ten numbers from 1 to 10, we have to draw three numbers. As the first step, we draw a number. Now, we have the choice of replacing or not replacing the number in the bag. If we replace the number, then this number can come up again. If the number is not replaced, then it can come up only once.

Sampling where each element of a population may be chosen more than once (i.e., where the chosen element is replaced) is called **sampling with replacement**. Sampling without replacement takes place when each element of a population can be chosen only once.

Remember that populations can be finite or infinite.

- **EXAMPLE**

A bag contains ten numbers. We choose two numbers without replacement. This is sampling from a finite population.

- **EXAMPLE**

A coin is tossed ten times and the number of tails is counted. This is sampling from an infinite population.

PROBLEM

The following sampling procedure is to be classified as producing a random sample or as producing a biased sample. Decide whether the procedure is random or biased.

In order to solve a particular problem, an investigator selects 100 people, each of which will provide 5 scores. The investigator will then take the average of each set of scores. This will yield 100 averages. Is this sample of average scores a random sample?

SOLUTION

A sample must meet the following conditions in order to be random:

(1) Equal Chance. A sample meets the condition of equal chance if it is selected in such a way that every observation in the entire population has an equal chance of being included in the sample.

(2) Independence. A sample meets this condition when the selection of any single observation does not affect the chances for selection of any other.

Samples that are not random are called biased.

The 100 elements are now independent. When repeated measures can be converted to a single score, so that each individual observed contributes just one summary observation (such as an average), the independence condition is met. Use of an average often helps to reduce the effects of chance variation within an individual's performance. Also, any observation would have an equal chance of being chosen. The sample is random.

PROBLEM

A wheat researcher is studying the yield of a certain variety of wheat in the state of Colorado. She has at her disposal five farms scattered throughout the state on which she can plant the wheat and observe the yield. Describe the sample and the target population. Under what conditions will this be a random sample?

SOLUTION

The sample consists of the wheat yields on the five farms. The target population consists of the yields of wheat on every farm in the state. This sample will be random if (1) every farm in the state has an equal chance of being selected and (2) the selection of any particular farm is independent of the selection of any other farm.

Sampling Distributions

A population is given from which we draw samples of size n, with or without replacement. For each sample, we compute a statistic, such as the mean, standard deviation, variance, etc. These numbers will depend on the sample, and they will vary from sample to sample. In this way, we obtain a distribution of the statistic which is called the **sampling distribution**.

For example, if for each sample we measure its mean, then the distribution obtained is the sampling distribution of means. We obtain the sampling distributions of variances, standard deviations, medians, etc. in the same way.

Correlation

Regression or estimation enables us to estimate one variable (the dependent variable) from one or more independent variables.

Correlation establishes the degree of relationship between variables. It answers the question: how well does a given equation describe or explain the relationship between independent and dependent variables?

Perfect Correlation

If all values of the variables fit the equation without errors, we say that the variables are perfectly correlated.

The area of a square S is in perfect correlation to its side d that

$$S = d^2.$$

Tossing two coins, we record the result for each coin. Assuming that the coins are fair, there is no relationship between the results for each coin, that is, they are uncorrelated.

Between perfectly correlated and uncorrelated situations, there are situations with some degree of correlation. The heights and weights of people show some correlation. We let x represent one variable (height) and let y represent the other variable (weight). We then try to determine the correlation between x and y.

Simple correlation and simple regression occur when only two variables are involved. When more than two variables are involved, we speak of multiple correlation.

Correlation Coefficient

The degree of relationship between two variables, x and y, is described by the correlation coefficient. If n observations are given

$$(x_i, y_i) \; i = 1, 2, \ldots, n$$

we can compute the sample correlation coefficient r.

$$r = \frac{\sum (x - \bar{x})(y - \bar{y})}{\sqrt{\sum (x - \bar{x})^2 \sum (y - \bar{y})^2}}$$

We shall list some properties of r:

1. $-1 \leq r \leq 1$

2. $r > 0$ indicates a positive linear relationship, and $r < 0$ indicates a negative linear relationship.

3. $r = 0$ indicates no linear relationship.

$r \approx 0$

If y tends to increase as x increases, the correlation is called positive.

Consider the linear model

$$y = a_0 + a_1 x + \varepsilon.$$

The total variability of the y's about their mean y can be expressed as

$$\sum (y - \bar{y})^2 = \sum (y - \hat{y})^2 + \sum (\hat{y} - \bar{y})^2$$

$\sum (\hat{y} - \bar{y})^2$ is that portion of the total variability that can be accounted for by the independent variable x. We have

$$\sum (y - \bar{y})^2 = \sum y^2 - \frac{\left(\sum \bar{y}\right)^2}{n}$$

$$\sum (y - \hat{y})^2 = \sum (y - \bar{y})^2 - \frac{\left(\sum (x - \bar{x})(y - \bar{y})\right)^2}{\sum (x - \bar{x})^2}$$

Hence,

$$\sum (\hat{y} - \bar{y})^2 = \frac{\left(\sum (x - \bar{x})(y - \bar{y})\right)^2}{\sum (x - \bar{x})^2}$$

and

$$\frac{\sum (y - \hat{y})^2}{\sum (y - \bar{y})^2} = 1 - r^2$$

$$\frac{\sum (\hat{y} - \bar{y})^2}{\sum (y - \bar{y})^2} = r^2$$

The total variation of y defined as

$$\sum (y - \bar{y})^2$$

is the sum of

$$\sum (y - \bar{y})^2 = \sum (y - \hat{y})^2 + \sum (\hat{y} - \bar{y})^2$$

where $\sum (y - \hat{y})^2$ is called the unexplained variation and $\sum (\hat{y} - \bar{y})^2$ is called the explained variation. The deviations $y - \hat{y}$ behave in a random manner, while $\hat{y} - \bar{y}$ have a definite pattern.

We define

$$\text{Coefficient of determination} = \frac{\text{explained variation}}{\text{total variation}}.$$

The value of coefficient of determination lies between zero and one. Note that

and $r^2 = $ coefficient of determination

$$r = \pm \sqrt{\frac{\text{explained variation}}{\text{total variation}}}.$$

Simple Linear Regression

Scatter Diagram

A *scatter diagram* is a graphic representation of the relationship between two variables. It consists of an X-axis for coding the **independent variable** and a Y-axis for coding the **dependent variable**. The data values are represented by points or dots within the grid and are plotted as they relate to both the X and Y variables.

- **EXAMPLE**

X = Speed of Machine (rpm)	Y = % Defectives Produced by Machine
50	1.5
75	1.9
60	2.0
65	1.5
90	3.0
70	2.5
55	1.0
45	1.2
80	1.7
70	2.0

The purpose of a scatter diagram is to allow for the comparison of the independent variable (X) with the dependent variable (Y) so that we may get a feel for how they are related. We can observe both the direction of the relationship, i.e., whether they are both changing in the same direction or in opposite directions, as well as the apparent strength of the relationship between the two variables. If we imagine a straight line through the middle of the points and then look at how close the points are to this imaginary line, we can get some idea about the strength of the relationship. The closer the points are to the line, and the sharper the slope of the line, the stronger the relationship between X and Y.

Regression Equation

Simple linear regression is a technique by which one dependent variable (Y) is regressed against one independent variable (X) and the relationship between the two is in the form of a straight line. The equation for calculation of the regression line is:

$$Y_i = a + bX_i$$

where:　Y_i = the ith value of the dependent variable,

X_i = the ith value of the independent variable.

$$b = \frac{\sum XY - n\bar{X}\bar{Y}}{\sum X^2 - n\bar{X}^2} \qquad a = \frac{\sum Y - b\sum X}{n}$$

• **EXAMPLE**

Assume that we use the data from the previous example and compute the regression equation where X = speed of machine measured in revolutions per minute and Y = percentage of defective items produced by the machine at the specified rates.

X (rpm)	Y (%)	XY	X²
50	1.5	75.0	2,500
75	1.9	142.5	5,625
60	2.0	120.0	3,600
65	1.5	97.5	4,225
90	3.0	270.0	8,100
70	2.5	175.0	4,900
55	1.0	55.0	3,025
45	1.2	54.0	2,025
80	1.7	136.0	6,400
70	2.0	140.0	4,900
TOTAL 660	18.3	1,265.0	45,300

$$\bar{X} = \sum X / n \qquad \bar{Y} = \sum Y / n$$
$$= 660/10 \qquad\quad = 18.3/10$$
$$= 66 \qquad\qquad = 1.83$$

$$b = \frac{\sum XY - n\bar{X}\bar{Y}}{\sum X^2 - n\bar{X}^2}$$

$$= \frac{1265 - 10(66)(1.83)}{45,300 - 10(66)^2}$$

$$= \frac{1265 - 1207.8}{45,300 - 43,560}$$

$$= \frac{57.2}{1740}$$

$$= .033$$

$$a = \frac{\sum Y - b\sum X}{n}$$

$$= \frac{18.3 - .033(660)}{10}$$

$$= \frac{18.3 - 21.78}{10}$$

$$= \frac{-3.48}{10}$$

$$= -.348$$

Therefore: $Y = a + bX$, i.e.,

$$Y = -.348 + .033X.$$

The value of "*b*" is the slope of the line. In this equation, $b = .033$ tells us that for every unit increase in rpm, the percentage of defective units produced increases by .033 percent. This is an indication of a positive relationship between X and Y; i.e., as X increases, Y also increases, as evident as well from the scatter diagram. The value of "*a*", which is the *y*-intercept, indicates that at the point where $X = 0$, the regression line

SCATTER DIAGRAM WITH REGRESSION LINE

crosses the Y-axis at $-.348$. A strict interpretation of this value would be that if we operate the machine at 0 rpm, we would produce $-.348$ defectives. Obviously, if we were operating the machine at 0 rpm, it would not be producing any items and, consequently, the percentage of defectives would be 0 also. We must keep in mind that the regression equation is valid only for a relevant range of X values. Two possible modifications (which are beyond the scope of this text) which would resolve this problem are regression through the origin and (even better) logistic regression.

Once we have plotted the data in a scatter diagram and calculated the regression equation, it is generally useful to plot a regression line. Since we know that this will be a straight line, we may substitute two values for X into the equation solve for Y, and plot the straight line

from these points. Using the previous example, we can illustrate this.

• **EXAMPLE**

If $X = 50$; $Y = -.348 + .033(50) = 1.30$
If $X = 80$; $Y = -.348 + .033(80) = 2.29$

Now we have a "real" line through the data points and we can observe that the points fall "relatively" close to the line, which implies that the relationship between the speed at which the machine operates and the percentage of defectives it produces is "relatively" strong. Also, we note that the relationship is positive in that the line has an upward slope. If the relationship is inverse or negative, the sign of "*b*" will be negative and the regression line will therefore slope downward.

Once we have measured the relationship between X and Y, of what value is this knowledge? If we are satisfied that the relationship is strong enough, we may use the regression equation X to predict the value of Y from predetermined values of X. For example, what percentages of defective items should we expect if we set the rpm rate at some prespecified value? We can answer this question by substituting this prespecified value into the equation for X and solving for Y.

• **EXAMPLE**

What percentage of defectives would we expect if we set the rpm rate at 95?

$$Y = a + bX$$

$$Y = -.348 + .033(95)$$

$$Y = 2.787 \text{ or } 2.79\%$$

What percentage of defectives would we expect if we set the rpm rate at 40?

$$Y = -.348 + .033(40)$$

$$= .972 \text{ or } .97\%$$

Note that when we use a regression equation to predict values of Y from X, we should not use X values that are extremely different from those which were used to build the equation. That is, we cannot expect the same linear relationship to hold indefinitely over all values of X. Also, we must be sure when predicting that the assumptions of the regression model are met.

Experimental Design

Each design of an experiment consists of the following steps:

1. Statement of an objective. It usually consists of a description of the population and a description of the parameters of the population we have to estimate.

2. Statement of the amount of information required about the parameters.

3. Experimental design which consists of selection of the appropriate experimental plan.

4. Estimation of test procedure.

Suppose the objective is to find the parameter μ of the population. We have to decide how accurate μ should be. For that purpose we can apply a bound on the error of estimate of μ. That bound can be $\pm A$ units of μ from μ.

Note that A can assume any value we choose.

Suppose μ is a mean yearly income of a construction worker. Then we can choose $A = \$1.00$ and estimate μ to be within $\$1.00$.

Often the sample mean is used as a point estimate of μ; then, the bound on the error of estimate is

$$\frac{2\sigma}{\sqrt{n}}$$

Solving the equation

$$A = \frac{2\sigma}{\sqrt{n}}$$

for n

$$n = \frac{u\sigma^2}{A^2}$$

we find the sample size required to estimate μ to within A units.

Two terms are used frequently in descriptions of experimental design.

Experimental Unit

Any object or person on which a measurement is made is called an experimental unit.

Treatment

A treatment is a factor level, or combination of factor levels, applied to an experimental unit.

Suppose our experimental objective is to estimate the parameters μ and $\mu_1 - \mu_2$ or to test a hypothesis about them.

It is important to determine the quantity of information in an experiment relative to the parameter.

Often we estimate a parameter $\hat{\lambda}$, using a point estimate $\hat{\lambda}$. For the sampling distribution of the point estimates approximately normal with mean $\hat{\lambda}$, and standard deviation $\sigma_{\hat{\lambda}}$

$$\text{the bound on the error of estimate} = 2\sigma_{\hat{\lambda}}$$

If we are looking for a point estimate of λ then we can set the bound on the error of estimate, say A.

In general

$$\sigma_{\hat{\lambda}} = \sigma_{\hat{\lambda}}(n)$$

that is $\sigma_{\hat{\lambda}}$ depends on n. Hence solving the equation

$$A = 2\sigma_{\hat{\lambda}}$$

for n we find the sample size n necessary to achieve the bound on the error equal A.

We summarize the results concerning sample sizes in the table

λ	$\hat{\lambda}$	$\sigma_{\hat{\lambda}}$	Sample Size
μ	$\bar{y}_1$	$\dfrac{\sigma}{\sqrt{n}}$	$n = \dfrac{\mu\sigma^2}{A^2}$
$\mu_1 - \mu_2$	$\bar{y}_1 - \bar{y}_2$	$\sqrt{\dfrac{\sigma_1^2}{n} + \dfrac{\sigma_2^2}{n}}$	$n = \dfrac{\mu(\sigma_1^2 + \sigma_2^2)}{A^2}$

Note that in estimating

$$\mu_1 - \mu_2$$

we use

$$\bar{y}_1 - \bar{y}_2$$

and determine the sample size by solving the equation

$$A = 2\sqrt{\frac{\sigma_1^2}{n} + \frac{\sigma_2^2}{n}}$$

We want to estimate $\mu_1 - \mu_2$ to within A units.

• EXAMPLE

A chemist wants to estimate the difference in mean melting temperatures for two different alloys. From previous experiments he knows that the range in melting temperatures for each alloy is approximately 400°. How many independent random samples of each kind of alloy must be checked to estimate

$$T_1 - T_2$$

within 50°?

The range of melting temperatures for both alloys is the same, thus we can assume that the population variances σ_1^2 and σ_2^2 are approximately the same.

$$\sigma_1^2 = \sigma_2^2 = \sigma^2$$

The range estimate of σ is

$$\hat{\sigma} = \frac{\text{range}}{4} = \frac{400}{4} = 100$$

The sample size formula

$$n = \frac{4(\sigma_1^2 + \sigma_2^2)}{A^2}$$
$$= \frac{4(100^2 + 100^2)}{50^2} = 32$$

Thus we should examine 32 samples of alloy of each type to estimate $T_1 - T_2$ with a bound on the error of estimate

$$A = 50°$$

Observe that increasing the desired bound on the error of estimate we decrease the number of required samples, i.e., decrease the cost of conducting the experiment.

For example for

$$A = 75°$$

$$n = \frac{4(100^2 + 100^2)}{75^2} = 14$$

Now, suppose the objective is to find an interval estimate of the parameter λ. Let $\hat{\lambda}$ be a point estimate of the parameter λ. We assume that the sampling distribution of the point estimates is approximately normal, with mean λ and standard deviation $\sigma_{\hat{\lambda}}$.

For confidence coefficient

$$1 - \alpha$$

the confidence interval for λ is

$$\hat{\lambda} \pm Z_{\frac{\alpha}{2}} \sigma_{\hat{\lambda}}$$

One of the accepted measures of the amount of information important to the parameter λ is the half width $Z_{\frac{\alpha}{2}} \sigma_{\hat{\lambda}}$ of the confidence interval.

$$A = Z_{\frac{\alpha}{2}} \sigma_{\hat{\lambda}}$$

Solving this equation for n we find the sample size required to estimate a parameter λ by using confidence coefficient

$$1 - \alpha$$

and a confidence interval $\pm Z_{\frac{\alpha}{2}} \sigma_{\hat{\lambda}}$

The table below shows the results of interval estimates of the parameters μ and $\mu_1 - \mu_2$.

λ	$\hat{\lambda}$	Confidence Interval	Sample Size
μ	$\bar{y}$	$\bar{y} \pm Z_{\frac{\alpha}{2}} \dfrac{\sigma}{\sqrt{n}}$	$n = \dfrac{Z_{\frac{\alpha}{2}}^2 \sigma^2}{A^2}$
$\mu_1 - \mu_2$	$\bar{y}_1 - \bar{y}_2$	$(\bar{y}_1 - \bar{y}_2) \pm Z_{\frac{\alpha}{2}} \sqrt{\dfrac{\sigma_1^2}{n} + \dfrac{\sigma_2^2}{n}}$	$n = \dfrac{Z_{\frac{\alpha}{2}}^2 \left(\sigma_1^2 + \sigma_2^2\right)}{A^2}$

Suppose we want to test the research hypothesis

$$h_a : \lambda > \lambda_0$$

Then the null hypothesis is

$$h_0 : \lambda = \lambda_0$$

Assume that the distribution of $\hat{\lambda}$ is approximately normal with mean λ_0 and standard deviation $\sigma_{\hat{\lambda}}$ under the null hypothesis. We want the probability of a type 1 error to be α and the probability of a type II error to be β or less for the actual value of λ such that

$$\lambda - \lambda_0 \geq \Delta$$

i.e., λ lies a distance of Δ or more above λ_0.

λ	h_0	Δ	Test Statistic	Sample Size
μ	$\mu = \mu_0$	$|\mu - \mu_0|$	$Z = \dfrac{\bar{y} - \mu_0}{\sigma} \sqrt{n}$	$n = \dfrac{\sigma^2 (Z_\alpha + Z_\beta)^2}{\Delta^2}$
$\mu_1 - \mu_2$	$\mu_1 - \mu_2 = \delta$	$|\mu_1 - \mu_2 - \delta|$	$Z = \dfrac{(\bar{y}_1 - \bar{y}_2) - \delta}{\sqrt{\dfrac{\sigma_1^2}{n} + \dfrac{\sigma_2^2}{n}}}$	$n = \dfrac{(\sigma_1^2 + \sigma_2^2)(Z_\alpha + Z_\beta)^2}{\Delta^2}$

Competency 7: Knowledge of Probability

Probability is defined as the likelihood of the occurrence of an event or as the chance that some particular event will occur.

- **EXAMPLE**

A weather report might indicate the chance of rain to be 70% which could be interpreted as the probability of rain = .70.

a) Objective Probability (Calculated)

In most instances, the probability that an event will occur is determined by a mathematical formula and is based on empirical evidence.

$$P(X) = \frac{\text{No. of outcomes corresponding to event } X}{\text{Total no. of possible outcomes}}$$

- **EXAMPLE**

The probability of drawing a queen from a deck of cards is defined as:

$$P(\text{Queen}) = \frac{\text{No. of queens in the deck}}{\text{Total no. of cards in the deck}}$$

$$= \frac{4}{52} = \frac{1}{13} \text{ or } .077.$$

b) Subjective Probability

When the probability of an event occurring is based on the personal (or professional) judgment of an individual or group of individuals, the probability is referred to as "subjective."

- **EXAMPLE**

The probability that sales will increase by $500,000 next year if we increase our advertising expenditure by $10,000 is .25.

Properties of Probabilities

The following three properties are characteristics of all probabilities:

1. $0 \leq P(X) \leq 1$; every probability is contained within the range 0 to 1, inclusive, where 0 represents absolute certainty that the event will not occur and 1 represents absolute certainty that the event will occur.

- **EXAMPLE**

  P (Head on Coin) = 1/2

  P (6 on Die) = 1/6

  P (Ace of Spades) = 1/52

2. $\sum_{i=1}^{n} P_i(X) = 1$; the probabilities of all possible simple events that can occur within a given experiment will sum to 1.

- **EXAMPLE**

  coin: $P(\text{Head}) + P(\text{Tail}) = 1/2 + 1/2 = 1$

  die: $P(1) + P(2) + P(3) + P(4) + P(5) + P(6) = 1/6 + 1/6 + 1/6 + 1/6 + 1/6 + 1/6 = 1$

  cards: $P(\text{Club}) + P(\text{Heart}) + P(\text{Spade}) + P(\text{Diamond}) = 1/4 + 1/4 + 1/4 + 1/4 = 1$

3. $P(X) + P(\text{Not } X) = 1$; the probability that event X occurs plus the probability that event X does not occur sums to 1.

- **EXAMPLE**

  coin: P (Head) + P (Not a Head) = 1/2 + 1/2 = 1

  die: P (6) + P (Not a 6) = 1/6 + 5/6 = 1

  cards: P (Spade) + P (Not a Spade) = 1/4 + 3/4 = 1 or 13/52 + 39/52 = 1

Methods of Computing Probabilities

a) **Addition**

1. Mutually Exclusive Events - those which cannot occur simultaneously. In order to determine the probability that either event X occurs or event Y occurs, the individual probabilities of event X and event Y are added.

   $P(X \text{ or } Y) = P(X) + P(Y)$

- **EXAMPLE**

  The probability that either a club or a spade is drawn from a deck of cards in a single draw is defined as:

  P (Club or Spade) = P (Club) + P (Spade)

  $= 13/52 + 13/52$

  $= 26/52$

  $= 1/2$ or .5

Note: That this concept applies to three or more events as well.

2. Non-Mutually Exclusive Events - those which can occur simultaneously. In order to determine the probability that either event X occurs or event Y occurs, the individual probabilities of event X and event Y are added and the probability that the two occur simultaneously is subtracted from the total.

$$P(X \text{ or } Y) = P(X) = P(Y) - P(X \& Y)$$

- **EXAMPLE**

  The probability that either a Queen or a Spade is drawn from a deck of cards in a single draw is defined as:

  P (Queen or Spade) = P (Queen) + P (Spade) − P (Queen & Spade)

  $= 4/52 + 13/52 − 1/52$

  $= 16/52$

  $= 4/13$.

  Notice in this example that we must subtract 1/52 from the total since the Queen of Spades is counted in the total number of Queens and it is also counted in the total number of Spades. If we do not subtract P (Queen & Spade), we are counting that one card twice.

b) **Multiplication**

1. Independent Events

   Two (or more) events are independent if the occurrence of one event has no effect upon whether or not the other event occurs. In order to determine the probability that event X occurs and event Y occurs, the individual probability of event X and event Y are multiplied together.

$$P(X \text{ and } Y) = P(X) \times P(Y)$$

- **EXAMPLE**

1. The probability of tossing a 6 on a single die followed by the toss of a 3 is:

   P (6 and 3) = P (6) × P (3)

$$= 1/6 \times 1/6$$

$$= 1/36.$$

2. The probability of tossing three heads in 3 tosses of a coin:

$$P\,(H, H, H) = P\,(H) \times P\,(H) \times P\,(H)$$

$$= 1/2 \times 1/2 \times 1/2$$

$$= 1/8.$$

3. The probability of drawing a heart from a deck of cards, replacing the first card, and drawing a club on the second draw:

$$P\,(H \text{ and } C) = P(H) \times P\,(C)$$

$$= 13/52 \times 13/52$$

$$= 1/4 \times 1/4$$

$$= 1/16.$$

2. Dependent Events

Two (or more) events are dependent if the occurrence of one event has some effect upon whether or not the other event occurs. In order to determine the probability that event X occurs and event Y occurs, when X and Y are dependent, the formula is:

$$\boxed{P(X \text{ and } Y) = P\,(X) \times P(Y \mid X)}$$

or

$$\boxed{P(X \text{ and } Y) = P\,(Y) \times P(X \mid Y)}$$

where: $P\,(Y \mid X)$ is read as the probability that event Y will occur, given that event X has already occurred.

And: $P\,(X \mid Y)$ is read as the probability that event X will occur given that event Y has already occurred.

• **EXAMPLE**

1. A box contains 6 red balls, 4 green balls, and 5 purple balls. What is the probability that a red ball is drawn on the first draw and a purple ball is drawn on the second draw, if the first ball is not replaced prior to the second ball being drawn

$$P\,(\text{Red and Purple}) = P(R) \times P(P \mid R)$$

$$= 6/15 \times 5/14$$

$$= 30/210$$

$$= 1/7$$

2. Three cards are drawn from a deck. What is the probability that the first is a Queen, the second is a Queen, and the third is a King? Assume that each card is **not** replaced prior to the next one being drawn.

$$P\,(Q1, Q2, K) = P\,(Q1) \times P\,(Q2 \mid Q1) \times P\,(K \mid Q1 \,\&\, Q2)$$

$$= 4/52 \times 3/51 \times 4/50$$

$$= 48/132{,}600$$

$$= .0004$$

Bayesian Decision Analysis

Sometimes the probability of an event occurring is influenced by the occurrence of a previous event. When this occurs, the probability is referred to as a conditional probability. Conditional probability is denoted by $P\,(X \mid Y)$ and is read as "the probability of event X occurring given that event Y has already occurred." $P\,(X \mid Y)$ may be calculated using the following formula:

$$\boxed{P(X \mid Y) = \frac{P(X \text{ and } Y)}{P(Y)}}$$

This formula is frequently "broken down" further and written this way:

$$\boxed{P(Y \mid X) = \frac{P(X) \times P(Y \mid X)}{P(X) \times P(Y \mid X) + P(\text{Not } X)\, P(Y \mid \text{Not } X)}}$$

This latter version is called **Bayes Theorem** and the use of it is called Bayesian Analysis.

• **EXAMPLE**

Two workers assemble parts from a production process. The probability that worker A makes a mistake in assembling a part is .02 and the probability that worker B makes a mistake is .03. However, worker A assembles 55% of the parts while worker B assembles the remaining 45%. If an assembled part is randomly selected from all of those produced during a given time period and it is determined to be defective, what is the probability that worker A assembled this part?

Let A = Assembled by worker A

B = Assembled by worker B (Same as "not A")

D = Defective

$$P(A|D) =$$

$$\frac{P(A)P(D|A)}{P(A) \times P(D|A) + P(B) \times P(D|B)} =$$

$$\frac{.55 \times .02}{(.55)(.02) + (.45)(.03)} = \frac{.011}{.025} = .449$$

Probability Tables

A tabular approach is often easier to understand when calculating probabilities.

- **EXAMPLE**

For the previous example, the probability table looks as follows:

ASSEMBLED PARTS

		GOOD	DEFECTIVE	TOTAL
Worker	A	.5390	.0110	.55
	B	.4365	.0135	.45
TOTAL		.9755	.0245	1.00

The **cell** probabilities are referred to as **joint probabilities** which represent the combined probability of the two events (row and column) occurring; e.g., the probability that worker A assembled the part and it is good is .539. The **total** row and column probabilities are referred to as **marginal probabilities** which are the sums of the joint probabilities over the rows or columns. For example, .45 is a marginal probability representing the probability that worker B assembled the part. It is the sum of .4365 (probability that worker B assembled it and it is good) plus .0135 (the probability that B assembled it and it is defective).

Counting Methods

Sampling and Counting

There are many instances in the application of probability theory where it is desirable and necessary to count

the outcomes in the sample space and the outcomes in an event. For example, in the special instance of a uniform probability function, the probability of an event is known when the number of outcomes that comprises the event is known; that is, as soon as the number of outcomes in the subset that defines the event is known.

If a sample space $S = \{e_1, e_2, \ldots, e_n\}$ contains n simple events, $E_i = \{e_i\}$, $i = 1, 2, \ldots, n$, then using a uniform probability model, we assign probability $1/n$ for each point in S; that is, $P(E_i) = 1/n$. To determine the probability of an event A, we need,

1. The number of possible outcomes in S.

2. The number of outcomes in the event A.

Then,

$$P(A) = \frac{\text{number of outcomes corresponding to } A}{\text{number of possible outcomes in } S}$$

Frequently, it may be possible to enumerate fully all the sample space points in S and then count how many of these correspond to the event A. For example, if a class consists of just three students, and the instructor always calls on each student once and only once during each class, then if we label the students 1, 2, and 3, we can easily enumerate the points in S as

$$S = \{(1, 2, 3), (1, 3, 2), (2, 1, 3), (2, 3, 1), (3, 1, 2),$$
$$(3, 2, 1)\}$$

Assume that the instructor chooses a student at random, it would seem reasonable to adopt a uniform probability model and assign probability 1/6 to each point in S. If A is the event that John is selected last, then

John = B

$A = \{(1, 2, 3), (2, 1, 3)\}$

$P(A) = 2/6 = 1/3$

It would be most unusual for a class to consist of only three students. The total enumeration of the sample space becomes more complicated even if we increase the class size to 6 students. To deal with these situations in which the sample space contains a large number of points, we need to have an understanding of basic counting or combinatorial procedures.

The Fundamental Principle of Counting

Suppose a man has four ways to travel from New York to Chicago, three ways to travel from Chicago to

Denver, and six ways to travel from Denver to San Francisco, how many ways can he go from New York to San Francisco via Chicago and Denver?

If we let A_1 be the event "going from New York to Chicago," A_2 be the event "going from Chicago to Denver," and A_3 be the event "going from Denver to San Francisco," then because there are four ways to accomplish A_1, 3 ways to accomplish A_2, and 6 ways to accomplish A_3, the number of routes the man can follow is

$$(4) \times (3) \times (6) = 72$$

We can now generalize these results and state them formally as the fundamental principle or multiplication rule of counting.

Fundamental Principle of Counting

If an operation consists of a sequence of k separate steps of which the first can be performed in n_1 ways, followed by the second in n_2 ways, and so on until the kth can be performed in n_k ways, then the operation consisting of k steps can be performed in

$$n_1 \times n_2 \times n_3 \ldots \ldots n_k$$

ways.

Tree Diagrams

A tree diagram is a device that can be used to list all possible outcomes of a sequence of experiments where each experiment can occur only in a finite number of ways.

The following tree diagram list the different ways three different flavors of ice cream, chocolate (c), vanilla (v), and strawberry (s), can be arranged on a cone, with no flavor used more than once.

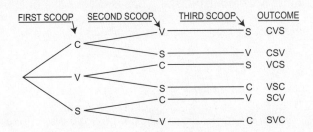

The tree starts with three branches in the first stage, representing the three possibilities for first stage. For each outcome at the first stage, there are two possibilities at the second stage. Then, for each outcome in the second stage, there is only one possibility at the third stage.

Consequently, there are $3 \times 2 \times 1$, or 6, different arrangement.

Using a tree diagram, we can develop the sample space for an experiment consisting of tossing a fair coin and then rolling a die as follows:

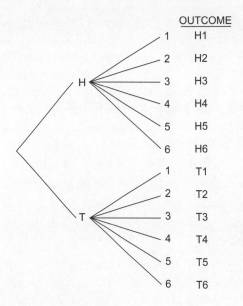

Factorial Notation

Consider how many ways the owner of an ice cream parlor can display ten ice cream flavors in a row along the front of the display case. The first position can be filled in ten ways, the second position in 9 ways, and the third position in 8 ways, and so on. By the fundamental counting principle, there are

$$(10) \times (9) \times (8) \times (7) \times \ldots \times (2) \times (1)$$

or 3,628,800 ways to display the flavor. If there are 16 flavors, there would be $(16) \times (15) \times (14) \times \ldots \times (3) \times (2) \times (1)$ ways to arrange them. In general

If n is a natural number, then the product from 1 to n inclusive is denoted by the symbol $n!$ (read as "n factorial" or as "factorial n" and is defined as

$$n! = n(n-1)(n-2) \ldots (3)(2)(1)$$

where n is a positive natural number.

There are two fundamental properties of factorials:

1. By definition, $0! = 1$

2. $n(n-1)! = n!$

   For example, $(6)(5!) = 6!$

Counting Procedures Involving Order Restrictions (Permutations)

Suppose a class consists of 5 students. The instructor calls on exactly three students out of the 5 students during each class period to answer three different questions. To apply the uniform probability model, we need to know how many points there are in the sample space S. Note that each point in S is an ordered triplet; that is, the point $(3, 5, 1)$ is different from the point $(5, 3, 1)$. The same three people were called upon to respond, but the order of response is different. Such arrangement is referred to as a permutation.

A permutation of a number of objects is any arrangement of these objects in a definite order.

For example if a class consists of 3 students, then there are $3 \times 2 \times 1 = 6$ ways in which the students might be called upon.

In general, if the class had consisted of n students and all of them had been called upon, then the responses could have taken place in

$$n(n-1)(n-2) \ldots (3)(2)(1)$$

ways. Hence,

The number of permutations of a set of n distinct objects, taken all together, is $n!$.

In our example of the class consisting of five students, only three students were to be called on to respond; that is, we are interested in an ordered subset.

An arrangement of r distinct objects taken from a set of n distinct objects, $r \leq n$, is called a permutation of n objects taken r at a time. The total number of such orderings is denoted by nPr, and defined as

$$nPr = \frac{n!}{(n-r)!}$$

In our example, $n = 5$, $r = 3$,

$$5P3 = \frac{5!}{(5-3)!} = 5 \times 4 \times 3 = 60$$

If we have n items with r objects alike, then the number of distinct permutations taking all n at a time is

$$\frac{n!}{r!}$$

In general,

In a set of n elements having r_1 elements of one type, r_2 elements of a second type and so on to r_k element of a kth type, then the number of distinct permutations of the n elements, taken all together, is given by

$$nPn = \frac{n!}{r_1! r_2! r_3! \ldots r_k!}$$

where $\displaystyle\sum_{i=1}^{k} r_i = n$

For example, the number of ways a group of 10 of which 6 are females and 4 are males can line up for theatre tickets, if we are interested only in distinguishing between sexes, is given by

$$10P10 = \frac{10!}{6!4!} = 210$$

Counting Procedures Not Involving Order Restrictions (Combinations)

Suppose that a class of 12 students selects a committee of 3 to plan a party. A possible committee is John, Sally, and Joe. In this situation, the order of the three is not important because the committee of John, Sally, and Joe, is the same as the committee of Sally, Joe, and John.

When choosing committee members and in other cases of selection where order is not important, we are interested in combinations, not permutations.

A subset of r objects selected without regard to order from a set of n different objects, $r \leq n$, is called a combination of n objects taken r at a time. The total number of combinations of n things taken r at a time is denoted by nCr or $\binom{n}{r}$ and is defined as

$$nCr = \binom{n}{r} = \frac{n!}{r!(n-r)!}$$

In our example, the number of possible committees that could plan the party can be calculated by

$$12C3 = \binom{12}{3} = \frac{12!}{3!(12-3)!} = 220$$

PROBLEM

> A deck of playing cards is thoroughly shuffled and a card is drawn from the deck. What is the probability that the card drawn is the ace of diamonds?

SOLUTION

The probability of an event occurring is

$$\frac{\text{the number of ways the event can occur}}{\text{the number of possible outcomes}}$$

In our case there is one way the event can occur, for there is only one ace of diamonds and there are 52 possible outcomes (for there are 52 cards in the deck). Hence, the probability that the card drawn is the ace of diamonds is 1/52.

PROBLEM

> A bag contains four black and five blue marbles. A marble is drawn and then re-placed, after which a second marble is drawn. What is the probability that the first is black and the second blue?

SOLUTION

Let C = event that the first marble drawn is black.

D = event that the second marble drawn is blue.

The probability that the first is black and the second is blue can be expressed symbolically:

$P(C \text{ and } D) = P(CD)$.

We can apply the following theorem. If two events, A and B, are independent, then the probability that A and B will occur is

$P(A \text{ and } B) = P(AB) = P(A) \times P(B)$.

Note that two or more events are said to be independent if the occurrence of one event has no effect upon the occurrence or non-occurrence of the other. In this case the occurrence of choosing a black marble has no effect on the selection of a blue marble and vice versa;

since, when a marble is drawn it is then replaced before the next marble is drawn. Therefore, C and D are two independent events.

$$P(CD) = P(C) \times P(D)$$

$$P(C) = \frac{\text{number of ways to choose a black marble}}{\text{number of ways to choose a marble}}$$

$$= \frac{4}{9}$$

$$P(D) = \frac{\text{number of ways to choose a blue marble}}{\text{number of ways to choose a marble}}$$

$$= \frac{5}{9}$$

$$P(CD) = P(C) \times P(D) = \frac{4}{9} \times \frac{5}{9} = \frac{20}{81}$$

PROBLEM

> A traffic count at a highway junction revealed that out of 5,000 cars that passed through the junction in one week, 3,000 turned to the right. Find the probability that a car will turn (A) to the right and (B) to the left. Assume that the cars cannot go straight or turn around.

SOLUTION

(A) If an event can happen in s ways and fail to happen in f ways, and if all these ways $(s + f)$ are assumed to be equally likely, then the probability (p) that the event will happen is

$$p = \frac{s}{s+f} = \frac{\text{successful ways}}{\text{total ways}}.$$

In this case $s = 3,000$ and $s + f = 5,000$. Hence,

$$p = \frac{3,000}{5,000} = \frac{3}{5}.$$

(B) If the probability that an event will happen is

$\frac{a}{b}$, then the probability that this event will not happen

is $1 - \frac{a}{b}$. Thus, the probability that a car will not turn right, but left, is $1 - \frac{3}{5} = \frac{2}{5}$. This same conclusion can also be arrived at using the following reasoning:

Since 3,000 cars turned to the right, 5,000 − 3,000 = 2,000 cars turned to the left. Hence, the probability that a car will turn to the left is

$$\frac{2,000}{5,000} = \frac{2}{5}.$$

Drill: Permutations, Combinations, and Probability

1. How many games would it take a baseball coach to try every possible batting order with his nine players?

   (A) 9

   (B) 45

   (C) 81

   (D) 362,880

   (E) 3.8742×10^8

2. What is the probability of drawing an ace from a well-shuffled deck of 52 cards?

   (A) 0.0769

   (B) 0.0192

   (C) 0.0196

   (D) 0.0385

   (E) 0.5000

3. In how many different ways can the letters *a*, *b*, *c*, and *d* be arranged if they are selected three at a time?

   (A) 8

   (B) 12

   (C) 24

   (D) 4

   (E) 48

4. What is the probability that in a single throw of two dice the sum of 10 will appear?

   (A) $\frac{10}{36}$

   (B) $\frac{1}{6}$

   (C) $\frac{1}{12}$

   (D) $\frac{2}{10}$

   (E) $\frac{11}{12}$

5. A bag contains four white balls, six black balls, three red balls, and eight green balls. If one ball is drawn from the bag, find the probability that it will be either white or green.

   (A) $\frac{1}{3}$

   (B) $\frac{2}{3}$

   (C) $\frac{4}{7}$

   (D) $\frac{4}{13}$

   (E) $\frac{8}{21}$

6. A box contains 30 blue balls, 40 green balls, and 15 red balls. What is the probability of choosing a red ball first followed by a blue ball?

   (A) 0.3571

   (B) 0.1765

   (C) 0.3529

   (D) 0.0620

   (E) 0.0630

7. When rolling a six-sided die, what is the probability of getting either a four or five?

   (A) 0.5000

   (B) 0.3333

   (C) 0.2500

   (D) 0.1670

   (E) 3.0000

8. What is the probability of getting at most one head in three coin tosses?

   (A) 0

   (B) $\frac{1}{4}$

   (C) $\frac{1}{2}$

   (D) $\frac{3}{4}$

   (E) $\frac{7}{8}$

9. In how many ways can we arrange four letters (*a*, *b*, *c*, and *d*) in different orders?

   (A) 4

   (B) 8

   (C) 16

   (D) 24

   (E) 48

10. Six dice are thrown. What is the probability of getting six ones?

   (A) 0.0000214

   (B) 0.0278

   (C) 0.00001

   (D) 0.1667

   (E) 0.1

Answer Key

1.	(D)	6.	(E)
2.	(A)	7.	(B)
3.	(C)	8.	(C)
4.	(C)	9.	(D)
5.	(C)	10.	(A)

Chapter 8

Competency 8: Knowledge of Discrete Mathematics

Sequences and Series

A sequence is a function whose domain is the set of all natural numbers. All the sequences described in this section will have a subset in the set of all real numbers as their range. It is common to let a_n represent the nth term of the sequence. For example, if

$$a_n = 10n$$

then the sequence is 10, 20, 30, 40 . . .

The sum of the first n terms of the sequence,

$$a_1, a_2, a_3, \ldots a_n,$$

is indicated by

$$a_1 + a_2 + a_3 + \ldots + a_n,$$

and the sum of these terms is called a series. The Greek letter Σ is used to represent this sum as indicated below.

$$\sum_{k=1}^{n} a_k = a_1 + a_2 + a_3 + \ldots + a_n$$

For a fixed number a and a fixed number d, the sequence

$$a, a + d, a + 2d, a + 3d, \ldots$$

is called an arithmetic sequence, and the nth term of this sequence is given by

$$a_n = a + (n - 1)d$$

The number a is called the first term and d is called the common difference. The symbol S_n is used to represent the corresponding series and

$$\sum_{K=1}^{n} a + (K - 1)d$$

or $S_n = n\left(\dfrac{a_1 + a_n}{2}\right)$

A sequence of the form

$$a, ar, ar^2, \ldots$$

is called a geometric sequence, where a is the first term and r is the common ratio. The nth term of such a sequence is

$$a_n = ar^{n-1}$$

The symbol S_n is used to represent the corresponding series and

$$S_n = \dfrac{a(1 - r^n)}{1 - r}.$$

Expressions of the form

$$a + ar + ar^2 \ldots$$

are called infinite geometric series. When $|r| < 1$, the sum S of the infinite geometric series exists and

$$S = \frac{a}{1-r}$$

PROBLEM

In an arithmetic sequence, $a_1 = 29$ and $a_8 = 78$. Find the common difference d and the sixth term a_6.

SOLUTION

The nth term in an arithmetic sequence is given by $a_n = a + (n-1)d$ where a is the initial term and d is the common difference. Using the given information we can first find d.

$$78 = 29 + (8-1)d$$

$$78 = 29 + 7d$$

$$49 = 7d$$

$$7 = d$$

Thus the common difference is 7. We may now use this information to obtain a_6.

$$a_6 = 29 + (6-1)(7)$$

$$= 29 + 35$$

$$= 64$$

thus the sixth term is 64.

Linear Equations and Matrices

A linear equation is an equation of the form $a_1x_1 + a_2x_2 + \ldots + a_nx_n = b$, where $a_1, \ldots, a_n$ and b are real constants.

- **EXAMPLES**

    a) $2x + 6y = 9$
    b) $x_1 + 3x_2 + 7x_3 = 5$

c) $\alpha - 2 = 0$

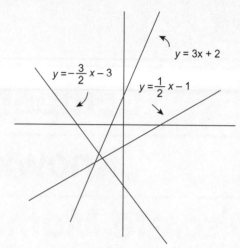

$y = 3x + 2$

$y = -\frac{3}{2}x - 3$

$y = \frac{1}{2}x - 1$

Linear equations in two variables are always straight lines.

A system of linear equations is a finite set of linear equations, all of which use the same set of variables.

- **EXAMPLES**

    a) $2x_1 + x_2 + 5x_3 = 4$
        $x_2 + 3x_3 = 0$
        $7x_1 + 3x_2 + x_3 = 9$

    b) $y - z = 5$
        $z = 1$

The solution of a system of linear equations is that set of real numbers which, when substituted into the set of variables, satisfies each equation in the system. The set of all solutions is called the solution set S of the system.

- **EXAMPLE**

    $y + z = 9$ $S = \{5, 4\}$
    $z = 4$

A consistent system of linear equations has at least one solution, while an inconsistent system has no solutions.

- **EXAMPLES**

    (a) $y + z = 9$ $S = \{5, 4\}$ (consistent system)
        $z = 4$

b) $x_1 + x_2 = 7$ $S = \varnothing$ (inconsistent system)
$$x_1 = 3$$
$$x_1 - x_2 = 7$$

Consistent System

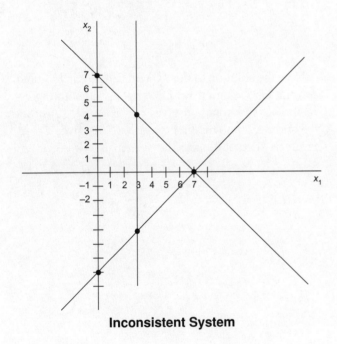

Inconsistent System

Every system of linear equations has either one solution, no solution, or infinitely many solutions.

A system of linear equations with infinitely many solutions is called a dependent system of linear equations.

The augmented matrix for a system of linear equations is the matrix of the form:

$$\begin{bmatrix} a_{11} & a_{12}\cdots & a_{1n} & b_1 \\ a_{21} & a_{22}\cdots & a_{2n} & b_2 \\ \vdots & & & \\ a_{m1} & a_{m2}\cdots & a_{mn} & b_m \end{bmatrix}$$

where a_{ij} represents each coefficient in the system and b_i represents each constant in the system.

- **EXAMPLE**

$$\begin{array}{l} x_1 + 6x_2 - 2x_3 = 4 \\ 3x_1 \qquad + x_3 = 7 \\ 5x_1 - 3x_2 + x_3 = 0 \end{array} \qquad \begin{bmatrix} 1 & 6 & -2 & 4 \\ 3 & 0 & 1 & 7 \\ 5 & -3 & 1 & 0 \end{bmatrix}$$

Elementary row operations are operations on the rows of an augmented matrix, which are used to reduce that matrix to a more solvable form. These operations are the following:

a)   Multiply a row by a non-zero constant.

b)   Interchange two rows.

c)   Add a multiple of one row to another row.

PROBLEM

By forming the augmented matrix and row reducing, determine the solutions of the following system:

$$2x - y + 3z = 4$$
$$3x \qquad + 2z = 5$$
$$-2x + y + 4z = 6$$

SOLUTION

The augmented matrix of the system is:

$$\begin{bmatrix} 2 & -1 & 3 & 4 \\ 3 & 0 & 2 & 5 \\ -2 & 1 & 4 & 6 \end{bmatrix}.$$

Add the first row to the third row:

$$\begin{bmatrix} 2 & -1 & 3 & | & 4 \\ 3 & 0 & 2 & | & 5 \\ 0 & 0 & 7 & | & 10 \end{bmatrix}$$

This is the augmented matrix of:

$$2x - y + 3z = 4$$
$$3x \quad\;\; + 2z = 5$$
$$7z = 10$$

The system has been sufficiently simplified now so that the solution can be found.

From the last equation we have $z = {}^{10}\!/_{7}$. Substituting this value into the second equation and solving for x gives $x = {}^{5}\!/_{7}$. Substituting $x = {}^{5}\!/_{7}$ and $z = {}^{10}\!/_{7}$ into the first equation and solving for y yields $y = {}^{12}\!/_{7}$. The solution to the system is, therefore,

$$x = \frac{5}{7}, \;\; y = \frac{12}{7}, \;\; z = \frac{10}{7}.$$

PROBLEM

Solve the following linear system of equations:

$$2x + 3y - 4z = 5$$
$$-2x \quad\;\;\; + z = 7$$
$$3x + 2y + 2z = 3$$

SOLUTION

The augmented matrix for the system is:

$$\begin{bmatrix} 2 & 3 & -4 & | & 5 \\ -2 & 0 & 1 & | & 7 \\ 3 & 2 & 2 & | & 3 \end{bmatrix}$$

which can be reduced by using the following sequence of row operations:

Add the first row to the second row.

$$\begin{bmatrix} 2 & 3 & -4 & | & 5 \\ 0 & 3 & -3 & | & 12 \\ 3 & 2 & 2 & | & 3 \end{bmatrix}$$

Divide the first row by 2 and the second row by 3.

$$\begin{bmatrix} 1 & \frac{3}{2} & -2 & | & \frac{5}{2} \\ 0 & 1 & -1 & | & 4 \\ 3 & 2 & 2 & | & 3 \end{bmatrix}$$

Add –3 times the first row to the third row.

$$\begin{bmatrix} 1 & \frac{3}{2} & -2 & | & \frac{5}{2} \\ 0 & 1 & -1 & | & 4 \\ 0 & -\frac{5}{2} & 8 & | & -\frac{9}{2} \end{bmatrix}$$

Add $\tfrac{5}{2}$ times the second row to the third row.

$$\begin{bmatrix} 1 & \frac{3}{2} & -2 & | & \frac{5}{2} \\ 0 & 1 & -1 & | & 4 \\ 0 & 0 & \frac{11}{2} & | & \frac{11}{2} \end{bmatrix}$$

This is the augmented matrix for the system:

$$x + \tfrac{3}{2} y - 2z = \tfrac{5}{2}$$
$$y - z = 4$$
$${}^{11}\!/_{2}\, z = {}^{11}\!/_{2}$$

Now the solution to this system can be easily found. From the last equation we have $z = 1$. Substituting $z = 1$ in the second equation gives $y = 5$. Next, substitute $y = 5$ and $z = 1$ into the first equation. This gives $x = -3$. Therefore, the solution to the system is $x = -3$, $y = 5$, $z = 1$.

PROBLEM

Solve the following system:

$$x + \;\; y + 2z = 9$$
$$2x + 4y - 3z = 1$$
$$3x + 6y - 5z = 0$$

SOLUTION

The augmented matrix for the system is:

$$\begin{bmatrix} 1 & 1 & 2 & | & 9 \\ 2 & 4 & -3 & | & 1 \\ 3 & 6 & -5 & | & 0 \end{bmatrix}.$$

It can be reduced by elementary row operations.

Add –2 times the first row to the second row and –3 times the first row to the third row.

$$\begin{bmatrix} 1 & 1 & 2 & 9 \\ 0 & 2 & -7 & -17 \\ 0 & 3 & -11 & -27 \end{bmatrix}$$

Multiply the second row by ½.

$$\begin{bmatrix} 1 & 1 & 2 & 9 \\ 0 & 1 & -\frac{7}{2} & -\frac{17}{2} \\ 0 & 3 & -11 & -27 \end{bmatrix}$$

Add –3 times the second row to the third row.

$$\begin{bmatrix} 1 & 1 & 2 & 9 \\ 0 & 1 & -\frac{7}{2} & -\frac{17}{2} \\ 0 & 0 & -\frac{1}{2} & -\frac{3}{2} \end{bmatrix}$$

Multiply the third row by –2 to obtain

$$\begin{bmatrix} 1 & 1 & 2 & 9 \\ 0 & 1 & -\frac{7}{2} & -\frac{17}{2} \\ 0 & 0 & 1 & 3 \end{bmatrix}.$$

This is the augmented matrix for the system:

$$x + y + 2z = 9$$
$$y - \frac{7}{2}z = -\frac{17}{2}$$
$$z = 3$$

Solving this system gives $x = 1$, $y = 2$, and $z = 3$.

PROBLEM

For the following system, find the augmented matrix; then, by reducing, determine whether the system has a solution.

$$3x - y + z = 1$$
$$7x + y - z = 6 \qquad (1)$$
$$2x + y - z = 2$$

SOLUTION

The augmented matrix for the system is

$$\begin{bmatrix} 3 & -1 & 1 & 1 \\ 7 & 1 & -1 & 6 \\ 2 & 1 & -1 & 2 \end{bmatrix}.$$

This can be reduced by performing the following row operations. Divide the first row by 3.

$$\begin{bmatrix} 1 & -\frac{1}{3} & \frac{1}{3} & \frac{1}{3} \\ 7 & 1 & -1 & 6 \\ 2 & 1 & -1 & 2 \end{bmatrix}$$

Now add –7 times the first row to the second row and –2 times the first row to the third row.

$$\begin{bmatrix} 1 & -\frac{1}{3} & \frac{1}{3} & \frac{1}{3} \\ 0 & \frac{10}{3} & -\frac{10}{3} & \frac{11}{3} \\ 0 & \frac{5}{3} & -\frac{5}{3} & \frac{4}{3} \end{bmatrix}$$

Divide the second row by $^{10}\!/_3$, and add $-\,^{5}\!/_3$ times the second row to the third row.

Matrices

A matrix is a rectangular array of numbers, called entries.

- **EXAMPLES**

a) $$\begin{bmatrix} 6 & 2 \\ 3 & 1 \\ 0 & 0 \end{bmatrix}$$

b) $$\begin{bmatrix} 3 \\ 1 \end{bmatrix}$$

c) $$[1 \quad 7 \quad 2 \quad 1]$$

A matrix with n rows and n columns is called a square matrix of order n.

- **EXAMPLE**

$$\begin{bmatrix} 2 & 10 & 1 \\ 6 & 2 & 9 \\ 3 & 3 & 7 \end{bmatrix}$$ is a square matrix of order 3.

Two matrices are called equal if they have the same size and entries in corresponding positions are the same.

Entries starting at the top left and proceeding to the bottom right of a square matrix are said to be on the main diagonal of that matrix.

- **EXAMPLE**

main diagonal

The sum $B + D$ is the matrix obtained when two matrices, B and D, are added together; they must both be of the same size. $B - D$ is obtained by subtracting the entries of D from the corresponding entries of B.

- **EXAMPLES**

a) $\begin{bmatrix} 1 & 2 \\ 2 & 6 \end{bmatrix} + \begin{bmatrix} -4 & 7 \\ 1 & 1 \end{bmatrix} = \begin{bmatrix} -3 & 9 \\ 3 & 7 \end{bmatrix}$

b) $\begin{bmatrix} 1 & 2 \\ 2 & 6 \end{bmatrix} - \begin{bmatrix} -4 & 7 \\ 1 & 1 \end{bmatrix} = \begin{bmatrix} 5 & -5 \\ 1 & 5 \end{bmatrix}$

The product of a matrix A by a scalar k is obtained by multiplying each entry of A by k.

- **EXAMPLE**

If $A = \begin{bmatrix} 4 & 7 \\ -1 & 2 \end{bmatrix}$ and $k = 3$, then $Ak = \begin{bmatrix} 12 & 21 \\ -3 & 6 \end{bmatrix}$.

When multiplying two matrices A and B, the matrices must be of the sizes $m \times n$ and $n \times p$ (the number of columns of A must equal the number of rows of B); to obtain the (ij) entry of AB, multiply the entries in row i of A by the corresponding entries in column j of B. Add up the resulting products; this sum is the (ij) entry of AB. If $AB = C$, then $C_{ij} = \sum_{k=1}^{n} a_{ik} b_{kj}$.

The size of C will be $m \times p$.

- **EXAMPLE**

If $A = \begin{bmatrix} 2 & 3 \\ 4 & 5 \end{bmatrix}$ and $B = \begin{bmatrix} 3 & 3 \\ 7 & 2 \end{bmatrix}$, then

$AB = \begin{bmatrix} 27 & 12 \\ 47 & 22 \end{bmatrix}$.

A matrix which contains entries corresponding to the coefficients of a system of linear equations, but excludes the constants of that system, is called a coefficient matrix.

- **EXAMPLE**

$\begin{aligned} x_1 + 6x_2 - 2x_3 &= 4 \\ 3x_1 + x_3 &= 7 \\ 5x_1 - 3x_2 + x_3 &= 0 \end{aligned}$ $\begin{bmatrix} 1 & 6 & -2 \\ 3 & 0 & 1 \\ 5 & -3 & 1 \end{bmatrix}$

PROBLEM

Find $A + B$ where:

$A = \begin{bmatrix} 1 & -2 & 4 \\ 2 & -1 & 3 \end{bmatrix}$, $B = \begin{bmatrix} 0 & 2 & 4 \\ 1 & 3 & 1 \end{bmatrix}$.

SOLUTION

Using the definition of matrix addition, add the (ij) entry of A to the (ij) entry of B. Thus,

$A + B = \begin{bmatrix} 1+0 & -2+2 & 4-4 \\ 2+1 & -1+3 & 3+1 \end{bmatrix} = \begin{bmatrix} 1 & 0 & 0 \\ 3 & 2 & 4 \end{bmatrix}$

PROBLEM

Let $A = \begin{bmatrix} 2 & 3 & 7 \\ 4 & m & \sqrt{3} \\ 1 & 5 & a \end{bmatrix}$, $B = \begin{bmatrix} \alpha & \beta & \delta \\ \sqrt{5} & 3 & 1 \\ p & q & 4 \end{bmatrix}$.

Find $A + B$.

SOLUTION

Using the definition of matrix addition, add the (*ij*) entry of A to the (*ij*) entry of B. Thus,

$$A + B = \begin{bmatrix} 2 & 3 & 7 \\ 4 & m & \sqrt{3} \\ 1 & 5 & a \end{bmatrix} + \begin{bmatrix} \alpha & \beta & \delta \\ \sqrt{5} & 3 & 1 \\ p & q & 4 \end{bmatrix}$$

$$= \begin{bmatrix} 2+\alpha & 3+\beta & 7+\delta \\ 4+\sqrt{5} & m+3 & \sqrt{3}+1 \\ 1+p & 5+q & a+4 \end{bmatrix}$$

PROBLEM

If $A = \begin{bmatrix} 2 & 3 & 4 \\ 1 & 2 & 1 \end{bmatrix}$ and $B = \begin{bmatrix} 0 & 2 & 7 \\ 1 & -3 & 5 \end{bmatrix}$, find $A - B$.

SOLUTION

$A - B$ is obtained by subtracting the entries of B from the corresponding entries of A.

$$A - B = \begin{bmatrix} 2 & 3 & 4 \\ 1 & 2 & 1 \end{bmatrix} - \begin{bmatrix} 0 & 2 & 7 \\ 1 & -3 & 5 \end{bmatrix}$$

$$= \begin{bmatrix} 2-0 & 3-2 & 4-7 \\ 1-1 & 2-(-3) & 1-5 \end{bmatrix}$$

$$= \begin{bmatrix} 2 & 1 & -3 \\ 0 & 5 & -4 \end{bmatrix}$$

PROBLEM

If $A = \begin{bmatrix} 2 & -2 & 4 \\ -1 & 1 & 1 \end{bmatrix}$ and $B = \begin{bmatrix} 0 & 1 & -3 \\ 1 & 3 & 1 \end{bmatrix}$, find $2A + B$.

SOLUTION

$$2A = 2\begin{bmatrix} 2 & -2 & 4 \\ -1 & 1 & 1 \end{bmatrix}$$

$$= \begin{bmatrix} 2\times 2 & 2\times(-2) & 2\times 4 \\ 2\times(-1) & 2\times 1 & 2\times 1 \end{bmatrix}$$

$$= \begin{bmatrix} 4 & -4 & 8 \\ -2 & 2 & 2 \end{bmatrix}$$

Then,

$$2A + B = \begin{bmatrix} 4 & -4 & 8 \\ -2 & 2 & 2 \end{bmatrix} + \begin{bmatrix} 0 & 1 & -3 \\ 1 & 3 & 1 \end{bmatrix}$$

$$= \begin{bmatrix} 4+0 & -4+1 & 8-3 \\ -2+1 & 2+3 & 2+1 \end{bmatrix}$$

$$2A + B = \begin{bmatrix} 4 & -3 & 5 \\ -1 & 5 & 3 \end{bmatrix}$$

PROBLEM

If $A = \begin{bmatrix} 1 & 2 & 4 \\ 2 & 6 & 0 \end{bmatrix}$ and $B = \begin{bmatrix} 4 & 1 & 4 & 3 \\ 0 & -1 & 3 & 1 \\ 2 & 7 & 5 & 2 \end{bmatrix}$, find AB.

SOLUTION

Since A is a 2×3 matrix and B is a 3×4 matrix, the product AB is a 2×4 matrix.

$$AB = \begin{bmatrix} 1 & 2 & 4 \\ 2 & 6 & 0 \end{bmatrix}\begin{bmatrix} 4 & 1 & 4 & 3 \\ 0 & -1 & 3 & 1 \\ 2 & 7 & 5 & 2 \end{bmatrix}$$

$$= \begin{bmatrix} 1\cdot 4+2\cdot 0+4\cdot 2 & 1\cdot 1+2\cdot(-1)+4\cdot 7 & 1\cdot 4+2\cdot 3+4\cdot 5 & 1\cdot 3+2\cdot 1+4\cdot 2 \\ 2\cdot 2+6\cdot 0+0\cdot 2 & 2\cdot 1+6\cdot(-1)+0\cdot 7 & 2\cdot 4+6\cdot 3+0\cdot 5 & 2\cdot 3+6\cdot 1+0\cdot 2 \end{bmatrix}$$

$$= \begin{bmatrix} 4+0+8 & 1-2+28 & 4+6+20 & 3+2+8 \\ 8+0+0 & 2-6+0 & 8+18+0 & 6+6+0 \end{bmatrix}$$

$$AB = \begin{bmatrix} 12 & 27 & 30 & 13 \\ 8 & -4 & 26 & 12 \end{bmatrix}$$

Matrix Arithmetic

Rules of Matrix Arithmetic

a) $A + B = B + A$ (Commutative Law of Addition)

b) $A + (B + C) = (A + B) + C$ (Associative Law of Addition)

c) $A(BC) = (AB)C$ (Associative Law of Multiplication)

d) $A(B \pm C) = AB \pm AC$ (Distributive Law)

e) $a(B + C) = aB + aC$

f) $(a \pm b)C = aC \pm bC$

g) $(ab)C = a(bC)$

h) $a(BC) = (aB)C = B(aC)$

A matrix whose entries are all zero is called a zero matrix, $\mathbf{0}$.

- **EXAMPLES**

a) $\begin{bmatrix} 0 & 0 \\ 0 & 0 \end{bmatrix}$

b) $\begin{bmatrix} 0 \\ 0 \\ 0 \end{bmatrix}$

c) $\begin{bmatrix} 0 & 0 & 0 \\ 0 & 0 & 0 \\ 0 & 0 & 0 \end{bmatrix}$

Theorem

If the size of the matrices are such that the indicated operations can be performed, the following rules of matrix arithmetic are valid:

a) $A + \mathbf{0} = \mathbf{0} + A = A$

b) $A - A = \mathbf{0}$

c) $\mathbf{0} - A = -A$

d) $A\mathbf{0} = \mathbf{0}$

An identity matrix (I) is a square matrix with ones on the main diagonal and zeros everywhere else.

- **EXAMPLES**

a) $\begin{bmatrix} 1 & 0 \\ 0 & 1 \end{bmatrix}$

b) $\begin{bmatrix} 1 & 0 & 0 & 0 \\ 0 & 1 & 0 & 0 \\ 0 & 0 & 1 & 0 \\ 0 & 0 & 0 & 1 \end{bmatrix}$

If A is a square matrix and a matrix B exists such that $AB = BA = I$, then A is invertible and B is the inverse of A, (A^{-1}). An invertible matrix has one and only one inverse.

Theorem

If A and B are invertible matrices of the same size, then:

a) AB is invertible

b) $(AB)^{-1} = (B^{-1})(A^{-1})$

The formula for inverting a 2×2 matrix is

If $A = \begin{bmatrix} a & b \\ c & d \end{bmatrix}$, then $A^{-1} = \dfrac{1}{ad - bc}\begin{bmatrix} d & -b \\ -c & a \end{bmatrix}$.

- **EXAMPLE**

If $A = \begin{bmatrix} 1 & 2 \\ 3 & 4 \end{bmatrix}$, then $A^{-1} = \begin{bmatrix} -2 & 1 \\ \frac{3}{2} & -\frac{1}{2} \end{bmatrix}$.

Theorem

If A is an invertible matrix, then:

a) A^{-1} is invertible; $(A^{-1})^{-1} = A$

b) kA is invertible (where k is a non-zero scalar); $(kA)^{-1} = \dfrac{1}{k}A^{-1}$

c) A^n is invertible; $(A^n)^{-1} = (A^{-1})^n$

If A is a square matrix and x and y are positive integers, then:

a) $A^x A^y = A^{x+y}$

b) $(A^x)^y = A^{xy}$

PROBLEM

Show that

a) $A + B = B + A$ where:

$$A = \begin{bmatrix} 3 & 1 & 1 \\ 2 & -1 & 1 \end{bmatrix} \text{ and } B = \begin{bmatrix} 4 & 2 & -1 \\ 0 & 0 & 2 \end{bmatrix}.$$

b) $(A + B) + C = A + (B + C)$ where

$$A = \begin{bmatrix} -2 & 6 \\ 2 & 1 \end{bmatrix}, B = \begin{bmatrix} 2 & 1 \\ 0 & 3 \end{bmatrix}, \text{ and } C = \begin{bmatrix} -1 & 0 \\ 7 & 2 \end{bmatrix}.$$

C) If A and the zero matrix have the same size, then $A + \mathbf{0} = A$ where:

$$A = \begin{bmatrix} 2 & 1 \\ 1 & 2 \end{bmatrix}.$$

d) $A + (-A) = \mathbf{0}$ where:

$$A = \begin{bmatrix} 2 & 1 \\ 1 & 2 \end{bmatrix}.$$

e) $(ab)A = a(bA)$ where $a = -5$, $b = 3$, and:

$$A = \begin{bmatrix} 6 & -1 & 0 \\ 1 & 2 & 1 \end{bmatrix}.$$

f) Find B if $2A - 3B + C = \mathbf{0}$ where:

$$A = \begin{bmatrix} -1 & 3 \\ 0 & 0 \end{bmatrix} \text{ and } C = \begin{bmatrix} -2 & -1 \\ -1 & 1 \end{bmatrix}.$$

SOLUTION

a) By the definition of matrix addition,

$$A + B = \begin{bmatrix} 3 & 1 & 1 \\ 2 & -1 & 1 \end{bmatrix} + \begin{bmatrix} 4 & 2 & -1 \\ 0 & 0 & 2 \end{bmatrix}$$

$$= \begin{bmatrix} 3+4 & 1+2 & 1+(-1) \\ 2+0 & -1+0 & 1+2 \end{bmatrix}$$

$$= \begin{bmatrix} 7 & 3 & 0 \\ 2 & -1 & 3 \end{bmatrix}$$

and

$$B + A = \begin{bmatrix} 4 & 2 & -1 \\ 0 & 0 & 2 \end{bmatrix} + \begin{bmatrix} 3 & 1 & 1 \\ 2 & -1 & 1 \end{bmatrix}$$

$$= \begin{bmatrix} 4+3 & 2+1 & -1+1 \\ 0+2 & 0+(-1) & 2+1 \end{bmatrix}$$

$$= \begin{bmatrix} 7 & 3 & 0 \\ 2 & -1 & 3 \end{bmatrix}$$

Thus, $A + B = B + A$.

b) $$A + B = \begin{bmatrix} -2 & 6 \\ 2 & 1 \end{bmatrix} + \begin{bmatrix} 2 & 1 \\ 0 & 3 \end{bmatrix}$$

$$= \begin{bmatrix} -2+2 & 6+1 \\ 2+0 & 1+3 \end{bmatrix}$$

$$= \begin{bmatrix} 0 & 7 \\ 2 & 4 \end{bmatrix}$$

and

$$(A + B) + C = \begin{bmatrix} 0 & 7 \\ 2 & 4 \end{bmatrix} + \begin{bmatrix} -1 & 0 \\ 7 & 2 \end{bmatrix}$$

$$= \begin{bmatrix} 0+(-1) & 7+0 \\ 2+7 & 4+2 \end{bmatrix}$$

$$= \begin{bmatrix} -1 & 7 \\ 9 & 6 \end{bmatrix}$$

$$B + C = \begin{bmatrix} 2 & 1 \\ 0 & 3 \end{bmatrix} + \begin{bmatrix} -1 & 0 \\ 7 & 2 \end{bmatrix}$$

$$= \begin{bmatrix} 2+(-1) & 1+0 \\ 0+7 & 3+2 \end{bmatrix}$$

$$= \begin{bmatrix} 1 & 1 \\ 7 & 5 \end{bmatrix}$$

and

$$A + (B + C) = \begin{bmatrix} -2 & 6 \\ 2 & 1 \end{bmatrix} + \begin{bmatrix} 1 & 1 \\ 7 & 5 \end{bmatrix}$$

$$= \begin{bmatrix} -2+1 & 6+1 \\ 2+7 & 1+5 \end{bmatrix}$$

$$= \begin{bmatrix} -1 & 7 \\ 9 & 6 \end{bmatrix}$$

Thus, $(A + B) + C = A + (B + C)$.

c) $A = \begin{bmatrix} 2 & 1 \\ 1 & 2 \end{bmatrix}$ $0 = \begin{bmatrix} 0 & 0 \\ 0 & 0 \end{bmatrix}$.

Thus,

$$A + 0 = \begin{bmatrix} 2 & 1 \\ 1 & 2 \end{bmatrix} + \begin{bmatrix} 0 & 0 \\ 0 & 0 \end{bmatrix}$$

$$= \begin{bmatrix} 2+0 & 1+0 \\ 1+0 & 2+0 \end{bmatrix}$$

$$= \begin{bmatrix} 2 & 1 \\ 1 & 2 \end{bmatrix}$$

Hence, $A + \mathbf{0} = A$.

d) $-A = -1 \times \begin{bmatrix} 2 & 1 \\ 1 & 2 \end{bmatrix}$

$$= \begin{bmatrix} -1\times2 & -1\times1 \\ -1\times1 & -1\times2 \end{bmatrix}$$

$$= \begin{bmatrix} -2 & -1 \\ -1 & -2 \end{bmatrix}$$

Thus,

$$A + (-A) = \begin{bmatrix} 2 & 1 \\ 1 & 2 \end{bmatrix} + \begin{bmatrix} -2 & -1 \\ -1 & -2 \end{bmatrix}$$

$$= \begin{bmatrix} 2+(-2) & 1+(-1) \\ 1+(-1) & 2+(-2) \end{bmatrix}$$

$$= \begin{bmatrix} 0 & 0 \\ 0 & 0 \end{bmatrix}$$

Therefore, $A + (-A) = \mathbf{0}$.

e) $bA = 3\begin{bmatrix} 6 & -1 & 0 \\ 1 & 2 & 1 \end{bmatrix} = \begin{bmatrix} 3\times6 & 3\times(-1) & 3\times0 \\ 3\times1 & 3\times2 & 3\times1 \end{bmatrix}$

$$= \begin{bmatrix} 18 & -3 & 0 \\ 3 & 6 & 3 \end{bmatrix}$$

and

$$a(bA) = -5\begin{bmatrix} 18 & -3 & 0 \\ 3 & 6 & 3 \end{bmatrix}$$

$$= \begin{bmatrix} -90 & 15 & 0 \\ -15 & -30 & -15 \end{bmatrix}$$

$$(ab)A = ((-5)(3))\begin{bmatrix} 6 & -1 & 0 \\ 1 & 2 & 1 \end{bmatrix}$$

$$= -15\begin{bmatrix} 6 & -1 & 0 \\ 1 & 2 & 1 \end{bmatrix}$$

$$= \begin{bmatrix} -90 & 15 & 0 \\ -15 & -30 & -15 \end{bmatrix}$$

Thus, $(ab)A = a(bA)$.

f) $2A - 3B + C = 2A + C - 3B = 0$ since matrix addition is commutative.

Now, add $3B$ to both sides of the equation,

$$2A + C - 3B = 0,$$

to obtain $2A + C - 3B + 3B = 0 + 3B$.   (1)

Using the laws we exemplified in parts a) through d), (1) becomes $2A + C = 3B$. Now,

$$\frac{1}{3}(2A + C) = \frac{1}{3}(3B)$$

which implies

$$B = \frac{1}{3}(2A + C).$$

$$2A + C = \begin{bmatrix} 2(-1) & 2(3) \\ 2(0) & 2(0) \end{bmatrix} + \begin{bmatrix} -2 & -1 \\ -1 & 1 \end{bmatrix} = \begin{bmatrix} -4 & 5 \\ -1 & 1 \end{bmatrix}$$

Thus,

$$B = \frac{1}{3}(2A + C) = \frac{1}{3}\begin{bmatrix} -4 & 5 \\ -1 & 1 \end{bmatrix} = \begin{bmatrix} -\frac{4}{3} & \frac{5}{3} \\ -\frac{1}{3} & \frac{1}{3} \end{bmatrix}.$$

PROBLEM

Let $A = \begin{bmatrix} 1 & 1 \\ 3 & 7 \end{bmatrix}$ and $B = \begin{bmatrix} 2 & 5 \\ 4 & 0 \end{bmatrix}$. Show $AB \neq BA$.

SOLUTION

$$AB = \begin{bmatrix} 1 & 1 \\ 3 & 7 \end{bmatrix}\begin{bmatrix} 2 & 5 \\ 4 & 0 \end{bmatrix} = \begin{bmatrix} 1 \cdot 2 + 1 \cdot 4 & 1 \cdot 5 + 1 \cdot 0 \\ 3 \cdot 2 + 7 \cdot 4 & 3 \cdot 5 + 7 \cdot 0 \end{bmatrix}$$

$$= \begin{bmatrix} 2 + 4 & 5 + 0 \\ 6 + 28 & 15 + 0 \end{bmatrix}$$

$$= \begin{bmatrix} 6 & 5 \\ 34 & 15 \end{bmatrix}$$

$$BA = \begin{bmatrix} 2 & 5 \\ 4 & 0 \end{bmatrix}\begin{bmatrix} 1 & 1 \\ 3 & 7 \end{bmatrix} = \begin{bmatrix} 2 \cdot 1 + 5 \cdot 3 & 2 \cdot 1 + 5 \cdot 7 \\ 4 \cdot 1 + 0 \cdot 3 & 4 \cdot 1 + 0 \cdot 7 \end{bmatrix}$$

$$= \begin{bmatrix} 2 + 15 & 2 + 35 \\ 4 + 0 & 4 + 0 \end{bmatrix}$$

$$= \begin{bmatrix} 17 & 37 \\ 4 & 4 \end{bmatrix}$$

Therefore, $AB \neq BA$.

Competency 9:
Knowledge of
Calculus

Limits

Definition

Let f be a function that is defined on an open interval containing a, but possibly not defined at a itself. Let L be a real number. The statement

$$\lim_{x \to a} f(x) = L$$

defines the limit of the function $f(x)$ at the point a. Very simply, L is the value that the function has as the point a is approached.

Problem Solving Examples:

PROBLEM

$$\lim_{x \to 2} f(x) = 2x + 1$$

SOLUTION

As $x \to 2, f(x) \to 5$. Therefore, $\lim_{x \to 2} (2x + 1) = 5$

PROBLEM

$$\text{Find } \lim_{x \to 3} f(x) = \frac{x^2 - 9}{x + 1}$$

SOLUTION

$$\lim_{x \to 3} = \frac{x^2 - 9}{x + 1} = \frac{0}{4} = 0.$$

Theorems on Limits

The following are important properties of limits:

Consider $\lim_{x \to a} f(x) = L$ and $\lim_{x \to a} g(x) = K$, then

A) Uniqueness – If $\lim_{x \to a} f(x)$ exists then it is unique.

B) $\lim_{x \to a} [f(x) + g(x)] = \lim_{x \to a} f(x) + \lim_{x \to a} g(x) = L + K$

C) $\lim_{x \to a} [f(x) - g(x)] = \lim_{x \to a} f(x) - \lim_{x \to a} g(x) = L - K$

D) $\lim_{x \to a} [f(x) \cdot g(x)] = \lim_{x \to a} f(x) \cdot \lim_{x \to a} g(x) = L \cdot K$

E) $\lim_{x \to a} \dfrac{f(x)}{g(x)} = \dfrac{\lim_{x \to a} f(x)}{\lim_{x \to a} g(x)} = \dfrac{L}{K}$ provided $K \neq 0$

F) $\lim_{x \to a} \dfrac{1}{g(x)} = \dfrac{1}{K},\ K \neq 0$

G) $\lim_{x \to a} [f(x)]^n = [\lim_{x \to a} f(x)]^n$ for $n > 0$

H) $\lim_{x \to a} [cf(x)] = c[\lim_{x \to a} f(x)], c \in R$

I) $\lim_{x \to a} cx^n = c \lim_{x \to a} x^n = ca^n, c \in R$

J) If f is a polynomial function then $\lim_{x \to a} f(x) = f(a)$ for all $a \in R$.

K) $\lim_{x \to a} \sqrt[n]{x} = \sqrt[n]{a}$ when $a \geq 0$ and n is a positive integer or when $a \leq 0$ and n is an odd positive integer.

L) $\lim_{x \to a} \sqrt[n]{f(x)} = \sqrt[n]{\lim_{x \to a} f(x)}$ when n is a positive integer

M) If $f(x) \leq h(x) \leq g(x)$ for all x in an open interval containing a, except possibly at a, and if $\lim_{x \to a} f(x) = L = \lim_{x \to a} g(x)$ then $\lim_{x \to a} h(x) = L$.

PROBLEM

Find $\lim_{x \to 0} (x\sqrt{x-3})$

SOLUTION

In checking the function by simple substitution, we see that:

$$x\sqrt{x-3} = 0$$

if $x = 0$.

However, this function does not have real values for values of x less than 3. Therefore, since x cannot approach 0, $f(x)$ does not approach 0 and the limit does not exist. This example illustrates that we cannot properly find

$$\lim_{x \to a} f(x)$$

by finding $f(a)$, even though they are equal in many cases. We must consider values of x near a, but not equal to a.

One-Sided Limits

Suppose f is a function such that it is not defined for all values of x. Rather, it is defined in such a way that it "jumps" from one y value to the next instead of smoothly going from one y value to the next. Examples are shown in figures below.

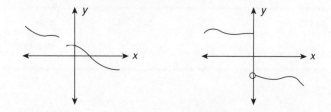

Fig 9.1 $y = f(x)$ is not defined for all x values.

Fig 9.2 $y = f(x)$ "jumps" from a positive value to a negative one.

The statement $\lim_{x \to a^+} f(x) = R$ tells us that as x approaches "a" from the right or from positive infinity, the function f has the limit R.

Similarly, the statement $\lim_{x \to a^-} f(x) = L$ says that as x approaches "a" from the left-hand side or from negative infinity, the function f has the limit L.

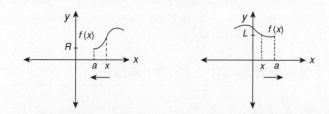

Fig 9.3 Right-hand limit

Fig 9.4 Left-hand limit

If f is defined in an open interval containing a, except possibly at a, then

$$\lim_{x \to a} f(x) = L \text{ if and only if}$$

$$\lim_{x \to a^+} f(x) = L = \lim_{x \to a^-} f(x)$$

Notice that in Fig. 2 the right-hand limit is not the same as the left-hand limit, as it is in Fig. 5.

Fig 9.5

PROBLEM

Let $f(x)$ and $g(x)$ be defined by:

$$f(x) = \begin{cases} x^2 + 2x, & x \leqq 1, \\ 2x, & x > 1, \end{cases}$$

$$g(x) = \begin{cases} 2x^3, & x \leqq 1, \\ 3, & x > 1. \end{cases}$$

Find $\lim\limits_{x \to 1} [f(x) \cdot g(x)]$ if it exists.

SOLUTION

Neither $f(x)$ nor $g(x)$ have limits as $x \to 1$, but one-sided limits exist for both functions. It is possible that the product of two functions may have a limit, even though the two functions do not have limits individually.

$$\lim_{x \to 1^-} f(x) = 3, \qquad \lim_{x \to 1^+} f(x) = 2,$$

$$\lim_{x \to 1^-} g(x) = 2, \qquad \lim_{x \to 1^+} g(x) = 3.$$

Therefore,

$$\lim_{x \to 1^-} [f(x) \cdot g(x)] = 6$$

and

$$\lim_{x \to 1^+} [f(x) \cdot g(x)] = 6$$

Consequently,

$$\lim_{x \to 1} [f(x) \cdot g(x)] = 6$$

PROBLEM

Given that f is the function defined by:

$$f(x) = \begin{cases} x - 3 & \text{if } x \neq 4 \\ 5 & \text{if } x = 4, \end{cases}$$

Find $\lim\limits_{x \to 4} f(x)$.

SOLUTION

When plotting $f(x)$ to obtain a visual representation, it is seen that $f(x) = x - 3$ is a straight line which has a break or discontinuity at the point $x = 4$. At $x = 4$, the value of $f(x)$ is given as 5, and not as 1 - the value that $f(x)$ would assume if the line were continuous. However, when evaluating $\lim\limits_{x \to 4} f(x)$, we are considering values of x close to 4 but not equal to 4. Thus we have

$$\lim_{x \to 4} f(x) = \lim_{x \to 4}(x - 3)$$
$$= 1.$$

In this example,

$$\lim_{x \to 4} f(x) = 1 \text{ but } f(4) = 5; \text{ therefore,}$$

$$\lim_{x \to 4} f(x) \neq f(4).$$

Special Limits

A) $\lim\limits_{x \to 0} \dfrac{\sin x}{x} = 1, \quad \lim\limits_{x \to 0} \dfrac{1 - \cos x}{x} = 0$

B) $\lim\limits_{n\to\infty}(1+\dfrac{1}{n})^n = e,$ $\lim\limits_{n\to 0}(1+n)^{1/n} = e$

C)   For $a > 1$ $\lim\limits_{x\to +\infty} a^x = +\infty,$ $\lim\limits_{x\to -\infty} a^x = 0$

     $\lim\limits_{x\to +\infty} \log_a x = +\infty,$ $\lim\limits_{x\to 0} \log_a x = -\infty$

D)   For $0 < a < 1,$ $\lim\limits_{x\to +\infty} a^x = 0,$ $\lim\limits_{x\to -\infty} a^x = +\infty$

     $\lim\limits_{x\to +\infty} \log_a x = -\infty,$ $\lim\limits_{x\to 0} \log_a x = +\infty$

Some nonexistent limits which are frequently encountered are:

A) $\lim\limits_{x\to 0}\dfrac{1}{x^2},$ as x approaches zero, x^2 gets very small and also becomes zero therefore $\dfrac{1}{0}$ is undefined and the limit does not exist.

B) $\lim\limits_{x\to 0}\dfrac{|x|}{x}$ does not exist.

Proof:

If $x > 0$, then $\dfrac{|x|}{x} = \dfrac{x}{x} = 1$ and hence lies to the right of the y-axis, the graph of f coincides with the line $y = 1$. If $x < 0$ then $\dfrac{-x}{x} = -1$ and the graph of f coincides with the line $y = -1$ to the left of the y-axis.

If it were true that $\lim\limits_{x\to 0}\dfrac{|x|}{x} = L$ for some L, then the preceding remarks imply that $-1 \le L \le 1$.

If we consider any pair of horizontal lines $y = L \pm \theta$, where $0 < \theta < 1$, then there exists points on the graph which are not between these lines for some non-zero x in every interval $(-\theta, \theta)$ containing 0. It follows that the limit does not exist.

Fig 9.6

PROBLEM

Find $\lim\limits_{x\to 3} f(x) = \dfrac{1}{(x-3)^2},$ $x \ne 3$

SOLUTION

Sketching the graph of this function about $x = 3$, we see that it increases without bound as x tends to 3.

Using the method of simple substitution, we find that $\lim\limits_{x\to 3} f(x) = \infty$. There is no limit.

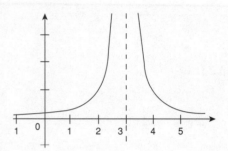

PROBLEM

Find $\lim\limits_{x\to 3}\dfrac{5x}{6-2x}.$

SOLUTION

$\lim\limits_{x\to 3} 5x = 15$

and

$\lim\limits_{x\to 3}[6 - 2x] = 0$

Therefore,

$\lim\limits_{x\to 3}\dfrac{5x}{6-2x} = \dfrac{15}{0} = \infty.$

The function has no limit.

Continuity

A function f is continuous at a point a if

$\lim\limits_{x\to a} f(x) = f(a).$

This implies that three conditions are satisfied:

a) $f(a)$ exists, that is, f is defined at a

b) $\lim\limits_{x\to a} f(x)$ exists, and

c)   the two numbers are equal.

To test continuity at a point $x = a$ we test whether

$\lim\limits_{x\to a^+} F(x) = \lim\limits_{x\to a^-} F(x) = F(a)$

PROBLEM

Investigate the continuity of the function:

$$h(x) = \begin{cases} 3+x & \text{if } x \leq 1 \\ 3-x & \text{if } 1 < x. \end{cases}$$

SOLUTION

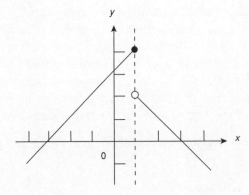

Because there is a break in the graph at the point $x = 1$, we investigate the three conditions for continuity at the point $x = 1$. The three conditions are: (1) $f(x_0)$ is defined, (2) $\lim_{x \to x_0} f(x)$ exists,

(3) $\lim_{x \to x_0} f(x) = f(x_0)$. At $x = 1$, $h(1) = 4$; therefore, condition (1) is satisfied.

$$\lim_{x \to 1^-} h(x) = \lim_{x \to 1^-} (3+x) = 4$$

$$\lim_{x \to 1^+} h(x) = \lim_{x \to 1^+} (3-x) = 2.$$

Because $\lim_{x \to 1^-} h(x) \neq \lim_{x \to 1^+} h(x)$, we conclude that $\lim_{x \to 1} h(x)$ does not exist. Therefore, condition (2) fails to hold at 1.

Hence, h is discontinuous at 1.

PROBLEM

Investigate continuity of:

$$F(x) = \begin{cases} |x-3| & \text{if } x \neq 3 \\ 2 & \text{if } x = 3. \end{cases}$$

SOLUTION

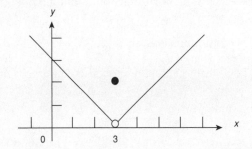

We investigate the three conditions for continuity at the point $x = 3$. The three conditions are: (1) $f(x_0)$ is defined,

(2) $\lim_{x \to x_0} f(x)$ exists, (3) $\lim_{x \to x_0} f(x) = f(x_0)$. At $x = 3$ we have $F(3) = 2$; therefore, condition (1) is satisfied.

$\lim_{x \to 3^-} F(x) = 0$ and $\lim_{x \to 3^+} F(x) = 0$. Therefore, $\lim_{x \to 3} F(x)$ exists and is 0; therefore, condition (2) is satisfied.

$\lim_{x \to 3} F(x) = 0$ but $F(3) = 2$. Therefore, condition (3) is not satisfied. F is thus discontinuous at 3.

Theorems of Continuity

A) A function defined in a closed interval $[a,b]$ is continuous in $[a,b]$ if and only if it is continuous in the open interval (a,b), as well as continuous from the right at "a" and from the left at "b".

B) If f and g are continuous functions at a, then so are the functions $f + g, f-g, fg$ and f/g where $g(a) \neq 0$.

C) If $\lim_{x \to a} g(x) = b$ and f is continuous at b, then $\lim_{x \to a} f(g(x)) = f(b) = f[\lim_{x \to a} g(x)]$.

D) If g is continuous at a and f is continuous at $b = g(a)$, then

$$\lim_{x \to a} f(g(x)) = f[\lim_{x \to a} g(x)] = f(g(a)).$$

E) Intermediate Value Theorem. If f is continuous on a closed interval $[a, b]$ and if $f(a) \neq f(b)$, then f takes on every value between $f(a)$ and $f(b)$ in the interval $[a, b]$.

F) $f(x) = k$, $k \in R$ is continuous everywhere.

G) $f(x) = x$, the identity function is continuous everywhere.

H) If f is continuous at a, then $\lim_{n \to \infty} f\left(a + \frac{1}{n}\right) = f(a)$.

I) If f is continuous on an interval containing a and b, $a < b$, and if $f(a) \cdot f(b) < 0$ then there exists at least one point c, $a < c < b$ such that $f(c) = 0$.

PROBLEM

Let h be defined by:

$$h(x) = \begin{cases} 4 - x^2 & \text{if } x < 1 \\ 2 + x^2 & \text{if } 1 < x \end{cases}$$

Find each of the following limits if they exist:

$$\lim_{x \to 1^-} h(x), \lim_{x \to 1^+} h(x), \lim_{x \to 1} h(x).$$

SOLUTION

It is desirable to sketch the given function to aid in visualizing the problem.

Now,

$$\lim_{x \to 1^-} h(x) = \lim_{x \to 1^-} - (4 - x^2) = 3$$

$$\lim_{x \to 1^+} h(x) = \lim_{x \to 1^+} + (2 + x^2) = 3$$

Therefore, $\lim_{x \to 1} h(x)$ exists and is equal to 3. Note that $h(1) = 3$. This holds because the function is continuous.

PROBLEM

If $h(x) = \sqrt{4 - x^2}$, prove that $h(x)$ is continuous in the closed interval $[-2, 2]$.

SOLUTION

To prove continuity we employ the following definition: A function defined in the closed interval $[a,b]$ is said to be continuous in $[a,b]$ if and only if it is continuous in the open interval (a,b), as well as continuous from the right at a and continuous from the left at b. The function h is continuous in the open interval $(-2,2)$. We must show that the function is continuous from the right at -2 and from the left at 2. Therefore, we must show that $f(-2)$ is defined and $\lim_{x \to -2^+} f(x)$ exists and that these are equal. Also, we must show that $f(2) = \lim_{x \to 2^-} f(x)$. We have:

$$\lim_{x \to -2^+} \sqrt{4 - x^2} = 0 = h(-2),$$

and

$$\lim_{x \to 2^-} \sqrt{4 - x^2} = 0 = h(2).$$

Thus, h is continuous in the closed interval $[-2,2]$.

The Derivative

The Definition and Δ-Method

The derivative of a function expresses its rate of change with respect to an independent variable. The derivative is also the slope of the tangent line to the curve.

Consider the graph of the function f in the figure. Choosing a point x and a point $x + \Delta x$ (where Δx denotes a small distance on the x-axis) we can obtain both, $f(x)$ and $f(x + \Delta x)$. Drawing a tangent line, l, of the curve through the points $f(x)$ and $f(x + \Delta x)$, we can measure the rate of change of this line. As we let the distance, Δx, approach zero, then

$$\lim_{\Delta x \to 0} \frac{f(x + \Delta x) - f(x)}{\Delta x}$$

becomes the instantaneous rate of change of the function or the derivative.

We denote the derivative of the function f to be f'. So we have

$$f'(x) = \lim_{\Delta x \to 0} \frac{f(x + \Delta x) - f(x)}{\Delta x}$$

If $y = f(x)$, some common notations for the derivative are

$$y' = f'(x)$$

$$\frac{dy}{dx} = f'(x)$$

$$D_x y = f'(x) \text{ or } Df = f'$$

PROBLEM

Find the slope of each of the following curves at the given point, using the Δ-method.

    a) $y = 3x^2 - 2x + 4$ at $(1,5)$

    b) $y = x^3 - 3x + 5$ at $(-2,3)$.

SOLUTION

The slope of a given curve at a specified point is the derivative, in this case $\dfrac{\Delta y}{\Delta x}$, evaluated at that point.

a) From the Δ-method we know that:

$$\frac{\Delta y}{\Delta x} = \frac{f(x + \Delta x) - f(x)}{\Delta x}.$$

For the curve $y = 3x^2 - 2x + 4$, we find:

$$\frac{\Delta y}{\Delta x} = \frac{3(x + \Delta x)^2 - 2(x + \Delta x) + 4 - (3x^2 - 2x + 4)}{\Delta x}$$

$$= \frac{3x^2 + 6x\Delta x + 3(\Delta x)^2 - 2x - 2\Delta x + 4 - 3x^2 + 2x - 4}{\Delta x}$$

$$= \frac{6x\Delta x + 3(\Delta x)^2 - 2\Delta x}{\Delta x}$$

$$= 6x + 3\Delta x - 2.$$

$$\lim_{\Delta x \to 0} \frac{\Delta y}{\Delta x} = \lim_{\Delta x \to 0} 6x + 3\Delta x - 2 = 6x - 2.$$

At $(1,5)$ $\dfrac{\Delta y}{\Delta x} = 4$ is the required slope.

b) Again using the Δ-method, $\dfrac{\Delta y}{\Delta x}$ for the curve:

$y = x^3 - 3x + 5$, can be found as follows:

$$\frac{\Delta y}{\Delta x} = \frac{f(x + \Delta x) - f(x)}{\Delta x}$$

$$\frac{\Delta y}{\Delta x} = \frac{(x + \Delta x)^3 - 3(x \, \Delta x) + 5 - (x^3 - 3x + 5)}{\Delta x}.$$

$$\frac{\Delta y}{\Delta x} = \frac{(x + \Delta x)^3 - 3(x + \Delta x) + 5 - (x^3 - 3x + 5)}{\Delta x}$$

$$= \frac{x^3 + 3x^2\Delta x + 3x(\Delta x)^2 + (\Delta x)^3 - 3x - 3\Delta x + 5 - x^3 + 3x - 5}{\Delta x}$$

$$= \frac{3x^2\Delta x + 3x(\Delta x)^2 + (\Delta x)^3 - 3\Delta x}{\Delta x}$$

$$= 3x^2 + 3x\Delta x + (\Delta x)^2 - 3.$$

$$\lim_{\Delta x \to 0} \frac{\Delta y}{\Delta x} = \lim_{\Delta x \to 0} 3x^2 + 3x\Delta x + (\Delta x)^2 - 3 = 3x^2 - 3.$$

At $(-2,3)$, $\dfrac{\Delta y}{\Delta x} = 9$ is the required slope.

PROBLEM

Find the average rate of change, by the Δ process, for:

$$y = \frac{1}{x}.$$

SOLUTION

$$y = f(x) = \frac{1}{x}$$

The average rate of change is defined to be

$\dfrac{\Delta y}{\Delta x}$ with $\Delta y = f(x + \Delta x) - f(x)$.

Since

$$f(x) = \dfrac{1}{x}, \; f(x + \Delta x) = \dfrac{1}{x + \Delta x},$$

and

$$\Delta y = \dfrac{1}{x + \Delta x} - \dfrac{1}{x} = \dfrac{x - (x + \Delta x)}{x(x + \Delta x)}$$

$$= \dfrac{-\Delta x}{x(x + \Delta x)}.$$

Now,

$$\dfrac{\Delta y}{\Delta x} = \dfrac{-\Delta x}{x(x + \Delta x)\Delta x} = -\dfrac{1}{x(x + \Delta x)}.$$

Therefore, the average rate of change is $\dfrac{-1}{x(x + \Delta x)}$.

The Derivative at a point

If f is defined on an open interval containing "a", then

$$f'(a) = \lim_{x \to a} \dfrac{f(x) - f(a)}{x - a},$$

provided the limit exists.

PROBLEM

Find the instantaneous rate of the function:

$$y = \dfrac{2x}{x + 1}$$

for any value of x and for $x = 2$.

SOLUTION

The instantaneous rate of change of a function is defined as,

$$\lim_{\Delta x \to 0} \dfrac{\Delta y}{\Delta x} = \lim_{\Delta x \to 0} \dfrac{f(x + \Delta x) - f(x)}{\Delta x}$$

Therefore,

$$\Delta y = f(x + \Delta x) - f(x).$$

In this case,

$$f(x) = \dfrac{2x}{x + 1}, \text{ therefore,}$$

$$f(x + \Delta x) = \dfrac{2(x + \Delta x)}{x + \Delta x + 1}$$

Substituting, we have:

$$\Delta y = \dfrac{2x + 2 \cdot \Delta x}{x + \Delta x + 1} - \dfrac{2x}{x + 1}$$

$$= \dfrac{(2x + 2 \cdot \Delta x)(x + 1) - 2x(x + \Delta x + 1)}{(x + \Delta x + 1)(x + 1)}$$

$$= \dfrac{2x^2 + 2x \cdot \Delta x + 2x + 2 \cdot \Delta x - 2x^2 - 2x \cdot \Delta x - 2x}{(x + \Delta x + 1)(x + 1)}$$

$$= \dfrac{2 \cdot \Delta x}{(x + \Delta x + 1)(x + 1)}.$$

$$\dfrac{\Delta y}{\Delta x} = \dfrac{2 \cdot \Delta x}{(x + \Delta x + 1)(x + 1)(\Delta x)}$$

$$= \dfrac{2}{(x + \Delta x + 1)(x + 1)}$$

Now,

$$\lim_{\Delta x \to 0} \dfrac{\Delta y}{\Delta x} = \lim_{\Delta x \to 0} \dfrac{2}{(x + \Delta x + 1)(x + 1)}.$$

Substituting 0 for Δx we have,

$$\lim_{\Delta x \to 0} \dfrac{\Delta y}{\Delta x} = \dfrac{2}{(x + 1)^2},$$

the instantaneous rate of change for any value of x.

For $x = 2$, we have,

$$\dfrac{2}{(x + 1)^2} = \dfrac{2}{(2 + 1)^2} = \dfrac{2}{9}.$$

PROBLEM

> Find the rate of change of y with respect to x at the point $x = 5$, if
> $$2y = x^2 + 3x - 1.$$

SOLUTION

Rate of change is defined as

$$\lim_{\Delta x \to 0} \frac{\Delta y}{\Delta x}, \text{ with}$$

$$\Delta y = f(x + \Delta x) - f(x).$$

We have:

$$2\Delta y = (x + \Delta x)^2 + 3(x + \Delta x) - 1 - (x^2 + 3x - 1)$$
$$= x^2 + 2x \cdot \Delta x + (\Delta x)^2 + 3x + 3\Delta x - 1 - x^2 - 3x + 1$$
$$= 2x \cdot \Delta x + (\Delta x)^2 + 3\Delta x.$$

Dividing by Δx,

$$\frac{2\Delta y}{\Delta x} = \frac{2x \cdot \Delta x}{\Delta x} + \frac{(\Delta x)^2}{\Delta x} + \frac{3\Delta x}{\Delta x}$$
$$= 2x + \Delta x + 3$$

and

$$\frac{\Delta y}{\Delta x} = x + \frac{\Delta x}{2} + \frac{3}{2}.$$

Now,

$$\lim_{\Delta x \to 0} \frac{\Delta y}{\Delta x} = \lim_{\Delta x \to 0} x + \frac{\Delta x}{2} + \frac{3}{2} = x + \frac{3}{2}.$$

For $x = 5$,

$$\lim_{\Delta x \to 0} \frac{\Delta y}{\Delta x} = 5 + \frac{3}{2} = 6\frac{1}{2}.$$

Rules for Finding the Derivatives

General rule:

A) If f is a constant function, $f(x) = c$, then $f'(x) = 0$.

B) If $\boxed{f(x) = x, \text{ then } f'(x) = 1.}$

C) If f is differentiable, then $\boxed{(cf(x))' = cf'(x)}$

D) Power Rule: If $f(x) = x^n$, $n \in z$, then
$f'(x) = nx^{n-1}$; if $n < 0$ then x^n is not defined at $x = 0$.

E) If f and g are differentiable on the interval (a,b) then:

a) $\boxed{(f + g)'(x) = f'(x) + g'(x)}$

b) Product Rule: $\boxed{(fg)'(x) = f(x)g'(x) + g(x)f'(x)}$

Example: Find $f'(x)$ if $f(x) = (x^3 + 1)(2x^2 + 8x - 5)$.
$$f'(x) = (x^3 + 1)(4x + 8) + (2x^2 + 8x - 5)(3x^2)$$
$$= 4x^4 + 8x^3 + 4x + 8 + 6x^4 + 24x^3 - 15x^2$$
$$= 10x^4 + 32x^3 - 15x^2 + 4x + 8$$

c) Quotient Rule: $\boxed{\left(\dfrac{f}{g}\right)(x) = \dfrac{g(x)f'(x) - f(x)g'(x)}{[g(x)]^2}}$

Example: Find $f'(x)$ if $f(x) = \dfrac{3x^2 - x + 2}{4x^2 + 5}$

$$f'(x) = \frac{-(3x^2 - x + 2)(8x) + (4x^2 + 5)(6x - 1)}{(4x^2 + 5)^2}$$
$$= \frac{-(24x^3 - 8x^2 + 16x) + (24x^3 - 4x^2 + 30x - 5)}{(4x^2 + 5)^2}$$
$$= \frac{4x^2 + 14x - 5}{(4x^2 + 5)^2}$$

F) If $f(x) = x^{m/n}$, then $f'(x) = \dfrac{m}{n} x^{\frac{m}{n} - 1}$
where $m, n \in Z$ and $n \neq 0$

G) Polynomials. If $f(x) = (a_0 + a_1 x + a_2 x^2 + \ldots + a_n x^n)$ then $f'(x) = a_1 + 2a_2 x + 3a_3 x^2 + \ldots + na_n x^{n-1}$

This employs the power rule and rules concerning constants.

H) Chain Rule. Let $f(u)$ be a composite function, where $u = g(x)$.

Then $f'(u) = f'(u)g'(x)$ or if $y = f(u)$ and $u = g(x)$ then $D_x y = (D_u y)(D_x u) = f'(u)g'(x)$

PROBLEM

> Find the derivative of: $y = x^{3b}$.

SOLUTION

Applying the theorem for $d(u^n)$,

$$\frac{dy}{dx} = 3b \cdot x^{3b-1}.$$

PROBLEM

Find the derivative of: $y = (x^2 + 2)^3$.

SOLUTION

Method 1. We may expand the cube and write:

$$\frac{dy}{dx} = \frac{d}{dx}[(x^2 + 2)^3] = \frac{d}{dx}(x^6 + 6x^4 + 12x^2 + 8)$$

$$= 6x^5 + 24x^3 + 24x.$$

Method 2. Let $u = x^2 + 2$, then $y = (x^2 + 2)^3 = u^3$;

Using the chain rule we have:

$$\frac{dy}{dx} = \frac{dy}{du} \cdot \frac{du}{dx} = \frac{d(u^3)}{du} \cdot \frac{d(x^2 + 2)}{dx} = 3u^2(2x)$$

$$= 3(x^2 + 2)^2 \cdot (2x) = 3(x^4 + 4x^2 + 4) \cdot (2x)$$

$$= 6x^5 + 24x^3 + 24x.$$

Implicit Differentiation

An implicit function of x and y is a function in which one of the variables is not directly expressed in terms of the other. If these variables are not easily or practically separable, we can still differentiate the expression.

Apply the normal rules of differentiation such as the product rule, the power rule, etc. Remember also the chain rule which states $\dfrac{du}{dx} \times \dfrac{dx}{dt} = \dfrac{du}{dt}$.

Once the rules have been properly applied we will be left with as in the example of x and y, some factors of $\dfrac{dy}{dx}$.

We can then algebraically solve for the derivative $\dfrac{dy}{dx}$ and obtain the desired result.

PROBLEM

If $x^2 + y^2 = 16$, find $\dfrac{dy}{dx}$ as an implicit function of x and y.

SOLUTION

Since y is a function of x, we differentiate the equation implicitly in terms of x and y. We have:

$$2x + 2y \cdot \frac{dy}{dx} = 0 \quad \text{or} \quad 2y \frac{dy}{dx} = -2x.$$

$$\frac{dy}{dx} = -\frac{x}{y}.$$

PROBLEM

Find $\dfrac{dy}{dx}$ for the expression:
$2x^4 - 3x^2y^2 + y^4 = 0$.

SOLUTION

The equation $2x^4 - 3x^2y^2 + y^4 = 0$, could be solved for y and then differentiated to obtain $\dfrac{dy}{dx}$, but an easier method is to differentiate implicitly and then solve for $\dfrac{dy}{dx}$.

Hence, from $2x^4 - 3x^2y^2 + y^4 = 0$ we obtain:

$$8x^3 - 6x^2y \frac{dy}{dx} - 6xy^2 + 4y^3 \frac{dy}{dx} = 0.$$

Solving for $\dfrac{dy}{dx}$,

$$4y^3 \frac{dy}{dx} - 6x^2y \frac{dy}{dx} = 6xy^2 - 8x^3.$$

$$(4y^3 - 6x^2y) \frac{dy}{dx} = 6xy^2 - 8x^3.$$

$$\frac{dy}{dx} = \frac{6xy^2 - 8x^3}{4y^3 - 6x^2y}$$

$$= \frac{3xy^2 - 4x^3}{2y^3 - 3x^2y}.$$

Trigonometric Differentiation

The three most basic trigonometric derivatives are:

$$\frac{d}{dx}(\sin x) = \cos x,$$

$$\frac{d}{dx}(\cos x) = -\sin x,$$

$$\frac{d}{dx}(\tan x) = \sec^2 x,$$

Given any trigonometric function, it can be differentiated by applying these basics in combination with the general rules for differentiating algebraic expressions.

The following will be most useful if committed to memory:

$$D_x \sin u = \cos u\, D_x u$$

$$D_x \cos u = -\sin u\, D_x u$$

$$D_x \tan u = \sec^2 u\, D_x u$$

$$D_x \sec u = \tan u \sec u\, D_x u$$

$$D_x \cot u = -\csc^2 u\, D_x u$$

$$D_x \csc u = -\csc u \cot u\, D_x u$$

PROBLEM

Find the derivative of: $y = \sin ax^2$.

SOLUTION

Applying the theorem for the derivative of the sine of a function,

$$\frac{dy}{dx} = \cos ax^2 \cdot \frac{d}{dx}(ax^2)$$
$$= 2\, ax \cos ax^2.$$

PROBLEM

Find the derivative of: $y\, \tan 3\theta$.

SOLUTION

Let $u = 3\theta$

Then, $y = \tan u$, and

$$\frac{dy}{d\theta} = \frac{dy}{du} \cdot \frac{du}{d\theta}$$

$$\frac{du}{d\theta} = 3,$$

and $\dfrac{dy}{du} = \sec^2 u$.

Therefore,

$$\frac{dy}{d\theta} = \frac{dy}{du} \cdot \frac{du}{d\theta} = \sec^2 u \cdot 3 = 3\sec^2(3\theta).$$

Inverse Trigonometric Differentiation

Here are the derivatives for the inverse trigonometric functions which can be found in a manner similar to the above function. If u is a differentiable function of x then:

$$D_x \sin^{-1} u = \frac{1}{\sqrt{1-u^2}} D_x u \quad , \quad |u| < 1$$

$$D_x \cos^{-1} u = \frac{-1}{\sqrt{1-u^2}} D_x u \quad , \quad |u| < 1$$

$$D_x \tan^{-1} u = \frac{1}{1+u^2} D_x u \quad ,$$

$$D_x \sec^{-1} u = \frac{1}{|u|\sqrt{u^2-1}} D_x u, u = f(x), |f(x)| > 1$$

$$D_x \cot^{-1} u = \frac{-1}{1+u^2} D_x u \quad ,$$

$$D_x \csc^{-1} u = \frac{-1}{|u|\sqrt{u^2-1}} D_x u, u = f(x), |f(x)| > 1$$

PROBLEM

Find the derivative of $y = $ arc sin $4x$.

SOLUTION

We use the formula for differentiation of the $\sin^{-1}$ or arc sin function, which states:

$$\frac{d}{dx} \sin^{-1} u = \frac{1}{\sqrt{1-u^2}}.$$

Hence

$$\frac{dy}{dx} = \frac{1}{\sqrt{1-16x^2}}(4) = \frac{4}{\sqrt{1-16x^2}}$$

PROBLEM

Given: $y = \text{arc } \tan \frac{3}{x}$, find $\frac{dy}{dx}$.

SOLUTION

In this example, we use the formula:

$$\frac{d(\text{arc } \tan u)}{dx} = \frac{1}{1+u^2} \cdot \frac{du}{dx}.$$

For

$$y = \text{arc } \tan \frac{3}{x}, \quad u = \frac{3}{x}, \quad \text{and} \quad du = \frac{-3}{x^2}.$$

Therefore,

$$\frac{dy}{dx} = \frac{1\left(\dfrac{-3}{x^2}\right)}{1+\left(\dfrac{3}{x}\right)^2} = \frac{\dfrac{-3}{x^2}}{\dfrac{x^2+9}{x^2}} = \frac{-3}{x^2+9}.$$

Exponential and Logarithmic Differentiation

The exponential function e^x has the simplest of all derivatives. Its derivative is itself.

$$\frac{d}{dx} e^x = e^x$$

and

$$\frac{d}{dx} e^u = e^u \frac{du}{dx}$$

Since the natural logarithmic function is the inverse of $y = e^x$ and $\ln e = 1$, it follows that

$$\frac{d}{dx} \ln y = \frac{1}{y} \frac{dy}{dx}$$

and

$$\frac{d}{dx} \ln u = \frac{1}{u} \frac{du}{dx}$$

If x is any real number and a is any positive real number, then

$$a^x = e^{x \ln a}$$

From this definition we can obtain the following:

a) $\dfrac{d}{dx} a^x = a^x \ln a$ and $\dfrac{d}{dx} a^u = a^u \ln a \dfrac{du}{dx}$

b) $\dfrac{d}{dx}(\log_a x) = \dfrac{1}{x \ln a}$ and $\dfrac{d}{dx}\log_a |u| = \dfrac{1}{u \ln a}\dfrac{du}{dx}$

where $u \neq 0$

Sometimes it is useful to take the logs of a function and then differentiate since the computation becomes easier (as in the case of a product).

PROBLEM

If $y = e^{\frac{1}{x^2}}$, find $D_x y$.

SOLUTION

To find $D_x y = \dfrac{dy}{dx}$, we use the differentiation formula:

$$\frac{d}{dx} e^u = e^u \frac{du}{dx}, \text{ with } u = \frac{1}{x^2}. \text{ We obtain:}$$

$$D_x y = e^{\frac{1}{x^2}}\left(-\frac{2x}{x^4}\right)$$

$$= e^{\frac{1}{x^2}}\left(-\frac{2}{x^3}\right) = -\frac{2e^{\frac{1}{x^2}}}{x^3}.$$

PROBLEM

Find the derivative of:

$$y = \left(e^{\frac{1}{x}} \right)^2.$$

SOLUTION

We can first rewrite the function as:

$$y = e^{\frac{2}{x}}.$$

Now we use the formula:

$$\frac{d}{dx} e^u = e^u \frac{du}{dx},$$

letting $u = \dfrac{2}{x}$. Then,

$$\frac{du}{dx} = \frac{(x)(0) - (2)(1)}{x^2} = -\frac{2}{x^2}.$$

Applying the formula, we obtain:

$$\frac{dy}{dx} = e^{\frac{2}{x}} \cdot -\frac{2}{x^2}$$

$$= -\frac{2e^{\frac{2}{x}}}{x^2}.$$

Steps in Logarithmic Differentiation

1. $y = f(x)$ given
2. $\ln y = \ln f(x)$ take logs and simplify
3. $D_x (\ln y) = D_x (\ln f(x))$ differentiate implicitly
4. $\dfrac{1}{y} D_x y = D_x (\ln f(x))$
5. $D_x y = f(x) D_x (\ln f(x))$ multiply by $y = f(x)$

To complete the solution it is necessary to differentiate $\ln f(x)$. If $f(x) < 0$ for some x then step 2 is invalid and we should replace step 1 by $|y| = |f(x)|$, and then proceed.

Example: $y = (x+5)(x^4+1)$

$\ln y = \ln[(x+5)(x^4+1)] = \ln(x+5) + \ln(x^4+1)$

$$\frac{d}{dx} \ln y = \frac{d}{dx} \ln(x+5) + \frac{d}{dx} \ln(x^4+1)$$

$$\frac{1}{y} \frac{dy}{dx} = \frac{1}{x+5} + \frac{4x^3}{x^4+1}$$

$$\frac{dy}{dx} = (x+5)(x^4+1) \left[\frac{1}{x+5} + \frac{4x^3}{x^4+1} \right]$$

$$= (x^4+1) + 4x^3(x+5)$$

This is the same result as obtained by using the product rule.

PROBLEM

Find the derivative of $y = \ln(1 - 2x)^3$

SOLUTION

It is best to rewrite the equation as:

$$y = 3 \ln(1 - 2x).$$

Then we apply the formula:

$$\frac{d}{dx} \ln u = \frac{1}{u} \frac{du}{dx},$$

letting $u = (1 - 2x)$. Then $\dfrac{du}{dx} = -2$. We obtain:

$$\frac{dy}{dx} = 3 \left(\frac{1}{1-2x} \right) (-2) = \frac{-6}{1-2x}.$$

High Order Derivatives

The derivative of any function is also a legitimate function which we can differentiate. The second derivative can be obtained by:

$$\frac{d}{dx} \left[\frac{d}{dx} u \right] = \frac{d^2}{dx^2} u = u'' = D^2 u,$$

where $u = g(x)$ is differentiable.

The general formula for higher orders and the nth derivative of u is,

$$\underbrace{\frac{d}{dx} \frac{d}{dx} \cdots \frac{d}{dx}}_{n \text{ times}} u = \frac{d^{(n)}}{dx^n} u = u^{(n)} = D_x^{(n)} u.$$

The rules for first order derivatives apply at each stage of higher order differentiation (e.g., sums, products, chain rule).

A function which satisfies the condition that its nth derivative is zero, is the general polynomial

$$p_{n-1}(x) = a_{n-1}x^{n-1} + a_{n-2}x^{n-2} + \ldots + a_0.$$

PROBLEM

Find the sixth derivative of $y = x^6$.

SOLUTION

First derivative $= 6x^{6-1} = 6x^5$

Second derivative $= 5 \cdot 6x^{5-1} = 30x^4$

Third derivative $= 4 \cdot 30x^{4-1} = 120x^3$

Fourth derivative $= 3 \cdot 120x^{3-1} = 360x^2$

Fifth derivative $= 2 \cdot 360x^{2-1} = 720x^1 = 720x$

Sixth derivative $= 1 \cdot 720x^{1-1} = 720x^0 = 720$

The seventh derivative is seen to be zero, and therefore the function $y = x^6$ has seven derivatives.

PROBLEM

Find y'' for the expression $xy^3 = 1$.

SOLUTION

To find the second derivative, y'', we must first find the first derivative and then differentiate that to obtain the second derivative. We could solve for y and then differentiate to obtain y', but an alternative is implicit differentiation,

$$xy^3 = 1.$$

Differentiating implicitly,

$$3xy^2 \cdot y' + y^3 = 0.$$
$$3xy^2 \cdot y' = -y^3.$$
$$y' = \frac{-y^3}{3xy^2}$$

$$= -\frac{y}{3x}.$$

Now we take the derivative of y' to find y''.

$$y'' = -\frac{1}{3}\left[\frac{x \cdot y' - y}{x^2}\right].$$

Substituting $y' = -\dfrac{y}{3x}$ in the expression for y'' and simplifying

$$y'' = -\frac{1}{3}\left[\frac{-x\left(\dfrac{-y}{3x}\right) - y}{x^2}\right]$$

$$= -\frac{1}{3}\left[\frac{-\dfrac{y}{3} - y}{x^2}\right]$$

$$= -\frac{1}{3}\left[\frac{-\dfrac{4}{3}y}{x^2}\right]$$

$$= \frac{4y}{9x^2}.$$

Application of the Derivative

Rolle's Theorem

Let f be continuous on a closed interval $[a,b]$. Assume $f'(x)$ exists at each point in the open interval (a,b).

If $f(a) = f(b) = 0$ then there is at least one point (x_0) in (a,b) such that $f'(x_0) = 0$.

Three functions which satisfy the hypotheses, hence the conclusion, of Rolle's theorem.

The Mean Value Theorem

If f is continuous on $[a,b]$ and has a derivative at every point in the interval (a,b), then there is at least one number c in (a,b) such that

$$f'(c) = \frac{f(b) - f(a)}{b - a}$$

Notice in the Figure that the secant has slope

$$\frac{f(b) - f(a)}{b - a}$$

and $f'(x)$ has slope of the tangent to the point $(x, f(x))$. For some x_0 in (a,b) these slopes are equal.

PROBLEM

a) State and prove the Mean Value Theorem for the derivative of a real valued function of a single real variable.

b) Give a geometrical interpretation to this result.

SOLUTION

a) Let f be a real valued function of a real variable, x, which is continuous on a closed interval $[a,b]$ and has a derivative in the open interval (a,b). Then the Mean Value Theorem states that there exists a point c in (a,b) such that

$$f(b) - f(a) = f'(c)(b - a).$$

To prove this theorem, consider the function

$$\phi(x) = f'(x) - \left(f(a) + \frac{f(b) - f(a)}{b - a}(x - a) \right).$$

As can be seen from the Figure, θ is the difference of f and the linear function whose graph consists of the line segment passing through the points $(a, f(a))$ and $(b, f(b))$. Since f is continous on $[a,b]$, so is θ and since f has a derivative at all points in (a, b), so does θ. Furthermore, $\theta(a) = \theta(b) = 0$ so that all the conditions of Rolle's Theorem are satisfied for the function $\theta(x)$. Hence the conclusion of that theorem holds; i.e., there is a point $c \in (a, b)$ such that

$$\phi(c) = f'(c) - \frac{f(b) - f(a)}{b - a} = 0$$

or

$$f'(c) = \frac{f(b) - f(a)}{b - a}.$$

Thus, the theorem is proved.

b) The geometrical interpretation of the equation can be seen in the Figure. The equation states that there is a point c whose tangent line has the same slope as (i.e., is parallel to) the line connecting A and B.

PROBLEM

If $f(x) = 3x^2 - x + 1$, find the point x_0 at which $f'(x)$ assumes its mean value in the interval $[2,4]$.

SOLUTION

Recall the Mean Value Theorem. Given a function $f(x)$ which is continuous in $[a,b]$ and differentiable in (a, b), there exists a point x_0 where $a < x_0 < b$ such that:

$$\frac{f(b) - f(a)}{b - a} = f'(x_0).$$

Where x_0 is the mean point in the interval.

In our problem, $3x^2 - x + 1$ is continuous, and the derivative exists in the interval (2,4). We have:

$$\frac{f(4) - f(2)}{4 - 2} = \frac{[3(4)^2 - 4 + 1] - [3(2)^2 - 2 + 1]}{4 - 2}$$

$$= f'(x_0),$$

or

$$\frac{45 - 11}{2} = 17 = f'(x_0) = 6x_0 - 1.$$

$$6x_0 = 18$$

$$x_0 = 3.$$

$x_0 = 3$ is the point where $f'(x)$ assumes its mean value.

Consequences of the Mean Value Theorem

A) If f is defined on an interval (a,b) and if $f'(x) = 0$ for each point in the interval, then $f(x)$ is constant over the interval.

B) Let f and g be differentiable on an interval (a,b). If, for each point x in the interval, $f'(x)$ and $g'(x)$ are equal, then there is a constant, c, such that

$$f(x) + c = g(x) \text{ for all } x.$$

$f(x) + C = g(x)$ for all x

C) The Extended Mean Value Theorem. Assume that the function f and its derivative f' are continuous on $[a,b]$ and that f'' exists at each point x in (a,b), then there exists at least one point x_0, $a < x_0 < b$, such that

$$f(b) = f(a) + (b - a)f'(a) + \tfrac{1}{2}(b - a)^2 f''(x_0).$$

PROBLEM

Show: $e^x \geq 1 + x$ for all real numbers x.

SOLUTION

Divide the problem into 3 cases; $x = 0$, $x > 0$, $x < 0$.

Case 1. $x = 0$

For $x = 0$, we have $e^0 \geq 1 + 0$, or $1 = 1$.

Case 2. $x > 0$

For this case, we apply the Mean Value Theorem. We let

$$f(x) = e^x$$

and the interval will be $[0, x]$. Applying the theorem, we have

$$\frac{f(x) - f(0)}{x - 0} = \frac{e^x - e^0}{x - 0} = f'(x_0) = e^{x_0},$$

where $0 < x_0 < x$.

Simplifying, we have:

$$e^x = e^{x_0} \cdot x + e^0 = xe^{x_0} + 1$$

since $x_0 > 0$, $e^{x_0} > 1$. Therefore

$$e^x > x + 1$$

Case 3. $x < 0$

Solution is similar to Case 2 and will be left to the reader as an exercise.

Combining the three results, we have the desired inequality.

The Mean Value Theorem for the integral has a very simple geometric interpretation.

The Mean Value Theorem says that for a continuous function on the closed interval $[a, b]$, there exists a point x_0, where $a < x_0 < b$, such that:

$$f(x_0) = \frac{1}{b - a} \int_a^b f(x)\, dx.$$

If we multiply both sides by $(b - a)$ we have

$$(b - a) f(x_0) = \int_a^b f(x)\, dx,$$

which states that the integral from a to b is equal to the area of a rectangle of length $(b - a)$ and height $f(x_0)$. In the diagram, it means that the area in region 1 can be put in region 2, thus forming a rectangle.

PROBLEM

What is the mean value or mean ordinate of the positive part of the curve $y = 2x - x^2$?

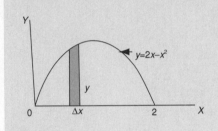

SOLUTION

First determine the length of the base to fix the limits of integration for the area by setting y equal to zero, or:

$0 = 2x - x^2 = x(2 - x)$.

Then, $x_1 = 0$, and $x_2 = 2$.

Now,

$$\bar{y}_x = \frac{1}{x_2 - x_1} \int y \cdot dx$$

$$= \frac{1}{2 - 0} \int_0^2 (2x - x^2) \, dx$$

$$= \int_0^2 \left(x - \frac{x^2}{2} \right) dx$$

$$= \frac{x^2}{2} - \frac{x^3}{6} \Big|_0^2 = \frac{4}{2} - \frac{8}{6} = \frac{2}{3},$$

the mean ordinate.

L'Hôpital's Rule

An application of the Mean Value Theorem is in the evaluation of

$$\lim_{x \to a} \frac{f(x)}{g(x)} \quad \text{where } f(a)=0 \text{ and } g(a)=0.$$

L'Hôpital's Rule states that if the $\lim_{x \to a} \dfrac{f(x)}{g(x)}$ is an indeterminate form (i.e., $\frac{0}{0}$ or $\frac{\infty}{\infty}$), then we can differentiate the numerator and the denominator separately and arrive at an expression that has the same limit as the original problem.

Thus, $\lim_{x \to a} \dfrac{f(x)}{g(x)} = \lim_{x \to a} \dfrac{f'(x)}{g'(x)}$

In general, if $f(x)$ and $g(x)$ have properties

1) $f(a) = g(a) = 0$

2) $f^{(k)}(a) = g^{(k)}(a) = 0$ for $k = 1, 2, \ldots n$

but 3) $f^{(n+1)}(a)$ or $g^{(n+1)}(a)$ is not equal to zero, then

$$\lim_{x \to a} \frac{f(x)}{g(x)} = \frac{f^{(n+1)}(x)}{g^{(n+1)}(x)}$$

PROBLEM

Evaluate $\lim_{x \to 2} \dfrac{(2x^2 - 4x)}{x - 2}$.

SOLUTION

The function takes the form $\frac{0}{0}$ and therefore we can apply L'Hôpital's rule to obtain:

$$\lim_{x \to 2} \frac{4x - 4}{1} = 4$$

We can also solve the problem in a different way by noting that the numerator can be factored.

$$\lim_{x \to 2} \frac{2x^2 - 4x}{x - 2} = \lim_{x \to 2} \frac{2x(x - 2)}{x - 2}$$

$$= \lim_{x \to 2} 2x$$

$$= 4.$$

PROBLEM

Find $\lim\limits_{x \to 3} \dfrac{x^2 - x - 6}{x - 3}$

SOLUTION

This limit may be found by writing

$$\frac{x^2 - x - 6}{x - 3} = \frac{(x+2)(x-3)}{x-3} = x + 2.$$

Hence $\lim\limits_{x \to 3} (x + 2) = 5$.

Since $\frac{0}{0}$ (indeterminate) is obtained by substitution in the original function, the limit may also be obtained by L'Hôpital's rule by differentiating separately the numerator and denominator. Thus

$$\lim_{x \to 3} \frac{x^2 - x - 6}{x - 3} = \lim_{x \to 3} \frac{2x - 1}{1} = 5.$$

The application of L'Hôpital's rule is the more systematic approach and should generally be tried first, if another method is not immediately apparent.

Tangents and Normals

Tangents

A line which is tangent to a curve at a point "a", must have the same slope as the curve. That is, the slope of the tangent is simply

$$m = \lim_{h \to 0} \frac{f(a+h) - f(a)}{h}$$

Therefore, if we find the derivative of a curve and evaluate for a specific point, we obtain the slope of the curve and the tangent line to the curve at that point.

A curve is said to have a vertical tangent at a point $(a, f(a))$ if f is continuous at a and $\lim\limits_{x \to a} |f'(x)| = \infty$.

PROBLEM

Using the Δ-method, find the points on the curve:
$y = \dfrac{x}{3} + \dfrac{3}{x}$, at which the tangent line is horizontal.

SOLUTION

When the slope of a curve equals zero, the curve has a horizontal tangent. We can find the points at which the tangent line is horizontal by calculating the slope $\dfrac{dy}{dx}$, setting it equal to zero and solving for x. By the Δ-method,

$$\frac{\Delta y}{\Delta x} = \frac{f(x + \Delta x) - f(x)}{\Delta x}$$

$$\frac{\Delta y}{\Delta x} = \frac{\dfrac{(x + \Delta x)}{3} + \dfrac{3}{(x + \Delta x)} - \left(\dfrac{x}{3} - \dfrac{3}{x} \right)}{\Delta x}$$

$$= \frac{\dfrac{x}{3} + \dfrac{\Delta x}{3} + \dfrac{3}{x + \Delta x} - \dfrac{x}{3} - \dfrac{3}{x}}{\Delta x}$$

$$= \frac{\dfrac{\Delta x}{3} + \dfrac{3}{x + \Delta x} - \dfrac{3}{x}}{\Delta x}.$$

$$\frac{\Delta y}{\Delta x} = \frac{\dfrac{x^2 \Delta x + x(\Delta x)^2 - 9 \Delta x}{3(x + \Delta x)x}}{\Delta x}$$

$$= \frac{x^2 + x\Delta x - 9}{3x^2 + 3x\Delta x}.$$

$$\frac{dy}{dx} = \lim_{\Delta x \to 0} \frac{\Delta y}{\Delta x} = \lim_{\Delta x \to 0} \frac{x^2 + x\Delta x - 9}{3x^2 + 3x\Delta x} = \frac{x^2 - 9}{3x^2}.$$

We can set this value, which is the slope, equal to zero and solve for x.

$$\frac{x^2 - 9}{3x^2} = 0$$

$$\frac{(x - 3)(x + 3)}{x(3x)} = 0$$

$$x = 3, \, x = -3.$$

(Remember that x cannot be zero, for that would give an infinite slope.)

Substituting these values for x back into $y = \dfrac{x}{3} + \dfrac{3}{x}$, we can obtain the y coordinates. We find $(3, 2)$ and $(-3, -2)$ to be the required points.

Normals

A line normal to a curve at a point must have a slope perpendicular to the slope of the tangent line. If

$f'(x) \neq 0$ then the equation for the normal line at a point (x_0, y_0) is

$$y - y_0 = \frac{-1}{f'(x_0)}(x - x_0).$$

PROBLEM

Find the equations of the tangent line and the normal to the curve: $y = x^2 - x + 3$, at the point $(2, 5)$.

SOLUTION

Since the equation of a straight line passing through a given point can be expressed in the form: $y - y_1 = m(x - x_1)$, this is appropriate for finding the equations of the tangent and normal. Here $x_1 = 2$ and $y_1 = 5$. The slope, m, of the tangent line is found by taking the derivative, $\frac{dy}{dx}$, of the curve: $y = x^2 - x + 3$.

$$\frac{dy}{dx} = 2x - 1.$$

At $(2, 5)$, $\frac{dy}{dx} = 2(2) - 1 = 3$, therefore the slope, m, of the tangent line is 3. Substituting x_1, y_1 and m into the equation $y - y_1 = m(x - x_1)$ we obtain:

$$y - 5 = 3(x - 2),$$

as the equation of the tangent line, or

$$3x - y - 1 = 0.$$

Since the slope of the normal is given by: $m' = -\frac{1}{m}$,

and since $m = 3$, the slope of the normal is $m' = -\frac{1}{3}$. Substituting $x_1 = 2$, $y_1 = 5$

and the slope of the normal, $m' = -\frac{1}{3}$, into the equation: $y - y_1 = m'(x - x_1)$, we obtain:

$$y - 5 = -\frac{1}{3}(x - 2).$$

or

$$x + 3y - 17 = 0.$$

This is the equation of the normal.

Minimum and Maximum Values

If a function f is defined on an interval I, then

a) f is increasing on I if $f(x_1) < f(x_2)$ whenever x_1, x_2 are in I and $x_1 < x_2$.

b) f is decreasing on I if $f(x_1) > f(x_2)$ whenever $x_1 < x_2$ in I.

Increasing function   Decreasing function

c) f is constant if $f(x_1) = f(x_2)$ for every x_1, x_2 in I.

Suppose f is defined on an open interval I and c is a number in I then,

a) $f(c)$ is a local maximum value if $f(x) \leq f(c)$ for all x in I.

b) $f(c)$ is a local minimum value if $f(x) \geq f(c)$ for all x in I.

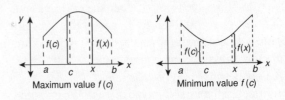

Maximum value $f(c)$ Minimum value $f(c)$

In the figure above in the interval $[a,b]$, the local maxima occur at c_1, c_3, c_5, with an absolute maximum at c_5 and local minima occur at c_2, c_4.

To find Absolute Extrema for functions, first calculate $f(c)$ for each critical number c, then calculate $f(a)$ and $f(b)$. The absolute extrema of f on $[a,b]$ will then be the largest and the smallest of these functional values. If $f(a)$ or $f(b)$ is an extremum we call it an endpoint extremum.

Viewing the derivative as the slope of a curve, there may be points (or critical values) where the curve has a zero derivative. At these values the tangent to the curve is horizontal.

Conversely, if the derivative at a point exists and is not zero, then the point is not a local extrema.

PROBLEM

Find the maxima and minima of the function $f(x) = x^4$.

SOLUTION

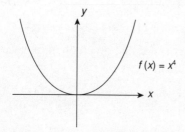

$f(x) = x^4$

To determine maxima and minima we find $f'(x)$, set it equal to 0, and solve for x to obtain the critical points. We find: $f'(x) = 4x^3 = 0$, therefore $x = 0$ is the critical value. We must now determine whether $x = 0$ is a maximum or minimum value. In this example the Second Derivative Test fails because $f''(x) = 12x^2$ and $f''(0) = 0$. We must, therefore, use the First Derivative Test. We examine $f'(x)$ when $x < 0$, and when $x > 0$. We find that for $x < 0$, $f'(x)$ is negative, and for $x > 0$, $f'(x)$ is positive. Therefore there is a minimum at $(0, 0)$. (See figure.)

PROBLEM

Locate the maxima and minima of $y = 2x^2 - 8x + 6$.

SOLUTION

To obtain the minima and maxima we find $\dfrac{dy}{dx}$, set it equal to 0 and solve for x. We find:

$$\frac{dy}{dx} = 4x - 8 = 0.$$

Therefore, $x = 2$ is the critical point. We now use the Second Derivative Test to determine whether $x = 2$ is a maximum or a minimum. We find:

$\dfrac{d^2y}{dx^2} = 4$, (positive). The second derivative is positive, hence $x = 2$ is a minimum.

Now substitute this back into the original equation to get the corresponding ordinate.

$$y = 2x^2 - 8x + 6 = 2 \cdot 2^2 - 8 \cdot 2 + 6 = 8 - 16 + 6$$
$$= -2.$$

Therefore, the minimum is at $x = 2$, $y = -2$.

Solving Maxima and Minima Problems

Step 1. Determine which variable is to be maximized or minimized (i.e., the dependent variable y).

Step 2. Find the independent variable x.

Step 3. Write an equation involving x and y. All other variables can be eliminated by substitution.

Step 4. Differentiate with respect to the independent variable.

Step 5. Set the derivative equal to zero to obtain critical values.

Step 6. Determine maxima and minima.

PROBLEM

Locate the maxima and minima of

$$y = \frac{x^3}{3} - \frac{5x^2}{2} + 6x + 4.$$

SOLUTION

To find the maxima and minima we find $\dfrac{dy}{dx}$, set it to 0, and solve for x, obtaining the critical points. Doing this we have:

$$\frac{dy}{dx} = x^2 - 5x + 6 = 0, \quad (x-2)(x-3) = 0$$

therefore,

$x = 3$ and 2.

We now use the Second Derivative Test to determine whether the critical values are maximum, minimum, or neither. We find:

$$\frac{d^2y}{dx^2} = 2x - 5.$$

For $x = 3$,

$$\frac{d^2y}{dx^2} = 2x - 5 = 2\cdot 3 - 5 = +(positive),$$

which indicates a minimum.
For $x = 2$,

$$\frac{d^2y}{dx^2} = 2x - 5 = 2\cdot 2 - 5 = -(negative),$$

which indicates a maximum.

Therefore, we have a minimum at $x = 3$ and a maximum at $x = 2$. We now wish to find the corresponding ordinates. Going back to the original equation, we have:

For $x = 3$,

$$y = \frac{x^3}{3} - \frac{5x^2}{2} + 6x + 4 = \frac{3^3}{3} - \frac{5\cdot 3^2}{2} + 6\cdot 3 + 4$$

$$= 9 - \frac{45}{2} + 18 + 4 = 8\frac{1}{2}.$$

For $x = 2$,

$$y = \frac{x^3}{3} - \frac{5x^2}{2} + 6x + 4 = \frac{2^3}{3} - \frac{5\cdot 2^2}{2} + 6\cdot 2 + 4$$

$$= \frac{8}{3} - 10 + 12 + 4 = 8\frac{2}{3}.$$

Therefore, minimum is at $x = 3$, $y = 8\frac{1}{2}$, and maximum is at $x = 2$, $y = 8\frac{2}{3}$.

Curve Sketching and the Derivative Tests

Using the knowledge we have about local extrema and the following properties of the first and second derivatives of a function, we can gain a better understanding of the graphs (and thereby the nature) of a given function.

A function is said to be smooth on an interval (a,b) if both f' and f'' exist for all $x \in (a,b)$.

The First Derivative Test

Suppose that c is a critical value of a function, f, in an interval (a,b), then if f is continuous and differentiable we can say that,

a) if $f'(x) > 0$ for all $a < x < c$ and $f'(x) < 0$ for all $c < x < b$, then $f(c)$ is a local maximum.

b) if $f'(x) < 0$ for $a < x < c$ and $f'(x) > 0$ for $c < x < b$, then $f(c)$ is a local minimum.

c) if $f'(x) > 0$ or if $f'(x) < 0$ for all $x \in (a,b)$ then $f(c)$ is not a local extrema.

PROBLEM

Find the maxima and minima of $f(x) = 3x^5 - 5x^3$.

SOLUTION

To determine maxima and minima we find $f'(x)$, set it equal to 0 and solve for x, obtaining the critical points. We find:

$$f'(x) = 15x^4 - 15x^2 = 15x^2(x^2 - 1).$$

Therefore, $x = 0, \pm 1$ are the critical points. We must now determine whether the function reaches a maximum, minimum or neither at each of these values. To do this we will use the second Derivative Test. Computing the second derivative f'', we have:

$$f''(x) = 60x^3 - 30x = 30(2x^2 - 1).$$

$f''(1) = 30 > 0$. Therefore, $x = 1$ is a relative minimum point and $x = -1$ is a relative maximum since $f''(-1) = -30 < 0$. Now, $f''(0) = 0$. Therefore the Second Derivative Test indicates a point which is neither maximum nor minimum. This is known as a point of inflection. For further study of the behavior of f at 0 we must use the First Derivative Test. We examine $f'(x)$ when $-1 < x < 0$ and when $0 < x < 1$. Let us select a representative value from each interval. We

will use

$$x = -\frac{1}{2} \quad \text{and} \quad x = \frac{1}{2}. \quad \text{For } f'\left(-\frac{1}{2}\right) \text{ we obtain a}$$

negative value, and for $f'\left(\frac{1}{2}\right)$ we again obtain a negative value. Because there is no change in sign we conclude that at $x = 0$ there is neither a maximum nor a minimum, as can also be seen from the graph.

Concavity

If a function is differentiable on an open interval containing c, then the graph at this point is

a) concave upward (or convex) if $f''(c) > 0$;

b) concave downward if $f''(c) < 0$.

If a function is concave upward than f' is increasing as x increases. If the function is concave downward, f' is decreasing as x increases.

Upward concavity

Downward concavity

PROBLEM

Find the intervals of x for which the curve

$$y = 2x^3 - 9x^2 + 12x - 3$$

is concave downward and concave upward,

SOLUTION

Differentiating twice,

$$\frac{dy}{dx} = 6(x^2 - 3x + 2)$$

and

$$\frac{d^2y}{dx^2} = 6(2x - 3)$$

By setting $\frac{d^2y}{dx^2} = 0$, we have $x = \frac{3}{2}$

y'' is positive or negative according to $x > \frac{3}{2}$ or $< \frac{3}{2}$.

Hence the graph is concave downward to the left of $x = \frac{3}{2}$ and concave upward to the right of $x = \frac{3}{2}$.

Points of Inflection

Points which satisfy $f''(x) = 0$ may be positions where concavity changes. These points are called the points of inflection. It is the point at which the curve crosses its tangent line.

PROBLEM

Investigate the function $y = (x - a)^{\frac{1}{3}}$ $(2x - a)^{\frac{2}{3}}$ for maxima and minima.

SOLUTION

Differentiating

$$y' = \frac{(2x-a)^{\frac{2}{3}}}{3(x-a)^{\frac{2}{3}}} + \frac{4(x-a)^{\frac{1}{3}}}{3(2x-a)^{\frac{1}{3}}} = \frac{6x-5a}{3(x-a)^{\frac{2}{3}}(2x-a)^{\frac{1}{3}}}.$$

From $y' = 0$, and $\frac{1}{y'} = 0$, the critical points are

$$x = \frac{a}{2}, \; x = \frac{5a}{6}, \; x = a.$$

We must now determine whether each of these critical points is a maximum, minimum or neither. We choose a value of x less than and a value greater than each of the critical values and evaluate y' at these values. If the sign changes from positive to negative, we have a maximum. If it changes from negative to positive, we have a minimum. If the sign does not change there is neither one at that critical value.

Setting $x = \frac{a}{3}$ and $\frac{2a}{3}$ in turn, we have y' positive and negative respectively. Hence $x = \frac{a}{2}$ makes y a maximum.

Test $x = \frac{5a}{6}$, using values $\frac{2a}{3}$ and $\frac{9a}{10}$.

These show y' to be successively negative and positive, so the function has a minimum value at $x = \frac{5a}{6}$.

Apply the test to $x = a$, with the values $\frac{9a}{10}$ and $2a$. These show y' positive in both cases, therefore, at $x = a$ there is neither a maximum or a minimum. We observe that $y' = \frac{a}{0} = \infty$ at $x = a$, therefore the graph has a vertical tangent at this value. At $x = a$ there is a point of inflection as shown. The maximum point at $(\frac{a}{2}, 0)$ is called a cusp.

Graphing a Function Using the Derivative Tests

The following steps will help us gain a rapid understanding of a function's behavior.

A) Look for some basic properties such as oddness, evenness, periodicity, boundedness, etc.

B) Locate all the zeros by setting $f(x) = 0$.

C) Determine any singularities, $f(x) = \infty$.

D) Set $f'(x)$ equal to zero to find the critical values.

E) Find the points of inflection by setting $f''(x) = 0$.

F) Determine where the curve is concave, $f''(x) < 0$, and where it is convex $f''(x) > 0$.

G) Determine the limiting properties and approximations for large and small $|x|$.

H) Prepare a table of values $x, f(x), f'(x)$ which includes the critical values and the points of inflection.

I) Plot the points found in Step H and draw short tangent lines at each point.

J) Draw the curve making use of the knowledge of concavity and continuity.

PROBLEM

Find the maxima and minima of:
$$y = \frac{4}{x^2 - 4}, \text{ and trace the curve.}$$

SOLUTION

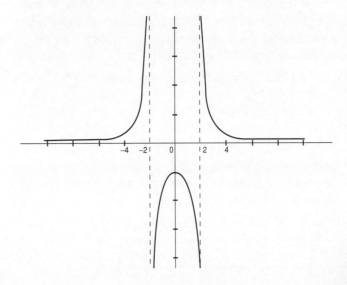

To find the maxima and minima we determine $\dfrac{dy}{dx}$, equate it to 0, and solve for x, obtaining the critical value. We find:

$$\frac{dy}{dx} = \frac{(x^2 - 4)(0) - 4(2x)}{(x^2 - 4)^2} = -\frac{8x}{(x^2 - 4)^2}.$$

$\dfrac{-8x}{(x^2 - 4)^2} = 0$, therefore $x = 0$. Substituting $x = 0$, into the original equation, $y = -1$, therefore the critical point is $(0, -1)$.

To determine whether a maximum, minimum, or neither occurs at this point, we use the First Derivative Test. We examine $\dfrac{dy}{dx}$ at a point less than 0, (use -1), and at a point greater than 0 (use 1). If $\dfrac{dy}{dx}$ changes sign from $+$ to $-$, a maximum occurs at $x = 0$, from $-$ to $+$, a minimum occurs, and if there is no change in sign, neither a maximum nor a minimum occurs. We find that at $x = -1$, $\dfrac{dy}{dx} = \dfrac{8}{9}$, a positive value, and at $x = 1$, $\dfrac{dy}{dx} = -\dfrac{8}{9}$, a negative value. Therefore, at the point $(0, -1)$, a maximum occurs.

Upon further investigation of the curve: $y = \dfrac{4}{x^2 - 4}$, we observe that for the values $x = 2, -2$, y is undefined or $y = \pm \infty$. Therefore, the graph of the curve has asymptotes at 2 and -2, as shown in the accompanying graph.

Rectilinear Motion

When an object moves along a straight line we call the motion rectilinear motion. Distance s, velocity v, and acceleration a, are the chief concerns of the study of motion.

Velocity is the proportion of distance over time.

$$\boxed{v = s/t}$$

Average velocity $= \dfrac{s(t_2) - s(t_1)}{t_2 - t_1}$

where t_1, t_2 are time instances and $s(t_2) - s(t_1)$ is the displacement of an object.

Instantaneous velocity at time t is defined as

$$\boxed{v = D\,s(t) = \lim_{h \to 0} \frac{s(t + h) - s(t)}{h}}$$

We usually write $\boxed{v(t) = \dfrac{ds}{dt}}$.

Acceleration, the rate of change of velocity with respect to time is

$$\boxed{a(t) = \frac{dv}{dt}.}$$

It follows clearly that

$$a(t) = v'(t) = s''(t).$$

When motion is due to gravitational effects, $g = 32.2$ ft/sec^2 or $g = 9.81$ m/sec^2 is usually substituted for acceleration.

Speed at time t is defined as $|v(t)|$. The speed indicates how fast an object is moving without specifying the direction of motion.

PROBLEM

A rope attached to a boat is being pulled in at a rate of 10 ft/sec. If the water is 20 ft below the level at which the rope is being drawn in, how fast is the boat approaching the wharf when 36 ft of rope are yet to be pulled in?

SOLUTION

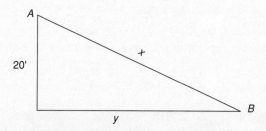

The length AB denotes the rope, and the position of the boat is at B. Since the rope is being drawn in at a rate of 10ft/sec.

$$\frac{dx}{dt} = 10.$$

To find how fast the boat is being towed in when 36 ft. of rope are left,

$\dfrac{dy}{dt}$ must be found at $x = 36$.

From the right triangle, $20^2 + y^2 = x^2$ or $y = \sqrt{x^2 - 400}$. Differentiating with respect to t,

$$\frac{dy}{dt} = \frac{dy}{dx} \cdot \frac{dx}{dt} = \frac{1}{2}(x^2 - 400)^{-\frac{1}{2}}(2x)\frac{dx}{dt} = \frac{x\frac{dx}{dt}}{\sqrt{x^2 - 400}}.$$

Substituting the conditions that:

$$\frac{dx}{dt} = -10 \text{ and } x = 36,$$

$$\frac{dy}{dt} = \frac{-360}{\sqrt{896}} = -\frac{45}{\sqrt{14}}.$$

It has now been found that, when there are 36 ft of rope left, the boat is moving in at the rate of:

$$\frac{45}{\sqrt{14}} \text{ ft/sec.}$$

PROBLEM

A boat is being hauled toward a pier at a height of 20 ft above the water level. The rope is drawn in at a rate of 6ft/sec. Neglecting sag, how fast is the boat approaching the base of the pier when 25 ft of rope remain to be pulled in?

SOLUTION

Formulating the given data, we have:
$\frac{dz}{dt} = 6$, $z = 25$, and $\frac{dx}{dt}$ is to be found.

At any time t we have, from, the Pythagorean theorem,

$$20^2 + x^2 = z^2$$

By differentiation, we obtain:

$$x\frac{dx}{dt} = z\frac{dz}{dt}$$

When $z = 25$, $x = \sqrt{25^2 - 20^2} = 15$; therefore

$$15\frac{dx}{dt} = 25(-6)$$

$$\frac{dx}{dt} = -10 \text{ ft/sec}$$

(The boat approaches the base at 10 ft/sec).

Rate of Change and Related Rates

Rate of Change

In the last section we saw how functions of time can be expressed as velocity and acceleration. In general, we can speak about the rate of change of any function with respect to an arbitrary parameter (such as time in the previous section).

For linear functions $f(x) = mx + b$, the rate of change is simply the slope m.

For non-linear functions we define the

1) average rate of change between points c and d to be

$$\frac{f(d) - f(c)}{d - c}$$

2) instantaneous rate of change of f at the point x to be

$$f'(x) = \lim_{h \to 0} \frac{f(x+h) - f(x)}{h}$$

If the limit does not exist, then the rate of change of f at x is not defined.

The form, common to alt related rate problems, is as follows:

a) Two variables, x and y are given. They are functions of time, but the explicit functions are not given.

b) The variables, x and y are related to each other by some equation such as $x^2 + y^3 - 2x - 7y^2 + 2 = 0$.

c) An equation which involves the rate of change $\dfrac{dx}{dt}$ and $\dfrac{dy}{dt}$ is obtained by differentiating with respect to t and using the chain rule.

As an illustration, the previous equation leads to

$$2x\frac{dx}{dt} + 3y^2\frac{dy}{dt} - 2\frac{dx}{dt} - 14y\frac{dy}{dt} = 0$$

The derivatives $\dfrac{dx}{dt}$ and $\dfrac{dy}{dt}$ in this equation are called the related rates.

PROBLEM

> Compute the average rate of change of $y = f(x) = x^2 - 2$ between $x = 3$ and $x = 4$.

SOLUTION

Average rate of change is defined as:

$\dfrac{\Delta y}{\Delta x}$ with $\Delta y = f(x + \Delta x) - f(x)$.

Given: $x = 3$, $\Delta x = 4 - 3 = 1$,

$y = f(x) = f(3) = 3^2 - 2 = 7$

For $x = 4$,

$y + \Delta y = f(x + \Delta x) = 4^2 - 2 = 14$

$$\Delta y = f(x + \Delta x) - f(x) = f(4) - f(3)$$
$$= (4^2 - 2) - (3^2 - 2) = 14 - 7 = 7$$

$\dfrac{\Delta y}{\Delta x} = \dfrac{7}{1} = 7$, the average rate of change.

PROBLEM

> Find the rate of change of y with respect to x at the point $x = 5$, if $2y = x^2 + 3x - 1$.

SOLUTION

Rate of change is defined as

$\displaystyle\lim_{\Delta x \to 0}\frac{\Delta y}{\Delta x}$, with

$\Delta y = f(x + \Delta x) - f(x)$.

We have:

$$2\Delta y = (x + \Delta x)^2 + 3(x + \Delta x) - 1 - (x^2 + 3x - 1)$$
$$= x^2 + 2x \cdot \Delta x + (\Delta x)^2 + 3x + 3\Delta x - 1 - x^2 - 3x + 1$$
$$= 2x \cdot \Delta x + (\Delta x)^2 + 3\Delta x.$$

Dividing by Δx,

$$\frac{2\Delta y}{\Delta x} = \frac{2x \cdot \Delta x}{\Delta x} + \frac{(\Delta x)^2}{\Delta x} + \frac{3\Delta x}{\Delta x}$$

$$= 2x + \Delta x + 3$$

and

$$\frac{\Delta y}{\Delta x} = x + \frac{\Delta x}{2} + \frac{3}{2}.$$

Now,

$$\lim_{\Delta x \to 0}\frac{\Delta y}{\Delta x} = \lim_{\Delta x \to 0} x + \frac{\Delta x}{2} + \frac{3}{2} = x + \frac{3}{2}.$$

For $x = 5$,

$$\lim_{\Delta x \to 0}\frac{\Delta y}{\Delta x} = 5 + \frac{3}{2} = 6\frac{1}{2}$$

This means that the instantaneous rate of change of the function represented by the curve at the point $x = 5$ is $6\dfrac{1}{2}$.

The function, it is seen, changes $6\dfrac{1}{2}$ times as fast as the independent variable x at $x = 5$.

The slope of the tangent at $x = 5$ is $6\dfrac{1}{2}$.

The Definite Integral

Antiderivatives

Definition:

If $F(x)$ is a function whose derivative $F'(x) = f(x)$, then $F(x)$ is called the antiderivative of $f(x)$.

THEOREM:

If $F(x)$ and $G(x)$ are two antiderivatives of $f(x)$, then $F(x) = G(x) + c$, where c is a constant.

Power Rule for Antidifferentiation

Let "a" be any real number, "r", any rational number not equal to -1 and "c" an arbitrary constant.

$$\text{If } f(x) = ax^r, \text{ then } F(x) = \frac{a}{r+1}x^{r+1} + c.$$

THEOREM:

An antiderivative of a sum is the sun of the antiderivatives.

$$\frac{d}{dx}(F_1 + F_2) = \frac{d}{dx}(F_1) + \frac{d}{dx}(F_2) = f_1 + f_2$$

Area

To find the area under the graph of a function f from a to b, we divide the interval $[a,b]$ into n subintervals, all having the same length $(b-a)/n$. This is illustrated in the Figure.

Since f is continuous on each subinterval, f takes on a minimum value at some number u_i in each subinterval.

We can construct a rectangle with one side of length $[x_{i-1}, x_i]$, and the other side of length equal to the minimum distance $f(u_i)$ from the x-axis to the graph of f.

The area of this rectangle is $f(u_i)\Delta x$. The boundary of the region formed by the sum of these rectangles is called the inscribed rectangular polygon.

The area (A) under the graph of f from a to b is

$$A = \lim_{\Delta x \to 0} \sum_{i=1}^{n} f(u_i)\Delta x.$$

The area A under the graph may also be obtained by means of circumscribed rectangular polygons.

In the case of the circumscribed rectangular polygons the maximum value of f on the interval $(x_{i-1}, x_i]$, v_i, is used.

Note that the area obtained using circumscribed rectangular polygons should always be larger than that obtained using inscribed rectangular polygons.

PROBLEM

> Determine the area under the curve: $y = f(x) = x^2$ between $x = 2$ and $x = 3$.

SOLUTION

It is given that the area to be evaluated is between $x = 2$ and $x = 3$, therefore, these are the limits of the integral which gives us the required area. Area is equal to the integral of the upper function minus the lower function. From the diagram it is seen that the required area is between $y = x^2$ as the upper function and $y = 0$ (the x-axis) as the lower function. Therefore, we can write:

$$A = \int_2^3 (x^2 - 0)dx$$
$$= \int_2^3 x^2 dx$$
$$= \frac{x^3}{3}\Big]_2^3$$
$$A = \frac{3^3}{3} - \frac{2^3}{3} = \frac{19}{3}.$$

Definition of Definite Integral

A partition P of a closed interval $[a, b]$ is any decomposition of $[a, b]$ into subintervals of the form,

$[x_0, x_1], [x_1, x_2], [x_2, x_3], \dots, [x_{n-1}, x_n]$

where n is a positive Integer and x_i are numbers, such that

$$a = x_0 < x_1 < x_2 < \dots < x_{n-1} < x_n = b.$$

The length of the subinterval is $\Delta x_i = x_i - x_{i-1}$. The largest of the numbers $\Delta x_1, \Delta x_2 \dots \Delta x_n$ is called the norm of the partition P and denoted by $\|P\|$.

Definition:

Let f be a function that is defined on a closed interval $[a,b]$ and let P be a partition of $[a,b]$. A Riemann Sum of f for P is any expression R_p of the form,

$$R_p = \sum_{i=1}^{n} f(w_i)\Delta x_i,$$

where w_i is some number in $[x_{i-1}, x_i]$ for $i = 1,2, \dots ,n$.

Definition:

Let f be a function that is defined on a closed interval $[a,b]$. The definite integral of f from a to b, denoted by

$\int\limits_a^b f(x)\,dx$ is given by

$$\int\limits_a^b f(x)\,dx = \lim_{\|P\| \to 0} \sum_i f(w_i)\Delta x_i$$

provided the limit exists.

THEOREM:

If f is continuous on $[a,b]$, then f is integrable on $[a,b]$ that is, the limit $\int\limits_b^a f(x)\,dx$ exists.

THEOREM:

If $f(a)$ exists, then $\int\limits_a^a f(x)\,dx = 0$.

PROBLEM

$\dfrac{dy}{dx} = (a - bx)^n$. What is $y = F(x)$ when $n = 2$?

SOLUTION

$\dfrac{dy}{dx} = (a - bx)^n$ can be rewritten as $dy = (a - bx)^n dx$. We can now write: $\int dy = \int (a - bx)^n dx$ or, $y = \int (a-bx)^n dx$. To integrate, we consider the formula: $\int u^n du = \dfrac{u^{n+1}}{n+1} + C$, with $u = (a - bx)$ and $du = -b\,dx$. Applying the formula, we obtain:

$$y = \int (a - bx)^n dx = -\frac{1}{b} \cdot \frac{(a-bx)^{n+1}}{n+1}$$

$$= -\frac{(a-bx)^{n+1}}{b(n+1)} + C,$$

the integral in the general form.
For $n = 2$,

$$y = \int (a - bx)^2 \cdot dx = -\frac{(a-bx)^3}{3b} + C.$$

PROBLEM

$\dfrac{dy}{dx} = (a + bx)^n$. What is $y = F(x)$ when $n = 1$, $n = 2$, and $n = -2$?

SOLUTION

In solving, we first find the integral in the general form and then substitute and find the integral for $n = 1$, $n = 2$, and $n = -2$.

$\dfrac{dy}{dx} = (a + bx)^n$ can be rewritten as

$dy = (a + bx)^n dx$. To find the integral, we write: $\int dy = \int (a + bx)^n dx$ or, $y = \int (a + bx)^n dx$.

We now consider the formula:

$$\int u^n du = \frac{u^{n+1}}{n+1} + C, \text{ with } u = (a + bx) \text{ and } du = b\,dx.$$

Applying the formula, we have:

$$y = \int (a+bx)^n \cdot dx$$

$$= \frac{(a+bx)^{n+1}}{b(n+1)} + C,$$

the integral in the general form.

For $n = 1$,

$$\int (a+bx)^1 \, dx = \frac{(a+bx)^{1+1}}{b(1+1)} = \frac{(a+bx)^2}{2b} + C.$$

For $n = 2$,

$$\int (a+bx)^2 \, dx = \frac{(a+bx)^{2+1}}{b(2+1)} = \frac{(a+bx)^3}{3b} + C.$$

For $n = -2$,

$$\int \frac{dx}{(a+bx)^2} + \int (a+bx)^{-2} \cdot dx = \frac{(a+bx)^{-2+1}}{b(-2+1)}$$

$$= \frac{1}{b(a+bx)} + C.$$

Properties of Definite Integral

A) If f is integrable on $[a,b]$, and k is any real number, then kf is integrable on $[a,b]$ and

$$\int_a^b kf(x)dx = k \int_a^b f(x)dx.$$

B) If f and g are integrable on $[a,b]$, then $f+g$ is integrable on $[a,b]$ and

$$\int_a^b [f(x)+g(x)]dx = \int_a^b f(x)dx + \int_a^b g(x)dx.$$

C) If $a < c < b$ and f is integrable on both $[a,c]$ and $[c,b]$ then f is integrable on $[a,b]$ and

$$\int_a^b f(x)dx = \int_a^c f(x)dx + \int_c^b f(x)dx.$$

D) If f is integrable on a closed interval and if a, b, and c are any three numbers in the interval, then

$$\int_a^b f(x)dx = \int_a^c f(x)dx + \int_c^b f(x)dx.$$

E) If f is integrable on $[a,b]$ and if $f(x) \geq 0$ for all x in $[a,b]$, then $\int_a^b f(x)dx \geq 0$.

PROBLEM

Evaluate the expression: $\int_2^3 \frac{(x+1)dx}{\sqrt{x^2+2x+3}} dx$.

SOLUTION

We can rewrite the given integral as:

$$\int_2^3 (x^2+2x+3)^{-\frac{1}{2}} (x+1)dx,$$

and make use of the formula: $\int u^n du = \frac{u^{n+1}}{n+1}$.

Let $u = x^2 + 2x + 3$. Then $du = (2x+2)dx$, and $n = -\frac{1}{2}$. Applying the formula, we obtain:

$$\int_2^3 \frac{(x+1)dx}{\sqrt{x^2+2x+3}} = \frac{1}{2}\int_2^3 (x^2+2x+3)^{-\frac{1}{2}} 2(x+1)dx$$

$$= \frac{1}{2}\left[\frac{(x^2+2x+3)^{\frac{1}{2}}}{\frac{1}{2}} \right]_2^3 = \sqrt{x^2+2x+3} \, \Big]_2^3.$$

We now evaluate the definite integral between 3 and 2, obtaining:

$$\sqrt{3^2+(2)(3)+3} - \sqrt{2^2+(2)(2)+3} = \sqrt{18} - \sqrt{11}.$$

PROBLEM

Evaluate the expression: $\int_0^2 2x^2\sqrt{x^3+1} \, dx$.

SOLUTION

We wish to convert the given integral into a form, to which we can apply the formula for $\int u^n du$, with $u = (x^3 + 1)$, $du = 3x^2$ and $n = \dfrac{1}{2}$. We obtain:

$$\int_0^2 2x^2\sqrt{x^3+1}\ dx = \frac{2}{3}\int_0^2 (x^3+1)^{\frac{1}{2}}\left(\frac{3}{2}\cdot 2x^2 dx\right).$$

Applying the formula for $\int u^n du$, we obtain:

$$\frac{2}{3}\left[\frac{(x^3+1)^{\frac{3}{2}}}{\frac{3}{2}}\right]_0^2 = \frac{4}{9}(x^3+1)^{\frac{3}{2}}\Big]_0^2.$$

Evaluating between 2 and 0, we have:

$$\frac{4}{9}(8+1)^{\frac{3}{2}} - \frac{4}{9}(0+1)^{\frac{3}{2}}$$

$$= \frac{4}{9}(27-1)$$

$$= \frac{104}{9}.$$

The Fundamental Theorem of Calculus

The fundamental theorem of calculus establishes the relationship between the indefinite integrals and differentiation by use of the mean value theorem.

Mean Value Theorem for Integrals

If f is continuous on a closed interval $[a,b]$, then there is some number P in the open interval (a,b) such that

$$\int_a^b f(x)\,dx = f(P)(b-a)$$

To find $f(P)$ we divide both sides of the equation by $(b-a)$ obtaining

$$f(P) = \frac{1}{b-a}\int_a^b f(x)\,dx.$$

PROBLEM

What is the mean value or mean ordinate of the positive part of the curve $y = 2x - x^2$?

SOLUTION

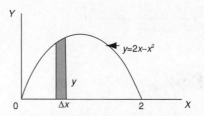

First determine the length of the base to fix the limits of integration for the area by setting y equal to zero, or:

$$0 = 2x - x^2 = x(2 - x).$$

Then, $x_1 = 0$, and $x_2 = 2$.

Now,

$$\bar{y}_x = \frac{1}{X_2 - X_1}\int y \cdot dx$$

$$= \frac{1}{2-0}\int_0^2 (2x - x^2)\,dx$$

$$= \int_0^2 \left(x - \frac{x^2}{2}\right)dx$$

$$= \frac{x^2}{2} - \frac{x^3}{6}\Big|_0^2 = \frac{4}{2} - \frac{8}{6} = \frac{2}{3},$$

the mean ordinate.

Definition of the Fundamental Theorem

Suppose f is continuous on a closed interval $[a,b]$, then

a) If the function G is defined by

$$G(x) = \int_a^x f(t)\,dt,$$

for all x in $[a,b]$, then G is an antiderivative of f on $[a,b]$.

b) If F is any antiderivative of f, then

$$\boxed{\int_a^b f(x)\,dx = F(b) - F(a)}$$

PROBLEM

Find the mean value of the ordinates of the circle $x^2 + y^2 = a^2$ in the first quadrant.

a) With respect to the radius along the x-axis

b) With respect to the arc-length.

SOLUTION

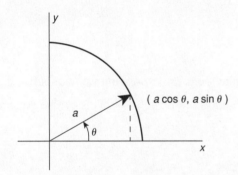

$(a\cos\theta, a\sin\theta)$

a) Noting that the mean value is defined by:

$$f(x_o) = \frac{1}{b-a}\int_a^b f(x)\,dx, \text{ where } a < x_o < b,$$

we have:

$$f(x_o) = \frac{1}{a-o}\int_0^a \sqrt{a^2 - x^2}\,dx,$$

where $f(x) = y = \pm\sqrt{a^2 - x^2}$. We take $y = \sqrt{a^2 - x^2}$, because we are in the first quadrant. Also, noting that:

$$\int \sqrt{a^2 - x^2}\,dx = \frac{1}{2}\,x\sqrt{a^2 - x^2}$$

$$+\frac{1}{2}\,a^2 \arcsin\frac{x}{a} + C,$$

we have:

$$f(x_o) = \frac{1}{4}\pi a.$$

(b) The coordinates of any point on the circle can be expressed in terms of θ by the following method. For the point in question, drop a perpendicular line to the x-axis. We have a right triangle with hypotenuse of length a.

$$\cos(\theta) = \frac{x}{a},$$

or

$$x = a\cos(\theta). \qquad \sin(\theta) = \frac{y}{a},$$

or

$$y = a\sin(\theta).$$

Now an element of the arc length is $a\Delta\theta$. (Recall that the length of an arc of a circle is equal to $S = R\theta$ where R is the radius and θ the angle in radians.) Therefore the length of the arc of the circle in the first quadrant is $\frac{1}{2}\pi a$.

By taking the limit, $a\Delta\theta$ becomes $a\,d\theta$

$$f(\theta) = \frac{1}{\frac{1}{2}\pi a}\int_0^{\frac{\pi}{2}} a\sin\theta(a\,d\theta)$$

$$= \frac{2a}{\pi}\int_0^{\frac{\pi}{2}} \sin\theta\,d\theta = \frac{2a}{\pi}\,[\cos\theta]_0^{\frac{\pi}{2}}$$

$$= \frac{2a}{\pi}(1-0) = \frac{2a}{\pi}.$$

Indefinite Integral

The indefinite integral of $f(x)$, denoted by $\int f(x)\,dx$, is the most general integral of $f(x)$, that is

$$\int f(x)\,dx = F(x) + C.$$

$F(x)$ is any function such that $F'(x) = f(x)$. C is an arbitrary constant.

Integration of Formulas

1. $\int x^n\,dx = \dfrac{x^{n+1}}{n+1} + C,\ n \neq -1$

2. $\int \dfrac{dx}{x} = \ln|x| + C$

3. $\int \dfrac{dx}{x-a} = \ln|x-a| + C$

4. $\int \dfrac{xdx}{x^2+a^2} = \dfrac{1}{2}\ln|x^2+a^2| + C$

5. $\int \dfrac{dx}{x^2+a^2} = \dfrac{1}{a}\tan^{-1}\dfrac{x}{a} + C$

6. $\int \dfrac{dx}{(a^2-x^2)^{\frac{1}{2}}} = \sin^{-1}\dfrac{x}{a} + C$

7. $\int \sin ax\,dx = \dfrac{1}{a}\cos ax + C$

8. $\int \cos ax\,dx = \dfrac{1}{a}\sin ax + C$

9. $\int \sec^2 x\,dx = \tan x + C$

10. $\int e^{ax}\,dx = \dfrac{e^{ax}}{a} + C$

11. $\int \sinh ax\,dx = -\dfrac{1}{a}\cosh ax + C$

12. $\int \cosh ax\,dx = \dfrac{1}{a}\sinh ax + C$

$\ln x \equiv \log_e x$ is called the logarithm of base e where $e \equiv 2.7182818$ ---

PROBLEM

Integrate the expression: $\int \dfrac{dx}{1+e^x}$.

SOLUTION

We wish to convert the given integral into the form $\int \dfrac{du}{u}$. If we multiply $\dfrac{1}{1+e^x}$ by $\dfrac{e^{-x}}{e^{-x}}$ (which is equal to 1) we obtain:

$$\dfrac{e^{-x}(1)}{e^{-x}(1+e^x)} = \dfrac{e^{-x}}{e^{-x}+e^0} = \dfrac{e^{-x}}{e^{-x}+1}.$$

In integrating this, we apply the formula, $\int \dfrac{du}{u} = \ln|u| + C$, letting $u = e^{-x}+1$. Then $du = -e^x dx$. We obtain:

$$\int \dfrac{e^{-x}}{e^{-x}+1}\,dx = -\int \dfrac{-e^{-x}dx}{e^{-x}+1} = -\ln(1+e^{-x}) + C.$$

Algebraic Simplification

Certain apparently complicated integrals can be made simple by simple algebraic manipulations.

Example: Find $\int \dfrac{x}{x+1}\,dx$

Write $\dfrac{x}{x+1} = \dfrac{x+1-1}{x+1} = 1 - \dfrac{1}{x+1}$

$\int \dfrac{x}{x+1}\,dx = \int dx - \int \dfrac{dx}{x+1} = x - \ln|x+1| + c$

PROBLEM

Integrate: $\int \dfrac{2x}{x+1}\,dx$.

SOLUTION

To integrate the given expression we manipulate the integrand to obtain the form $\int \dfrac{du}{u}$. This can be done as follows:

$$\int \dfrac{2x}{x+1}\,dx = 2\int \dfrac{x}{x+1}\,dx$$

$$= 2\int \left(\dfrac{x+1}{x+1} - \dfrac{1}{x+1}\right)dx$$

$$= 2\int \left(1 - \dfrac{1}{x+1}\right)dx$$

$$= 2\int dx - 2\int \dfrac{dx}{x+1}.$$

Now, applying the formula $\int \dfrac{du}{u} = \ln u$, we obtain:

$$\int \dfrac{2x}{x+1}\,dx = 2x - 2\ln(x+1) + C.$$

Substitution of Variables

Suppose $F(x)$ is expressed as a composite function, $F(x) = f(u(x))$,

then $F'(x) = f'(u)\dfrac{du}{dx}$, and $F'(x)dx = f'(u)du$.

Therefore,

$$\int F'(x)\,dx = \int f'(u)\,du = f(u) + C$$
$$= f(u(x)) + C = F(x) + C.$$

THEOREM:

Let f and u be functions satisfying the following conditions:

a) f is continuous on a domain including the closed interval $\{x : a \leq x \leq b\}$.

b)   For each point t in the closed interval $\{t : \alpha \leq t \leq \beta\}$, the value $u(t)$ is a point in $\{x : a \leq x \leq b\}$.

c) $u(\alpha) = a$, and $u(\beta) = b$.

d) u is continuous on $\{t : \alpha \leq t \leq \beta\}$.

The $\int\limits_{a}^{b} f(x)\,dx = \int\limits_{\alpha}^{\beta} f(u(t)) \cdot u'(t)\,dt$.

Example: Evaluate $\int \dfrac{x}{x^2 + a^2}\,dx$

Let $u = x^2 + a^2$

$$du = 2x\,dx$$

$$\frac{1}{2}du = x\,dx$$

$$\int \frac{x}{x^2 + a^2}\,dx = \frac{1}{2}\int \frac{du}{u} = \frac{1}{2}\ln|u| + C$$
$$= \frac{1}{2}\ln|x^2 + a^2| + C$$

PROBLEM

Evaluate the expression: $\int_{0}^{3} x\sqrt{1+x}\ dx$.

SOLUTION

We wish to convert the given integral into a form, to which we can apply the formula for $\int u^n du$. To evaluate the indefinite integral $\int x\sqrt{1+x}\,dx$, we let

$u = \sqrt{1+x}$, $u^2 = 1 + x$, $x = u^2 - 1$, $dx = 2u\,du$

Substituting, we have:

$$\int x\sqrt{1+x}\,dx = \int (u^2 - 1)\,u\,(2u\,du)$$
$$= 2\int (u^4 - u^2)\,du.$$

We can now apply the formula for $\int u^n du$, and we obtain:

$$\frac{2}{5}u^5 - \frac{2}{3}u^3 + C = \frac{2}{5}(1+x)^{\frac{5}{2}} - \frac{2}{3}(1+x)^{\frac{3}{2}} + C,$$

by substitution. Therefore, the definite integral

$$\int_{0}^{3} x\sqrt{1+x}\,dx = \frac{2}{5}(1+x)^{\frac{5}{2}} - \frac{2}{3}(1+x)^{\frac{3}{2}}\bigg]_{0}^{3}$$
$$= \frac{2}{5}(4)^{\frac{5}{2}} - \frac{2}{3}(4)^{\frac{3}{2}} - \frac{2}{5}(1)^{\frac{5}{2}} + \frac{2}{3}(1)^{\frac{3}{2}}$$
$$= \frac{64}{5} - \frac{16}{3} - \frac{2}{5} + \frac{2}{3}$$
$$= \frac{116}{15}.$$

Change of Variables

Example: Evaluate $\int\limits_{0}^{1} x(1+x)^{\frac{1}{2}}dx$

Let $u = 1+x$, $du = dx$, $x = u - 1$

$$\int\limits_{0}^{1} x(1+x)^{\frac{1}{2}} = \int\limits_{1}^{2} (u-1)u^{\frac{1}{2}}\,du.$$

*Notice the change in the limits for $x=0$, $u=1$ and for $x=1$ $u=2$.

$$\int\limits_{1}^{2} (u-1)u^{\frac{1}{2}}\,du = \int\limits_{1}^{2} u^{3/2} - u^{\frac{1}{2}}\,du$$
$$= 2/5\,u^{5/2} - 2/3\,u^{3/2}\bigg|_{1}^{2}$$
$$= [(2/5)\sqrt{32} - (2/3)\sqrt{8})] - \left(\frac{2}{5} - \frac{2}{3}\right)$$
$$= \frac{4\sqrt{2}}{15} - \frac{4}{15} = \frac{4}{15}(\sqrt{2} - 1).$$

PROBLEM

Evaluate the expression: $\int_{1}^{2} \dfrac{x}{(1+2x)^3}\,dx$.

SOLUTION

This integral is difficult because of the expression: $1 + 2x$, in the denominator. Hence we choose our substitution to eliminate this expression. We let

$u = 1 + 2x$, then $x = \dfrac{u-1}{2}$ and $dx = \dfrac{1}{2}\ du$.

Now

$u = 3$ when $x = 1$

$u = 5$ when $x = 2$,

giving us new limits. Using the substitution, we obtain:

$$\int_1^2 \frac{x}{(1+2x)^3}\ dx = \int_3^5 \left(\frac{\frac{u-1}{2}}{u^3}\right)\left(\frac{1}{2}\right) du$$

$$= \frac{1}{4}\int_3^5 \left(\frac{1}{u^2} - \frac{1}{u^3}\right) du.$$

We can now use the formula for $\int u^n du$ on both terms of the integrand, obtaining:

$$\frac{1}{4}\left[-\frac{1}{u} + \frac{1}{2u^2}\right]_3^5 = \frac{11}{450}.$$

Integration of Parts

This method is based on the formula

$d(uv) = u\ dv + v\ du$.

The corresponding integration formula,

$uv = \int u\ dv + \int v\ du$, is applied in the form

$$\boxed{\int u\ dv = uv - \int v\ du}$$

This procedure involves the identification of u and dv and their manipulation into the form of the latter equation. v must be easily determined. If a definite integral is

$$\int_a^b u\ \frac{dv}{dx}\ dx = uv\ \Big]_a^b - \int_a^b v\ \frac{du}{dx}\ dx.$$

Example: Evaluate $\int x \cos x\ dx$

$u = x$ \qquad $dv = \cos x\ dx$

$du = dx$ \qquad $v = \sin x$

$$\int x \cos x\ dx = x \sin x - \int \sin x\ dx$$

$$= x \sin x - (-\cos x) + C$$

$$= x \sin x + \cos x + C$$

PROBLEM

Integrate by parts the expression: $\dfrac{dy}{dx} = x^2 \ln x.$

SOLUTION

$dy = x^2 \ln x \cdot dx.$

$y = \int x^2 \ln x\ dx.$

To integrate by parts we use the equation:

$\int u\ dv = uv - \int v\ du.$

Now, let $u = \ln \cdot x.$

Then, $du = \dfrac{1}{x} \cdot dx.$

Let $dv = x^2 \cdot dx.$

Then, $v = \int dv = \int x^2 dx = \dfrac{x^3}{3},$

by use of the formula for $\int u^n du$. Substituting into the above equation, we have:

$$y = \int \overset{u}{\ln x} \cdot \overset{dv}{x^2 \cdot dx} = \frac{x^3}{3}\ \ln x - \int \frac{x^3}{3} \cdot \frac{1}{x} \cdot dx.$$

We can now integrate

$$\int \frac{x^3}{3} \cdot \frac{1}{x} \cdot dx,$$

by using the formula for $\int u^n du$, with $u = x$, $du = dx$, and $n = 2$. Doing this, we obtain:

$$y = \frac{x^3}{3} \ln x - \frac{x^3}{9} + C.$$

Trigonometric Integrals

Integrals of the form $\int \sin^n x\ dx$ or $\int \cos^n x dx$ can be evaluated without resorting to integration by parts. This is done in the following manner;

We write $\int \sin^n x\, dx = \int \sin^{n-1} \sin x\, dx$, if n is odd.

Since the integer $n-1$ is even, we may then use the fact that $\sin^2 x = 1 - \cos^2 x$ to obtain a form which is easier to integrate.

Example: $\int \sin^5 x\, dx = \int \sin^4 x \sin x\, dx$
$$= \int (\sin^2 x)^2 \sin x\, dx$$

but $\sin^2 x = 1 - \cos^2 x$.

Hence, $\int \sin^5 x\, dx = \int (1 - \cos^2 x)^2 \sin x\, dx$
$$= \int (1 - 2\cos^2 x + \cos^4 x)\sin x\, dx$$

Substitute $u = \cos x$, $du = -\sin x\, dx$

$$= -\int (1 - 2u^2 + u^4)\, du = -u + \frac{2}{3}u^3 - \frac{u^5}{5}$$

$$= -\cos x + \frac{2}{3}\cos^3 x - \frac{1}{5}\cos^5 x + C.$$

A similar technique can be employed for odd powers of $\cos x$.

If the integrand is $\sin^n x$ or $\cos^n x$ and n is even, then the half angle formulas,

$$\sin^2 x = \frac{1 - \cos 2x}{2} \quad or$$

$$\cos^2 x = \frac{1 + \cos 2x}{2}$$

may be used to simplify the integrand.

Example: $\int \cos^2 x\, dx = \frac{1}{2}\int (1 + \cos 2x)\, dx$
$$= \frac{1}{2}x + \frac{1}{4}\sin 2x + C$$

PROBLEM

Integrate the expression: $\int \cos^2 x \sin x\, dx$.

SOLUTION

In evaluating this integral we use the formula:

$$\int u^n du = \frac{u^{n+1}}{n+1}.$$

Let $u = \cos x$, $du = -\sin x\, dx$, and $n = 2$. Applying the formula, we obtain:

$$\int \cos^2 x \sin x\, dx = -\frac{\cos^3 x}{3} + C.$$

Applications of the Integral

Area

If f and g are two continuous functions on the closed interval $[a,b]$, then the area of the region bounded by the graphs of these two functions and the ordinates $x = a$ and $x = b$ is

$$A = \int_a^b [f(x) - g(x)]\, dx.$$

where $f(x) \geq 0$ and $f(x) \geq g(x)$

$a \leq x \leq b$

This formula applies whether the curves are above or below the x-axis.

The area below $f(x)$ and above the x-axis is represented by $\int_a^b f(x)$. The area between $g(x)$ and the x-axis is represented by $\int g(x)$.

Example: Find the area of the region bounded by the curves $y = x^2$ and $y = \sqrt{x}$.

$$\text{Area} = A = \int_0^1 (\sqrt{x} - x^2)\, dx$$

$$= \int_0^1 \sqrt{x}\, dx - \int_0^1 x^2\, dx$$

$$= \left[\frac{2}{3}x^{\frac{3}{2}} - \frac{1}{3}x^3\right]_0^1$$

$$A = \left[\frac{2}{3} - \frac{1}{3}\right] = \frac{1}{3}$$

PROBLEM

Find the area between the curve: $y = x^3$, and the x-axis, from $x = -2$ to $x = 3$.

SOLUTION

It is generally advantageous to sketch the curve, since parts of the curve may have to be considered separately, particularly when positive and negative limits are given. The desired area is composed of the two parts: BOC and ODE. To find the total area, we can evaluate each area separately and then add. The area is the integral of the upper function minus the lower function. In the first quadrant, the upper function is the curve $y = x^3$, the lower function is $y = 0$, (the x-axis) and the limits are $x = 0$ and $x = 3$. In the third quadrant, the upper function is $y = 0$, the lower function is the curve $y = x^3$, and the limits are $x = -2$ and $x = 0$. Hence, we can write,

$$A_{total} = \int_0^3 (x^3 - 0)dx + \int_{-2}^0 (0 - x^3)\,dx$$

$$= \int_0^3 x^3\,dx + \int_{-2}^0 -x^3\,dx$$

$$= \left[\frac{x^4}{4}\right]_0^3 + \left[-\frac{x^4}{4}\right]_{-2}^0$$

$$= \frac{81}{4} + \frac{16}{4}$$

$$= 24\frac{1}{4}\text{ sq. units.}$$

Note that refusal to consider this problem in two parts does <u>not</u> give area, but gives "net area" with one area considered positive and the other negative.

PROBLEM

Find the area of the region bounded by the x-axis, the curve: $y = 6x - x^2$ and the vertical lines: $x = 1$ and $x = 4$.

SOLUTION

The limits of the integral which give the required area are $x = 1$ and $x = 4$. The function: $y = 6x - x^2$ is above the function $y = 0$ (the x-axis), therefore the area can be found by taking the integral of the upper function minus the lower function, or, $y = 6x - x^2$ minus $y = 0$, from $x = 1$ to $x = 4$. Therefore, we obtain:

$$A = \int_1^4 (6x - x^2) - 0\ dx = \left[3x^2 - \frac{x^3}{3}\right]_1^4$$

$$= \frac{80}{3} - \frac{8}{3} = 24.$$

Volume of a Solid of Revolution

If a region is revolved about a line, a solid called a solid of revolution is formed. The solid is generated by the region. The axis of revolution is the line about which the revolution takes place.

There are several methods by which we may obtain the volume of a solid of revolution. We shall now discuss three such methods.

Disk Method

The volume of the solid generated by the revolution of a region about the x-axis is given by the formula

$$V = \pi \int_a^b [f(x)]^2\,dx,$$

provided that f is a continuous, nonnegative function on the interval $[a, b]$.

PROBLEM

Find the volume of the solid generated by revolving about the *y*-axis the region bounded by the parabola: $y^2 = 4x$, the *y*-axis and the tine $y = 2$.

SOLUTION

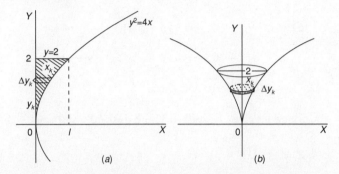

(a)   (b)

An element of volume is the disk generated by rotating a strip: *x* by *dy*, about the *y*-axis. The volume of the disk is: $dV = \pi x^2 dy$.

Hence,

$$V = \pi \int_0^2 x^2 \, dy$$

$$= \pi \int_0^2 \frac{1}{16} Y^4 \, dy = \frac{2}{5}\pi.$$

Shell Method

This method applies to cylindrical shells exemplified by

The volume of a cylindrical shell is

$$V = \pi r_2^2 h - \pi r_1^2 h$$

$$= \pi(r_2 + r_1)(r_2 - r_1)h$$

$$= 2\pi\left(\frac{r_2 + r_1}{2}\right)(r_2 - r_1)h$$

where r_1 = inner radius

r_2 = Outer radius

h = height.

Let $r = \dfrac{r_1 + r_2}{2}$ and $\Delta r = r_2 - r_1$, then the volume of a shell becomes

$$\boxed{V = 2\pi r h \Delta r}$$

The thickness of the shell is represented by Δr and the average radius of the shell by r.

Thus, $\boxed{V = 2\pi \int_a^b x f(x) \, dx}$

is the volume of a solid generated by revolving a region about the *y*-axis. This is illustrated by the figure below.

PROBLEM

Find the volume of the solid generated by revolving about the *y*-axis the region bounded by the parabola: $y = -x^2 + 6x - 8$, and the *x*-axis.

SOLUTION

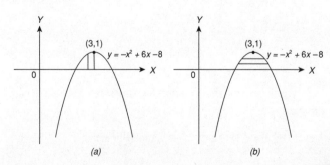

(a)   (b)

Method 1. We use the method of cylindrical shells. The curve:

$$y = -x^2 + 6x - 8,$$

cuts the x-axis at $x = 2$ and $x = 4$.

The cylindrical shells are generated by the strip formed by the two lines parallel to the y-axis, at distances x and $x + \Delta x$ from the y-axis, $2 \le x \le 4$, as shown in figure (a). When this strip is revolved about the y-axis, it generates a cylindrical shell of average height y^*, $y \le y^* \le y^* + \Delta y$, thickness Δx, and average radius x^*, $x < x^* \le x + \Delta x$. The volume of this element is:

$$\Delta V = 2\pi x^* y^* \Delta x,$$

where $2\pi x^* y^*$ is the surface area. Expressing y in terms of x and passing to the limits, the sum of the volumes of all such cylindrical shells is the integral:

$$V = 2\pi \int_2^4 x(-x^2 + 6x - 8)\, dx$$

$$= 2\pi \int_2^4 (-x^3 + 6x^2 - 8x)\, dx$$

$$= 2\pi \left(-\frac{x^4}{4} + 2x^3 - 4x^2 \right) \Big|_2^4$$

$$= 2\pi \left((-64 + 128 - 64) - (-4 + 16 - 16) \right)$$

$$= 8\pi.$$

Method 2. This can also be thought of as the volume comprising a series of concentric washers with variable outer and inner radii, as sectionally shown in figure (b). The variable radii are as follows: Since

$$y = -x^2 + 6x - 8,$$

we solve for x.

To complete the square, we require a 9, so that

$$x^2 - 6x + 9$$

constitutes a perfect square. Rewriting the equation,

$$x^2 - 6x + 9 - 9 + 8 = -y.$$

$$x^2 - 6x + 9 = 1 - y.$$

$$(x - 3)^2 = 1 - y.$$

Therefore,

$$x = 3 \pm \sqrt{1 - y}$$

which shows the washers, y units from the x-axis, have an

inner radius: $x_{in} = 3 - \sqrt{1 - y}$, and an

outer radius: $x_o = 3 + \sqrt{1 - y}$.

(The particular one on the x-axis has $x_{in} = 2$ and $x_o = 4$.)

The volume of this washer with thickness dy is:

$$dV = \pi(x_o^2 - x_{in}^2)\, dy,$$

or $dV = \pi \left[(x_o + x_{in})(x_o - x_{in}) \right] dy$.

Substituting the values for x_o and x_{in},

$$dV = \pi \Big(\big((3 + \sqrt{1-y}) + (3 - \sqrt{1-y}) \big) \cdot$$

$$\big((3 + \sqrt{1-y}) - (3 - \sqrt{1-y}) \big) \Big) dy$$

$$= \pi(12\sqrt{1-y})\, dy.$$

Since y varies from 0 to 1, the desired volume is:

$$V = 12\pi \int_0^1 (1-y)^{\frac{1}{2}}\, dy$$

$$= 12\pi \left(-\frac{2}{3}(1-y)^{\frac{3}{2}} \right) \Big|_0^1 = 8\pi.$$

Parallel Cross Sections

A cross section of a solid is a region formed by the intersection of a solid by a plane. This is illustrated by the figure.

If x is a continuous function on the interval [a,b], then the volume of the cross sectional area $A(x)$ is

$$V = \int_a^b A(x)\, dx.$$

PROBLEM

Rotate the curve $y = 2x$ about the line $x = 4$ and find the volume produced by the rotation of the shaded portion.

SOLUTION

Area of washer $= \pi\left(R_2^{\,2} - R_1^{\,2}\right)$

Increment of volume, $dV = \pi\left(R_2^{\,2} - R_1^{\,2}\right)dy$.

$V = \int_a^b \pi\left(R_2^{\,2} - R_1^{\,2}\right)dy$, where a and b are limits of y.

$V = \int_0^4 \pi\ \left((4-x)^2 - 2^2\right)dy$

$\quad = \int_0^4 \pi\ (16 - 8x + x^2 - 4)\ dy$

$\quad = \pi\int_0^4 (12 - 8x + x^2)\ dy.$

But the x terms must be in terms of y because of dy. We have: $x = \dfrac{y}{2}$, from the equation of the curve. Substituting,

$V = \pi\int_0^4\left(12 - 4y + \dfrac{y^2}{4}\right)dy$

$\quad = \pi\left(12y - \dfrac{4y^2}{2} + \dfrac{y^3}{12}\right)_0^4$

$\quad = \pi\left(48 - 32 + -\dfrac{16}{3}\right) = \dfrac{64\pi}{3}.$

This is the washer method. The important point to remember is to obtain the radii from the center line of rotation.

Competency 10: Knowledge of Number Sense and Mathematical Structure

Real Numbers and Their Components

The set of all real numbers has various components. These components are the set of all natural numbers, N, the set of all whole numbers, W, the set of all integers, I, the set of all rational numbers, Q, and the set of all irrational numbers, S. Then,

$N = \{1, 2, 3, ...\}$,

$W = \{0, 1, 2, 3, ...\}$,

$I = \{..., -3, -2, -1, 0, 1, 2, 3, ...\}$,

$Q = \left\{\dfrac{a}{b} \mid a,b \in I \text{ and } b \neq 0\right\}$;

and $S = \{x \mid x$ has a decimal name which is nonterminating and does not have a repeating block$\}$.

It is obvious that $N \subseteq W$, $W \subseteq I$, and $I \subseteq Q$, but a similar relationship does not hold between Q and S. More specifically, the decimal names for elements of Q are

(1) terminating or

(2) nonterminating with a repeating block.

For example, $\dfrac{1}{2} = .5$ and $\dfrac{1}{3} = .333....$ This means that Q and S have no common elements. Examples of irrational numbers include $.101001000...$, π and $\sqrt{2}$.

All real numbers are normally represented by R and $R = Q \cup S$. This means that every real number is either rational or irrational. A nice way to visualize real numbers geometrically is that real numbers can be put in a one-to-one correspondence with the set of all points on a line.

Real Number Properties of Equality

The standard properties of equality involving real numbers are:

Reflexive Property of Equality

For each real number a,

$a = a$

Symmetric Property of Equality

For each real number a, for each real number b,

if $a = b$, then $b = a$

Transitive Property of Equality

For each real number a, for each real number b, for each real number c,

if $a = b$ and $b = c$, then $a = c$

Real Number Operations and Their Properties

The operations of addition and multiplication are of particular importance. As a result many properties concerning those operations have been determined and named. Here is a list of the most important of these properties.

Closure Property of Addition

For every real number a, for every real number b,

$a + b$

is a real number.

Closure Property of Multiplication

For every real number a, for every real number b,

ab

is a real number.

Commutative Property of Addition

For every real number a, for every real number b,

$a + b = b + a$.

Commutative Property of Multiplication

For every real number a, for every real number b,

$ab = ba$.

Associative Property of Addition

For every real number a, for every real number b, for every real number c,

$(a + b) + c = a + (b + c)$.

Associative Property of Multiplication

For every real number a, for every real number b, for every real number c,

$(ab)c = a(bc)$.

Identity Property of Addition

For every real number a,

$a + 0 = 0 + a = a$.

Identity Property of Multiplication

For every real number a,

$a \times 1 = 1 \times a = a$.

Inverse Property of Addition

For every real number a, there is a real number $-a$ such that

$a + -a = -a + a = 0$.

Inverse Property of Multiplication

For every real number a, $a \neq 0$, there is a real number a^{-1} such that

$a \times a^{-1} = a^{-1} \times a = 1$.

Distributive Property

For every real number a, for every real number b, for every real number c,

$a(b + c) = ab + ac$.

The operations of subtraction and division are also important, but less important than addition and multiplication. Here are the definitions for these operations.

For every real number a, for every real number b, for every real number c,

$a - b = c$ if and only if $b + c = a$.

For every real number a, for every real number b, for every real number c,

$a \div b = c$ if and only if c is the unique real number such that $bc = a$.

The definition of division eliminates division *by* 0. Thus, for example, $4 \div 0$ is undefined, $0 \div 0$ is undefined, but $0 \div 4 = 0$.

In many instances, it is possible to perform subtraction by first converting a subtraction statement to an addition statement. This is illustrated below.

For every real number a, for every real number b,

$$a - b = a + (-b).$$

In a similar way, every division statement can be converted to a multiplication statement. Use the following model:

For every real number a, for every real number b, $b \neq 0$,

$$a \div b = a \times b^{-1}$$

Complex Numbers

A **complex number** is a number that can be written in the form $a + bi$, where a and b are real numbers and $i = \sqrt{-1}$. The number a is the **real part,** and the number b is the **imaginary part** of the complex number.

Returning momentarily to real numbers, the square of a real number cannot be negative. More specifically, the square of a positive real number is positive, the square of a negative real number is positive, and the square of 0 is 0. Then i is defined to be a number with a property that

$$i^2 = -1.$$

Obviously i is not a real number. C is then used to represent the set of all complex numbers and

$$C = \{a + bi \mid a \text{ and } b \text{ are real numbers}\}.$$

Here are the definitions of addition, subtraction, and multiplication of complex numbers.

Suppose $x + yi$ and $z + wi$ are complex numbers. Then

$$(x + yi) + (z + wi) = (x + z) + (y + w)i$$

$$(x + yi) - (z + wi) = (x - z) + (y - w)i$$

$$(x + yi) \times (z + wi) = (xz - y) + (xw + yz)i.$$

To add, subtract, or multiply complex numbers, compute in the usual way, replace i^2 with -1, and simplify.

$$(a + bi) + (c + di) = (a + c) + (b + d)i$$

$$(a + bi) - (c + di) = (a - c) + (b - d)i$$

$$(a + bi)(c + di) = ac + adi + bci + bdi^2$$
$$= ac - bd + (ad + bc)i$$

PROBLEM

Simplify the following $(3 + i)(2 + i)$.

SOLUTION

$$(3 + i)(2 + i) = 3(2 + i) + i(2 + i)$$
$$= 6 + 3i + 2i + i^2$$
$$= 6 + (3 + 2)i + (-1)$$
$$= 5 + 5i$$

Complex numbers, $a + bi$, may be obtained when using the quadratic formula to solve quadratic equations.

PROBLEM

Solve the equation $x^2 - x + 1 = 0$.

SOLUTION

In this equation, $a = 1$, $b = -1$ and $c = 1$. Substitute into the quadratic formula.

$$x = \frac{-(-1) \pm \sqrt{(-1)^2 - 4(1)(1)}}{2(1)}$$

$$= \frac{1 \pm \sqrt{1 - 4}}{2}$$

$$= \frac{1 \pm \sqrt{-3}}{2}$$

$$= \frac{1 \pm \sqrt{3}i}{2}$$

$$x = \frac{1 + \sqrt{3}i}{2} \text{ or } x = \frac{1 - \sqrt{3}i}{2}$$

Division of two complex numbers is usually accomplished with a special procedure that involves the conjugate of a complex number. The conjugate of $a + bi$ is denoted by

$$\overline{a + bi} \text{ and } \overline{a + bi} = a - bi.$$

Also, $(a + bi)(a - bi) = a^2 + b^2$.

The usual procedure for division is illustrated below.

$$\frac{x + yi}{z + wi} = \frac{x + yi}{z + wi} \times \frac{z - wi}{z - wi}$$

$$= \frac{(xz + yw) + (-xw + yz)i}{z^2 + w^2}$$

$$= \frac{xz + yw}{z^2 + w^2} + \frac{-xw + yz}{z^2 + w^2}i$$

All the properties of real numbers described in the previous section carry over to complex numbers, however, those properties will not be stated again.

If a is a real number, then a can be expressed in the form $a = a + 0i$. Hence, every real number is a complex number and $R \subseteq C$.

Drill: Real and Complex Numbers

DIRECTIONS: Solve the following equations.

1. $3i^3 =$
   (A) $-3i$ (C) $9i$
   (B) $3i$ (D) $-i$

2. $2i^7 =$
   (A) $-128i$ (C) $14i$
   (B) $2i$ (D) $-2i$

3. $-4i^4 =$
   (A) 4 (C) $4i$
   (B) -4 (D) $-4i$

4. $-5i^6 =$
   (A) -5 (C) $-i$
   (B) $-5i$ (D) 5

5. $(3 + 2i)(2 + 3i) =$
   (A) $12 + 13i$ (C) $13i$
   (B) $-12 - 13i$ (D) $-13i$

6. $(2 - i)(2 + i) =$
   (A) -5 (C) $-5i$
   (B) $5i$ (D) 5

7. $(5 - 4i)^2 =$
   (A) $9 - 40i$ (C) $41 - 40i$
   (B) $-9 - 40i$ (D) $9 + 40i$

8. $x^2 + 16 = 0$
   (A) ± 4 (C) $4 \pm i$
   (B) $\pm 4i$ (D) $-4 \pm i$

9. $4y^2 + 1 = 0$
   (A) $\pm\dfrac{1}{2}$ (C) $-i \pm \dfrac{1}{2}$
   (B) $i \pm \dfrac{1}{2}$ (D) $\pm\dfrac{1}{2}i$

10. $x^2 - 4x + 13 = 0$
   (A) $3 \pm 2i$ (C) $\pm 5i$
   (B) $\pm 6i$ (D) $2 \pm 3i$

Answer Key

1.	(A)	6.	(D)
2.	(D)	7.	(A)
3.	(B)	8.	(B)
4.	(D)	9.	(D)
5.	(C)	10.	(D)

Detailed Explanations of Answers

$$= 25 - 40i + 16(-1)$$
$$= 9 - 40i$$

1.   (A)

$$3i^3 = 3i(i)^2 = 3i(-1) = -3i$$

8.   (B)

$$x^2 + 16 = 0$$
$$x^2 = -16$$
$$x^2 = (16)(-1)$$
$$x = \pm 4i$$

2.   (D)

$$2i^7 = 2i(i^2)(i^2)(i^2) = 2i(-1)(-1)(-1) = -2i$$

3.   (B)

$$-4i^4 = -4(i^2)(i^2) = -4(-1)(-1) = -4$$

9.   (D)

$$4y^2 + 1 = 0$$
$$4y^2 = -1 \Rightarrow y^2 = -\frac{1}{4} \quad y = \pm\frac{1}{2}i$$

4.   (D)

$$-5i^6 = -5(i^2)(i^2)(i^2) = -5(-1)(-1)(-1) = 5$$

5.   (C)

$$(3 + 2i)(2 + 3i) = 6 + \underbrace{9i + 4i} + 6i^2$$
$$= 6 + \quad 13i \quad -6$$
$$= 13i$$

10.   (D)

$$x^2 - 4x + 13 = 0$$

by the quadratic formula

$$\frac{-b \pm \sqrt{b^2 - 4ac}}{2a} = \frac{4 \pm \sqrt{16 - 4(1)(13)}}{2}$$

$$= \frac{4 \pm \sqrt{\overset{2}{)16 - 52}}}{2}$$

$$= \frac{4 \pm \sqrt{\overset{2}{)-36}}}{2}$$

$$= \frac{4 \pm 6i}{2}$$

$$= 2 \pm 3i$$

6.   (D)

$$(2 - i)(2 + i) = 4 + 2i - 2i - i^2$$
$$= 4 + 0 - (-1)$$
$$= 5$$

7.   (A)

$$(5 - 4i)^2 = (5 - 4i)(5 - 4i)$$
$$= (25 - 20i - 20i + 16i^2)$$

Competency 11: Knowledge of Mathematics as Communication

The teacher has knowledge of the nature of mathematics as a form of communication and is able to apply this knowledge to provide meaningful instruction to the student.

- Identify statements that correctly communicate mathematical definitions or concepts.

- Interpret written presentations of mathematics.

- Select or interpret appropriate concrete examples, pictorial illustrations, and symbolic representations in developing mathematical concepts.

It is necessary for students, parents, and teachers to understand that mathematics is a means of communication, complete with its own syntax, grammar, dialects, and slang. A simple and common rule that many math teachers share is the translation of the word 'is' into '=' when teaching students to decode word problems. This is a useful piece of information but it is just a very small example of what it means to communicate using mathematics. Although mathematics is indeed a language in which symbols can be translated into nouns and verbs and equations into sentences, it is also pictures, graphs, proofs, diagrams, and abstractions. Teachers must appreciate and understand the complexity

and importance of mathematical language and language about mathematics. Moreover, being able to effectively communicate about and communicate with mathematics allows teachers to reach more students in more meaningful ways.

Defining Objects and Concepts in Mathematics

One of the most attractive and yet daunting characteristics of mathematics is that the rules and objects used in doing math in Moscow are the same as in Singapore or in Kigali or in Miami. The emphases in curricula may differ and the styles of teaching may reflect different cultural norms but a *square* in London must also be a *square* in New Delhi. Therefore, a mathematics teacher should be knowledgeable of the necessary and sufficient conditions required to define mathematical objects and concepts and be careful in the sharing of this knowledge with students.

Of key importance is the difference between descriptions and definitions. A description may in its fullness accidentally include enough information to define a mathematical object but will likely contain information that is not essential and may lack information that is. A good definition in mathematics provides the information that is necessary to distinguish one object or concept from another—no more and no less. In the table below are some likely 'definitions' of a square along with an evaluation of each.

Possible Definition of a Square

Definitions	Comments
A shape with four right angles.	Does not contain sufficient information to determine that the shape is a quadrilateral or the necessary information to distinguish the shape from a rectangle. This is not an adequate definition.
A four-sided quadrilateral with opposite sides parallel, all sides congruent, and four right angles.	Although accurate the definition is unwieldy and contains redundant and, therefore, unnecessary information. This is not a good definition.
A quadrilateral with congruent sides and four right angles.	Contains the necessary and sufficient information to distinguish a shape as square or not a square. This is a good definition.

Many advocates of education reform, including the *National Council of Teachers of Mathematics*, suggest that teachers introduce content related jargon after students have developed a need for the term in order to make communication about the problem that they are solving or the idea that they are exploring more coherent. This is quite different from the tradition of providing students with a list of terms and definitions at the start of each chapter or section. However, regardless of instructional strategy, mathematics teachers need to ensure that the definitions students develop or work with are good ones.

The Language of Mathematics

Along with a careful approach to defining terms and concepts, teachers of mathematics should be accurate and precise in their understanding and use of language when talking or writing about math. Beyond being able to recite definitions, axioms, and formulas, teachers need to have a working knowledge of mathematical jargon. Teachers need to understand and be able to use terms like *at least one, direct variation, rate of change, if and only if, or mutually exclusive*. It is this ability that will help tie one mathematical concept to another. Also, teachers need to recognize the difference between mathematical terminology, like *rate of change*, and mathematical slang, such as *rise over run*. The use of mathematical slang is not necessarily a bad thing but meaning and understanding are more important than expedient turns of phrase.

Beyond Words

In addition to using concise mathematical language, a skilled mathematics teacher often uses analogies and concrete examples to illustrate ideas or to help students make connections. Physical representations, even if they are approximations to the mathematical ideal, are a powerful tool in engaging minds. A good example is the concept of *slope*. Math teachers commonly use a hill or a flight of stairs as a model and then equate the slope of a line with the *steepness* of the model. Physical experiences of doing mathematics or observing mathematical constructs afford students with an immediacy of experience that often goes beyond words. The same is true for pictorial representations of an idea. For example, Leonardo da Vinci's anatomical sketch *Vitruvian Man* is great for the study of proportions or a guided discovery of the golden mean.

Although an effective mathematics teacher will choose appropriate physical and pictorial examples, the careful teacher should ensure that student understanding is rooted in the mathematics. The teacher needs to be sure that the learner can go beyond the model or representation to use his or her mathematical knowledge of the concept in a meaningful way. Being able to compare slope to steepness is valuable but if the student can not calculate the slope of a line—or the steepness of a flight of stairs—then the mathematics has been lost.

Finally, it is important that teachers foster this attention to the language of mathematics among their students. Carelessness or ambiguity in language is a good indicator of insufficient understanding.

Competency 12: Knowledge of Mathematics as Reasoning

Basic Concepts of Logic

Sentences

Logic is concerned with declarative sentences that are unambiguous and definite, and either true or false (though we may not know which).

Truth Values

There are two truth values: Truth and Falsity.

Every sentence to which standard logic applies has exactly one of the two truth values (that is, is either true or false, but not both). No sentence can be both true and false.

Arguments

An *argument* is a set of sentences, one of which is the *conclusion*. The remaining sentences are the *premises* of the argument, where the *premises* are taken to present evidence or reasons in support of the *conclusion*.

Conclusion-Indicator Words

To identify arguments in a text or conversation, it is important to understand what function each sentence in the discourse is performing. English offers some "indicator words" as clues to help identify what function sentences are serving. These serve only as a guide and do not guarantee that an argument is present. (This is because these words, like most words of English, have several different meanings.)

Conclusion-indicator words include: *therefore, thus, hence, so, consequently, it follows that*.

Premise-Indicator words

Premise-indicator words include: *since, because, for, given that, inasmuch as, for the reason that, on account of*.

Evaluating Arguments

Arguments may be evaluated according to a variety of criteria or standards.

One such standard is the FACT standard: are all of the premises true? Is the data (evidence) offered in the premises actually, as a matter of fact, true? Are the reasons offered correct? Logic generally offers no help regarding the question of the truth or falsity of premises.

Logic is concerned with the LOGIC question: the evaluation of arguments in terms of the strength of support the premises provide for the conclusion. That is, logic develops standards for determining how strongly the premises, if all true, support the conclusion. This is an evaluation of how relevant the evidence or reasons given in the premises is to the claim made by the conclusion. Deductive logic formulates the most demanding standards by which to evaluate arguments.

Deductive Validity and Invalidity

An argument is (deductively) valid if and only if it is *impossible* that all its premises be true while its conclusion is false. That is, the premises of a valid argument, if they were all true, *guarantee* the truth of the conclusion; to accept all the premises and deny the conclusion would be inconsistent.

An argument is invalid if and only if it is not valid. That is, even if the premises are or were assumed (imagined) to be all true, the conclusion could still be false.

The relationship of evidential strength that premises lend to a conclusion can be seen in the following table:

The premises of a valid argument are said to entail its conclusion.

The following table summarizes these relationships between truth values of premises and conclusion and the validity and invalidity of arguments.

Premises	Conclusion	Validity
all true	true	can't tell
all true	false	invalid
one or more false	true	can't tell
one or more false	false	can't tell

Inductive Strength and Weakness

Invalid arguments may still be good arguments when evaluated by other acceptable standards. Inductive logic develops different standards by which arguments are evaluated.

An argument is *inductively strong* if and only if it is *improbable* that all its premises be true while its conclusion is false. Inductive strength is typically measured as a real number value from zero (false) to one (certain).

An argument is inductively weak if and only if it is not inductively strong.

Examples:

The following argument is invalid, but inductively strong:

Ninety percent of restaurants in Chicago are owned by Greeks.

Evidential Strength between Premises and Conclusion		
Example of an argument that . . .	**Valid** (The truth of the premises guarantees the truth of the conclusion.)	**Invalid** (The truth of the premises does not guarantee the truth of the conclusion.)
All true premises, true conclusion	If Chicago is in Illinois, then it is in the USA. Chicago is in Illinois. Therefore, Chicago is in the USA.	Clinton was President in 1995. Therefore, Washington was the 1st US President.
All true premises, false conclusion	**By definition of "valid," none exist**	Either Bush or Clinton have been presidents. Bush was a president. Therefore, Clinton has not been President.
One or more false premises, true conclusion	Either Reagan was a President or Bush was a Vice-President. Reagan was not a President. Therefore, Bush was a Vice-President.	Bush was not a President. Therefore, Bush was a Vice-President.
One or more false premises, false conclusion	Clinton was a President and Dukakis was a President. Therefore, Dukakis was a President.	Bush was not a President. Therefore, Bush was not a Vice President.

Lou Mitchell's is a restaurant in Chicago.
Therefore, Lou Mitchell's is owned by Greeks.

This argument is inductively strong, because given the truth of the premises, the chances are that Lou Mitchell's will be among the 90 percent of restaurants that are Greek-owned. The argument is invalid because there is some chance that Lou Mitchell's may be among the 10 percent that are not Greek-owned; so it is not *impossible* that even should the premises be true, the conclusion may still be false.

The following argument is valid:

100 percent (that is, all) of restaurants in Chicago are owned by Greeks.

Lou Mitchell's is a restaurant in Chicago.

Therefore, Lou Mitchell's is owned by Greeks.

Note that while the premises in fact are not true, if they were, the conclusion would have to be true. Also note that any percentage in the first premise less than 100 percent would give an invalid argument; as long as the percentage is greater than 0 percent, the argument has some inductive strength; as the percentage approaches 0 percent, the reason to accept the conclusion, given the evidence supplied by the premises, approaches no reason at all.

Symbolic logic is concerned only with deductive standards for evaluating arguments and with matters related to these standards.

Logical Properties of Sentences

Consistency

A sentence is *consistent* if and only if it is *possible* that it is true.

A sentence is *inconsistent* if and only if it is not consistent; that is, if and only if it is *impossible* that it is true.

Example: At least one odd number is not odd.

Logical Truth

A sentence is *logically true* if and only if it is *impossible* for it to be false; that is, the denial of the sentence is inconsistent.

Example: Either Mars is a planet or Mars is not a planet.

Logical Falsity

A sentence is *logically false* if and only if it is *impossible* for it to be true; that is, the sentence is inconsistent.

Example: Mars is a planet and Mars is not a planet.

Logical Indeterminacy (Contingency)

A sentence is *logically indeterminate* (*contingent*) if and only if it is neither logically true nor logically false.

Example: Einstein was a physicist and Pauling was a chemist.

Logical Equivalence of Sentences

Two sentences are *logically equivalent* if and only if it is *impossible* for one of the sentences to be true while the other sentence is false; that is, if and only if it is impossible for the two sentences to have different truth values.

Example: "Chicago is in Illinois and Pittsburgh is in Pennsylvania" is logically equivalent to "Pittsburgh is in Pennsylvania and Chicago is in Illinois."

Method of Proof

Logic

Definition 1

A statement is a sentence which is either true or false, but not both.

Definition 2

If a and b are statements, then a statement of the form "a and b" is called the conjunction of a and b, denoted by $a \wedge b$.

Definition 3

The disjunction of two statements a and b is shown by the compound statement "a or b," denoted by $a \vee b$.

Definition 4

The negation of a statement q is the statement "not q," denoted by $\sim q$.

Definition 5

The compound statement "if *a*, then *b*," denoted by $a \rightarrow b$, is called a conditional statement or an implication.

"If *a*" is called the hypothesis or premise of the implication, "then *b*" is called the conclusion of the implication.

Further, statement *a* is called the antecedent of the implication, and statement *b* is called the consequent of the implication.

Definition 6

The converse of $a \rightarrow b$ is $b \rightarrow a$.

Definition 7

The contrapositive of $a \rightarrow b$ is $\sim b \rightarrow \sim a$.

Definition 8

The inverse of $a \rightarrow b$ is $\sim a \rightarrow \sim b$.

Definition 9

The statement of the form "*p* if and only if *q*," denoted by $p \leftrightarrow q$, is called a biconditional statement.

Definition 10

An argument is valid if the truth of the premises means that the conclusion must also be true.

Definition 11

Intuition is the process of making generalizations on insight.

Problem Solving Example:

PROBLEM

Write the inverse for each of the following statements. Determine whether the inverse is true or false. (a) If a person is stealing, he is breaking the law. (b) If a line is perpendicular to a segment at its midpoint, it is the perpendicular bisector of the segment. (c) Dead men tell no tales.

SOLUTION

The inverse of a given conditional statement is formed by negating both the hypothesis and conclusion of the conditional statement.

(a) The hypothesis of this statement is "a person is stealing;" the conclusion is "he is breaking the law." The negation of the hypothesis is "a person is not stealing." The inverse is "if a person is not stealing, he is not breaking the law."

The inverse is false, since there are more ways to break the law than by stealing. Clearly, a murderer may not be stealing but he is surely breaking the law.

(b) In this statement, the hypothesis contains two conditions: (1) the line is perpendicular to the segment; and (2) the line intersects the segment at the midpoint. The negation of (statement a *and* statement b) is (not statement a *or* not statement b). Thus, the negation of the hypothesis is "The line is not perpendicular to the segment or it doesn't intersect the segment at the midpoint." The negation of the conclusion is "the line is not the perpendicular bisector of a segment."

The inverse is "if a line is not perpendicular to the segment or does not intersect the segment at the midpoint, then the line is not the perpendicular bisector of the segment."

In this case, the inverse is true. If either of the conditions holds (the line is not perpendicular; the line does not intersect at the midpoint), then the line cannot be a perpendicular bisector.

(c) This statement is not written in if-then form, which makes its hypothesis and conclusion more difficult to see. The hypothesis is implied to be "the man is dead"; the conclusion is implied to be "the man tells no tales." The inverse is, therefore, "If a man is not dead, then he will tell tales."

The inverse is false. Many witnesses to crimes are still alive but they have never told their stories to the police, either out of fear or because they didn't want to get involved.

Basic Principles, Laws, and Theorems

1. Any statement is either true or false. (The law of the Excluded Middle)

2. A statement cannot be both true and false. (The Law of Contradiction)

3. The converse of a true statement is not necessarily true.

4. The converse of a definition is always true.

5. For a theorem to be true, it must be true for all cases.

6. A statement is false if one false instance of the statement exists.

7. The inverse of a true statement is not necessarily true.

8. The contrapositive of a true statement is true and the contrapositive of a false statement is false.

9. If the converse of a true statement is true, then the inverse is true. Likewise, if the converse is false, the inverse is false.

10. Statements which are either both true or false are said to be logically equivalent.

11. If a given statement and its converse are both true, then the conditions in the hypothesis of the statement are both necessary and sufficient for the conclusion of the statement.

If a given statement is true but its converse is false, then the conditions are sufficient but not necessary for the conclusion of the statement.

If a given statement and its converse are both false, then the conditions are neither sufficient nor necessary for the statement's conclusion.

Deductive Reasoning

An arrangement of statements that would allow you to deduce the third one from the preceding two is called a syllogism. A syllogism has three Parts:

The first part is a general statement concerning a whole group. This is called the major premise.

The second part is a specific statement which indicates that a certain individual is a member of that group. This is called the minor premise.

The last part of a syllogism is a statement to the effect that the general statement which applies to the group also applies to the individual. This third statement of a syllogism is called a deduction.

Example A: Properly Deduced Argument

A) Major Premise: All birds have feathers.

B) Minor Premise: An eagle is a bird.

C) Deduction: An eagle has feathers.

The technique of employing a syllogism to arrive at a conclusion is called deductive reasoning.

If a major premise which is true is followed by an appropriate minor premise which is true, a conclusion can be deduced which must be true, and the reasoning is valid. However, if a major premise which is true is followed by an inappropriate minor premise which is also true, a conclusion cannot be deduced.

Example B: Improperly Deduced Argument

A) Major Premise: All people who vote are at least 18 years old.

B) Improper Minor Premise: Jane is at least 18.

C) Illogical Deduction: Jane votes.

The flaw in example B is that the major premise stated in A makes a condition on people who vote, not on a person's age. If statements B and C are interchanged, the resulting three-part deduction would be logical.

Indirect Proof

Indirect proofs involve considering two possible outcomes — the result we would like to prove and its negative — and then showing, under the given hypothesis, that a contradiction of prior known theorems, postulates, or definitions is reached when the negative is assumed.

Postulate 1

A proposition contradicting a true proposition is false.

Postulate 2

If one of a given set of propositions must be true, and all except one of those propositions have been proved to be false, then this one remaining proposition must be true.

The method of indirect proof may be summarized as follows:

Step 1. List all the possible conclusions.

Step 2. Prove all but one of those possible conclusions to be false (use Postulate 1 given).

Step 3. The only remaining possible conclusion is proved true according to Postulate 2.

• EXAMPLE

When attempting to prove that in a scalene triangle the bisector of an angle cannot be perpendicular to the opposite side, one method of solution could be to consider the two possible conclusions:

1) the bisector can be perpendicular to the opposite side, or

2) the bisector cannot be perpendicular to the opposite side.

Obviously, one and only one of these conclusions can be true; therefore, if we can prove that all of the possibilities, except one, are false, then the remaining possibility must be a valid conclusion. In this example, it can be proven that, for all cases, the statement which asserts that the bisector of an angle of a scalene triangle can be perpendicular to the opposite side is false. Therefore, the contradicting possibility—the bisector cannot be perpendicular to the opposite side—is in fact true.

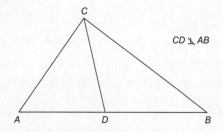

$CD \perp AB$

Problem Solving Example:

PROBLEM

Prove, by indirect method, that if two angles are not congruent, then they are not both right angles.

SOLUTION

Indirect proofs involve considering two possible outcomes, the result we would like to prove and its negative, and then showing, under the given hypothesis, that a contradiction of prior known theorems, postulates, or definitions is reached when the negative is assumed.

In this case, the outcomes can be that the two angles are not right angles or that the two angles are right angles. Assume the negative of what we want to prove—that the two angles are right angles.

The given hypothesis in this problem is that the two angles are not congruent. A previous theorem states that all right angles are congruent. Therefore, the conclusion we have assumed true leads to a logical contradiction. As such, the alternative conclusion must be true. Therefore, if two angles are not congruent, then they are not both right angles.

Inductive Reasoning

Inductive reasoning is a method of reasoning by which one draws a conclusion or generalization based on a pattern of specific cases. Observing a well-defined pattern can lead us to predict an answer for the unknown portion of the pattern.

For example, observing the numbers 2, 5, 8, 11, . . ., we find that a pattern is defined based on a difference of 3 between each two consecutive numbers. Extrapolating this pattern, we can conclude that the number immediately following 11 is $11 + 3 = 14$.

In mathematics, we use the following steps as the general method of inductive reasoning.

Let $P(n)$ be a statement or proposition, where n is a positive integer.

Try to verify that $P(1)$ is a true statement. That is, replace n with 1 in the given statement or proposition to see whether the statement is true or false. If the statement is true, assume that it is also true for all the following values of n, up to k. That is, assume that $P(n)$ is true for $n = k$.

Next, using the true statements $P(1)$ and $P(k)$, try to verify that $P(n)$ is true for $n = k + 1$ as well. If you succeed in verifying this step, you can claim that the statement or proposition $P(n)$ is true for all integer values of n.

PROBLEM

Prove by mathematical induction that
$$1 + 7 + 13 + \ldots + (6n - 5) = n(3n - 2).$$

SOLUTION

Denote $1 + 7 + 13 + ... + (6n - 5)$ by $P(n)$.

So, (1) $P(n) = 1 + 7 + 13 + ... + (6n - 5)$

Step 1. Check the statement to see whether it is true for $n = 1$. To do so, simply replace n with 1 in the given statement.

(2) $P(1) = [6(1) - 5] = 1[3(1) - 2]$

Computing both sides of (2) indicates the statement is true for $n = 1$.

Step 2. Assume that the statement is true for $n = k$. This means that

(3) $P(k) = 1 + 7 + 13 + ... + (6k - 5) = k(3k - 2)$.

Step 3. Now, try to prove that the statement is true for $n = k + 1$ as well. To do so, add $6k + 1$ to the right side equation in (3).

(4) $1 + 7 + 13 + ... + (6k - 5) + 6k + 1 = k(3k - 2) + 6k + 1$

We know that

(5) $(6k - 5) + 6k + 1 = 6k - 5 + 6k + 1 - 6 + 6$

$= (6k - 5) + (6k + 6) - 5$

$= (6k - 5) + [6(k + 1) - 5]$

Next, simplify and rearrange the right side of (4) as follows

(6) $k(3k - 2) + 6k + 1 = 3k^2 - 2k + 6k + 1$

$= 3k^2 + 4k + 1$

$= 3k^2 + 3k + k + 1$

$= 3k(k + 1) + (k + 1)$

$= (k + 1)(3k + 1)$

$= (k + 1)[3(k + 1) - 2]$

$= (k + 1)(3k + 3 - 2)$

$= (k + 1)[3(k + 1) - 2]$

Placing the final results obtained through (5) and (6) into (4), we get

(7) $1 + 7 + 13 + ... + (6k - 5) + [6(k + 1) - 5]$

$= k(3k - 2) + (k + 1)[3(k + 1) - 2]$.

That is, $P(n)$ is true for $n = k + 1$.

Defined and Undefined Terms: Axioms, Postulates, and Assumptions; Theorems and Corollaries

To build a logical system of mathematics, the first step is to take a known and then move to what is not known. The terms which we will accept as known are called undefined terms. We accept certain basic terms as undefined, since their definition would of necessity include other undefined terms. Examples of some important undefined terms with characteristics that you must know are:

A) Set: The sets we will be concerned with will have clearly defined characteristics.

B) Point: Although we represent points on paper with small dots, a point has no size, thickness, or width. A point is denoted by a capital letter.

C) Line: A line is a series of adjacent points which extends indefinitely. A line can be either curved or straight; however, unless otherwise stated, the term "line" refers to a straight line. A line is denoted by listing two points on the line and drawing a line with arrows on top, i.e., $\overleftrightarrow{AB}$.

D) Plane: A plane is the collection of all points lying on a flat surface which extends indefinitely in all directions. Imagine holding a record cover in a room and imagine that the record cover divides the entire room. Remember that a plane has no thickness.

We use these undefined terms to construct defined terms so we can describe more sophisticated expressions.

Necessary characteristics of a good definition are:

A) It names the term being defined.

B) It uses only known terms or accepted undefined terms.

C) It places the term into the smallest set to which it belongs.

D) It states the characteristics of the defined term which distinguish it from the other members of the set.

E) It contains the least possible amount of information.

F) It is always reversible.

Axioms, postulates, and assumptions are the statements in geometry which are accepted as true without proof, whereas theorems are the statements in geometry which are proven to be true.

A corollary is a theorem that can be deduced easily from another theorem or from a postulate.

In this text, the term postulate is used exclusively, instead of axiom or assumption.

Postulate 1

A quantity is equal to itself (reflexive law).

Postulate 2

If two quantities are equal to the same quantity, they are equal to each other (transitive law).

Postulate 3

If *a* & *b* are any quantities, and *a* = *b*, then *b* = *a* (symmetric law).

Postulate 4

The whole is equal to the sum of its parts.

Postulates 5

If equal quantities are added to equal quantities, the sums are equal quantities.

Postulate 6

If equal quantities are subtracted from equal quantities, the differences are equal quantities.

Postulate 7

If equal quantities are multiplied by equal quantities, the products are equal quantities.

Postulate 8

If equal quantities are divided by equal quantities (not 0), the quotients are equal quantities.

Postulates 9

There exists one and only one straight line through any two distinct points.

Postulate 10

Two straight lines can intersect at only one point.

PROBLEM

In the figure shown, the measure of ∢*DAC* equals the measure of ∢*ECA* and the measure of ∢1 equals the measure of ∢2. Show that the measure of ∢3 equals the measure of ∢4.

SOLUTION

This proof will require the subtraction postulate, which states that if equal quantities are subtracted from equal quantities, the differences are equal.

Given: ∢*DAC* ≅ ∢*ECA*, ∢1 ≅ ∢2

Prove: ∢3 ≅ ∢4

Statement	Reason
1. $m\angle DAC = m\angle ECA$ $m\angle 1 = m\angle 2$	1. Given.
2. $m\angle DAC - m\angle 1 =$ $m\angle ECA - m\angle 2$	2. Subtraction Postulate.
3. $m\angle 3 = m\angle 4$	3. Substitution Postulate.

Competency 13: Knowledge of Mathematical Connections

The teacher understands the connections within the structure of mathematics and is able to use those connections to further student understanding as well as provide more avenues of access to mathematics ideas.

- Identify equivalent representations of the same concept or procedure (e.g., graphical, algebraic, verbal, numeric).

- Interpret relationships between mathematical topics (e.g., multiplication as repeated addition, powers as repeated multiplication).

- Interpret descriptions, diagrams, and representations of arithmetic operations.

Connections

The study of mathematics has developed over several millennia into ever more specialized fields. In our public schools, the distinctions are being made even at the middle and elementary school levels but are most pronounced in high schools where student receive mathematics instruction in year-long doses of algebra, geometry, or calculus. This is advantageous with regard to course scheduling and high mobility rates among students but it neglects the interconnectedness of mathematics as a whole and limits student exploration of the field. An effective mathematics teacher should have knowledge of these connections and use them to give students a more comprehensive picture of mathematics.

Using these *mathematical* connections, teachers will be able to give students more chances to make mental connections to multiple ideas resulting in an increase in retention and more depth in understanding. Furthermore, teachers that understand these links in the underlying structure of mathematics are better able to make meaningful long-term instructional and curricular plans by using already mastered concepts to develop new ones.

Equivalent Representations

A good test for depth of understanding of any topic is a person's ability to communicate about the subject in multiple ways. Teachers should use several different but equivalent representations of a concept or procedure to build mathematical understanding and encourage flexible thinking. For example, in creating a lesson on linear relationships, a teacher can have students a) collect and organize data using a chart or table, b) explore the data using graphs or pictograms, c) analyze the graphs for more information, d) develop a symbolic model for the phenomenon and e) write an evaluation of the experiment and a summary of conclusions. Throughout the process, the teacher needs to reinforce the concept of linearity as it manifests in each of the representations.

It is also essential that students learn how each representation highlights different aspects of the same idea. Numeric information draws our attention to patterns within data and the degree of the relationship between variables. Tables and charts allow us to organize data in ways that make looking for patterns easier. Graphs or pictograms afford us with a way to see trends in data as well as provide visual information that can sometimes match the actual physical behavior of objects. Written or verbal communications offer the opportunity for providing explanations or setting conditions. Symbolic representations allow us to make generalizations and explore the phenomenon under different conditions. Students should be able to determine what representation is best to highlight the periodic behavior in a pendulum or the possible permutations of a 5-letter combination.

Finally, the teacher needs to use multiple representations often enough that students become competent in selecting and constructing the most appropriate representation or representations for their needs. Students should come to see the multitude of representations as tools that they can create and then use to explore and solve concrete, real-world problems.

Relationships Between Mathematical Topics

In addition to being able to represent one idea or procedure in multiple ways, teachers must understand that topics within and between fields of mathematical study are connected. The seemingly disjointed courses of algebra and geometry are rife with connections such as the concept of linearity, the usefulness of coordinate systems, number sequences and the properties of geometric shapes, etc. Sometimes the connections are so important that one concept is actually defined by the other. A good example is the relationship between addition and multiplication. At the elementary level, the fact that multiplication is simply *multiple* additions helps students construct an understanding

of what multiplications is and does. However, at more advanced levels this understanding can help students simplify or manipulate complex expressions.

It is also important for teachers to recognize themes and behaviors that extend throughout mathematics. For example, dilation and translation are concepts that appear in Algebra I, Geometry, and Algebra II again and again and teachers should plan for and take advantage of the repetition.

The idea of building models from collected data is another important, ongoing theme that becomes increasingly important in the study of mathematics and its applications. Furthermore, mathematics teachers should be aware of the connections between mathematics and other fields of study. The vast majority of our students will not become theoretical mathematicians. They will become users of mathematics in the social, life, and physical sciences as well as in business, marketing, and service industries.

Representations of Arithmetic Operations

A particularly important series of connections are essential for the high school Algebra teacher. Teachers of elementary mathematics have long used base ten blocks, multiplication rectangles, and pictograms to help students learn the basic add, subtract, multiply, and divide operations. These diagrams and representations of the basic operations can be directly transferred to the teaching of algebra.

Teachers should be able to interpret and use these models to develop procedures such as distributing through a quantity or factoring an equation. Algebra tiles can take the place of base ten blocks and the multiplication rectangles can be set up in similar fashion to provide a model for the multiplication problem $(x + 3)(x + 1)$ or the factoring problem $3x^2 - 4x - 4$. Understanding these connections to the elementary models can help demystify many of these algebra procedures.

For in depth explanations of the base ten blocks and multiplication rectangles see J. A. Van de Walle's *Elementary and Middle School Mathematics: Teaching Developmentally* and for information on the use of algebra tiles see the manuals accompanying the tiles or visit one of the many dedicated sites on the internet.

Competency 14: Knowledge of Instruction

The teacher has knowledge of specific instructional resources, methods, and strategies appropriate to make mathematics applicable and accessible.

- Identify methods and strategies for teaching problem-solving skills and applications (e.g., constructing tables from given data, guess-and-check, working backwards, reasonableness, estimation).

- Select appropriate resources for a classroom activity (e.g., manipulatives, mathematical models, technology, other teaching tools).

Instruction as Pedagogical Content Knowledge

Effective teachers are individuals that not only know what they teach but also how to teach it. This specialized knowledge is often called pedagogical content knowledge. Pedagogical content knowledge is the combination of subject matter knowledge with the instructional strategies needed to teach at grade level. It requires an understanding of how to design and present materials in a manner that is accessible to learners at a given level of understanding. Lee Shulman (1986) defines pedagogical content knowledge as "the transformation of subject matter knowledge through the lenses of belief about learners and learning mathematics, beliefs about mathematics, and pedagogical knowledge."

Subject Matter Knowledge

A teacher's subject matter knowledge of high school mathematics requires detailed knowledge of the concepts and topics in high school mathematics rather than expertise in Advanced Differential Equations or Number theory. The advanced mathematics courses should act as a foundation for deeper exploration and understanding of the mathematics that the teacher will actually teach.

For example, a geometry teacher needs to have deep understanding of such concepts as deductive and inductive reasoning, axiomatic structures, plane geometry, the Pythagorean Theorem, and the nine-point circle, while a teacher of algebra needs to have in-depth knowledge about functions, dependent and independent variables, coordinate systems, data collection and data analysis. This detailed knowledge of high school mathematics will allow the teacher to select exercises where mathematical reasoning is a part of the solution process rather than low-complexity, procedural exercises. Also, as discussed earlier, an important part of this knowledge is the ability to anticipate and address student errors and misconceptions.

Beliefs about Learning and Learners

What mathematics teachers believe about their students and how their students learn mathematics is an essential component in how teachers facilitate the learning process. Teachers with the *tabula rasa*, or blank slate, perspective spend class time explaining to students very carefully how to solve each particular exercise type appearing in the textbook. They also assign large numbers of procedural practice exercises believing that the opportunity to practice on a large number of exercises will lead to mastery.

However, in order to develop the ability to reason and communicate mathematically, teachers should provide opportunities for students to work on real problems in which the solution process must be determined, designed, and implemented by the students rather than copied from the teacher.

Teachers should also introduce children to open-ended problems in which there are a multitude of reasonable interpretations and solutions. Good teachers will be wary of trivial solutions and will discourage them by asking challenging questions about the student's solution process. Generally speaking, the students should be doing the mathematics rather than the teacher.

Beliefs about Mathematics

One of the key goals of the National Council of Teachers of Mathematics (NCTM) is to alter the perception that teachers and, subsequently, their students have about the nature of mathematics (2004). For some teachers and most students, mathematics is a collection of mysterious rules, randomly applied to algebraic expressions that have no apparent relation to anything in the real world.

The common belief is that there is always a correct procedure that will lead to a number and that the number is *the* answer. Unfortunately, teachers that do hold this narrow perspective of math are still able to succeed in teaching some students very efficient procedures that, in the right circumstances, result in the correct answers. This makes it more difficult to change a teacher's perspective because they already know how to get the *right* answer. However, in order to fully appreciate and become skillful users of mathematics, teachers and students needed to gain a perspective of mathematics as a means of building models that describe the physical world.

Pedagogical Knowledge

Pedagogical knowledge is the collected skills, practices, and strategies a teacher employs to manage the learning experience and the learning environment. Examples of pedagogical knowledge might include the use of wait time, equitable means for dividing students into groups, knowing what the essential components of a lesson plan are, knowing Bloom's taxonomy of higher order thinking, and having the organizational and managerial skills to maintain the discipline of a class full of students.

Additionally, mode of delivery is an important pedagogical skill. Teachers' pedagogical knowledge extends to the use of lecture, collaborative learning, discovery learning, problem-based learning, or any number of other methods of delivery. Other pedagogical concerns involve ensuring that boys and girls get called on the same number of times with the same level of questions, incorporating English as a Second Language strategies throughout the activity, and how to teach mathematics through reading.

The combination of subject matter knowledge, belief about learners and learning mathematics, beliefs about mathematics, and pedagogical knowledge defines a teacher's approach to instruction and should guide the choices regarding the strategies and resources used to teach mathematics.

Teaching Problem-Solving

It is probably necessary to define the term *problem* before discussing effective ways to teach mathematics through problem-solving. A problem is a question in which the solver does not already know the mathematical procedure or process necessary to arrive at an answer. Therefore, students need to use their existing knowledge and possibly develop new knowledge to solve the problem. Although this is a realistic representation of what it means to 'do mathematics', this process is difficult and discouraging if the problem solver does not have appropriate problem-solving skills. Teachers need to develop these skills in themselves and model them for their students. The instruction in problem solving skills should be explicit.

How teachers teach problem-solving can range from instructing students in individual strategies as appropriate problem types appear in the course of classroom activities to teaching problem-solving as a separate unit at the beginning of the school year. In either case, the teacher needs to select problems in which the problematic area is mathematics rather than some other complexity such as access to data, understanding of technical jargon, or wording of the problem. As well, teachers should provide students with regular feedback on the problem-solving techniques they use as well as on the mathematical concept and procedures they employ.

At the start of a problem-solving session, teachers can engage the interest of the students as well as provide them with some groundwork for the problem by thinking aloud, brainstorming with students, or breaking down the problem into a less complex one. After several problem solving sessions, students should be encouraged to do these things with each other.

Once the students are engaged in the actual problem-solving task, the teacher should circulate among the students providing feedback and encouragement through careful questioning and, possibly, small hints. Teachers should avoid giving enough information that they actually guide the students through the solution process. However, on occasion, it may become necessary for the teacher to suggest a student takes another approach. Presentations of the solutions and classroom discussions focusing on the mathematical tools used in those solutions will allow the teacher to tie the learning experience to previous, current, and future mathematics topics.

The Problem-Solving Process

Problem-solving begins with understanding the problem being asked. This means that the problem-solver needs to isolate such information as what is being asked, given, needed, and assumed. Gathering this information will allow the student to organize the problem and begin to devise a plan or strategy for actually solving the problem. Characteristics of the problem itself such as the number of possible solutions or the presence of an equation may indicate that one particular strategy is a better choice than another.

Mathematics students need to become knowledgeable about specific problem solving strategies so that they can use them appropriately. Once a strategy is used and a solution is found, the student should return to the problem and determine whether or not that solution makes sense and whether there are any constraints on the solution from either the assumptions made in the organization process or by the mathematics performed. Finally, the solution should be stated within the context of the problem. Teachers may teach students variations of this process as outlined in any number of problem-solving resources, but the key is that it must be taught. Teachers should not assume that students will develop the ability to solve problems by simply being given problems to solve.

Some Problem Solving Strategies and Skills

Reasonableness and Estimation

Throughout the problem solving process the student should be asking whether or not the steps and the results of those steps make sense. This can mean knowing if a particular strategy is a good choice for the problem at hand, being able to determine when factoring a polynomial is prudent or not, or recognizing when a quantity is either considerably larger or smaller than what is reasonable to expect. These skills can be developed by asking students to defend their work to each other and to themselves while that work is in progress. Asking students to estimate the answer to a problem or part of a problem on a regular basis will encourage the practice and will also build students mathematical self-confidence as they become better mathematical thinkers. The responses to reasonableness and estimation questions can serve as excellent informal assessments of student comprehension and readiness for additional or accelerated work.

Constructing a Table

When a problem provides a data set that can be organized by specific characteristics or groups, constructing a table or several tables will make the student start thinking about the data and possible connections between one group of data and another. This is also an important strategy if the problem requires students to make measurements or record data or when a problem asks students to determine the possible combinations of certain events. Tables are also important in problems where formulas and equations are present. A table of values can provide insight into a pattern or anomaly that may not be apparent otherwise. The act of creating the table itself may or may not provide the solution but it will organize the information and it may lead the student to another strategy.

Guess-and-Check

Although it may seem odd, guessing is a valid problem-solving strategy that should be used when there are a relatively small number of possible solutions or when all of the solutions can be tested easily. Technology makes this an even more appealing option when a computer or calculator can be programmed to do the testing. Guessing is also useful when the student has narrowed down the possible solutions through the use of other methods or has some other indication of what the solution might be. The key to the guess-and-check strategy is the checking. To make this clear to the learner, the teacher can require a guess-and-check solution to show each guess and subsequent check.

Working Backwards

Working backwards is a strategy used when the answer is already known. Geometry proofs and algebraic derivations of formulas are good examples of problems where working backwards should be applied. It is important to point out that this strategy is really a back and forth effort that fills in proofs and derivations from the bottom up and from the top down and sometimes from the middle out. Teachers can guide students in this strategy by making the process overt. Since this is likely a strategy that the he employs quite well, the teacher can model it for students while saying out loud the thinking process that he is going through.

Solving an Easier Problem

When confronted with a complex or difficult problem it is often advantageous to simplify the problem and attempt to solve the easier version first. This can be done by reducing the number of components and/or variables in the problematic situation. However, in doing so, it is important not to alter the essence of the mathematics in the original problem. For example, in a routing question about a delivery company with five hubs, the problem-solver might wish to reduce the number of hubs to two but reducing the number of hubs to one would result in a fundamental change in the mathematics of the situation. It would no longer be a routing or graph theory problem.

Teaching Tools

Mathematical understanding is closely connected to the ability to turn mathematics information such as numbers, relationships between variables, and graphs into pictures or even movies within the mind. This ability is generally called *visualization*. A teacher may have a well established picture of the mathematics topic being taught in her mind but find that transmitting it to others by attempting to share the resulting mathematical artifacts is difficult at best. In fact, constructivist theory tells us that in order to make meaningful connections to other knowledge and achieve higher levels of understanding, students need to construct those pictures and movies themselves. The teacher's role is to select the most appropriate resources to aid students in constructing their own pictures.

Manipulatives and Mathematical Models

Manipulatives are physical objects that are used to represent abstract ideas. Examples of this are counter beads that are used to represent numbers, algebra tiles that are used to represent variables in an algebraic expression or equation, or pieces of metal on an air track that represents objects moving on a frictionless surface. Students group, move, or otherwise manipulate these objects in accordance with some mathematical property or rule. For example, students told to make three groups of two and then use another set of counters to make two groups of three see the commutative property of multiplication by adding the counters. The teacher's role is to guide the student in the use of the manipulatives, lead the students to recognize the property or rule, and then help them articulate and communicate their findings.

On the other hand, a mathematical model can be an object, picture, diagram, or equation that provides the learner the opportunity to see particular characteristics of a mathematics concept. Examples are as varied as a square cut out of construction paper to the diagram of a function box in an algebra text to a set of base-ten blocks. The mathematical model is different from a manipulative because it has some characteristic of a mathematics concept built in. Again, the teacher guides the student to use the model to discover this mathematical idea.

More complex mathematical models are often built by mathematicians, scientists, or statisticians. These models allow researchers to simplify real world phenomena so that individual processes can be observed, examined, or predicted. Recently, the construction of these complex mathematical models has made its way into the classroom as an instructional strategy. The approach to mathematical modeling instruction is similar to teaching through problem-solving but emphasizes overarching models that connect one mathematical idea to another.

Manipulatives and mathematical models can also be used as a means of exploration. Providing opportunities for free, unguided exploration of mathematical ideas allows learners to reinforce things that they already know and encourages creativity in a field that many students perceive as rigid, fixed, and, therefore, boring. Informal questions about what, why, and how students are exploring should be used to maintain both individual and class momentum. Teachers can also ask students to share their ideas with rest of the class to spark interest or even debate. Unfortunately, this kind of free activity can easily fall into unproductive, mathematically meaningless play time. It should be introduced to students over time with the amount of time spent exploring increased gradually.

Teachers need to gauge when productive efforts are winding down and bring the students together to discuss what they did. The discussions should serve to validate the time spent and inspire questions for future exploration.

Manipulatives and mathematical models do have a down side. While the connection between the manipulative or model and the mathematical concept that it is representing is clear to the teacher, the student needs to be guided to developing that connection. Unless this is done, the activity involving the manipulative or model becomes an exercise in following instructions. In this case, the purpose of the activity is obscure and the student may create incorrect or incomplete conceptions of the mathematics involved. Or, the activity is relegated to the 'busy work' file in the student's head and is promptly dismissed as material 'that will not be on the test'.

Teachers should also be conscious of who is using the manipulatives and models in the classroom. If the teachers is pointing to, talking about, and manipulating these objects then there is a good likelihood that the students are not. In order for mathematical models or manipulatives to be useful the learning process students must use them.

Technology

In this discussion the term *technology* will be defined as electronic devices such as computers, graphing calculators, hand-held scientific probes, and digital cameras. Using technology in the mathematics classroom makes mathematics more accessible by helping students visualize mathematics in a way that traditional teaching tools such as pencil and paper, transparencies, and chalk boards can not. Technology allows students to explore mathematics interactively. Teachers should create opportunities for students to discover mathematical properties through cause and effect observations. For example, students can use a graphing calculator or computer to see what happens to a graph when a given coefficient in its equation is changed. The dynamic nature of some software packages allows students to watch the changes in the graphs while they control the changes in the coefficients.

Although a similar activity is possible with paper and pencil exercises, the process is tedious and the number of times a student must graph very similar equations in order to draw conclusions on her own turns the lesson into a graphing exercise with the key ideas showing up only briefly at the end. The other, more common alternative is that the teacher draws the graphs as well as the conclusions for the students while the students sit and watch.

Unfortunately, even though technology offers a wide array of learning opportunities for students, resistance to using calculators or computers to do mathematics exists among parents, administrators, and even some teachers. The idea that students should learn to do math 'by hand' is still strong mainly because teachers, parents, and administrators feel comfortable with the way that they learned mathematics.

In order to overcome this bias, teachers should use technology to introduce and explore mathematical ideas on a regular basis and should encourage students to use the calculators to make and check hypotheses whenever they are 'stuck'. Students should be required to use appropriate technology to implement problem solving strategies and asked questions that measure conceptual understanding rather than technical skill. Although technology can be used for drilling students on factual knowledge or procedural skills, the more it is used as a tool in solving complex, elaborate problems the more teachers, students, and parents will recognize its value.

Competency 15: Knowledge of Assessment

The teacher has knowledge of the methods and uses of various forms of assessment and is able to apply this knowledge for the purposes of guiding classroom instruction and providing meaningful feedback to the student.

- Identify appropriate alternative methods of assessment (e.g., performance, portfolios, projects).

- Identify students' errors, including multiple errors that result in correct or incorrect answers (e.g., algorithms, properties, drawings, procedures).

Assessment in the Mathematics Classroom

Assessment is a key component of classroom teaching and lesson planning. The effective and efficient mathematics teacher uses a variety of assessment tools as a means of not only evaluating student understanding and progress but also as a means to plan for future instruction. By fully answering the questions *"What do I want my students to learn?"* and *"How do I want them to demonstrate their understanding?"* a teacher must identify the big ideas underlying the content objectives and determine the types of activities that are most appropriate and accessible for the individuals that he or she is teaching. This process

will lead the teacher to more complex questions of understanding and will lay the groundwork for all levels of evaluation: informal, formal, formative, and summative.

Informal Assessment

Informal assessment provides teachers and students with immediate, non-threatening feedback on a student's understanding of a single concept, the level of readiness of the class to move on, or the success or failure of a particular lesson. This type of evaluation can be done by talking to individuals or to small groups of students while the class is engaged in problem-solving or project work. Questions might start with broad sweeps such as "Why did you solve for m?" and move progressively toward a question that requires conceptual understanding such as "What does knowing the slope of this line tell you about the variables s and t?" These questions can lead to important guided discussions that can be used to address misunderstandings and misconceptions.

Effective teachers should consider these types of questions and the likely responses during the planning process. Teachers can also provide written feedback on practice assignments to point out strengths and weaknesses and give students an appreciation of their own understanding of a concept before they are expected to perform in a formal setting.

Formal Assessment

Formal assessment is used as a means of informing both the student and the teacher of the student's level of understanding and competence in specific skills. Formal evaluations can be short quizzes completed independently or complex group projects but all should be valid measures of what has occurred in the classroom.

Asking a student to solve a system of equations that has no solution is not reasonable if they have not experienced such examples in class. Also, as with other disciplines, rubrics that are known to the students and that have been used to provide them with regular feedback are essential. Most importantly, teachers of mathematics should always work out solutions to all questions on a formal assessment before giving it. Aside from avoiding embarrassment when confronted with questions he or she is unprepared to answer, the teacher should be sure that each question is testing the desired concept rather than miring students in unnecessary arithmetic or algebraic manipulation.

Formative and Summative Assessment

Formative assessments are either informal or formal and provide both the teacher and the students with knowledge about their progress toward stated learning objectives. On the other hand, summative assessments are generally formal and provide teachers and students with a measure of student understanding at the close of a specific unit of instruction such as a chapter test or a unit project. It is important to note that in mathematics summative evaluations over the course of a school year are also formative evaluations. For example, the accumulation of assessments of variation, relation between quantities, linear functions, and non-linear functions provide a measure of a student's growing understanding of algebra. In either case, the nature of the evaluation is important.

In some mathematics classrooms, teachers limit evaluation to quizzes and tests that require only the ability to follow procedures and, while there is value in being able to use algorithms, this provides a limited view of student understanding and propagates the misunderstanding of the nature of doing mathematics. Procedural assessments do not translate into students being able to solve problems, think critically, or reason mathematically. In order to support the development of these skills,

teachers need to assess students doing exactly these things and that requires a varied collection of assessment tools and methods.

Methods of Assessment

Instruments that test factual or procedural knowledge can be useful but should be crafted carefully so that math content and skills rather than test taking ability are being measured. Multiple choice items should include solutions that are the result of common misconceptions or errors and true/false questions should be clearly true or false according to a concept of mathematics rather than a question of semantics. Procedural exercises associated with instructions such as "Solve for x" or "Find the derivative $f'(x)$" evaluate the ability of the student to reproduce a series of steps but are not necessarily a measure of conceptual understanding or mathematical reasoning. Although these kinds of assessments are familiar and therefore comfortable to both teachers and students, they are limited in scope and, if used to the exclusion of other forms of evaluation, leave students with an inaccurate vision of what it means to do mathematics and discourages independent mathematical thinking.

In order to use assessment as a means of determining a student's conceptual understanding, effective assessment should include tasks that encourage reflection, communication, and reasoning. Assessments should be an opportunity to learn. Such alternative assessments include but are not limited to performance tasks, projects, presentations, debates, and portfolios.

Performance tasks in mathematics may require a student to complete a geometry proof or to solve a real-world problem. Success is measured not only by completing the task but in how the task was completed. The teacher can observe how the student organizes given information, works with others to develop a mathematical strategy, deals with roadblocks, determines the correctness of a solution, etc. In evaluating students based on performance, the teacher should determine the skills and behaviors that are desirable in advance. Teachers should model these behaviors and skills, identifying and explaining them explicitly so that students will understand what is expected of them.

Projects are generally long term individual or group efforts that are useful in exploring a topic or concept in depth or in tying together seemingly unconnected topics in order to reveal big mathematical ideas. Teachers commonly allow students to select their own project topics as a means of increasing personal interest but they should provide specific project guidelines, develop an appropriate rubric, and regularly monitor progress to ensure that the project does not become an exercise in reporting or is mathematically trivial. For example, in a project on the golden ratio, a teacher might require the student to evaluate a favorite poster or song for evidence of the ratio. Incremental deadlines will keep students on track and will allow teachers to redirect students that may have started down the 'cut and paste' path.

Teacher designed projects can reduce such problems and can be molded to guide students to important revelations about mathematical ideas but teachers may wish to limit situations where everyone is working on the same project. There should be opportunities for students to become experts on an idea or topic and be able to share that expertise with their classmates.

Presentations of exercises, problems, proofs, and projects emphasize mathematical communication and can be a great way to solidify a student's understanding. Teachers should encourage students to focus on explaining the 'why' of their work rather than the 'how'. Vague statements and inaccurate wording often mask incomplete or incorrect understanding so teachers should not fill in the blanks or assume that 'they knew what they meant'. Socratic questioning by the teacher and fellow students can strengthen understanding by forcing students to defend mathematical choices and articulate math ideas. Giving students plenty of opportunities to present their work informally will build self-confidence and provide practice for more formal presentations of research projects or solutions to complex problems.

Debates can be used to gauge and challenge not only individual understanding but also the collective understanding of the class itself. Asking students to choose and defend the best method for finding the roots of a 4th degree polynomial not only requires students to understand the mathematics of many possible methods but also requires them to make a judgment regarding the definition of 'best'. As well, taking sides in a debate on a problem involving the concept of infinity or a question of chaos theory can motivate students to explore advanced or abstract concepts that they might otherwise reject as being too difficult. In monitoring the debate, teachers should require students to supply logical or mathematical reasoning as arguments. This experience should provide students with valuable insight into the nature of mathematics and mathematicians.

Portfolios are collections of student work that highlight important learning objectives along each student's individual path to understanding. This often includes examples of a student's best work but can also include samples of work that led to a significant learning event. These items might include an ungraded homework assignment in which it is clear that the student finally mastered the concept of slope, a quiz that the student originally failed but later corrected, or a video clip that shows a student's mathematical epiphany during a debate on the definition of limit. Teachers will need to aid students in the development of the portfolios but, if they are used regularly as a resource of the individual student's constructed knowledge, then they become meaningful representations of the learning process and students will begin to add to them on their own.

Identifying Errors

An important part of a mathematics teacher's special knowledge regarding the assessment of mathematical understanding is recognizing student errors and determining what they indicate about that student's understanding. The 'careless mistake' is more often due to misunderstanding than inattention. The teacher who pays attention to student errors will gain a greater insight into what is being learned in the classroom and what is not. In fact, effective teachers will anticipate the multiple sources of error in a procedure or algorithm, determine what misconceptions those errors represent, and plan how and when to address the errors and their associated misconceptions.

Anticipating the errors that students will make can be difficult for teachers because they are often so facile with the content, as well as the foundations of mathematics, that procedures may appear trivial or obvious. Teachers need to examine what types of questions and exercises they intend to give and then determine the key understandings that a student must have in order to succeed in the task(s). The next step is to strip away each understanding and attempt to complete the task in its absence. The results will be the errors that students produce. For example, "Solve for x where $(x + 3)^2 = 16$" may result in one student proceeding with $x^2 + 9 = 16$

where another student may conclude that $x + 3 = 4$. Such errors should be addressed as errors in concept rather than simply showing the student 'how to do it again'.

It is possible to address the most likely errors at the time of instruction but this could confuse the lesson and may actually reinforce the errors rather than the intended concepts. Unless a fair percentage of the class is making the same or similar mistakes (in which case the teacher should consider reteaching) the teacher should approach students on a small group or individual basis. In this manner the teacher can lead students to recognizing their own mistakes through careful questioning or by providing concrete examples that will counter-indicate the student's erroneous procedure.

Some Common Errors

Error	Associated Misunderstanding/Misconception
$(x + 3)^2 = x^2 + 9$	Student does not recognize that $(x + 3)^2$ means $(x + 3)$ times $(x + 3)$ or does not distribute the first $(x + 3)$ to each term in the second $(x + 3)$. This problem may arise from being taught the FOIL algorithm without the explanation of why it works.
Given the right triangle prove: $a^2 + b^2 = c^2$ $3^2 + 4^2 = 5^2$ $9 + 16 = 25$ $25 = 25$	Student does not understand the value of being able to generalize a property or condition. As well, the student may be assuming what he is trying to prove. The practice of working both sides of the equation indicates a limited understanding of the nature of equality.
Graph $f(x) = \dfrac{x^2 + 9x - 10}{x^2 + 12x + 20}$	While correct for $0 \le x \le 10$, the graph does not provide important information about the function. The student is unaware of the importance of domain and has not identified the asymptote at $x = -10$.

FTCE

Florida Teacher Certification Examination
Mathematics 6–12

Practice Test

Answer Sheet

1. (A) (B) (C) (D)
2. (A) (B) (C) (D)
3. (A) (B) (C) (D)
4. (A) (B) (C) (D)
5. (A) (B) (C) (D)
6. (A) (B) (C) (D)
7. (A) (B) (C) (D)
8. (A) (B) (C) (D)
9. (A) (B) (C) (D)
10. (A) (B) (C) (D)
11. (A) (B) (C) (D)
12. (A) (B) (C) (D)
13. (A) (B) (C) (D)
14. (A) (B) (C) (D)
15. (A) (B) (C) (D)
16. (A) (B) (C) (D)
17. (A) (B) (C) (D)
18. (A) (B) (C) (D)
19. (A) (B) (C) (D)
20. (A) (B) (C) (D)

21. (A) (B) (C) (D)
22. (A) (B) (C) (D)
23. (A) (B) (C) (D)
24. (A) (B) (C) (D)
25. (A) (B) (C) (D)
26. (A) (B) (C) (D)
27. (A) (B) (C) (D)
28. (A) (B) (C) (D)
29. (A) (B) (C) (D)
30. (A) (B) (C) (D)
31. (A) (B) (C) (D)
32. (A) (B) (C) (D)
33. (A) (B) (C) (D)
34. (A) (B) (C) (D)
35. (A) (B) (C) (D)
36. (A) (B) (C) (D)
37. (A) (B) (C) (D)
38. (A) (B) (C) (D)
39. (A) (B) (C) (D)
40. (A) (B) (C) (D)

41. (A) (B) (C) (D)
42. (A) (B) (C) (D)
43. (A) (B) (C) (D)
44. (A) (B) (C) (D)
45. (A) (B) (C) (D)
46. (A) (B) (C) (D)
47. (A) (B) (C) (D)
48. (A) (B) (C) (D)
49. (A) (B) (C) (D)
50. (A) (B) (C) (D)
51. (A) (B) (C) (D)
52. (A) (B) (C) (D)
53. (A) (B) (C) (D)
54. (A) (B) (C) (D)
55. (A) (B) (C) (D)
56. (A) (B) (C) (D)
57. (A) (B) (C) (D)
58. (A) (B) (C) (D)
59. (A) (B) (C) (D)
60. (A) (B) (C) (D)

61. (A) (B) (C) (D)
62. (A) (B) (C) (D)
63. (A) (B) (C) (D)
64. (A) (B) (C) (D)
65. (A) (B) (C) (D)
66. (A) (B) (C) (D)
67. (A) (B) (C) (D)
68. (A) (B) (C) (D)
69. (A) (B) (C) (D)
70. (A) (B) (C) (D)
71. (A) (B) (C) (D)
72. (A) (B) (C) (D)
73. (A) (B) (C) (D)
74. (A) (B) (C) (D)
75. (A) (B) (C) (D)
76. (A) (B) (C) (D)
77. (A) (B) (C) (D)
78. (A) (B) (C) (D)
79. (A) (B) (C) (D)
80. (A) (B) (C) (D)

FTCE Mathematics 6-12 Practice Test

TIME: 150 minutes (2 hours and 30 minutes)
80 questions.

> **Directions:** Read each item and select the best response.

1. Of a freshman class, half of the students are enrolled in 15 class hours, most of the remaining freshmen are taking 12 hours with a few students taking 18 hours. Select the statement which is true about this distribution.

   (A) The mode is the same as the mean.

   (B) The median is less than the mean.

   (C) The mean is greater than the mode.

   (D) The mean is less than the median.

2. In the triangle shown below, $\cos\omega$ is equal to

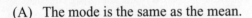

   (A) $\dfrac{1}{56}$.

   (C) $\dfrac{1}{28}$.

   (B) $\dfrac{\sqrt{2}}{2}$.

   (D) $\dfrac{\sqrt{3}}{3}$.

3. Calculate the area of the nonshaded region within the square.

   (A) $s^2 - \pi s^2$

   (C) $s^2 - \dfrac{\pi s^2}{4}$

   (B) $\dfrac{\pi s^2}{4 - s^2}$

   (D) $\dfrac{\pi s^2}{4}$

4. Given that:

   I.   Some shrubs flower.

   II. An Alamanda is a shrub.

   determine which conclusion can be logically deduced.

   (A) An Alamanda flowers.

   (B) An Alamanda does not flower.

   (C) An Alamanda is not a shrub.

   (D) None of the above.

5. While students are working in small groups on a discovery activity involving linear functions, the teacher circulates through the class asking

individual student's questions like "Why did you choose to assign the height variable to the vertical axis?" and "What happens to the graph if you use different sized cups for the experiment?" The purpose of the questions is to

(A) Provide a formal assessment that can be used to encourage students to work harder.

(B) Gauge student progress in developing conceptual understanding in a way that will not penalize the student.

(C) Show the students that the teacher cares about the work that they are doing.

(D) Provide an informal, summative assessment that can be used to determine the student's grade for the assignment.

6. What is the range of values for which $|6x - 5| \leq 8$ is satisfied?

(A) $-\dfrac{1}{2} \leq x \leq \dfrac{1}{2}$

(C) $-1 \leq x \leq \dfrac{1}{2}$

(B) $0 \leq x \leq \dfrac{5}{6}$

(D) $-\dfrac{1}{2} \leq x \leq \dfrac{13}{6}$

7. $\sin\left(\dfrac{1}{2}\pi + t\right) =$

(A) $\sin\dfrac{\pi}{2} + \sin t$

(C) $\sin t$

(B) $\cos t$

(D) $\cos 2t$

8. How many games would it take a baseball coach to try every possible batting order with his nine players?

(A) 9

(C) 81

(B) 45

(D) 362,880

9. The fraction

$$\dfrac{\dfrac{2}{b^2 a^2}}{\dfrac{1}{b^2 - 2b}}$$

may be expressed more simply as

(A) $\dfrac{2a}{b}$.

(C) $\dfrac{2b - 4}{a^2 b}$.

(B) $\dfrac{b - 4}{b}$.

(D) $\dfrac{b - a}{a}$.

10. A new teacher is assigned to teach Honors Geometry. He is excited because geometry and logic were his favorite courses in college. He decides that it is important that his students learn formal proofs and is determined to begin immediately. During the first lesson he writes on the board: "Axiom 1: ∃ a pt. X." In similar fashion, he continues with his lessons for a few days but on the third day he gives a quiz and discovers that only a few students have passed. What is likely to be a part of the problem?

(A) High school students are mature enough to pass a proof-based course if and only if they are gifted.

(B) There is exactly one teaching method appropriate for geometry instruction, guided discovery, and it does not include proofs.

(C) At most, a few of his students have understood the language being used or can grasp the format of the lessons.

(D) The learning of proof-based, formal geometry and high levels of achievement are mutually exclusive.

11. If there exist positive integers a and b such that $8a + 12b = c$, then c must be divisible by

(A) 3.

(C) 18.

(B) 4.

(D) 24.

12. If a function is defined as $f(x) = |2 - 5x| < 3$, then the interval which does not contain any solution for x is

(A) $0 < x < 1$.

(C) $-\dfrac{1}{25} < x < 0$.

(B) $0 < x < 2$.

(D) $-\dfrac{3}{5} < x < -\dfrac{1}{2}$.

13. If $27^x = 9$ and $2^{x-y} = 64$, then $y =$

(A) -5

(C) $-\dfrac{2}{3}$

(B) -3

(D) $-\dfrac{16}{3}$

14. The sum of 3 angles of a triangle is $180°$. The second angle is $11°$ less than the first angle. The third angle is twice the measure of the first angle increased by 3. If x represents the number of degrees in the first angle, which equation correctly represents the relationship among the three angles?

(A) $x + (11 - x) + (2x + 3) = 180$

(B) $x + (x - 11) + 2(x + 3) = 180$

(C) $x + (x - 11) + (2x + 3) = 180$

(D) $x + (x - 11) + (2x - 3) = 180$

15. Point A has coordinates $(2, 5)$ and point B has coordinates $(-3, -3)$. What is the distance between point A and point B?

(A) 5.6

(C) 8.1

(B) 9.4

(D) 2.4

16. A man can do a job in nine days and his son can do the same job in 16 days. They start working together. After four days the son leaves and the father finishes the job alone. How many days did the man take to finish the job alone?

(A) $2\dfrac{3}{4}$

(C) $3\dfrac{3}{4}$

(B) $1\dfrac{1}{2}$

(D) $2\dfrac{1}{4}$

17. Find a, b for the parabola

$$y = ax^2 + bx + 3$$

if the vertex is $(2, 4)$.

(A) $a = -\dfrac{1}{4}, b = 1$

(C) $a = 1, b = 2$

(B) $a = -1, b = -2$

(D) $a = -\dfrac{1}{3}, b = 1$

18. Which functions(s) below is(are) symmetric with respect to the origin?

I. $f(x) = x^3 - x$

II. $f(x) = 2x + x^5$

III. $f(x) = 2x + 4$

(A) I and II.

(C) I and III.

(B) I only.

(D) II and III.

19. The position of a particle moving along a straight line at any time t is given by $s(t) = 2t^3 - 4t^2 + 2t - 1$. What is the acceleration of the particle when $t = 2$?

(A) 32

(C) 4

(B) 16

(D) 8

20. An AP statistics teacher wants to provide her students with a concrete example of a data set that illustrates the normal curve. Select her best choice from the examples below.

(A) The shoe sizes of the 15 students in her class.

(B) The weight of all the 17 year olds in the country.

(C) The number of times of one hundred that a flipped penny will land on its head.

(D) The height of the students in the high school.

21. A function is defined as $f(x) = x^2 + 2$. What is the numerical value of $3f(0) + f(-1)f(2)$?

(A) 6

(C) 18

(B) 24

(D) 36

22. If the probability of a certain team winning is $\frac{3}{4}$, what is the probability that this team will win its first 3 games and lose the fourth?

(A) $\dfrac{3}{256}$

(C) $\dfrac{27}{256}$

(B) $\dfrac{9}{256}$

(D) $\dfrac{81}{256}$

23. Which of the following assessments will allow a teacher to measure a student's conceptual understanding of systems of equations?

(A) Solve the following system

$$4x + 2y = 6$$
$$x - y = 3$$

(B) Prove that if one equation in a system of equations is multiplied by a constant c, where $c \neq 0$, then the solution to the system remains unchanged.

(C) Shelby is 15 years older than David. Also, if you triple David's age and then subtract Shelby's age the total is 27. How old are Shelby and David?

(D) Select or invent a situation that can be represented using a system of equations. Create a graphical or algebraic model of that system. Prepare a presentation to your classmates during which you explain your model and how it can be used to provide information about the situation.

24. $\int_{1}^{e^2} \dfrac{\ln(x^2)}{x} \, dx$ is approximately

(A) $\dfrac{8}{3}$ (C) 0.805

(B) 2 (D) 4

25. If $f(x) = 3x - 5$ and $g(f(x)) = x$, then $g(x) =$

(A) $\dfrac{x-5}{3}$. (C) $\dfrac{2x+5}{3}$.

(B) $\dfrac{x+5}{3}$. (D) $\dfrac{x+5}{4}$.

26. $\int_{1}^{e} x \ln x \, dx = ?$

(A) e (C) $\dfrac{e^2+1}{4}$

(B) $\dfrac{e^2-1}{2}$ (D) $\dfrac{e-1}{2}$

27. Select the geometric figure that possesses all of the following characteristics:

I. Quadrilateral

II. At least one pair of parallel sides

III. Diagonals are always perpendicular to each other

(A) Rectangle (C) Trapezoid

(B) Rhombus (D) Parallelogram

28. Select the shaded region which graphically represents the conditions $x \geq 0$ and $-3 < y < 3$.

(A)

(B)

(C)

(D)

29. The first three terms of a progression are $3, 6, 12, \ldots$. What is the value of the tenth term?

(A) 1,200   (C) 188

(B) 2,468   (D) 1,536

30. $\lim\limits_{x \to 1} \dfrac{\dfrac{1}{x+1} - \dfrac{1}{2}}{x-1} =$

(A) $-\dfrac{1}{4}$ (C) $\dfrac{1}{4}$

(B) -1 (D) 0

31. An equation of the line normal to the graph of $y = x^4 - 3x^2 + 1$ at the point where $x = 1$ is

(A) $2x - y + 3 = 0$ (C) $2x - y - 3 = 0$

(B) $x - 2y + 3 = 0$ (D) $x - 2y - 3 = 0$

32. The scatter plot below shows the relationship between grade level and hours of reading each week. Which statement describes this relationship?

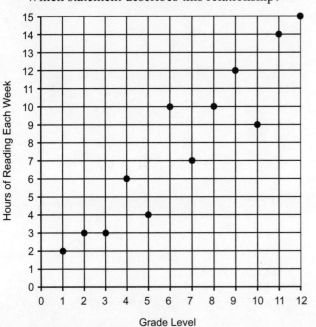

Grade Level

(A) As grade level goes down, the number of reading hours goes up.

(B) As grade level goes up, the number of reading hours goes down.

(C) As grade level goes up, the number of reading hours goes up.

(D) Grade level and reading hours are unrelated.

33. If $f(x) = 2x + 4$ and $g(x) = x^2 - 2$, then $(f \circ g)(x)$, where $(f \circ g)(x)$ is a composition of functions, is

(A) $2x^2 - 8$ (C) $2x^2$

(B) $2x^2 + 8$ (D) $2x^3 + 4x^2 - 4x - 8$

34. If two fair dice are thrown, what is the probability that the sum of the number of dots on the top faces will be 7?

(A) $\dfrac{1}{2}$ (C) $\dfrac{1}{9}$

(B) $\dfrac{1}{6}$ (D) $\dfrac{1}{12}$

35. At what value of x does $f(x) = \dfrac{x^3}{3} - x^2 - 3x + 5$ have a relative minimum?

(A) -1 only   (C) $+1$ only

(B) -1 and 3   (D) 3 only

36. Solve the following quadratic equation.

$$2x^2 - 1 = 3x$$

(A) $\dfrac{3 \pm \sqrt{17}}{2}$ (C) $\dfrac{3 \pm \sqrt{17}}{4}$

(B) $1, \frac{1}{2}$ (D) $\dfrac{-3 \pm \sqrt{17}}{4}$

37. If $\log_8 3 = x\log_2 3$ then x equals

(A) $\dfrac{1}{3}$ (C) 3

(B) $\log_4 3$ (D) $\log_8 9$

38. Ten white balls and 19 blue balls are in a box. If a man draws a ball from the box at random, what are the odds in favor of him drawing a blue ball?

    (A) 10:29   (C) 19:10

    (B) 19:29   (D) 29:10

39. If $f(x) = 2x^2 + 4x + k$, what should the value of k be in order to have the graph of this function intersect the x-axis in only one place?

    (A) −2   (C) 1

    (B) 4   (D) 2

40. The sum of the first 50 terms of an arithmetic series is 100. If the common difference is 2, what is the first term?

    (A) 47   (C) −48

    (B) 48   (D) −47

41. Choose the correct solution set for the system of linear equations.

    $$4x + 2y = -1$$
    $$5x - 3y = 7$$

    (A) $\{(2, 1)\}$

    (B) $\{(\frac{1}{2}, -\frac{3}{2})\}$

    (C) $\{(x, y) \mid 4x + 2y = -1\}$

    (D) The empty set

42. Given the triangle below, what is the value of θ?

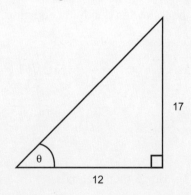

    (A) 54.8°   (C) 45.0°

    (B) 35.2°   (D) 42.8°

43. Read the statements below and answer the question.

    1. All people who exercise have blue eyes.

    2. Some of the people have brown eyes.

    3. All people who have blue eyes enjoy movies.

    4. People who have brown eyes like baseball.

    5. Sarah has blue eyes.

    Which must be true?

    (A) Sarah has brown eyes.

    (B) Sarah enjoys movies.

    (C) Sarah exercises.

    (D) Sarah likes baseball.

44. Making connections within the structure of mathematics requires teachers to

    (A) communicate mathematics ideas clearly.

    (B) understand mathematics at high level.

    (C) be able to recite properties, rules, and axioms of mathematics.

    (D) understand topics at the most basic level.

45. The area enclosed by the graphs of $y = x^2$ and $y = 2x + 3$ is

    (A) $\dfrac{38}{3}$ (C) $\dfrac{32}{3}$

    (B) $\dfrac{40}{3}$ (D) $\dfrac{16}{3}$

46. $\sqrt{108} + 3\sqrt{12} - 7\sqrt{3} =$

    (A) $3 - 3\sqrt{3}$ (C) $4\sqrt{3}$

    (B) 0 (D) $5\sqrt{3}$

47. $t = -9$ is a root of the equation $t^2 + 4t - 45 = 0$. Which of the following statements is (are) correct for the equation?

    I. $t + 9$ is a factor of the equation.

II. Division of the equation by $t - 9$ yields the other factor of the quadratic equation.

III. $t = -5$ is another root of the equation.

(A) I only.　　　　(C) III only

(B) II and III only.　(D) I, II, and III.

48. If $x = 3 + 2i$ and $y = 1 + 3i$, where $i^2 = -1$, then $\dfrac{x}{y} =$

(A) $\dfrac{9}{10} - \dfrac{2}{3}i.$　　(C) $\dfrac{9}{10} + \dfrac{2}{3}i.$

(B) $\dfrac{9}{10} - \dfrac{7}{10}i.$　　(D) $3 - \dfrac{7}{10}i.$

49. A committee of 5 people is to be selected from a group of 6 men and 9 women. If the selection is made randomly, what is the probability that the committee consists of 3 men and 2 women?

(A) $\dfrac{1}{3}$　　　　(C) $\dfrac{1}{9}$

(B) $\dfrac{240}{1001}$　　(D) $\dfrac{1260}{3003}$

50. What is the equation of the line which is parallel to $6x + 3y = 4$ and has a y-intercept of -6?

(A) $y = 2x - 6$　　(C) $y = -2x - \dfrac{4}{3}$

(B) $y = 2x + \dfrac{4}{3}$　(D) $y = -2x - 6$

51. Which of the graphs below represents the function $y = 2 + \sin(x - \pi)$?

(A)

(B)

(C)

(D)

52. Answer the question based on the following:

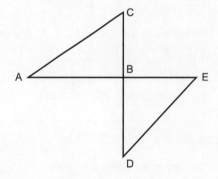

If $\overline{BC} \perp \overline{AE}, \overline{DB} \cong \overline{AB}$, and $\angle E = \angle C$, which of the following must be true?

(A) $\overline{AB} = 2\,\overline{BE}$　　(C) $\overline{BC} = \tfrac{2}{3}\,\overline{BD}$

(B) $\overline{BC} \cong \overline{AC}$　　(D) $\overline{BC} \cong \overline{BE}$

53. For which of the following intervals is the graph of $y = x^4 - 2x^3 - 12x^2$ concave down?

(A) $(-2, 1)$　　(C) $(-1, -2)$

(B) $(-1, 2)$　　(D) $(-\infty, -1)$

54. What is the range of values for which $|6x - 5| \le 8$ is satisfied?

    (A) $-\dfrac{1}{2} \le x \le \dfrac{1}{2}$ (C) $-1 \le x \le \dfrac{1}{2}$

    (B) $0 \le x \le \dfrac{5}{6}$ (D) $-\dfrac{1}{2} \le x \le \dfrac{13}{6}$

55. The teacher's knowledge of mathematics

    (A) is the most important factor in being able to teach mathematics well.

    (B) should reflect courses in advanced mathematics.

    (C) ensures that she can answer any math question that her students ask.

    (D) should be deepest in middle and high school mathematics.

56. If $f(x) = e^{\frac{x^3}{3} - x}$, then $f(x)$

    (A) increases in the interval $(-1, 1)$

    (B) decreases for $|x| > 1$

    (C) increases in the interval $(-1, 1)$ and decreases in the intervals $(-\infty, -1) \cup (1, \infty)$

    (D) increases in the intervals $(-\infty, -1) \cup (1, \infty)$ and decreases in the interval $(-1, 1)$

57. The equation $x^2 + 2x + 7 = 0$ has

    (A) two complex conjugate roots.

    (B) two real rational roots.

    (C) two real equal roots.

    (D) two real irrational roots.

58. The base of a right prism, shown here, is an equilateral triangle, each of whose sides measure

4 units. The altitude of the prism is 5 units. Find the volume of the prism.

    (A) $4\sqrt{3}$ (C) 60

    (B) $20\sqrt{3}$ (D) 40

59. An owner of a delicatessen is thinking of constructing a parking lot in back of his store. He would like to have 35 parking spaces, and will need 2 pounds of cement for each parking space. If he buys 40 more pounds of cement that he expects to use, how many pounds of cement does he buy?

    (A) 110 pounds   (C) 30 pounds

    (B) 70 pounds   (D) 1,470 pounds

60. A cube has total surface area 24 cm². The volume of the cube in cm³ is

    (A) 8   (C) 16

    (B) 12   (D) 20

61. Find the coordinates of the vertex of the parabola $y = x^2 - 8x + 15$.

    (A) $(2, 0)$ (C) $(4, -1)$

    (B) $(0, -1)$ (D) $(5, 0)$

62. Let T be a transformation function, $T(x, y) = (3.5x, 6.3y)$. Suppose the vertices of a rectangle of area 5 undergo the transformation $T(x, y)$. What is the area of the transformed rectangle?

    (A) 49   (C) 110.25

    (B) 4   (D) 259.7

63. If $y = \dfrac{3}{\sin x + \cos x}$ then $\dfrac{dy}{dx} =$

(A) $\dfrac{3(\sin x - \cos x)}{1 + 2\sin x \cos x}$ (C) $\dfrac{3}{\cos x - \sin x}$

(B) $\dfrac{6\sin x}{1 + 2\sin x \cos x}$ (D) $\dfrac{-3}{(\sin x + \cos x)^2}$

64. $5\sqrt{7} + 7\left(\sqrt{35} \times 4\sqrt{5}\right) - 2\sqrt{18} =$

(A) $145\sqrt{2} - 6\sqrt{7}$ (C) $151\sqrt{2}$

(B) $130\sqrt{5} - 4\sqrt{7}$ (D) $145\sqrt{7} - 6\sqrt{2}$

65. Two triangles are shown below.

Which of the following statements is true?

(A) The two triangles are congruent.

(B) The two triangles are *not* congruent.

(C) Only one side and one angle are equal.

(D) Both triangles are right triangles.

66. The polygons shown in the figure are similar. What is the length of k?

(A) 2.83.   (C) 3.53.

(B) 3.76.   (D) 4.57.

67.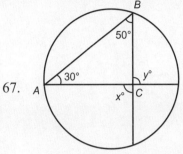

In the figure on the previous page, two chords of the circle intersect, making the angles shown. What is the value of $x + y$?

(A) 40°   (C) 80°

(B) 50°   (D) 160°

68. In triangle ABC, angle A is a right angle, and the length of BC is 7. What are the lengths of sides AB and AC?

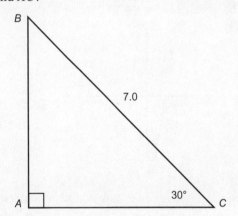

(A) 4.9, 4.9   (C) 3.5, 4.9

(B) 2.0, 6.1   (D) 3.5, 6.1

69. Which of the graphs below represents the equation
$$\frac{x^2}{9} - \frac{y^2}{9} = 1?$$

(A)

(B)

(C)

(D)

70. On a quiz designed to assess student understanding of rational equations, a teacher gives the following:

Given $\left|\dfrac{m+2}{m-3}\right| = \dfrac{4}{6}$, solve for m. This exercise is

(A) good because it requires the student to go through the solution process twice.

(B) easily solved just by looking at it and, so, is not valuable in assessing a student's understanding.

(C) testing more about the student's understanding of the absolute value operator than rational equations.

(D) purely procedural and will tell the teacher nothing about the student's understanding of rational equations.

71. $(x + 2)(x + 1)$ can be represented as

(A)

(B)

(C)

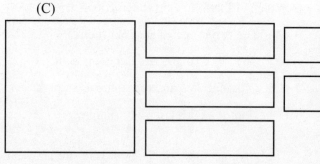

(D) $x^2 + 2$

72. Use this diagram to answer the question.

If segment $\overline{IG}$ meets line FH at point G, which is true?

(A) $\angle FGI$ and $\angle IGH$ are supplementary angles.

(B)   Segment $\overline{IG}$ is perpendicular to line *FH*.

(C) $\angle FGI$ and $\angle IGH$ are complementary angles.

(D) $\angle FGI$ and $\angle IGH$ are vertical angles.

73.   The rate of change of the area of an equilateral triangle with respect to its side *S* at *S* = 2 is

(A)   0.43   (C)   0.87

(B)   1.73   (D)   0.50

74.   Knowing how to do mathematics means all of the following EXCEPT

(A)   Communicate mathematics ideas clearly.

(B)   Solve an open-ended mathematics problem.

(C)   Recite properties, rules, and axioms of mathematics.

(D)   Work backwards to solve a problem.

75.   Triangle *ABC* is similar to triangle *ADE*. If the area of triangle *ABC* is 324, the area of triangle *ADE* is 441, and *AC* = 36, what is the length of $\overline{CE}$?

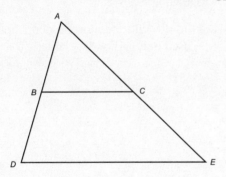

(A)   22   (C)   49

(B)   6   (D)   42

76.   Find the radius of the circle which has the following equation:

$x^2 + y^2 + 6x + 8y - 11 = 0$

(A)   6   (D)   12

(B)   8   (E) $6\sqrt{2}$

(C) $8\sqrt{2}$

77.   Use the diagram to answer the question.

A 17-foot ladder leans against a wall. If the ladder is 8 feet from the base of the wall, how far is it from the bottom of the wall to the top of the ladder?

(A)   9 feet

(B)   5 feet

(C)   15 feet

(D) $2\sqrt{34}$ feet

78.   Which of the following triangles A′ B′ C′ is the image of triangle ABC that results from reflecting the triangle ABC across the *y*-axis?

(A)

(B)

(C)

(D)

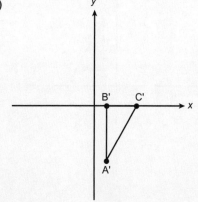

79. In the accompanying figure of a circle centered about point O, the measure of arc AB is $\dfrac{\pi}{5}$ radians. Find $\angle OBA$.

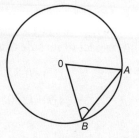

(A) 36°   (C) 90°

(B) 144°   (D) 72°

80. Teaching mathematics through problem-solving

(A) should be used after the students have learned the basic concepts.

(B) is too time consuming to work in a real classroom setting.

(C) encourages students to think and act like mathematicians.

(D) is too difficult for most students and should be used only in honors classes.

Answer Key

1. (D)	21. (B)	41. (B)	61. (C)
2. (A)	22. (C)	42. (A)	62. (C)
3. (C)	23. (D)	43. (B)	63. (A)
4. (D)	24. (D)	44. (D)	64. (D)
5. (B)	25. (B)	45. (C)	65. (A)
6. (D)	26. (C)	46. (D)	66. (C)
7. (B)	27. (B)	47. (A)	67. (D)
8. (D)	28. (A)	48. (B)	68. (D)
9. (C)	29. (D)	49. (B)	69. (A)
10. (C)	30. (A)	50. (D)	70. (C)
11. (B)	31. (D)	51. (B)	71. (A)
12. (D)	32. (C)	52. (D)	72. (A)
13. (D)	33. (C)	53. (B)	73. (B)
14. (C)	34. (B)	54. (D)	74. (C)
15. (B)	35. (D)	55. (D)	75. (B)
16. (A)	36. (C)	56. (D)	76. (A)
17. (A)	37. (A)	57. (A)	77. (C)
18. (A)	38. (C)	58. (B)	78. (A)
19. (B)	39. (D)	59. (A)	79. (D)
20. (D)	40. (D)	60. (A)	80. (C)

Practice Test

Detailed Explanations of Answers

1. (D)

is the correct choice. From the information given, the mode and median would be 15, and the mean would be less than 15. So, the mean is less than the median. (A) is incorrect because the mode is not the same as the mean. (B) is incorrect because the median is greater than the mean. (C) is incorrect because the mean is less than the mode.

2. (A)

To solve, we use the law of cosines:

$$c^2 = a^2 + b^2 - 2ab\cos(\text{included angle}).$$

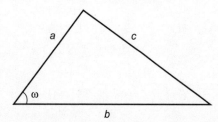

In the figure given, $a = 4$, $b = 7$, $c = 8$, and ω is the included angle.

We solve the law of cosine relation for $\cos\omega$:

$$c^2 = a^2 + b^2 - 2ab\cos\omega.$$

Transposing a^2 and b^2 and dividing through by $-2ab$, we obtain:

$$\frac{c^2 - a^2 - b^2}{-2ab} = \cos\omega.$$

Substituting for a, b, and c we obtain

$$\cos\omega = \frac{8^2 - 4^2 - 7^2}{-2(4)(7)} = \frac{64 - 16 - 49}{-56} = \frac{-1}{-56} = \frac{1}{56}.$$

3. (C)

The shaded section is $\frac{1}{4}$ of a circle with the radius s. The area of this section is $\frac{\pi s^2}{4}$; the nonshaded area is $\frac{s^2 - \pi s^2}{4}$.

4. (D)

Choices (A) and (B) cannot be logically deduced because only *some* shrubs flower. Choice (C) cannot be logically deduced because it is a contradiction of statement II "An Alamanda is a shrub." This leaves (D) as the correct answer.

5. (B)

Because no grades are being assigned the students will not be penalized if they can not answer the question. The questions themselves are focused on key concepts in linear functions such as the meaning of the y-intercept (question 1) and the linear function as a model of the physical world (question 2). Choice (A) is ruled out because the fact that the teacher is asking the questions in a conversational manner without mention of grades or marks being assigned makes this an informal assessment. Choice (D) is ruled out because the teacher is assessing the student as they work on the content. This means that it is a formative assessment. Although the Choice (C) is appealing it is not a correct response because a teacher that maintains a neutral relationship with her students can still perform these tasks effectively.

6. (D)

When given an inequality with an absolute value, recall the definition of absolute value:

$$|x| \equiv \begin{cases} x \text{ if } x \geq 0 \\ -x \text{ if } x < 0 \end{cases}$$

$$6x - 5 \leq 8 \text{ if } 6x - 5 \geq 0.$$

$$-6x + 5 \leq 8 \text{ if } 6x - 5 < 0.$$

7. (B)

$$\sin\left(\frac{\pi}{2} + t\right) = \sin\frac{\pi}{2}\cos t + \cos\frac{\pi}{2}\sin t$$

But $\sin\dfrac{\pi}{2} = 1$ and $\cos\dfrac{\pi}{2} = 0$

$$\therefore \quad \sin\left(\frac{\pi}{2} + t\right) = \cos t.$$

8. (D)

This is the possible combinations of nine items which is $n!$ (n-factorial). Most scientific calculators have a $x!$ button. Otherwise, the factorial formula is $9 \times 8 \times 7 \times 6 \times 5 \times 4 \times 3 \times 2 \times 1 = 362{,}880$.

9. (C)

The fraction is a complex fraction. To simplify, we must multiply both the numerator and denominator by $b^2 - 2b$:

$$\frac{\frac{2}{a^2b^2}}{\frac{1}{b^2 - 2b}} \times \frac{b^2 - 2b}{b^2 - 2b} = \frac{2(b^2 - 2b)}{a^2b^2}$$

Multiplying through in the numerator:

$$\frac{2b^2 - 4b}{a^2b^2}$$

The numerator is factored and like terms are cancelled:

$$\frac{b(2b - 4)}{a^2b^2} = \frac{2b - 4}{a^2b}$$

10. (C)

is the answer. Since the teacher had only a few passing grades it is likely that only a few students were

able to understand the language or the format of the class. Hence 'at most' only a few understood. Choice (A) is incorrect because understanding a proof-based does not require a student to be gifted. Choice (B) is incorrect because the term exactly excludes possibilities that are reasonable. It is quite likely that there are many ways of successfully teaching Honors Geometry. Choice (D) claims that proof-based, formal geometry and high levels of achievement can never occur simultaneously. This is patently untrue.

11. (B)

$$8a + 12b = c$$

$$4(2a + 3b) = c$$

Only 4 can be factored out.

12. (D)

The inequality $|2 - 5x| < 3$ may be rewritten as

$$-3 < 2 - 5x < 3.$$

Subtracting 2 from each side, we obtain:

$$-5 < -5x < 1$$

Dividing by -5 gives:

$$-\frac{1}{5} < x < 1$$

This is the interval over which all solutions lie. We are looking for an interval which does not contain any solutions to the inequality. The only interval given in the choices that satisfies this criterion is

$$-\frac{3}{5} < x < -\frac{1}{2}.$$

13. (D)

$$27^x = (3^3)^x = 3^{3x}$$

$$9 = 3^2$$

Thus, we have $3^{3x} = 3^2$, which implies $3x = 2$ or $x = \frac{2}{3}$ because the power function is one-to-one, which means that if

$$a^x_1 = a^x_2 \text{ then } x_1 = x_2.$$

Now $2^{x-y} = 64 = 2^6$

so $\quad x - y = 6$ or $\dfrac{2}{3} - y = 6$.

Hence, $y = \dfrac{2}{3} - 6 = -\dfrac{16}{3}$.

14. (C)

x = number of degrees in the first angle. The second angle is 11° less than the **first angle;** so the second angle = $x - 11$, where less than signifies subtraction (switching around), and the first angle (x) is the first term and 11° (11) is the second term.

The third angle is twice **the measure of the first angle** increased by 3; so the third angle = $2x + 3$, where twice represents multiplication by 2 and increased by means addition.

Since the **sum** of the angles of a triangle equals 180°, then

first angle + second angle + third angle = 180°

$\quad\downarrow\qquad\qquad$ and$\downarrow$

$\quad x \quad + \quad (x-11) \quad + \quad (2x+3) \; = \; 180°$

Answer choice (A) is wrong because of an error in interpretation of 11 less than x.

$$\angle 2 = (11 - x)$$

Answer choice (B) is wrong because of an error in interpretation of twice x increased by 3.

$$\angle 3 = 2(x + 3)$$

Answer choice (D) is wrong because of an error in interpretation of twice x increased by 3.

$$\angle 3 = (2x - 3)$$

15. (B)

Distance d between any two points (x_1, y_1), (x_2, x_2) in the two-dimensional coordinate system is

$$d = \sqrt{(x_1 - x_2)^2 + (y_1 - y_2)^2}$$

The problem can be calculated as:

$$d = \sqrt{(2 - (-3))^2 + (5 - (-3))^2} = \sqrt{89} = 9.434$$

16. (A)

Let x = the number of days it takes the man to finish the job.

Note that the man actually works ($x + 4$) days, and the son actually works 4 days.

The relationship used to set up the equation is: Part of job done by man + Part of job done by boy = 1 job

$$\frac{x+4}{9} + \frac{4}{16} = 1$$
$$16(x + 4) + 4(9) = 144$$
$$x = 2\frac{3}{4} \text{ days}$$

Check:

$$\frac{2\dfrac{3}{4} + 4}{9} + \frac{4}{16} = 1$$
$$\frac{3}{4} + \frac{1}{4} = 1$$

17. (A)

If the vertex is (2, 4) we can substitute this value into the equation of the parabola and obtain:

$$
\begin{aligned}
4 &= a(2)^2 + b(2) + 3 \\
4 &= \quad\;\; 4a + 2b + 3 \\
-3 &= \quad\qquad\qquad -3 \\
\hline
1 &= \quad\;\; 4a + 2b
\end{aligned}
\qquad\text{(I)}
$$

Also the x-coordinate of the vertex is given by

$$\frac{-b}{2a}$$

so $\quad 2 = \dfrac{-b}{2a}$ $\qquad\qquad$ (II)

From (I) and (II) we obtain

$$4a + 2b = 1 \qquad\qquad\text{(I)}$$
$$\frac{-b}{2a} = 2 \qquad\qquad\text{(II)}$$

From (II), $b = -4a$ and substituting into (I):

$$4a + 2 \times (-4a) = 1$$
$$4a - 8a = 1$$
$$-4a = 1$$
$$a = -\frac{1}{4}$$
$$b = 1$$

18. (A)

A function is symmetric with respect to the origin if replacing x by $-x$ and y by $-y$ produces an equivalent function.

(I) $\quad y = f(x) = x^3 - x$

$\quad\quad (-y) = (-x)^3 - (-x)$

$\quad\quad -y = -x^3 + x$

$\quad\quad y = x^3 - x$

(I) is symmetric.

(II) $\quad y = f(x) = 2x + x^5$

$\quad\quad -y = 2(-x) + (-x)^5$

$\quad\quad -y = -2x - x^5$

$\quad\quad y = 2x + x^5$

(II) is symmetric.

(III) $\quad y = f(x) = 2x + 4$

$\quad\quad -y = 2(-x) + 4$

$\quad\quad -y = -2x + 4$

$\quad\quad y = 2x - 4$

(III) is not symmetric.

19. (B)

$$a(t) = s''(t) = \frac{d}{dt}(6t^2 - 8t + 2) = 12t - 8$$

$$a''(2) = 24 - 8 = 16$$

20. (D)

is correct. The students in the statistics class have a reasonable chance at being able to sample a large enough portion of the students at their high school to get a reasonable estimate of the population and the data collected

would produce a normal curve under these circumstances. Therefore the choice is concrete and mathematically correct. Choice (A) is incorrect because there are not enough students and the data being collected is unlikely to yield a normal curve over such a small, homogeneous sample. Choice (B) does not work because there is no way to get the data. An internet source may provide a sample but the problem then becomes abstract – a mind exercise. Choice (C) is incorrect because the data collected would not produce a normal curve.

21. (B)

We are given $f(x) = x^2 + 2$. We must find $f(0)$, $f(-1)$, and $f(2)$.

Replacing x with zero, we obtain:

$$f(0) = 0^2 + 2 = 2$$

Similarly:

$$f(-1) = (-1)^2 + 2 = 3$$

Finally:

$$f(2) = (2)^2 + 2 = 6$$

Evaluating:

$$3f(0) + f(-1)f(2) = 3(2) + (3)(6)$$
$$= 6 + 18 = 24$$

22. (C)

Let's call the event winning A and not winning $\overline{A}$. We want the probability P given by the expression below:

$$P = P(A) \times P(A) \times P(A) \times P(\overline{A})$$
$$= \frac{3}{4} \times \frac{3}{4} \times \frac{3}{4} \times \frac{1}{4} = \frac{27}{256}$$

23. (D)

This last task requires the student to understand and then recognize the characteristics of a situation that make it appropriate to model as a system of equations. Asking the student to produce a graphic or algebraic model evaluates his ability to communicate the situation mathematically. The presentation provides the teacher with the opportunity to delve into the students understanding with questions about his mathematical choices.

Choices (A) and (B) are procedural and do not require conceptual understanding. Choice (B) is more a test of the ability to manipulate algebraic expressions and understanding what it means to prove something. Option (C) will likely result in the student using a guess and test strategy.

24. (D)

Since $\ln (x^2) = 2 \ln x$, we have

$$\int_1^{e^2} \frac{\ln(x^2)}{x}\, dx = 2\int_1^{e^2} \frac{\ln x}{x}\, dx.$$

This integral can be evaluated by using the substitution $u = \ln x$. The integrand becomes, u, with $du = \dfrac{dx}{x}$, and the limits of integration change to

$$u(1) = \ln 1 = 0$$
$$u(e^2) = \ln(e^2) = 2.$$

We get

$$2\int_0^2 u\, du = u^2\Big|_0^2$$

$$= 2^2 - 0 = 4$$

25. (B)

$$f(x) = 3x - 5 \text{ and } g(f(x)) = x$$

We want to know what value of x (in terms of x) would cause $g(3x - 5)$ to equal x. To distinguish one x from the other, we can represent the x from $3x - 5$ with a y. This will result in:

$$3y - 5 = x$$
$$3y = x + 5$$
$$y = \frac{x+5}{3}$$
$$g(y) = g(3x-5) = \frac{3x-5+5}{3} = x$$

<u>Note:</u> $g(x)$ is the inverse of $f(x)$, since $g(f(x)) = f(g(x)) = x$.

26. (C)

Use integration by parts with

$u = \ln x$	$du = \dfrac{1}{x}dx$
$dv = x$	$v = \dfrac{x^2}{2}$

$$\int_1^e x \ln x\, dx = \frac{x^2}{2}\ln x - \int_1^e \frac{x}{2}\, dx$$

$$= \left(\frac{x^2}{2}\ln x - \frac{x^2}{4} \right)\Big|_1^e$$

$$= \frac{e^2 + 1}{4}$$

27. (B)

A rhombus is a quadrilateral, has at least one pair of parallel sides, and its diagonals are always perpendicular to each other.

28. (A)

is the correct response. The inequality $x \geq 0$ identifies the region to the right of the y-axis, eliminating choices (C) and (D). The double inequality of $-3 < y < 3$ represents dotted horizontal lines passing through 3 and -3 on the y-axis with the area between the lines shaded. Of the two remaining choices, (A) is the only one which satisfies this constraint.

29. (D)

The progression given is a geometric progression. The expression for the nth term of a geometric progression is:

$$L_n = a_1 r^{n-1}$$

where a_1 is the first term and r is the common ratio between terms.

In the given sequence, the first term is 3. The common ratio is found to be $\dfrac{6}{3} = \dfrac{12}{6} = 2$.

Therefore, letting $n = 10$ (for the tenth term), we have:

$$L_{10} = 3(2)^{10-1} = 3(2)^9.$$

Since $2^9 = 512$:

$$L_{10} = 3(512) = 1,536$$

30. (A)

$$\lim_{x \to 1} \frac{\frac{1}{x+1} - \frac{1}{2}}{x-1}$$

Obtain a common denominator in the main numerator.

$$\lim_{x \to 1} \frac{\frac{2-(x+1)}{2(x+1)}}{x-1} = \lim_{x \to 1} \frac{1-x}{2(x+1)(x-1)}$$
$$= \lim_{x \to 1} \frac{-1}{2(x+1)}$$
$$= \frac{-1}{2(1+1)} = -\frac{1}{4}$$

Note: $\dfrac{1-x}{x-1} = -1$ for $x \neq 1$

31. (D)

The normal line is the line that is perpendicular to the curve at the given point. Its equation is $y = y_0 + m(x - x_0)$ where (x_0, y_0) is the given point and m is the slope. At the point where $x = 1$,

$$y = x^4 - 3x^2 + 1$$
$$= (1)^4 - 3(1)^2 + 1$$
$$= -1$$

Thus, $(x_0, y_0) = (1, -1)$. The slope m of the normal line is the negative reciprocal of the slope of the tangent line, which is the value of the derivative at the given point;

i.e., $m = \dfrac{-1}{\dfrac{dy}{dx}\bigg|_{x=1}}$

$$\frac{dy}{dx} = \frac{d}{dx}(x^4 - 3x^2 + 1)$$

Since
$$= 4x^3 - 6x,$$

$$m = \frac{-1}{(4x^3 - 6x)\big|_{x=1}}$$
$$= \frac{-1}{(4-6)}$$
$$= \frac{-1}{-2}$$
$$= \frac{1}{2}$$

Thus, the equation of the normal line is:

$$y = y_0 + m(x - x_0)$$
$$y = -1 + \frac{1}{2}(x-1)$$
$$2y = -2 + (x-1)$$
$$2y = x - 3$$
$$x - 2y - 3 = 0$$

32. C

Draw a line through the set of data points. Notice that low grade levels go with low hours of reading, and that high grade levels go with high hours of reading. Next, evaluate the truth of each possible answer. The graph shows that as the grade level goes up, the number of reading hours goes up.

33. (C)

$$(f \circ g)(x) = f(x) \circ g(x) = f(g(x)).$$

This is the definition of the composition of functions. For the functions given in this problem we have

$$2(g(x)) + 4 = 2(x^2 - 2) + 4$$
$$= 2x^2 - 4 + 4 = 2x^2.$$

34. (B)

There are 36 possible outcomes. Six of these produce the number 7:

$$(1, 6), (2, 5), (3, 4), (4, 3), (5, 2), \text{ and } (6, 1).$$

Hence the probability is

$$\frac{6}{36} = \frac{1}{6}.$$

35. (D)

$$f'(x) = x^2 - 2x - 3 = (x + 1)(x - 3)$$

$(x + 1)(x - 3) = 0 \Rightarrow x = -1$ and 3 are critical values.

The numbers -1 and 3 divide the x-axis into 3 intervals, from $-\infty$ to -1, -1 to 3, and 3 to $-\infty$.

$f(x)$ has a relative minimum value at $x = x_1$, if and only if $f'(x_1) = 0$ and the sign of $f'(x)$ changes from $-$ to $+$ as x increascs through x_1.

If $-1 < x < 3$, then $f'(x) = -$

If $x = 3$, then $f'(x) = 0$

If $x > 3$, then $f'(x) = +$

Therefore, $f(3)$ is a relative minimum.

Note that when $x < -1$, $f'(x) = +$. If $x = -1$, $f'(x) = 0$. If $-1 < x < 3$, $f'(x) = -$.

Thus, $f(-1)$ is a relative maximum, not minimum.

36. (C)

is the correct response. It is necessary to first write the quadratic in standard form: $2x^2 - 3x - 1 = 0$. This quadratic does not factor, so it is necessary to use the quadratic formula to find the solutions. The quadratic formula is as follows:

$$x = \frac{-b \pm \sqrt{b^2 - 4ac}}{2a} \text{ with } a = 2, b = -3, \text{ and } c = -1.$$

$$x = \frac{3 \pm \sqrt{9 - 4(2)(-1)}}{2(2)} = \frac{3 \pm \sqrt{17}}{4}$$

(A), (B), and (D) all contain errors in the use of the formula or with simplifying.

37. (A)

Let $y = \log_8 3 = x \log_2 3$.

Then $8^y = 3 \Rightarrow 2^{3y} = 3$ (1)

and $y = x\log_2 3 \Rightarrow 2^y = 3^x$ (2)

Substituting the expression for 2^y in (2) into (1) we obtain

$$3 = (2^y)^3 = (3^x)^3 = 3^{3x}.$$

Hence $3x = 1 \Rightarrow x = \frac{1}{3}.$

38. (C)

If an event can happen in p ways and fail to happen in q ways, then, if $p > q$, the odds are p to q in favor of the event happening.

If $p < q$, then the odds are q to p against the event happening. In this case, $p = 19$ and $q = 10$, $p > q$. Thus, the odds in favor of the event of drawing a blue ball are 19:10.

39. (D)

The function given is represented graphically by a parabola. A parabola will intersect the x-axis in only one place if both roots are equal, which means *discriminant* = 0.

$$discriminant = b^2 - 4ac = +(4)^2 - 4(2)k = 0$$

$$16 - 8k = 0$$

$$16 = 8k \therefore k = 2$$

40. (D)

The sum of n terms in arithmetic series with first term t_1, and common difference d is given by

$$S_n = \frac{n}{2}[2t_1 + (n-1)d]$$

In this problem $S_n = 100$, $n = 50$, $d = 2$, thus,

$$100 = \frac{50}{2}(2t_1 + (50-1)2)$$
$$100 = 25(2t_1 + 98)$$
$$\frac{100}{25} = 2t_1 + 98$$
$$4 = 2t_1 + 98$$
$$2t_1 = 4 - 98 = -94$$
$$t_1 = -\frac{94}{2} = -47$$

The values of $(50-1)2$, $\dfrac{94}{2}$ can be calculated by using the calculator.

Calculator: $(50-1) \times 2 = 98$

$94 \div 2 = 47$

41. (B)

Multiply the first equation by 3 and the second equation by 2. Then add them together.

$$3(4x+2y=-1)$$
$$2(5x-3y=\ 7)$$
$$\overline{12x+6y=-3}$$
$$\underline{10x-6y=14}$$
$$22x=11$$
$$x=\tfrac{1}{2}$$

Take this value of x and put it into either original equations, and solve for y.

$$4x+2y=-1$$
$$4\left(\tfrac{1}{2}\right)+2y=-1$$
$$2+2y=-1$$
$$2y=-3$$
$$y=-\tfrac{3}{2}$$

The answers are $x=\tfrac{1}{2}$ and $y=-\tfrac{3}{2}$ or $\left(\tfrac{1}{2},-\tfrac{3}{2}\right)$.

42. (A)

$\tan\theta=\dfrac{\text{opp}}{\text{adj}}$, so $\theta=\tan^{-1}\left(\dfrac{\text{opp}}{\text{adj}}\right)\Rightarrow$

Calculator:

$17 \div 12 = \boxed{\text{inv}} \boxed{\text{tan}}\ 54.80$

43. (B)

Statement 1 implies people who exercise have blue eyes. Statement 3 implies people who have blue eyes enjoy movies. If Sarah has blue eyes, then Sarah enjoys movies.

Answer (A) is wrong because it contradicts statement 5. Answer (C) is wrong because statement 1 says

"All people who exercise have blue eyes," not "All people with blue eyes exercise." Answer (D) is wrong because "People who have brown eyes like baseball," so this has no bearing on Sarah.

44. (D)

is the correct response. Teachers must understand mathematics at the most basic levels in order to make connections within the structure of mathematics. They need to understand the how and why of each nuance within a topic. Although communication is an invaluable tool, the question is asking what is needed by the teacher in order to make the connections not necessarily to communicate the connections to her students. So choice (A) is incorrect. Choice (B) is incorrect because although the understanding has to be deep the mathematics does not need to be at a high level. The connections being made can be about simple things like addition and multiplication. Choice (C) is incorrect because the ability to recite rules and axioms says little about understanding.

45. (C)

First determine where the graphs $y=x^2$ and $y=2x+3$ intersect.

$$x^2=2x+3$$
$$x^2-2x-3=0$$
$$(x-3)(x+1)=0$$
$$x=3,-1$$

$$A=\int_{-1}^{3}\left(2x+3-x^2\right)dx$$
$$=\int_{-1}^{3}\{(2x+3)-x^2\}dx$$
$$=\left(x^2+3x-\tfrac{1}{3}x^3\right)\Big|_{-1}^{3}$$
$$=3^2-(-1)^2+3(3-(-1))-\tfrac{1}{3}\left(3^3-(-1)^3\right)$$
$$=9-1+3(4)-\tfrac{1}{3}(27+1)$$
$$=20-\tfrac{28}{3}$$
$$=\tfrac{32}{3}$$

$y = 2x + 3$

$y = x^2$

46. (D)

$$\sqrt{108} + 3\sqrt{12} - 7\sqrt{3} = \sqrt{(36)(3)} + 3\sqrt{(4)(3)} = 7\sqrt{2}$$
$$= 6\sqrt{3} + 3\left(2\sqrt{3}\right) - 7\sqrt{3}$$
$$= 6\sqrt{3} + 6\sqrt{3} - 7\sqrt{3}$$
$$= 5\sqrt{3}.$$

47. (A)

Since $t = -9$ is a root of the equation

$$t^2 + 4t - 45 = 0$$

then $(t + 9)$ is a factor. Division of the equation by $(t + 9)$ would therefore yield the other factor of the quadratic, which is $(t - 5)$, giving the second root, $t = 5$.

48. (B)

$$\frac{x}{y} = \frac{3 + 2i}{1 + 3i}$$
$$= \frac{3 + 2i}{1 + 3i} \times \frac{1 - 3i}{1 - 3i}$$
$$= \frac{3 - 9i + 2i - 6i^2}{1^2 - 3^2 i^2}$$
$$= \frac{9 - 7i}{1 + 9}$$
$$= \frac{9}{10} - \frac{7}{10}i$$

49. (B)

There are 5 members to be selected from a group of 15 people. Therefore the total number of possible ways is

$$\binom{15}{5} = 3003.$$

We have to select 3 men out of 6 men, so the number of possible ways is

$$\binom{6}{3} = 20.$$

Two women have to be selected from 9 women. The total number of possible ways is

$$\binom{9}{2} = 36.$$

Hence the desired probability

$$= \frac{20 \times 36}{3003} = \frac{240}{1001}$$

Calculator: 15 INV nCr 5 = 3003

6 INV nCr 3 = 20

9 INV nCr 2 = 36.

50. (D)

We employ the slope intercept form for the equation to be written, since we are given the y-intercept. Our task is then to determine the slope.

We are given the equation of a line parallel to the line whose equation we wish to find. We know that the slopes of two parallel lines are equal. Hence, by finding the slope of the given line, we will also be finding the unknown slope. To find the slope of the given equation

$$6x + 3y = 4$$

we transform the equation $6x + 3y = 4$ into slope intercept form.

$$6x + 3y = 4$$
$$3y = -6x + 4$$
$$y = -\frac{6}{3}x + \frac{4}{3}$$
$$y = -2x + \frac{4}{3}$$

Therefore, the slope of the line we are looking for is -2. The y-intercept is -6. Applying the slope intercept form,

$$y = mx + b,$$

to the unknown line, we obtain,

$$y = -2x - 6$$

as the equation of the line.

51. (B)

There are three steps to build this graph.

First Step: Draw the graph $y = \sin x$

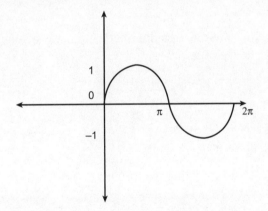

Second Step: Move the graph two units up, because it is $y = \sin(x - \pi) + 2$.

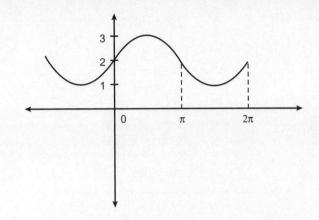

Third Step: Move the graph π units because it is $y = \sin(x - \pi) + 2$.

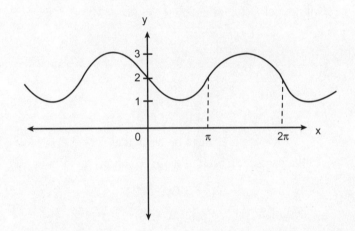

52. (D)

If $\overline{BC} \perp \overline{AE}$, then $\angle ABC$ and $\angle DBE$ are both $90°$. In addition, if $\angle E = \angle C$, then $\triangle ABC$ is similar to $\triangle DBE$ by the angle-angle correspondence. Therefore, $\underline{\angle A = \angle D}$. By Angle-Side-Angle, $\triangle CAB \cong \triangle EDB$. Thus, $\overline{BC} \cong \overline{BE}$ since they are corresponding parts of congruent triangles; so, Answer Choice (D) is correct.

Answer choices (A) and (C) do not apply since there are relationships between the line segments in the given triangles besides those relationships resulting from congruent triangles. Answer Choice (B) is wrong since the hypotenuse of a right triangle must be larger than either of its legs.

53. (B)

$$y = x^4 - 2x^3 - 12x^2$$
$$y' = 4x^3 - 6x^2 - 24x$$
$$y'' = 12x^2 - 12x - 24$$
$$= 12(x-2)(x+1)$$

$$+++++0------------0+++$$

(concave down)

54. (D)

When given an inequality with an absolute value, recall the definition of absolute value:

$$|x| \equiv \begin{cases} x \text{ if } x \geq 0 \\ -x \text{ if } x < 0 \end{cases}$$

$6x - 5 \leq 8$ if $6x - 5 \geq 0$.

$-6x + 5 \leq 8$ if $6x - 5 < 0$.

$-6x + 5 \leq 8$ can be written as $6x - 5 \geq -8$.

We can set up both of these equations as follows.

$$-8 \leq 6x - 5 \leq 8$$

adding 5: $-3 \leq 6x \leq 13$

dividing by 6: $-\dfrac{1}{2} \leq x \leq \dfrac{13}{6}$.

So the values of x which satisfy $|6x - 5| \leq 8$ are $[-\dfrac{1}{2}, \dfrac{13}{6}]$.

55. (D)

In order to teach mathematics to middle and high school students, the teacher needs to assign problems and provide information to the students to head off the anticipated misunderstandings and to address preexisting misconceptions. If the teacher does not have a deep understanding of the topic itself, attempts at explaining the more abstract concepts will be, at best, ineffectual and, at worst, will cause more confusion and misunderstanding. The level of understanding that was achieved when going through high school mathematics about high school mathematics is not sufficient to teach high school mathematics.

Choices (A) and (B): There are highly skilled mathematicians that are very poor mathematics instructors. High levels of math knowledge are not essential in teaching high school mathematics. Choice (C): There will always be times when a teacher can not answer a student's question regardless of how well she planned.

56. (D)

$$f(x) = e^{\frac{x^3}{3} - x}$$

$$\Rightarrow f'(x) = (x^2 - 1) e^{\frac{x^3}{3} - x}, \text{ by the chain rule.}$$

We see $f(x) = e^{\frac{x^3}{3} - x} > 0$ for every real number x, and $x^2 - 1 = (x+1)(x-1)$

$$\Rightarrow x^2 - 1 < 0 \text{ when } x \in (-1, 1) \text{ and}$$
$$x^2 - 1 > 0 \text{ when } |x| > 1.$$

Hence,

$$f'(x) = (x^2 - 1) e^{\frac{x^3}{3} - x} < 0 \text{ for } x \in (-1, 1) \text{ and}$$

$$f'(x) = (x^2 - 1) e^{\frac{x^3}{3} - x} > 0 \text{ for } |x| > 1.$$

(D) is the answer.

57. (A)

To solve this quadratic equation, we invoke the quadratic formula:

$$x = \frac{-b \pm \sqrt{b^2 - 4ac}}{2a}$$

The equation is $x^2 + 2x + 7 = 0$.

So $a = 1$, $b = 2$, and $c = 7$.

Substituting into the formula:

$$x = \frac{-2 \pm \sqrt{2^2 - 4(1)(7)}}{2(1)}$$

$$= \frac{-2 \pm \sqrt{4 - 28}}{2} = -1 \pm \sqrt{-6}$$

Since $i = \sqrt{-1}$, $x = -1 \pm i\sqrt{6}$.

These roots are complex conjugates of each other.

58. (B)

We imagine the prism as a stack of equilateral triangles, congruent to the base of the prism. Let each of these triangles be one unit of measure thick. We can then calculate the area of the base, B, and multiply it by the number of bases needed to complete the height of the prism, h, to obtain the volume of the prism. Therefore,

$$V = Bh.$$

All prism volumes can be thought of in this way.

In this particular problem, the base is an equilateral triangle. Therefore

$$B = \frac{s^2\sqrt{3}}{4},$$

where s is the length of a side of the base. By substitution,

$$B = \frac{(4)^2\sqrt{3}}{4} = 4\sqrt{3}.$$

Since the prism is 5 units high,

$$V = Bh = (4\sqrt{3})5 = 20\sqrt{3}.$$

Therefore, the volume of the prism is $20\sqrt{3}$ cu. units.

59. (A)

2 pounds of cement/parking space × 35 parking spaces = 70 pounds of cement

70 pounds of cement + 40 extra pounds of cement = 110 pounds of cement

Answer choice (B) is incorrect because it does not add on the 40 extra pounds of cement.

2 pounds of cement/parking space × 35 parking spaces = 70 pounds

Answer choice (C) is incorrect because it subtracts the 40 extra pounds of cement.

(2 pounds of cement/parking space × 35 parking spaces) – 40 pounds = 30 pounds

Answer choice (D) is incorrect because it shows

(40 pounds + 2 pounds) × 35 parking spaces = 1,470 pounds

60. (A)

"Total surface area is 24" implies that the area of one face is

$$\frac{24}{6} = 4 \text{ cm}^2.$$

Hence the length of one side is 2 cm which implies the volume is

$$2^3 = 8 \text{ cm}^3.$$

61. (C)

$$y = x^2 - 8x + 15$$

The above equation is of the general quadratic form:

$$f(x) = ax^2 + bx + c,$$
here $a = 1$, and $b = -8$.

$$x = \frac{-b}{2a}$$

is the equation for the axis of symmetry of the parabola. Hence $x = -\frac{8}{2} = 4$ is the x value at the turning point.

When $x = 4$, we find y to be:

$$y = 4^2 - 8(4) + 15 = -1.$$

Hence the coordinates of the turning point are $(4, -1)$.

62. (C)

The width will be multiplied by 3.5 and the length by 6.3, so the area will be $3.5 \times 6.3 = 22.05$ times the original area $= 22.05 \times 5 = 110.25$.

Calculator: $3.5 \times 6.3 \times 5 = 110.25$

63. (A)

$$y = \frac{3}{\sin x + \cos x} = \frac{3}{u} \text{ where } u = \sin x + \cos x$$

So $\dfrac{dy}{dx} = 3(-1)u^{-1-1}\dfrac{du}{dx}$ using the derivative of a power and chain rule theorems.

Thus,

$$\frac{dy}{dx} = \frac{-3}{(\sin x + \cos x)^2}(\cos x - \sin x)$$

$$= \frac{3(\sin x - \cos x)}{\sin^2 x + 2\sin x \cos x + \cos^2 x}$$

$$\frac{dy}{dx} = \frac{3(\sin x - \cos x)}{1 + 2\sin x \cos x},$$

using the identity $\sin^2 x + \cos^2 x = 1$

64. (D) $5\sqrt{7} + 7\left(\sqrt{35} \times 4\sqrt{5}\right) - 2\sqrt{18}$

$$= 5\sqrt{7} + (7 \times 4)\left(\sqrt{35} \times \sqrt{5}\right) - 2\sqrt{18}$$

$$= 5\sqrt{7} + 28\left(\sqrt{7} \times \sqrt{5} \times \sqrt{5}\right) - 2\left(\sqrt{9} \times \sqrt{2}\right)$$

$$= 5\sqrt{7} + 28(5)\sqrt{7} - 2(3)\sqrt{2}$$

$$= 145\sqrt{7} - 6\sqrt{2}$$

65. (A)

First, make use of the fact that the sum of the angles of any triangle is 180 degrees. The missing angle in the second triangle can be found by adding the two angles and then subtracting from 180.

$$80 + 30 = 110$$

$$180 - 110 = 70$$

The missing angle equals 70 degrees. Now compare the two triangles. You can see that both triangles have an angle 70 degrees, a side 8 inches, and an angle 30 degrees. Therefore, by the Angle-Side-Angle postulate, the two triangles are congruent.

66. (C)

The lengths of corresponding sides are proportional. Thus:

$$\frac{16.3}{4.0} = \frac{14.4}{k}$$

$$k = \frac{4(14.4)}{16.3}$$

Calculator:

$$4 \boxed{\times} 14.41 \boxed{\div} 16.3 \boxed{=} 3.53$$

67. (D)

$$x = \angle CBA + \angle CAB$$

$$= 50° + 30°$$

$$= 80°$$

$x = y$ (vertically opposite angles)

Therefore, $x + y = 2(80°) = 160°$.

68. (D)

This is a 30°, 60°, and 90° triangle. The hypotenuse (BC) is twice the length of the shorter leg (AB), and the length of the longer leg (AC) is the length of the shorter leg multiplied by $\sqrt{3}$.

$$2AB = BC$$

$$AB = \frac{BC}{2}$$

$$AB = \frac{7.0}{2} = 3.5$$

and

$$AC = \sqrt{3} \times AB$$

$$= \sqrt{3} \times 3.5$$

Calculator:

$$3 \boxed{\sqrt{}} \boxed{\times} 3.5 \boxed{=} 6.1$$

69. (A)

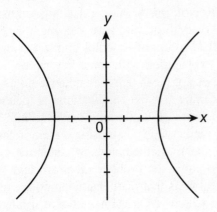

$$\frac{x^2}{9} - \frac{y^2}{9} = 1$$

is an equation of the form:

$$\frac{x^2}{a^2} - \frac{y^2}{b^2} = 1$$

with $a = 3$ and $b = 3$.

Therefore the graph is a hyperbola. The x-intercepts are found by setting $y = 0$:

$$\frac{x^2}{9} - \frac{0^2}{9} = 1$$
$$x^2 = 9$$
$$x = \pm 3.$$

Thus, the x-intercepts are at $(-3, 0)$ and $(3, 0)$. There are no y-intercepts since for $x = 0$ there are no real values of y satisfying the equation, i.e., no real value of y satisfies

$$\frac{2}{-1+1} - 3 = \frac{4(-1)+6}{-1+1}$$
$$\frac{2}{0} - 3 = \frac{-4+6}{0}$$

Since division by zero is impossible the above equation is not defined for $x = -1$. Hence we conclude that the equation has no roots for $x = -1$.

$$\left\{ x \left| \frac{2}{x+1} - 3 = \frac{4x+6}{x+1} \right. \right\} = \phi$$

70. (C)

The objective of the assessment is to determine the student's understanding of rational equations. Some of the key ideas for that topic include asymptotes and rational equations that lead to quadratic equations. The mathematical challenge in this exercise is for the student to recognize what the absolute value operator requires the student to do. After that the only concepts involved are whether the student can do the algebraic manipulations associated with a rational expression. The teacher may or may not wish to use the question but should be aware what is and is not measuring.

Choice (B) assumes that the student will see the problem in the same manner as an experienced user of mathematics. Choice (D) makes the assumption that procedural skills are not valuable. Choice (A) is not true because repeating a measure that is not very useful in the first place will not provide a good assessment.

71. (A)

is the correct answer. $(x + 2)$ is represented on the horizontal and $(x + 1)$ is represented on the vertical. The multiplication rectangle then represents the solution to the multiplication $(x + 2)(x + 1)$. Choices (B) and (C) are meaningless representations with regard to the given multiplication problem. Choice (D) is the result of a common error of multiplying the first terms and the last terms but ignoring the cross terms.

72. (A)

$\angle FGH$ is a straight angle. The number of degrees in a straight angle is $180°$. When the sum of two angles is $180°$, the angles are said to be supplementary. In the diagram,

$$\angle FGI + \angle IGH = \angle FGH$$

Therefore, $\angle FGI + \angle IGH = 180°$ and $\angle FGI$ and $\angle IGH$ are supplementary angles.

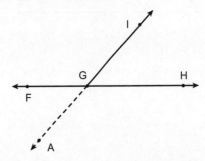

Answer choice (B) is incorrect because $\angle FGI \neq \angle IGH \neq 90°$ in the diagram.

Answer choice (C) is incorrect because complementary angles have a sum of 90°.

$$\angle FGI + \angle IGH = 180° \neq 90°$$

Answer choice (D) is incorrect because vertical angles are opposite angles formed when two lines cross each other.

$\angle AGH$ would be $\angle FGI$'s vertical angles.

73. (B)

$$\frac{\text{height}}{s} = \sin 60°$$

$$\Leftrightarrow \text{height} = s(\sin 60°)$$

$$= s\frac{\sqrt{3}}{3}$$

$$\Rightarrow \text{Area} = \frac{1}{2}h(S)$$

$$= \left(\frac{1}{2}\right)\frac{\sqrt{3}(s)(s)}{2}, \text{ substituting for } h$$

$$= \frac{\sqrt{3}s^2}{4}$$

$$\Rightarrow \frac{dA}{ds} = \frac{\sqrt{3}S}{2}$$

Therefore, when $s = 2$, $\dfrac{dA}{ds} = \dfrac{2\sqrt{3}}{2}$

$$= \sqrt{3}$$

$$\approx 1.73$$

74. (C)

Reciting properties, rules, algorithms, or axioms means very little. Students can memorize the Fundamental Theorem of Calculus and can even repeat parts of an explanation with some key words thrown in but that does not mean that they understand its importance, its meaning, or the implications associated with the idea. Choice (D): Working backwards is a more like doing mathematics than using a memorized algorithm. Choice (B): Mathematicians generally do not know how to solve the problems that are laid before them. The problems that mathematician do are usually open-ended. Choice (A): Mathematics is a language. In order to do mathematics, a student needs to communicate mathematically.

75. (B)

The ratio of the area of two similar polygons is equal to the square of the ratio of the lengths of any two corresponding sides. Thus:

$$\frac{\text{Area } \triangle ABC}{\text{Area } \triangle ADE} = \left(\frac{AC}{AE}\right)^2$$

$$(AE)^2 = \frac{(AC)^2 \,(\text{Area } \triangle ADE)}{\text{Area } \triangle ABC}$$

$$AE = \sqrt{\frac{(AC)^2 \,(\text{Area } \triangle ADE)}{\text{Area } \triangle ABC}}$$

$$= \sqrt{36^2 \left(\frac{441}{324}\right)}$$

Calculator:

$$441 \boxed{\div} 324 \boxed{\times} 36 \boxed{x^2} \boxed{=} 1764 \boxed{\sqrt{}} = 42$$

Thus, $AE = 42$. Since $AC + CE = AE$, then

$$CE = AE - AC$$

$$= 42 - 36$$

$$= 6$$

76. (A)

The circle has the following general equation:

$$x^2 + y^2 + cx + dy + e = 0$$

The radius is given by

$$\gamma = \frac{\sqrt{c^2 + d^2 - 4e}}{2}$$

In our equation $c = 6$, $d = 8$, and $e = -11$. Thus

$$\gamma = \frac{\sqrt{6^2 + 8^2 - 4(-11)}}{2} = \frac{\sqrt{36 + 64 + 44}}{2} = \frac{\sqrt{144}}{2} = \frac{12}{2} = 6$$

Calculator:

$$6\ \text{INV}x^2 + 8\ \text{INV}x^2 = -(4 \times 11\pm) = \sqrt{\ } \div 2 = 6$$

77. (C)

The triangle in the diagram is a right triangle. If the triangle is a right triangle, the lengths of the sides satisfy the Pythagorean property, namely $a^2 + b^2 = c^2$, where a, b are the lengths of the legs of the right triangle and c is the length of the hypotenuse. Therefore,

$a^2 + b^2 = c^2$ translates to

(length of base)^2 + (length of wall)^2 = (length of ladder)^2

or
$$\begin{aligned} 8^2 + b^2 &= 17^2 \\ 64 + b^2 &= 289 \qquad \text{Solving for } b^2, \\ -64 \qquad &-64 \\ \hline b^2 &= 225 \end{aligned}$$

and $b^2 = 225$ means to take the positive square root of both sides which yields $b = 15$ feet.

Answer choice (A) is incorrect due to the improper use of the Pythagorean property.

17 feet − 8 feet = 9 feet

Answer choice (B) is incorrect due to the improper use of the Pythagorean property.

17 feet + 8 feet = 25 feet

$\sqrt{25}$ = 5 feet

Answer choice (D) is also incorrect due to the improper use of the Pythagorean property.

$$\sqrt{(17)(8)} = \sqrt{136} = \sqrt{4}\sqrt{34} = 2\sqrt{34}$$

78. (A)

Find the y-axis. Find the side of the figure closest to the y-axis and measure the distance that this side is from the y-axis. A reflection of the figure will put this side the same distance from the y-axis, but on the other side.

Also, notice the point labeled C. A reflection of this point across the y-axis will also be the same distance from the y-axis, but on the other side.

79. (D)

From a theorem, we know that a central angle is equal in measurement to the arc it intercepts. The arc measurement is given as

$$m\overset{\frown}{AB} = \frac{1}{5}\pi \text{ radians.}$$

Converting this to degrees, we obtain

$$\left(\frac{1}{5}\pi\right)\left(\frac{180}{\pi}\right) = 36°.$$

Note that points A, O, and B form a triangle. Two sides of this triangle are equal to the radius of the circle. Thus, they are equal sides, and ΔAOB is isosceles (we know that the base angles of an isosceles triangle are equal). The vertex angle is 36°, and there are 180° in a triangle. The relation that is set up is

36° + 2 (base angle) = 180°.

Solving for the base angle:

$$\text{base angle} = \frac{180° - 36°}{2} = 72°.$$

Thus, $\angle OBA = 72°$.

80. (C)

Doing problem solving is doing mathematics. Although problem solving requires students to use mathematics, the act of solving a problem is also mathematics. Mathematicians are problem solvers. Choice (A): Problem solving should be used to teach the basic concepts.

Problems allow students to have concrete situations in which they can be guide to basic relationships and ideas. With the basic ideas firmly planted within a real situation, the students have a foundation on which more complex, abstract ideas can be developed. Choice (D): If the students are explicitly instructed in problem-solving skills and strategies, they can be guided to learn complex ideas well. Choice (B): It is hardly worth being able to move quickly if the students are not gaining conceptual understanding.

INDEX

Index

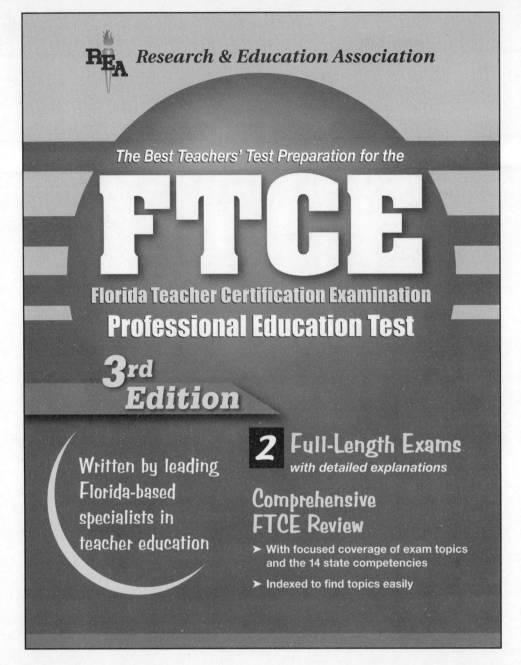